Bittersweet
Country

Bittersweet
Country

edited with an introduction by

Ellen Gray Massey

ANCHOR BOOKS

Anchor Press/Doubleday   Garden City, New York

1978

DEDICATION

The *Bittersweet* staff and I humbly dedicate this book to the preservation of our Ozark culture as remembered and practiced by the wonderful men and women who have shared their thoughts and skills with us, and as cherished by the first subscribers, whose faith and continued support give us the encouragement to continue.

Ellen Gray Massey teaches English at Lebanon High School in Lebanon, Missouri, and is the faculty adviser for *Bittersweet.* She organized the magazine following a workshop held in Rabun Gap, Georgia, in the summer of 1973 under the auspices of IDEAS and *Foxfire,* and has been one of the leading figures in the development of the Foxfire educational concept throughout the country.

ISBN: 0-385-12961-0
Library of Congress Catalog Card Number 77–12869

The Anchor Press edition is the first publication of BITTERSWEET COUNTRY in book form. It is published simultaneously in hard and paper covers.

Anchor Books edition: 1978

Lyrics from "Sweet, Sweet Spirit" Copyright © 1963 by Manna Music, Inc., 2111 Kenmere Ave., Burbank, Ca. 91504. Used by permission of the publishers.

Portions of this book first appeared in *Bittersweet* magazine.

CONTENTS

Acknowledgments

This book is possible only because the quarterly magazine *Bittersweet* succeeded. Its staff members and I would like to acknowledge the help of a few of the many who made our project work.

First, we'd like to express appreciation to Eliot Wigginton, of *Foxfire,* and IDEAS, of Washington, D.C., for getting us started. I'd also like to add that Wig encouraged us to go ahead with this book.

Of course, we wouldn't have accomplished anything without the permission and encouragement of the Lebanon R-III School Board. Our administrators, Vic Slaughter, Robert Payne, Gary Evans, and Robert Duncan, were always willing to help us—from being members of the Bittersweet, Inc., board to allowing us to run all over Missouri and Arkansas during school time to do our research.

We want to give special thanks to my son David, who steered us in the right direction in photographic work, and my daughter Ruth Ellen, who has been a sort of back-seat adviser and consultant from the beginning. After listening to me talk about *Bittersweet* so much at home she decided to join us.

Five adults in our community have been interested enough to serve on our board of directors. Our appreciation to James E. Baldwin, Sr., Dalton Wright, Esther Griffin, Bill Hawk, and a special thanks to George Kastler, who has also helped us with innumerable articles.

And last, we couldn't have stayed in business without continued promotional help. Our appreciation goes to all the news media that have covered us, especially The Lebanon *Daily Record* and Lebanon radio stations KLWT and KJEL, which feature us when each magazine appears.

INTRODUCTION

It's all Ralph's fault. The actual incentive for our beginning *Bittersweet* came from his interest in Eliot Wigginton's *Foxfire*, a student publication in Rabun Gap, Georgia. A long-time supporter of *Foxfire* and member of its advisory board, my brother Ralph Gray believed we had the potential in Lebanon High School to do a similar culturally oriented publication focused on the Ozarks. It was about that time that IDEAS (Institutional Development and Economic Affairs Service, Inc.), a non-profit private organization of Washington, D.C., began working with Wig to help other groups facilitate the cultural journalism concept of *Foxfire*. At Ralph's suggestion IDEAS called me and offered to send Wig to visit us, as well as give us other assistance to get started. From then on we became hooked.

We actually began working in the spring of 1973. With the support of the School Board and administration, the language arts department created a special English class open to grades ten through twelve which was to begin in the fall of the 1973–74 school year. But the students' enthusiasm was so great they couldn't wait. They began working that spring and summer to have the first issue ready to mail the first day of school.

One achievement led to another. Since that time we have published the quarterly regularly with each season. The students travel wherever needed to get their information: three to four enthusiastic boys and girls, loaded with battery-operated tape recorders, note paper, and cameras, climb into my car to drive to the home of some wonderful man or woman. There we watch, listen, ask a thousand questions, participate, learn, and record all we can. We are interested in anything about the Ozarks and its people—the traditions, customs, lore, crafts, music, and history, as well as the past and present ecological condition of our region.

To produce a publication devoted to such a broad range of interests is a large task for professional writers, researchers, and photographers. Yet we do it with fifteen-, sixteen-, and seventeen-year-old boys and girls who have never interviewed anyone, taken a photograph, or written anything more than an English assignment. Though they lack the knowledge and experience, they have managed to learn the fundamentals as they work, for these young people have something that is more valuable. They have an eagerness to learn, a willingness to spend much extra time (including their weekends and vacations), and, most of all, they have unending enthusiasm, ideas, and a youthful freshness. After the first semester the new staff are experienced workers; by the second year they begin training others.

In addition to publishing four issues of *Bittersweet* annually, the students also run their own business. They—along with a few interested community people—are the officers and board of directors of our not-for-profit, tax-exempt corporation. The staff makes all decisions for the corporation, keeps the books, handles correspondence and circulation, and constantly does publicity and promotion work to keep us solvent. Since its inception five years ago the project has been self-supporting; subscriptions and sales of magazines pay all our expenses.

All the chapters in this book have previously been published in *Bittersweet*. Over ninety per cent of the authors and photographers and all the artists are staff members. The only material not produced by students are the old photographs and articles that relate firsthand experiences which we could not re-create. In all cases the staff edited the material. Most of the students' stories are co-operative endeavors involving several different staff members who interview, transcribe, write, revise, and proofread each story.

We have included in this book only about one fourth of what we've published to date. If you like this sample, perhaps you'd like to read the articles as they happen by joining our subscribers. Write to Bittersweet, Inc., Lebanon High School, 777 Brice Street, Lebanon, Missouri 65536. A year's subscription of four issues is $8.00. Some back issues are available at $2.00 each plus postage.

There is no stopping a project such as this. New students eagerly apply each year, story ideas mount, and our readers encourage us daily. I hope you'll enjoy this sampling—welcome to *Bittersweet Country*.

ELLEN GRAY MASSEY

PROLOGUE

Bittersweet country is found wherever there are sorrowful and contented people living close to the soil, but the epitome of the bittersweet life seems to be the Ozarks. Over a hundred and fifty years ago ambitious family groups left their former homes in search of better opportunities, and settled in the hills, valleys, and on the plains of this area to raise their children and support their families through their labor and ingenuity. With help from neighbors and the guidance of their consciences trained by circuit riders and later their own preachers, they populated the country and established a way of life which did not change much until the 1940s.

Like the wild bittersweet vine that grew on the bluffs and bushes and soon covered their rail fences, the early pioneers were a hardy people who struggled to survive on the thin rocky soil. They succeeded because of their resourcefulness in using the corn, wheat, vegetables, and fruits they grew; the hogs and poultry they tended; and the wild nuts, greens, herbs, berries, animals, fish, and forest products already in abundance for those who were willing to hunt for and harvest them. They succeeded because of their willingness to work hard from early childhood to old age in order to provide the basic needs of living as well as a few small comforts like feather beds, pieced quilts, and musical instruments.

The prolific settlers attended first to the basic needs of food, clothing, and shelter for their large families. Though each family produced most of its needs, the settlers depended heavily on their neighbors, their church, and schools for companionship, help, and guidance. They established a culture and self-sufficient way of life which still exists today in the memories and habits of the older people—sweet both in reality and as seen in retrospect, but also bitter, sad, and hard.

Drab at times, uninteresting and common much of the time, their way of life shows its worth and beauty now when it is almost gone. "Ever' day was just like the next," Roy Gage said. "We did our morning chores, milking, feeding, and such, we'd work in the fields till dark, do our chores all over again in the evening, eat supper, and go to bed. Same thing ever' day."

But just as the bittersweet's red and orange berries color the dormant landscape in late fall after all the leaves have dropped, so have the warmth, neighborliness, humor, creativity, and skill of the Ozark people produced a brightness which is far more valuable and lasting than the dried bittersweet berries they gathered each fall to add a bit of color to their homes. Ashford Hough remembers, "We were a busy bunch, but we enjoyed life. We got together, had parties and things of that sort. We lived good lives." "We never lacked companionship. There was always a bunch of young people in farms all up and down the river ready to get together for picnics and such," Gene Chambers added.

Sickness and death fought with only home remedies, varmints like coyotes and grasshoppers which plagued the stock and crops, periodic droughts which threatened family food supplies and the crops they depended on for cash, wars that upset their lives at the core, and never-ending daily hard work were balanced with the joy of new births, homemade fun, plentiful companionships, and actual visible achievements and fruitfulness which resulted from the three-way partnership of men, women, and children, the land, and their God. Everyone remembers, "We never went hungry, and we always had something to wear. It wasn't much, but we were happy. Nobody had it any better."

The once widespread vine has almost disappeared from the land because of the burning, cutting, spraying, and bulldozing of the forests and the wanton gathering by "nature lovers." A new way of living came with the improved roads. The rest of the world entered the living rooms through radio and television. More physical comforts and relief from drudgery and hard physical labor came with the electric power lines which eventually reached even the most isolated home, barn, and hen house. Tourism and industry provided an income not dependent on the farm.

Most of this change was good. No one today really wants to go back. Myrtle Hough said, "It is easier now. If I had to I could go back, but I wouldn't like to. I can't say 'the good ole days.' We had fun in those days, but I think opportunities are greater now than they were then." But there remains a longing—a sadness. "Progress is wonderful," Ella Dunn said, "but even though we don't have to work so hard, we've lost something. We don't have time for our neighbors and families now." None of the older people are ever sorry they experienced the old way. They speak of it with pride, and those who did not live in the Ozarks years ago envy them. "You kids haven't ever experienced what we have," Elvie Hough said. "You missed it all."

Most of us in the present-day Ozarks like the technical progress. We are proud we can have automatic washers instead of having to pump and carry water from the well, heat it in an outdoor kettle, boil and scrub our clothes. We much prefer milking in our grade A dairy barns to squatting on a stool beside old Bessie under a shade tree with a milk bucket clasped between our knees and our cheek buried in her flank to escape her swishing tail. We would not exchange our cars, trucks, and tractors for a team of mules, nor would we walk four miles for the privilege of attending high school, and we'd hate to miss the morning and evening news on television each day. But as we enjoy these conveniences we see the Ozark traditions and lore slipping quietly away year by year with the deaths of each Fred Manes, Mary Moore, Charlie Grace, and Charlie McMicken.

These people have permitted us to become a part of their lives. With a hammer and forge we have helped Fred transform a rusty red-hot piece of metal into an ingenious nutcracker for the tough-shelled black walnuts, and we have sat very quietly to watch the mice in his blacksmith shop come up to his hands to get a nut meat each for their meal. We have basked in the reflection of Mary's contentment with her long work-filled life, which to us seemed so hard and so lonely. "We got along," she assured us. "We had just what we needed."

We have lost ourselves in the sounds of the fiddle and the tapping feet of an old-time jig-style, foot-stomping square dance, and became for a brief period a part of that era as Charlie Mc sang out, "You swing Sal and I'll swing Kate. Hurry up, boys, don't be late." We visited Charlie Grace in the hospital just days before his death and witnessed his strong faith and his joy at the prospect of soon being reunited in heaven with his wife.

As we catch these fleeting glimpses of that almost vanished way of life, we wonder why it is that to gain one thing we must lose something perhaps even more precious. Why must we destroy the wild bittersweet vine to have clean fence rows?

That is why we call this bittersweet country.

1. THE SETTING

The Ozarks region is a roughly two-hundred-mile-square area in southern Missouri and northern Arkansas. It is bounded by the Missouri River on the north, the Arkansas River on the south, the Mississippi River on the east, and the Great Plains on the west. Geologically it differs from the flat surrounding lands, being an ancient upraised plateau which has eroded for over fifty million years to form the present landscape of hills and valleys with some grasslands resistant to erosion.

In Indian times before 1800 the area was heavily forested with oak and hickory and some pine. The forest cover, underlaid with limestone and dolomite rock formations, created abundant springs which fed many small rocky-bottomed creeks and rivers. Bass, perch, goggle-eye, cat, buffalo, carp, and other fish filled the streams, while deer, bear, panther, turkey, quail, raccoon, possum, muskrat, and other fur-bearing animals lived in the woods and along the streams. Though much of the forest is gone, the Ozarks is still a beautiful region of wooded hills, open prairies, and rich river and creek bottomland.

Chronologically, the story of Ozark settlement by whites begins with the French who first came to the Ozarks from Canada, where they had been settled for some time along the St. Lawrence River. Prior to 1700 the French were well established on the Illinois side of the Mississippi opposite the Ozarks. Some French hunters, fur traders, and miners from the Illinois settlements were actively exploiting resources in the Ozarks by 1700. The resource that made the Ozarks important to the French was lead (the Missouri Ozarks still lead the world in lead production).

In 1735 the French established the village of Ste. Genevieve, Missouri's first permanent settlement. Thereafter numerous other settlements were founded by the French, including St. Louis, Cape Girardeau, and Potosi. Today only a few locations in the Ozarks retain vestiges of our French past. In Ste. Genevieve the homes of the French remain—possibly the finest collection of colonial French architecture in the United States. Some rural French remain in the vicinity of Old Mines, Missouri, where descendants of early miners live in conditions that are best described as bleak. Although the French were responsible for naming many places in Missouri, they are somewhat like the legendary Kilroy. They were here and then gone.

Control of Louisiana, including Missouri, passed from the French to the Spanish in 1762, and Missouri remained under Spanish control until 1802. However, the Spanish Crown sent very few Spaniards to Louisiana during this period. In fact, those who came to Missouri during the period of Spanish control were French, Americans, and even a few Germans. The Spanish contribution to the culture of the Ozarks is confined to Spanish land grants, a few place names, and myths of hidden treasure.

The area was opened to white settlement after the Louisiana Purchase in 1803. The few tribes of Osage Indians who had hunted the region for many generations were moved to Oklahoma by treaty before the white settlers came.

The frontier of settlement began its movement through or, rather, around the Ozarks. A rather important factor influencing the pattern of settlement was the price of land. The wealthier and presumably more successful settlers, such as the slaveholders along the Missouri and Mississippi rivers, obtained the best land paying as much as $2.50 an acre for it. In the interior Ozarks, more rugged land with thin cherty soils sold for as little as twelve and a half cents an acre. Thus, the wealthy settled on the best land and accumulated even more wealth while the poor continued to eke out a marginal living on the scrabble farms of the interior Ozarks, much as they had done in the Appalachians. These patterns, unfortunately, persist throughout much of the rural Ozarks to this day.

The settlers coming to Missouri after 1803 were mostly native-born Americans. In the early years they had come from states adjacent to Missouri on the east—Kentucky, Tennessee, and Illinois. Colonel Morgan's colony from Kentucky which settled New Madrid in 1788 was the first distinctly American settlement. Another early arrival was Daniel Boone, who had come from Kentucky in 1797 and settled along the Missouri River. Boone's son Nathan later settled in Greene County where his decaying cabin still stands.

Generally speaking, the early-arriving Americans came from western Tennessee and Kentucky, as well as southern Illinois. As time passed and the frontier pushed west, settlers began coming from the Appalachians proper and from areas to the north and east of the Appalachians. Some went west from Philadelphia and followed the Ohio Valley to Missouri. Others turned south at Philadelphia and followed the Great Valley (the National Road) down through Virginia. In western Virginia settlers passed through one of the few gaps in the Appalachians—Cumberland Gap—along a trail blazed by Daniel Boone. Once through the Gap settlers could follow either the Cumberland or the Tennessee River on their journey west. Both are tributary to the Ohio, and thus these settlers connected with those coming down the Ohio from Pittsburgh.

The fact that the Ozarks were similar to the Appalachians no doubt influenced many from that region to settle here. Of equal importance, those who settled early sent word back to the Appalachians, with the result that entire family clans frequently made the move to Missouri. This type of settlement, referred to as kin-based migration, accounts for the fact that many Ozarks settlements trace back to single counties in the Appalachians.

The mainstream of western migration in America avoided the Ozarks region because the many small rivers and creeks and the hilly terrain made travel difficult, and the thin rocky soil was not attractive to those wanting productive farm land. Most immigrants went north either on the Missouri River or by land across central and northern Missouri to Independence or St. Joseph.

However, these same land characteristics of rivers, creeks and hollows, and rocky wooded hills attracted from other hilly regions such as eastern Tennessee and Kentucky many immigrants who re-established in the Ozarks a way of life they had known in their homelands. Naturally these people brought their culture with them, and they did not have to change their customs a great deal. Isolated to a degree for over a hundred years, they continued their predominately rural way of life longer than most of the rest of America.

The Origins of Early Ozark Settlers

Though the greatest numbers of settlers came from eastern Tennessee, the Ozarks are more than simply an "Appalachian West." The origins of the Ozarks' population are far more complex and varied than most people realize.

Those who settled in the Ozarks came for a variety of reasons. There is of course the oft-told story of the pull of the frontier—the tale of the legendary ax-wielding frontiersmen seeking adventure in the unknown wilderness of the West. No doubt there is some truth in this, but many if not most moved for more practical reasons. Daniel Boone, for example, had to move—someone filed a claim to his land in Kentucky, something he had intended to do but never got around to. Many settlers in the Appalachians found themselves in similar circumstances. Many veterans of the War of 1812 came west of the

Mississippi River only because that was where the free bounty land for veterans was located. Some left their old areas because they could not conform. A good example of this was the pioneer distiller who would not succumb to the efforts by government to control whiskey making. Following the Whiskey Rebellion in Pennsylvania in 1794, many pioneer distillers packed their stills and other belongings and headed south and west where they could be free of government interference. Some made it all the way to the Ozarks, where they continue to resent government interference.

A good number, although no one knows how many, were plain criminals, guilty of everything from failure to house oxen properly to murder. A timely departure for the Ozarks saved many a Tom Dooley. Although some continued their lawless activities after arriving in the Ozarks, many became upstanding citizens.

An individual might depart from New Jersey and follow a series of routes, eventually ending in the Ozarks, but most families going west moved about a hundred miles per generation. So it might have taken a family coming from Pennsylvania a century or so before arriving in Missouri, and many remained in the Ozarks for only a generation or two before moving on. Thus many Tennesseans who migrated to Missouri were North Carolinians by birth and their ancestors might have been New Englanders.

For the Ozarks, a head count in 1860 would have indicated that the lead-ing states supplying settlers to Missouri, in order of importance, were Ken-tucky, Tennessee, and Virginia. Many of the Kentuckians and Virginians as well as some of the Tennesseans were wealthy slaveowners. They brought with them to Missouri a culture which was very Southern in character. They selected generally the better lands where slaves could be used and commer-cial crops grown. These areas included the Missouri and the Mississippi valleys, as well as some of the limestone basins in the eastern Ozarks. Several of the counties along the north of the Missouri River are included in the re-gion referred to as "Little Dixie," an area where political and cultural ties with the South have existed since the early days of settlement.

The remainder of the Ozarks was dominated by settlers from highland eastern Tennessee, with eastern Kentucky a distant second. Many, if not most, were of Scotch-Irish descent. They were yeoman farmers drawn from the poorest classes. They held few slaves, partly because the interior Ozarks would not support a slave economy, but also because slavery was not a part of their culture.

The settlement of the Ozarks continued and even intensified following the Civil War. The southern Appalachians continued to be a prime source of set-tlers, but changes were occurring. By 1890 settlers from the prairie states of Ohio, Indiana, and Illinois were coming in numbers equal to, and in some cases exceeding, those from the Appalachians.

In addition to native-born Americans, several hundred thousand Euro-

POPULATION ORIGINS IN RURAL MISSOURI

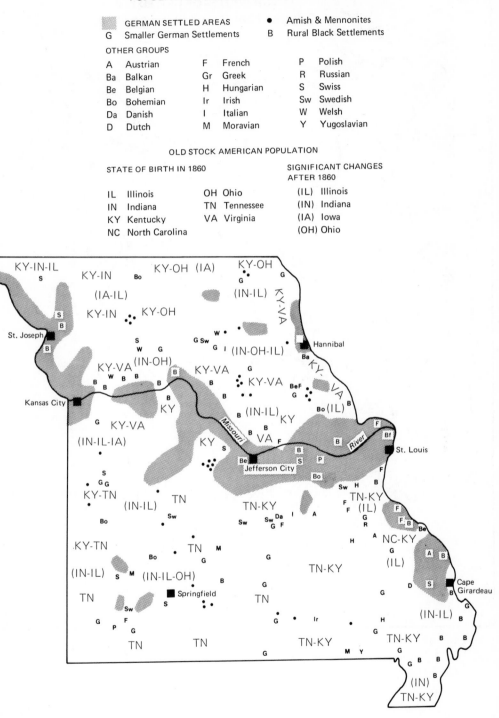

GERMAN SETTLED AREAS
G Smaller German Settlements

● Amish & Mennonites
B Rural Black Settlements

OTHER GROUPS

A	Austrian	F	French
Ba	Balkan	Gr	Greek
Be	Belgian	H	Hungarian
Bo	Bohemian	Ir	Irish
Da	Danish	I	Italian
D	Dutch	M	Moravian

P Polish
R Russian
S Swiss
Sw Swedish
W Welsh
Y Yugoslavian

OLD STOCK AMERICAN POPULATION

STATE OF BIRTH IN 1860

IL Illinois   OH Ohio
IN Indiana   TN Tennessee
KY Kentucky   VA Virginia
NC North Carolina

SIGNIFICANT CHANGES
AFTER 1860

(IL) Illinois
(IN) Indiana
(IA) Iowa
(OH) Ohio

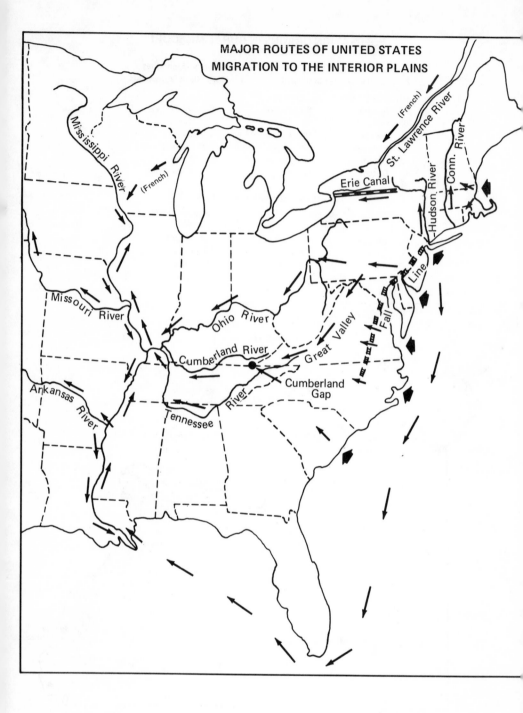

MAJOR ROUTES OF UNITED STATES
MIGRATION TO THE INTERIOR PLAINS

peans settled in the Ozarks during the nineteenth century. The largest numbers came from German-speaking lands. Although a few Germans, including the so-called Whitewater Dutch who established their settlements in Cape Girardeau County before 1800, had come to Missouri earlier, most came between 1830 and the Civil War. By 1830 more than a dozen travel books about the Ozarks were in circulation in the German language. These accounts presented a romanticized and exaggerated view of the Ozarks, and as a result countless thousands emigrated from the Old Country directly to Missouri. At one time Missouri was the focus of an effort to create a German-speaking state in America.

The Hermann settlement in Gasconade County has retained to this day the appearance of a village along the Rhine River. At the annual Maifest (May Festival) German food, music, and conversation abound in a genuinely Old World atmosphere. In Perry County the so-called Saxon Lutherans established several village settlements in 1839. From the small German-settled villages of Altenburg, Wittenberg, and Frohna has come the three-million-member Missouri Synod of the Lutheran Church. German settlements in the Ozarks are distinguished today by their large homes, often of brick, and by their religion—largely Lutheran and Catholic. Among the German-Americans live smaller numbers of Swiss, Belgian, Austrian, Bohemian, and Polish extraction.

Following the construction of railroads into the interior Ozarks in the 1870s and 1880s, there was a second influx of Europeans. The railroads had very active colonization programs which resulted in the location of more than twenty ethnic settlements in the Ozarks. The Italian community at Rosati brought large-scale viticulture to the area. Other groups included Polish (Pulaskifield), Germans (Freistatt, Lockwood, Billings), Swedes (Verona, Swede Hollow, Swedeborg), French Protestant Waldensians (Monett), and smaller numbers of Hungarians, Yugoslavs, Bohemians, and Irish.

Recently a most interesting group has made the Ozarks its home. In the last decade fifteen Amish and Mennonite settlements have sprung up in various parts of the Ozarks. The Amish and Mennonites are of German, Dutch, and Austrian background and many continue to use the German language. The more conservative groups have retained a very traditional life style, including simple dress, the use of horse-drawn machinery and buggies, and in general a refusal on religious grounds to employ modern technology. Without question, these people add a colorful cultural element to the region.

That in a nutshell is where the people we call Ozarkians have come from. The map summarizes nearly three hundred years of settlement in the Ozarks. As it clearly shows, the strands of many and varied cultures have been woven into the fabric of the Ozarks.

2. THE WOMAN

The core of Ozark life was the family. The church, the trading center, the schools—everything—depended on the family unit to support their very existence.

As the community depended on the family units, so the family needed and depended on each member. Their livelihood came from the family enterprise —the farm, store, mill, blacksmith shop, or some other community service— and the main source of labor was the immediate family.

Each member had his recognized place and job. Though these were stereotyped as to sex and age, no one thought much about inequality; someone had to do the work from which all benefited, and all worked equally hard. The man and his sons did the heavy outside work—the farming, haying, and working with the stock. As head of the family, he was in charge of the farm (or the business). His authority extended to the barns and fields but ended in the house.

The house was the woman's realm. She and her daughters did all the jobs inside and helped with those closely related to daily family life like tending the garden and the chickens and sometimes doing the milking. Her responsibilities included feeding and clothing the family, keeping the house comfortable, and caring for, training, and molding the children.

However, many jobs were done co-operatively, each helping the other whenever needed. If the man needed help gathering corn, the wife was beside him, often stooped over gathering the down row (the row knocked down by the team) while her husband gathered two or three rows beside the wagon. If she needed help with big house-cleaning jobs such as the annual task of taking up and cleaning the rag carpet, he gave a hand.

Country Kitchens

Though the yard and house were in the woman's sphere of influence, her special domain was the kitchen. There she was absolute monarch—cook, maid, and serving girl all rolled into one. The kitchen was the busiest room in the house and most of the essential activities of living took place there—preparing three meals a day for the family, extra hands, and friends; eating all meals; preparing food for canning and storing; washing and ironing; and washing up and bathing the family. From building the fire in the cookstove before cooking breakfast in early morning until late evening when the last family member washed up for bed, there was nearly always some activity going on. No other room had the same warm appeal, filled with pleasant odors and interesting activity.

Before electricity came to the rural areas in the late 1930s and early '40s, the normal kitchen did not have much furniture or built-in cabinets. There was usually just a big table and chairs or benches for eating, the iron cookstove, a cook table, a safe or cupboard, and often a pantry.

WOOD COOKSTOVES

Before the early pioneers had stoves, they used fireplaces for cooking their food. Cooking with a skillet or a kettle with little legs which permitted it to sit over the fire, they used the direct fire or coals for heat. When stoves became available, people continued to use wood for fuel but contained the fire in the stove which, with its dampers and flues, controlled the heat better and provided a convenient place to set pans. The wood stoves were such an improvement and so satisfactory that some people used them even after bottled gas and electricity came to the country.

Wood cookstoves were the most common and practical. Made from iron, they were durable and did not need much repair, nor were they expensive to buy or use. Though they needed wood to operate, the wood served a double duty by also giving off heat for the kitchen.

Bittersweet staff member Sally Moore remembers her experiences with these stoves not so long ago.

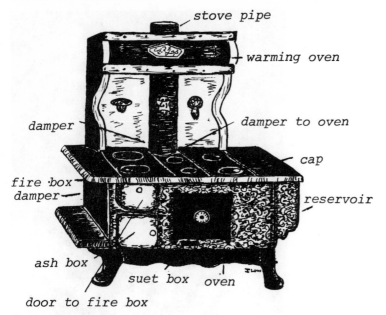

stove pipe

warming oven

damper

damper to oven

cap

fire ·box
damper

reservoir

ash box

suet box   oven

door to fire box

Deluxe model of wood cookstove.

"Before I started school and later during summer vacations I lived with my great-grandmother. Her way of life was completely different from what I was used to at home. One thing I remember so well was that she cooked on a wood cookstove, even though she had an electric range.

"I remember waking up early each morning to the smell of breakfast and jumping up to go help but Mama Keith and the wood stove were ahead of me. The eggs and bacon would be through at the same time as the biscuits. I never remember eating anything cold at breakfast, except for the orange juice.

"Every once in a while I was lucky enough to get up in time to help build the fire in the stove. To light the fire Mama Keith would remove the two lids and take out the crossbar above the firebox. She put scraps of paper, corn cobs, kindling, and sticks of wood up to eighteen inches long in the box. From above she would light the paper with a match, then replace the crossbar and lids as the wood started burning.

"To help the fire get started she would open the damper to let air into the fire. This helped the fire burn fast so that the stove would get hot quicker. As the stove began to get hot, she would close the damper to slow down and control the fire. One damper was located on the back side of the stove in the center. Another damper was under the door on the left side right by the firebox. She further controlled the fire by a damper in the stovepipe that moved a platelike valve in the flue that controlled the air flow.

Sally Moore (left) and Genetta Seeligman learn to cook on an old iron cookstove as Sally's great-grandmother did when Sally was a little girl.

Lighting the cookstove.

"While the stove was getting hot, Mama Keith would fix the orange juice, set the table, put the biscuits in the pan, and get the bacon and eggs ready to fry. She would sprinkle drops of water on the surface to see if the stove was hot enough. If they sizzled, popped, and danced the stove was ready. This usually took about a half an hour.

"I remember standing on a velvet-covered box on the right side of the stove away from the fire, so I could watch her cook. It was an adventure to look through the fire grate at the fire burning in the stove—much more exciting than looking at a sterile electric coil. I could hear the wood make popping sounds as it burned down and would notice the faint smell of wood smoke.

"When she started breakfast, she would put the skillet right above the firebox to get it hot enough to cook the bacon. If the fire was too hot, she would regulate the heat by moving the skillet and pots away from the hottest part of the fire. If some of the food was done before the rest of the meal was ready, she would set the pots on the right side of the stove to keep them warm. If she wanted something to cook faster, she would remove a lid from the stove and set the pan in the opening to have direct contact with the fire. She added more wood through the little door at the left. She always had a kettle sitting in the center of the stove at the back, sending steam into the air.

"By the time the top was hot enough to cook, so was the oven. After she opened the oven damper which sent the heat to the oven, she would test the oven by putting her hand in it. Her many years of experience told her when the oven was the right temperature to bake the biscuits. Some ovens had thermometers on the door to take the guesswork out of baking, but Mama Keith relied on feel.

"Her stove had a warming shelf above the cooking surface that made a handy place to put food to keep warm from the rising heat. Other styles of stoves had warming closets that were similar to the shelves, except that they were enclosed by doors.

"Some fancy or deluxe models had doors opening into the oven from two sides, or had a cap that had one or two smaller caps within it that could be removed to set smaller pans closer to the fire. Some stoves had little fancy shelves under the warming ovens and some had fancy decorations. Mama Keith said all that fanciness only made them harder to keep clean.

"While we ate breakfast, she put the kettle on the stove to heat water to wash the dishes. Some stoves had a reservoir on the right side that provided hot water whenever the stove was burning. When you needed hot water, you could dip it out with a dipper. This water could get boiling hot, depending on how hot the fire was.

"The stove top was easy to clean because there were no burners to clean around. If anything spilled while cooking, it would sizzle dry. To clean the top she rubbed an old piece of paper over it when it was cool. After breakfast we used her stove as a garbage disposal by throwing the egg shells, paper napkins, and scraps of food into the firebox.

"As the wood burned in the firebox, the ashes fell down through slots into

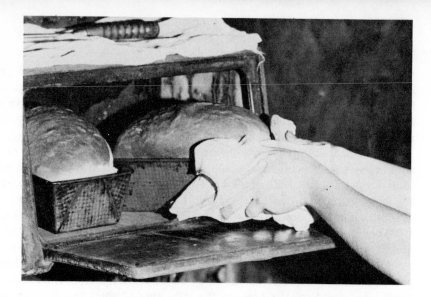

Hot light bread straight from the oven will keep warm in the warming oven of this old wood stove.

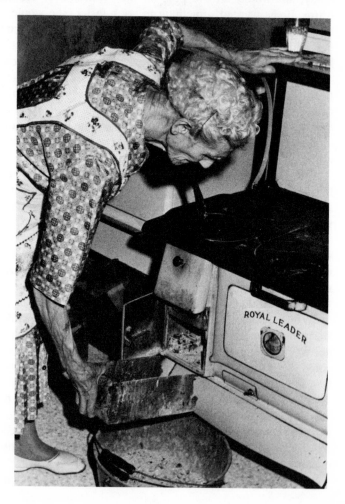

Sylvia Gunter still prefers her wood stove even if she has to clean out the ashes frequently.

the ash box. To clean the ashes we would open the door to the ash box, pull the box out, and empty it into a big pot that we later dumped. Then with a small shovel we cleaned out the area where the ash box sat in case ashes had fallen to the side. Ashes would also gather above the oven under the cooking surface, as well as in the little soot pan under the oven. We used a special T-shaped tool to rake out the ashes that collected under the oven.

"The biggest chore in caring for wood stoves was polishing. Mama Keith would apply stove black about every two weeks to make it black and shiny. She wouldn't cook any meal on the stove for company unless it had been cleaned and was in perfect order. She would say to me, 'Everything has to be perfect.' "

Even before electricity and bottled propane gas became available in the country, some women bought coal oil (kerosene) stoves, which usually had two or four burners. Some had a little oven that could be placed over a burner and used to bake bread and cakes, and others had ovens built permanently over one or two burners. This type of stove was not nearly as hot to cook on as the wood stove, and some families who had both would use the kerosene stove for summer and quick cooking, the wood stove for winter and heavy cooking. Some people thought kerosene gave off a displeasing odor, and while most people in the country had all the wood they wanted for free, they had to purchase the oil.

OTHER KITCHEN FURNISHINGS

Most of the food was prepared at a cook table which was usually close to the stove. Baking powder, soda, sugar, spices, and other staples were sometimes kept there so they would be in easy reach when mixing food. Some women would tack a curtain reaching to the floor around the table's edge behind which they would keep some pots and pans. Occasionally there might be a shelf above the table, which was used as a storage area for small utensils, and it, too, was often covered by a curtain.

When preparing a big dinner, the wife might use the eating table for rolling out pies or kneading bread. Most of the dinner tables were long with a backless bench placed against the wall where the older children sat. The father sat at the head of the table and the mother at the foot with the younger children between them. The youngest child usually sat by the mother and the next-to-youngest by the father.

Men would sometimes build their own tables. A handmade table may not have been fancy, but it was durable. Men made their own benches and sometimes made split-bottom chairs of hickory bark.

On the hot summer days the family frequently moved the table to an outside porch away from the stove in the hot kitchen. Carrying the food outside was a bit more work, but it made the kitchen less crowded and moved some of the activity out from underfoot of the cook.

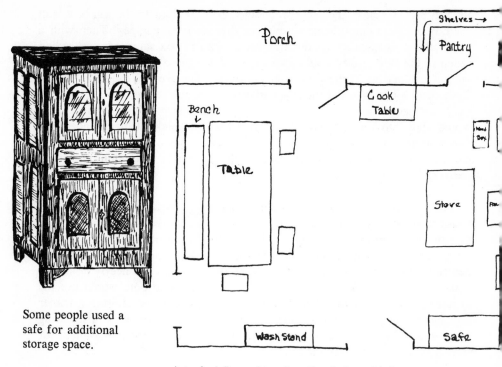

Some people used a safe for additional storage space.

A typical floor plan of an Ozark farm kitchen.

In addition to using the cook table as storage, some people used a safe. This was usually made of walnut and was tall, with glass doors and a drawer; it looked something like today's china cabinets. Everyday and Sunday dishes, silverware, and some staples might be kept there. Prepared food which would not spoil, such as pies and cakes, could also be stored.

In the kitchens of homes built after 1900 a little room called a pantry was often included. This was used to store large packages of coffee, flour, sugar, and other staple groceries bought at a store, as well as pots and pans, coffee and sausage mills, ice cream freezers, ironing boards, and many items of family living. Shelves were built on the walls with hooks to hang coats, pans, and other utensils. The pantry was not very big, usually five by eight feet, but provided the storage which built-in cabinets give today.

Floors of homes in the pioneer days were plain dirt, and the homemaker would simply sweep the hard-packed dirt floor. When local sawmills began operating, many built board floors of oak or sometimes pine. Using lye soap, the wife would scrub the floor with an old broom till it was clean. Some even crushed white sand rock to use as a cleaner. This would make the floors really shine.

Ceilings were at first plain, without paint or paper. Later kitchens were sealed and painted or papered. If the family could not afford paper, they might use newspaper to help seal the room and give the rough wooden interior a cleaner, brighter look.

Lighting was poor compared to modern standards. Most homes would have a kerosene lamp which had to be cleaned every day. Lanterns were also used, not only in the house, but to light the path to the barn or chicken house. Some people used a reflector lamp which was fueled by kerosene. It was kept on a shelf and had a metal reflector behind the flame to throw off more light. When electricity reached the farm, most people used it only for lighting, wiring their homes with one single light hanging from the ceiling in the middle of each room. If the kitchen had one wall outlet in it for electric appliances, it was lucky.

There could be many annoying little headaches for the lady of the house. Before doors and windows were screened the biggest problem in the summer was insects. In the country there was much to draw flies to the house—livestock, fruit trees, and water from the slop bucket dumped outside the kitchen door. Small tree branches or dish towels made handy items to shoo flies outside. Everything was covered to keep out flies. Women who left food on the table between meals covered everything carefully with a pretty cloth to protect the food from flies.

PROVIDING FOOD

Many farm families were practically self-sufficient, growing or producing most of what they needed, and buying only staples. The family usually had a few dairy cattle that provided milk for drinking and for making butter and cheese. Poultry houses furnished fresh eggs daily and chickens for baking, stewing, and frying.

Farm people usually butchered their own meat. They cured and stored pork in the smokehouse. Before pressure cookers became available and long before freezer lockers were common, farm people butchered beef for use only in the winter when it would keep. Usually two or three families would get together to butcher a steer so that all the beef was consumed before it spoiled.

Fresh vegetables like beans, potatoes, greens, lettuce, beets, and cucumbers were grown in the gardens and fruit from the orchards included apples, peaches, cherries, and pears. When winter came, root vegetables and fruits like potatoes, turnips, and apples were stored in the cellar or put in the ground and then covered with straw.

To add variety to the menu or stretch out the meat supply (and because it was great relaxation as well as fine eating), men would fish for crappie, bass, goggle-eye, catfish, or suckers, and would hunt wild rabbit, quail, squirrel, possum, and coon. Women and children picked wild dock and carpenter's square in early spring for a mess of greens. They gathered blackberries, dewberries, and huckleberries in the summer and hazel nuts, hickory nuts, and black walnuts in the fall.

BUYING FOOD

But not everything could be grown at home. Going to town on Saturday to get groceries was a weekly pilgrimage for many Ozark families. However, some people who lived a long distance from town would perhaps make the trip only once every three or four weeks. People who came to town so rarely had to make sure they got all they needed to last until they could get to town again.

Because most families baked their own bread, they used a large quantity of flour and meal. The smallest purchase was a twenty-five-pound sack, and in the winter when trips to town were even less frequent they would often get a hundred-pound sack.

Many households took their own grain to a nearby mill to be ground into flour or meal whenever they ran low. Some people who did not live near a mill had all the flour they would use ground once or twice a year.

Sugar was another product bought in large quantities, especially in the summer when it was used for canning fruits and making jellies and preserves. In the very early days, people used sorghum instead of sugar.

MENUS

Big breakfasts were common and necessary on the farm, for lots of energy was needed to do the chores and hard labor necessary to keep the farm running. In order to get all their work done, the entire family had to get up very early. The typical Ozark family would rise around four in the summer. The men would often do the morning chores while the women prepared breakfast. Since the chores took anywhere from one to two hours, they well deserved the large breakfast by the time it was ready.

A typical breakfast menu consisted of fried meat, flour gravy, biscuits, eggs, and coffee or milk. The variations in this menu came from frying a different meat. Pork was the most common; people ate tenderloin and sausage near butchering time and cured shoulder, ham, and side meat the rest of the time. Lean bacon as we know it was seldom cooked for breakfast. Bacon was called side meat and it was quite fat. Some women would dress a chicken and fry it for breakfast. While frying the meat, either in its own fat or home-rendered lard, the woman would mix and bake the biscuits.

When the meat was done, the woman would remove it from the pan and place it in the warming oven. She set aside part of the grease for the gravy before she fried the eggs in the same skillet as the meat. This gave them a special flavor. She put the eggs in the warming oven when they were cooked.

Gravy was the last thing to fix and it, too, was cooked in the same pan. The standard "recipe" for flour gravy went as follows: stirring constantly, add ½ cup of flour to equal amount of the grease left in the skillet. When thoroughly mixed, slowly add about 4 cups of milk, continuing to stir to prevent lumping and scorching. Cook until desired thickness is reached. Season to taste.

The jellies, butter, salt, pepper, sugar, and everything else used each meal were left on the table, covered with a colorful tablecloth. It was a simple matter to remove the cloth, set the table, and put all hot food on the table when the men had finished their chores. Everyone ate plenty because they knew there would be a lot of hard working hours between then and the country dinner.

The big meal was at noon and was called dinner. Since everyone needed this big meal to renew energy for the afternoon work, the women would take several hours to prepare it. A basic dinner menu consisted of meat, potatoes and gravy, dried beans, corn bread, vegetables, canned fruit, and frequently pie, cobbler, or cake.

The item that took the longest to prepare was the dried beans. Pinto or white beans were the most common. In order for them to be cooked by noon, the women would soak them overnight, cutting the cooking time from seven hours to about one and a half. To give the beans a good flavor a piece of fat pork was often boiled with the beans.

Most people preferred pork or chicken, and often both would be served at the same meal. Pork was cured and would keep without refrigeration, and chickens were dressed as needed.

Chicken was always a favorite, whether a young fryer or an old hen. If the choice was a hen, the housewife would dress it soon after breakfast and immediately boil it. A special treat was to use the broth to make either noodles or dumplings. Some preferred gravy.

Potatoes were a must at every meal, as they were easily grown in the garden and stored in the cellar. The potatoes were usually fried in meat grease, or boiled and mashed, or sometimes served soupy. They were cooked whole, halved, or sliced and the cooks added cream, milk, butter, and seasonings to the cooking water when they were finished. This was not thickened, but used as stock.

The vegetables were either fresh from the garden or home-canned, such as peas, tomatoes, greens, green beans, and corn. In the summer, corn was served on the cob or cut off. It was not unusual to have dried beans and fresh or canned green beans at the same meal. Sweet potatoes, squash, and turnips added variety in late summer and fall.

Almost everyone ate corn bread nearly every day, either with gravy or beans or with butter and jelly. Light bread (yeast bread) was reserved for special occasions in most homes. Sometimes both types were served.

The table was never complete without some fruit, which was eaten as often as bread and meat. Fresh fruit was peeled and sugared or stewed. When there was no fresh fruit, a trip to the cellar produced canned fruit such as peaches, apples, or strawberries. The fruit dish was not necessarily considered the dessert, but many times a fruit pie, cobbler, or shortcake would be fixed also.

Depending on personal preference, the beverage was coffee, milk, tea, or water.

Dinner was eaten leisurely—the entire family ate together. The noon hour provided a rest period for men and women. No one was in a hurry to go back to work, and everyone sat around the table visiting. After the rest period the family resumed working until night, when they gathered again for supper.

Afternoon was usually a slack time in the kitchen, so during this time the wife cleaned the house, sewed, or did other chores. When the sun began to set the family would come in, do their chores, and gather once more for supper, the lightest meal of the day, based on the leftovers from dinner.

If there was not enough food left over from dinner, the woman sometimes fried some meat or prepared a small roast in addition to the leftovers. When the family was hungry and tired the woman would prepare very simple meals. Two easy dishes using corn meal were mush and hush puppies.

Mush was usually made in large enough quantities to have some left to fry for breakfast the next day. It is good served with just butter when very hot, or with butter, sugar, molasses or honey, and milk. This is very much like Cream of Wheat or Malt-O-Meal.

Another common supper dish was leftover corn bread crumbled into milk. With some added sweetening it was like cereal today.

Fresh garden vegetables added variety. In season whole meals could be made of them—wilted lettuce (a mixture of hot grease and mild vinegar poured over cut-up leaf lettuce and green onions); cucumbers sliced into vinegar or pickle juice; buttered turnips or fresh corn.

There was always plenty of milk, eggs, and butter to supplement the meals, and jellies, jams, pickles, and relishes to satisfy every taste.

The whole family would sit down to eat together as they did at other meals. In summer the family often would not eat supper until eight or nine o'clock because of the long workdays, but in winter they usually finished their chores and were ready to eat by six or seven o'clock.

After the family ate supper everyone's chores and work for the day was finished—except for the women, who still had plenty to do. In summer the children went to bed shortly after supper but in winter there was time for everyone to sit around the fireplace or stove and entertain themselves by playing games, singing, or just munching apples and talking.

The women cleared the table of everything except the staples that were always left on the table, for instance, salt, pepper, sugar, butter, peanut butter, jelly, vinegar, toothpicks, and different spices and seasonings. The remaining food was fed to the farm animals.

The dogs got all the corn bread, potatoes, and meat left over from the meal. Since most people never purchased dog food years ago, some women would make twice as much corn bread as the family would eat so as to feed the dogs.

The chickens got the vegetables and eggshells and sometimes the peelings.

Everything else during the day went into the slop bucket—milk, dishwater, peelings, and any other food or waste water. The women carried this out and either poured it into the hog troughs or mixed it with wheat shorts (a by-product of milling) to feed to the hogs.

The women would clear the plates, glasses, and silverware from the table after every meal and wash them. They arranged the food that was left over neatly on the table and spread a clean tablecloth over everything. After they had washed and dried the dishes, they also stacked them under the cloth or stored them in the safe. There was usually a place to stand plates on end in the back of the shelves and space in front to store the bowls and glasses. One shelf was usually used to store the food that was already prepared, like pies and cakes.

The silverware was usually put in several different places. The spoons were placed in spoon holders on the table, one for serving spoons and one for teaspoons. The spoon holders were sometimes purchased as a set with the sugar bowl and cream pitcher. The knives and forks were stored in a drawer of the safe. However, some women would keep all the table settings needed for the family under the tablecloth because there wasn't enough storage space and it was easier to set the table for the next meal.

After the dishes were put away, the women would straighten up the kitchen, sweep the floors, fill the water buckets and the stove reservoir, and carry in enough wood for cooking the next day. Finally, they would be finished for the day.

On Thanksgiving, Christmas, the Fourth of July, or other special days, treats were included in the daily meal. Oranges, rarely seen the rest of the year, could be found in Christmas stockings and also on the Fourth of July. Lemonade was a summer treat, especially with ice from the icehouse. The children did not often have snacks, but when they did, they usually consisted of a cookie or bread-and-butter sandwich with a glass of milk.

WASHING

Washing the dishes after each meal was done differently than it is today. In most kitchens, sinks were not common until quite recently.

Some women were fortunate enough to have a well or cistern close enough to the house so they could have a hand pump inside, but most families carried the water inside in buckets which they placed on the washstand. This stand was really a small table where the water for all the household chores was stored. A dipper, washbasin, and soap dish sat beside the water bucket. The slop bucket sat under the table to eliminate a trip outside to empty the container each time water was used. All waste water, as well as garbage, was poured into this bucket.

As soon as they were strong enough, children were expected to keep the water bucket filled. The bucket held about two and a half gallons and was wooden, granite, or, later on, white enamel sometimes trimmed in red.

Bittersweet staff
members Kathy
Hawk and Kyra
Gibson draw water
for dinner.

The dishwashing chore was done by first heating the water, either in a tea-kettle or in the reservoir of the stove. Dishwashing took two pans, one for washing the dishes, the other for scalding. Without a sink to wash in, many women washed dishes on the broad, flat stove surface which kept the dish-water hot—sometimes too hot!

Homemade lye soap was put in the bottom of the dishpan, and hot water from the teakettle was poured directly on the soap to make suds. Cold water dipped from the water bucket was added to the dishwater to make it the right temperature. Some women had a metal utensil with a cage at the end of the handle which was just the right size to hold a cake of soap. This could be put into hot dishwater and stirred to make suds.

Dishes were washed and stacked into the other dishpan and hot scalding water was poured over them. The dishes were then dried and put away.

The kitchen was also used as a bathroom. Men shaved there, and all the family washed up and brushed their teeth there. One night a week the kitchen was used for bathing since it was convenient to heat the water there and it was the warmest place in the house to take a bath. The tub of water was usually placed near the stove and every member of the family took a turn bathing.

COOLING FOOD

In years past it was more difficult to keep food cool than it is today. Now freezers and refrigerators do our cooling for us, but before electricity came to the rural areas there were few ways to keep things cool enough to prevent spoilage. However, the Ozark people had several methods of cooling their food.

In the winter, people made use of the natural cold temperature. Food was sometimes covered and put in outdoor window boxes, and porches also served as winter refrigerators if the food was carefully covered so there would be no danger of animals eating it.

Storing perishables in hot weather posed a much greater problem. Some people were lucky enough to have a cave spring near their homes. The spring —clean, clear, and cold—would flow out of the ground from a cave opening. The farm wife would put the foods she wanted to keep cool in watertight jars, usually gallon or half-gallon size, and place them on shelves built inside the cave letting the 52° spring water flow over them. Sometimes, however, shelves were built on the cave's side walls. The food could be put on these shelves and the cool cave temperature would keep the food from spoiling so quickly. Often pans containing food to be cooled were set in the water but not completely submerged.

If a cave was not available, people built springhouses over the spring. The houses were small and had only one door. Food to be cooled could be put on shelves, submerged in the water, or hung from the rafter in buckets. The house protected the food from stock and wild animals.

Cisterns and dug wells were two other popular ways of keeping things cool. Both functioned in about the same way as the springs. The food was put into a pail or bucket and lowered on a rope or chain down into the water, or just down a few feet into the well, to take advantage of the cooler temperature.

In a similar manner, a pit several inches deep was often dug in the ground in a place protected from the sun, such as the north side of the house. River sand and gravel were placed in the bottom of the hole, and a frame with a lid was built around it so nothing would get into the food. Water was added from time to time to the sandy bottom and the natural coolness of the ground helped keep food somewhat cool.

As better transportation methods enabled people to get to town frequently to purchase ice, iceboxes became popular in summer months. They were usually small and square in size. Some of them had a square opening on one side of the top of the box so a block of ice could be put in from the top, while others had a door that opened from the front. The opening in the top had a cover which could be removed. In the compartment below fifty-, seventy-five-,

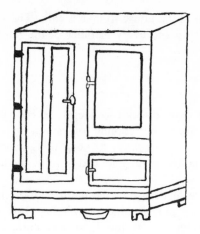

Ice was stored in the top right compartment. Note the pan to catch the drippings from the melting ice.

or hundred-pound blocks of ice could be stored in insulated compartments. Adjacent to and underneath the compartment were doors which opened to expose shelves for food storage.

Since the ice would melt little by little during the day a pan had to be kept under the side where it was stored to catch the dripping water. This pan had to be emptied frequently or puddles of water would form and run across the kitchen floor. The hundred-pound cake of ice would last about two days in hot weather. Because the ice had to be replaced so often, iceboxes were not practical for use very far from an ice plant. They were used mainly in or near towns and villages where there were sometimes ice routes.

There was another method of cooling that was available to those who had access to a river or pond and an ice shed. In winter ice cut out of the rivers would last until midsummer if stored well. Getting ice was usually a neighborhood undertaking, requiring several men to get the ice out of the river, load on wagons, and store. The men would stand on solid ice near the riverbank, and, using a crosscut saw with one handle removed, they would cut a long strip of ice. They then cut this strip into blocks small enough to handle and with ice tongs lifted the blocks out of the river and onto a wagon. The wagon was driven to a shed where they stacked the ice solidly and compactly.

The shed belonged to one of the men of the community, who would loan it for the storage of ice, and the ice was often used by the whole community. Anyone wanting the ice was welcome to help himself, taking what he needed.

Sawdust was used as insulation to keep the ice from melting. A space of about one foot would be left between the wall of the shed and the ice and sawdust would be closely packed in this space and piled at least a foot thick on top.

As ice was often difficult to get, it was not used regularly for drinking water, but mostly saved for making ice cream or served at dinners for threshing crews or other special occasions.

The housewife's tasks were done without the aid of modern kitchen appliances and surroundings. That old saying, "Man works from sun to sun, but a woman's work is never done," seems to have been written especially for the busy Ozark farm wife. But in spite of all the hard work, she led a satisfying life as she labored in her home and garden with her children to help with the chores. As she glanced around her kitchen before she blew out the lamp and went off to bed, she must have smiled a smile of contentment for a job well done, even though it would have to be done all over again tomorrow!

...and a Dash of Salt

"How much salt do you put in your cookies?" we asked.

"Oh, just a dash. Then add a couple big handfuls of flour, a chunk of butter the size of a walnut, and pour in enough milk until it looks right."

There has been no exact testing of the following recipes using wild or farm-grown foods which the women shared orally with us. The testing has been over the years through the cooks' experience in knowing just how much water to add or how much baking powder to dip out using their particular spoon. They can show how they make cookies, but sometimes have difficulty translating that knowledge to standardized cups and teaspoons. So experiment yourself with these foods and the measurements and directions that we found worked for us. But don't expect the result to be as good as Grandma's unless you also use garden-grown squash, wild gooseberries, home-butchered meat, or stone-ground meal.

No meal was ever complete without some kind of bread, which up to the 1940s was usually made from home-grown wheat or corn ground into flour or meal at the local mill.

CORN BREAD

Sift all corn meal to take out bran. Make the amount according to your pan (about 2 cups for 8×8×2-inch pan).

½ teaspoon salt
1 teaspoon baking soda
1 cup buttermilk (enough for a
    firm but pourable consistency)

1 egg
3 tablespoons melted shortening

Mix all together. Bake in a warm oven (375°) till brown. Serve while hot. Serves 6.

CRACKLING BREAD (CORN STICKS)

1 quart corn meal
3 teaspoons salt
Boiling water

1 pint cracklings (crisp remains of
fat after rendering lard)

Mix the corn meal and salt. Pour over this mixture enough boiling water to moisten, but not enough to make a mush. When meal has cooled, work the cracklings into it with your fingers. Form the dough into cakes about 4 inches long, 2 inches wide, and 1 inch thick. Bake at 450° around 30 minutes and serve while very hot. Serves 12–15 people.

CORN MEAL MUSH

Take about 1 quart boiling salted water, stir in 1½ cups meal until it gets thick (about like Cream of Wheat). Serve in sweet milk, or after cooling, slice and fry until brown. Or use your mush like breakfast food with cream and sugar.

HUSH PUPPIES

Hush puppies are made by simply dicing an onion in corn bread batter; dropping by spoonfuls into deep fat or meat grease, and cooking until golden brown. The meat grease gives it a good flavor.

BISCUITS

Flour
½ cup buttermilk
½ cup milk
1½ teaspoons baking powder

1 teaspoon baking soda
1 teaspoon salt
2 tablespoons shortening

Many women traditionally mixed their biscuits in a flour container, which was usually a large bowl or a pan approximately 12 to 18 inches across and 6 to 8 inches deep about half filled with flour. First, form a small hole in the flour. Put the above ingredients in it. With your hand, work flour into other ingredients until dough is just stiff enough to break off into small balls. It usually will take 2½ to 3 cups of flour to get the right consistency. Place pinched-off balls of dough in rows in a greased pan and bake at 500° for 15 minutes or until brown.

RAISED BISCUITS

1 cake yeast	3 tablespoons melted butter
3 tablespoons sugar	1 egg, unbeaten
1 cup warm water	2 teaspoons salt
1 cup milk	7 cups flour

Soak yeast and sugar in water for 30 minutes. Then add milk, melted butter, egg, and salt. Stir in about 7 cups of flour for a soft dough. Let rise and knead down 3 times. Make biscuits the size of an egg by cutting with a glass. Place in a greased pan—don't overcrowd. Cover with a clean white cloth and let stand overnight. Bake in hot oven (400°) until golden brown. Makes 2½ dozen.

OLD OZARKS BREAD RECIPE
(with everlasting yeast)

To the yeast starter, add 1½ cups of lukewarm water in a large milk crock or mixing bowl. Add sifted white flour to make a batter a little thicker than for pancakes. Cover and let stand overnight. The cover must be very tight in gnat season.

In the morning take out about ½ cup of the new starter. Add 1 tablespoon of sugar, or more if you take out a larger amount of starter. Put this in a jar with a lid and keep in a cool place. This will keep two to three weeks if 1 tablespoon of sugar is added from time to time.

To the remaining batter, add 3 teaspoons sugar (for dark bread use molasses and brown sugar), 1 tablespoon salt, 1 cup milk or lukewarm water, ½ cup fat, melted and cooled. Add sifted flour to make a stiff dough. Knead and let rise in greased crock until double in bulk. Form into loaves and let rise in a warm place until they double in size. Bake in hot oven (400°) for 15 minutes. Reduce heat and finish at 350° for 30 minutes. Variation: This recipe can be made of half white and half whole wheat flour.

It really takes experience to bake with everlasting yeast. Keeping the yeast alive in pioneer days was a must. It was also difficult to keep without refrigeration unless used at least twice each week, but with a large family this was no problem. If something happened to keep one from using it regularly, a neighbor was always willing to share hers.

HOT ROLLS

Dissolve 1 package yeast in 1¾ cups warm water. Add ⅓ cup sugar, ¼ cup melted shortening, 2 teaspoons salt, and flour enough to make dough stiff (about 4 to 5 cups). Knead until satiny. Leave this in a mixing bowl and let rise for 2 hours. Place on floured board and mold into a ball. Then break off into small balls and place in a greased pan and let rise 1½ to 2 hours. Bake in a 375° oven until brown.

PIE CRUST

1¼ cups shortening	1 egg
2 cups stone-ground whole wheat flour	1 tablespoon vinegar
	5 tablespoons water
1 cup white flour	1 teaspoon salt

Crumble shortening and flours together to a meal consistency. Beat the remaining ingredients together and add them to the first mixture. Mix lightly and roll on a floured board for pie.

NOODLES

Beat together 3 eggs, 3 tablespoons milk, 1 teaspoon salt. Add about 2 cups flour to the other ingredients, enough to make a thick dough. Roll thin and sprinkle the top with flour. Let stand 30 minutes. Starting at one edge, roll up the dough like a jelly roll. Beginning at one end, slice or shave off strips ⅛ inch thick. Let stand 2 hours. Drop into boiling broth and cook 10 minutes.

DUMPLINGS

Sift together 1 cup flour, ½ teaspoon salt, 1½ teaspoons baking powder. Add ½ cup milk and 2 tablespoons fat. Mix together. Drop with a spoon into boiling broth. Cover tightly and steam 10 to 15 minutes without lifting the lid.

WHOLE WHEAT BREAD

1 tablespoon white sugar
⅓ cup warm water
1 package dry yeast
¼ cup shortening
2 tablespoons brown sugar, 1 tablespoon molasses, and 1 tablespoon honey or ¼ cup brown sugar

1 tablespoon salt
1 egg
1 cup milk, scalded and cooled
3½ cups stone-ground whole wheat flour
½ cup unbleached white flour

Stir white sugar into water. Add yeast and let yeast rise. Combine shortening, brown sugar, molasses and honey, salt, egg, and scalded milk. Add 2 cups whole wheat flour. When lukewarm, add yeast and beat hard till smooth. Cover and let rise about ½ hour. Mix the remaining whole wheat flour with the unbleached flour and add enough to make a stiff dough. Knead in enough flour to make smooth and satiny. Let dough rise in a greased bowl until doubled. Knead lightly. Make into rolls or a loaf and let rise again. Bake in 325° oven 15 minutes, then 45 minutes at 350°.

WHOLE WHEAT MUFFINS

1 cup whole wheat flour
  (old-timers called this graham flour)
1 cup soft wheat white flour
3 teaspoons baking powder
1 teaspoon salt

1 egg
¾ cup milk
2 tablespoons molasses
3 tablespoons brown sugar
4 tablespoons melted shortening

Mix all ingredients together. Bake in greased muffin tins, 15 minutes in a moderate oven (400°).

Variation: You can add blueberries, nuts, huckleberries, or other fruits for a special taste.

WHEAT NUTS

This breakfast food is made with home-ground wheat flour. It requires:

3½ cups home-ground whole
   wheat flour
1 teaspoon baking soda
1 teaspoon salt

1 cup honey or syrup
Buttermilk or sour milk to
   moisten

Mix all ingredients together and bake in a moderate oven like a cake. When done, cool and crumble. If not dry enough, put it back in oven to crispen. Serve with hot rich cream.

Sugar was much harder to come by than flour, for the Ozark farmers never grew sugar cane or sugar beets. Sugar had to be purchased at the store, and thus the cook was economical in using sugar. But home-grown and wild fruit needed sugar to become pies and cakes, jellies and jams, so she would save her egg money to buy sugar. Sweets made from the following recipes completed many a country dinner and garnished many breakfast biscuits.

SQUASH PIE

Pastry for 1-crust pie
2 scant cups well-cooked squash
½ cup sugar
1 cup sweet cream
2 eggs separated

½ teaspoon allspice
½ teaspoon cinnamon
½ teaspoon lemon extract
Pinch of salt

Cook squash, sugar, cream, and egg yolk until mixture is the consistency of custard, then add allspice, cinnamon, and lemon extract, and salt. Mix and pour into a pan lined with rich pastry. Bake 40 to 50 minutes at 425°. Add meringue if desired, and brown ten minutes more.

GREEN TOMATO PIE

Pie dough
5 or 6 large green tomatoes
Salt

½ to ¾ cup sugar
Ground cinnamon and nutmeg
Butter

Line the pie pan with dough, leaving a small amount of dough for the top crust. Chop the green tomatoes in fine pieces in a bowl, using all the juice from the tomatoes. Sprinkle the tomatoes with a bit of salt to take out the sweet taste, and mix slightly. Pour into uncooked pie crust, sprinkle sugar and spice over the mixture, and dot with butter. Roll out the remaining dough and cut into strips. Crisscross the pastry across the pie for top crust. Bake in a hot oven (400°) until crust is brown.

GOOSEBERRY COBBLER

Ethel Massey remembers how her mother used to make gooseberry cobbler. In the latter part of May or early June, her mother would take the girls out to pick gooseberries that grew wild around bluffs and creek banks. They picked them green to use in pies, cobblers, and jellies. To prepare the gooseberries for use, they pinched off the blossom end as well as the stem.

Pie dough	Butter
4 tablespoons flour	2 cups gooseberries
2 cups sugar	½ cup water*

Spread the rolled pie dough in the bottom of the pan so that it hangs well over the edges of the pan. Instead of a separate top crust, the extra dough is folded to the center over the fruit. Mix together the flour and sugar. Spread half of the mixture over the pie dough in the bottom of the pan. Dot with butter. Add gooseberries and water. Sprinkle remaining flour and sugar mixture over the berries and dot with butter again. Fold over the extra dough to form the top crust. Sprinkle a little sugar on top and bake in a moderate oven.

Variation: Any fruit may be fixed in this manner. You might want to try peaches, blackberries, plums, or some other fruit.

RAW APPLE CAKE

1 cup butter	2 teaspoons cinnamon
2 cups sugar	1 teaspoon nutmeg
4 eggs	1 cup cold coffee
4 cups flour	2 cups raw apples sliced thin
1 teaspoon cloves	1 cup raisins
2 teaspoons baking soda	1 cup walnuts

Cream together butter and sugar. Add beaten eggs and mix. Sift all dry ingredients and add with coffee. Add sliced apples, raisins, and nuts. Pour into a greased and flour-dusted 13×9×2-inch pan. Bake for 1 hour at 350°.

* If using canned gooseberries, omit water and use less sugar.

FROSTING FOR RAW APPLE CAKE

2 tablespoons melted butter   ½ cup coconut
3 tablespoons cream   ½ cup chopped nuts
½ cup brown sugar

Mix all ingredients together. Spread on cake while warm, or broil after topping is added.

HICKORY NUT CAKE

1½ cups sugar   ½ teaspoon allspice
½ cup lard*   1 cup milk
2 cups flour   2 eggs
2½ teaspoons baking powder   1 teaspoon vanilla
½ teaspoon cinnamon   1 cup hickory nut meats
¼ teaspoon nutmeg

Cream sugar and lard together. Sift dry ingredients together and add to creamed mixture alternately with milk and beaten eggs until smooth and well mixed. Add vanilla and nut meats. Put in greased loaf cake pan and bake in a moderate (350° to 375°) oven. Cool the cake. Top with any boiled icing, and sprinkle generously with hickory nuts.

Persimmons, a small, round yellow-orange fruit, have found their way into many Ozark recipes. Their flavor is at its best when they are soft and wrinkled and look to be spoiled. They are best picked late in the fall, preferably after a frost when they are at the peak of flavor.

PERSIMMON CAKE

2 cups chopped nuts   2 teaspoons cinnamon
2 cups raisins   ½ teaspoon cloves
2 cups persimmon pulp   2 teaspoons baking soda
2 cups sugar   1 teaspoon salt
2 tablespoons oil   1 cup milk
3 cups sifted flour

Mix nuts, raisins, persimmon pulp, sugar, and oil. Sift dry ingredients, add to creamed mixture alternately with milk. Bake in an angel food cake pan, that has been greased and floured, at 350° for 30 minutes or until done.

* You may substitute butter or shortening if you have no lard.

PERSIMMON BREAD

1 cup persimmon puree
½ cup cooking oil
1½ cups sugar
2 eggs
½ teaspoon cloves
½ teaspoon nutmeg
½ teaspoon cinnamon

½ teaspoon allspice
1 teaspoon salt
¼ teaspoon baking powder
1 teaspoon baking soda
1¾ cups flour
½ cup raisins

Make a puree by rubbing persimmons through a sieve or food mill. Measure oil in mixing bowl, add sugar, and mix well. Then add eggs, persimmon puree, spices and salt sifted with baking powder, soda, and flour, and raisins. Turn into three or four oiled pans, filling each a half to two thirds full. Bake 45 minutes at 350° or until bread tests done.

PERSIMMON BARS

½ cup butter or oleo
2 eggs
1 cup persimmon pulp
½ teaspoon nutmeg
¼ teaspoon salt
1 cup chopped nuts
1 cup white sugar

1 teaspoon baking soda
2 cups flour
½ teaspoon cinnamon
¼ teaspoon cloves
1 teaspoon grated lemon rind
1 cup raisins

Mix well in order given and put in 9×12-inch greased pan. Bake about 20 minutes at 350° or until done. When cooled, frost with Brown Butter Frosting.

BROWN BUTTER FROSTING

Brown ¼ cup butter in heavy saucepan until amber-colored. Beat in 2 cups sifted powdered sugar, ½ teaspoon vanilla, ⅛ teaspoon salt, and 2 to 3 tablespoons light cream. Blend thoroughly and spread on cooled bars.

Here are two variations of the popular Persimmon Pudding.

PERSIMMON PUDDING I

1 cup flour	1 cup sugar
1 teaspoon salt	1 teaspoon baking soda
1 teaspoon cinnamon	¾ cup milk
1 cup persimmon pulp	1 teaspoon vanilla
2 tablespoons melted butter	3 egg yolks, beaten
1 cup chopped dates	1 cup chopped nuts

Combine and sift together all dry ingredients. Add the remaining ingredients, mix, and pour into a baking dish. Bake at moderate temperature (350°) until done.

PERSIMMON PUDDING II

2 cups buttermilk	½ teaspoon allspice
2 cups persimmon pulp	1 teaspoon cinnamon
1 cup sugar	½ teaspoon baking soda
1 egg	1 teaspoon baking powder
1 tablespoon butter	1½ cups flour
¼ teaspoon cloves	

Mix buttermilk, pulp, sugar, egg, and butter. Add spices, soda, and baking powder, sifted with flour. Pour into a 13×9×2-inch greased and floured pan. Bake at 350° for about 45 minutes. Serve with this sauce:

1 cup sugar	1 teaspoon vanilla
1 tablespoon flour	1 tablespoon butter
1 cup boiling water	Pinch of salt

Mix in order and cook until clear.

PERSIMMON SUGAR PLUMS

As late in the fall as possible, gather firm ripe persimmons. In the bottom of a dry container place a layer of hulled persimmons. Cover this with a layer of sugar and continue alternating layers until container is filled. Cover and let mellow in a cool, dry place. These tasty morsels will convince you that people in the Ozarks know how to eat.

PLUM BUTTER

The small wild plums that grow in the Ozarks have a delicious tart flavor that is excellent in jams, jellies, and butters.

3 quarts red plums   Sugar
½ cup water

After washing, put the plums in a large preserving kettle with ½ cup water, cover, and cook over low heat to simmering point. Simmer gently until plums burst and juice flows freely. Remove from fire and rub plums through a colander. This should produce about 9 cups of pulp.

For each cup of pulp add 1 cup sugar. Return pulp and sugar to the kettle and heat to simmering. Stir until well mixed. Bring to a boil and boil vigorously until mixture reaches the desired consistency. It should coat the spoon and drop off thickly and slowly in about 20 minutes. Be sure to stir constantly, as plums will burn easily. When done, pour into jelly glasses or jars and seal.

Variation: Cook the plum butter in the oven in an open, flat pan for about 1 to 1½ hours to avoid having to stir the butter and popping.

STRAWBERRY JAM

1 quart strawberries   1 tablespoon vinegar or lemon
1 quart sugar   juice

Wash strawberries before stemming, then cut each berry in half. Sprinkle sugar over berries. Let stand until juice rises. Bring to a boil slowly and boil for 10 minutes. Add vinegar or lemon juice and boil 3 minutes longer. Let stand for 24 hours, then seal. Make only 1 or 2 quarts at a time for best results.

CARROT MARMALADE

1 pound carrots   2 lemons
2 oranges   6½ cups sugar

Cook carrots until tender, then grind fine. Remove orange and lemon peel, making sure that the thin white skin is removed. Then grind the peel fine and add to carrots. After hard center and seeds have been removed, add lemon and orange pulp and juice. This should equal about 4 cups. Measure sugar and add to prepared ingredients. Put into a large kettle. Mix well and bring to a boil for 2 minutes. Stir constantly before and after cooking. Remove from heat and pour in jars. Seal at once.

PAWPAW JAM

Pawpaws are the fruit of a small tree that grows along the bluffs of river and creek bottoms. The elongated fruit is greenish brown with a soft pulp which tastes like a cross between a banana and an avocado. It ripens in the fall and is best when quite ripe. Those who enjoy the flavor usually eat the fruit raw, but they can be used in cakes like bananas or made into jam.

Put 3½ cups of pawpaw pulp and ½ cup water in a large pan. Add juice of 1 lemon and 1 box of Surejell or Certo and bring to a boil. Add 5½ cups sugar and bring to a rolling boil that cannot be stirred down. Boil for 3 minutes. Remove from heat and pour into sterilized glass jars. Cover with paraffin to seal. Serve with hot buttered biscuits for a real treat.

Hominy

While it was cooking, the mess in the pan looked like the worst batch of mud pies ever made, but it turned out to be fluffy white, mouth-watering hominy, a simple country dish made from dried corn, water, and a little lye. Ella Dunn had rotted the ashes from the fireplace so that they were just like strong lye, added some water and shelled corn, and cooked them on the stove.

This method of making hominy was undoubtedly used by Indians and older than other methods, which use either liquid lye from the ash hopper or purchased concentrated lye because it by-passes the process of isolating the lye. Ella doesn't think this method is any harder to do and she prefers the result. According to *Organic Gardening* (December 1976, p. 87), the finished product made with ashes probably has a higher nutritional value because of the chemical reactions that occur when ashes and corn are heated in water. The ash water adds calcium and trace minerals such as iron and magnesium to the kernel, increasing the natural nutritional value of the grain. The ash water also makes the protein and niacin already in the corn more available and digestible.

The Indians probably originated hominy to give variety to a diet that depended greatly on corn. Making hominy was a way to continue using corn after the growing season in some form other than corn meal. Since the stored dried corn would not spoil, the ingredients were always at hand and it could be made throughout the year as a vegetable dish. Either yellow or white corn can be used, though most preferred white corn because it makes such a pretty white fluffy product. The variety that most preferred was Hickory King (usually pronounced "cane").

To prepare the corn for making hominy, simply shell by rubbing the cobs together so that the kernels come off, then wash the kernels to remove parts of the cob and the silks. One gallon of dried corn will make two gallons of hominy.

The methods of making hominy differ only in the methods of obtaining the lye. The purpose of the lye is to remove the hard outside hull of the dried corn, leaving the edible kernel. The lye also loosens the dark eyes, which are not appealing to the eye.

Ella sifts the ashes as you would flour to remove the large pieces of char-

Kyra Gibson is not sure the muddy mess of ashes and corn Ella Dunn is cooking will ever be edible.

Shell the corn by rubbing the two ears together.

coal and rocks. She warned us not to use cedar ashes but to use hickory or any kind of oak. After sifting, she puts the ashes in a porcelain or enameled pan and dampens them so that they will rot. She covers the pan and leaves it for about a week until the ashes are ready to use.

To make hominy with these ashes, she spoons out about a quart of ashes for approximately three pints of corn. She puts the ashes in a big enameled pot and pours about a gallon of water over this, stirring until it is pretty well dissolved. Ella told us, "You don't want to put too much water. Too much would make it too weak and take away the value of your lye." Then she adds the corn and cooks the mixture, which looks like thick bubbling mud.

It is necessary to keep stirring the hot ash-water mixture to prevent the sediment and hulls from baking in the bottom of the pan. Use a wooden spoon, as the lye in the ashes will eat up a metal one.

When the hulls are loosened, she takes the pot of hominy off the stove and rinses and rerinses the hominy to remove the ash mud and wash away the hulls and eyes. Take the pan of cooked corn and ashes outside to rinse in a big sieve with the hose to dispose of the muddy ashes. While rinsing, Ella rubs the hominy through her fingers to take off all the eyes and hulls.

The result is raw hominy.

To make hominy, most people did not use ashes directly but gathered liquid lye in an ash hopper. Besides its use in hominy they needed lye for soap making, house cleaning, hog butchering (to loosen the hair before scraping), and for other farm and household tasks.

As they took wood ashes from the fireplace, cookstove, or heating stoves they would dump them outside into the ash hopper. When it rained, water would trickle through the ashes, leaching out the alkaline salts (sodium hydroxide) commonly known as lye.

The ash hoppers were made of wood. A frame of poles or 2×4s anchored into the ground held the V-shaped bin of 1×6s or 1×8s. The bin was wide at the top for ease in dumping ashes and to have a larger area to catch the rain. The bin, slanting down from back to front, narrowed to a very small opening or point at the bottom. A trough was placed along the bottom of the bin to catch the lye water, which would run down to the low end and be caught in an iron, stone, granite, or wooden container.

The trough was sometimes a split log, hollowed out, or one made of sawed oak lumber. The bucket to catch the lye had to be covered for safety. If an old hen got into it, the lye would take off all her feathers. The bucket was emptied into a bigger covered barrel kept in the smokehouse or shed out of the reach of small children. When lye was needed, it was dipped out with a granite or stone cup.

The amount of lye made by the rain was usually sufficient for daily use. However, in the spring or when a large amount of lye was needed—such as before making soap or butchering—people would pour water into the ash hopper.

Even without an ash hopper, liquid lye can be made quickly by putting

Rinse the hominy
repeatedly to dispose of
the ashes.

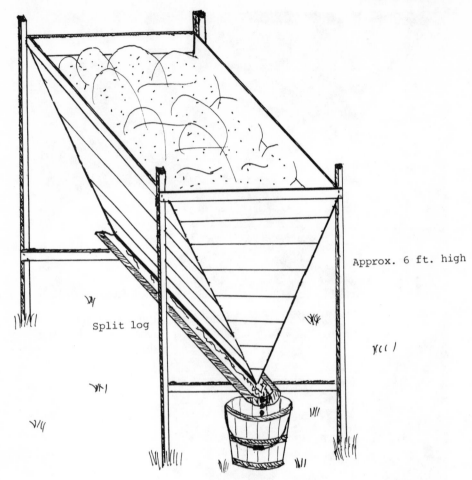

Approx. 6 ft. high

Split log

An old-time ash hopper.

about one gallon of ashes in a cloth, tying the top, and putting it in a granite pan with two gallons of water. Set the pan on the heating stove to keep it warm overnight.

The ash hopper served as a very useful piece of equipment, but due to the production of concentrated lye, the ash hopper is seldom used today.

To see how hominy using liquid or concentrated lye was made, we went to the Hough farm one rainy day to help Elvie and Myrtle and their friend Annie Fike make hominy the same way their parents and grandparents did. They put the clean corn kernels into an iron kettle or other suitable container with enough lye water to cover it. They used two tablespoons of concentrated lye to a quart of corn. Build a fire under the kettle and cook until the husk is loosened, about twenty to twenty-five minutes. Then wash the corn in hot water to remove the skins and the lye. The lye will cause white corn to turn yellow, but after three or four washings and boilings it will return to its natural color. After washing, put the corn in clean water, boil again about twenty minutes, and rewash. Repeat this washing and boiling in fresh water until the corn is tender enough to be eaten and the husks and black hearts are removed. Season with salt and pepper and serve.

Today we can make large quantities of hominy and then freeze or can it for later use. To freeze, just seal in airtight containers and quick-freeze. Most people can hominy in the pressure cooker. They put a teaspoon of salt in each quart jar and fill the jar only two thirds full of hominy because it will swell some more. Then they fill the jar to within ½ inch of the top with water and seal. They pressure-cook it at 10 pounds pressure for an hour and a half to two hours.

No matter which method is used in making hominy, the hot steamy dish, seasoned and garnished with butter, is good, nutritious food.

Christmas Goose

Though geese were a common sight on many Ozark farms of the past, they were not used for food as much as for their feathers. Few but those Ozarkians of German descent appreciated and included goose on their tables. Ella Hough said her mother, Louise Schneider, felt she had not adequately celebrated a holiday or birthday in their home if goose wasn't the main dish. To keep a steady supply she raised geese every spring. In late fall she would pen them up to fatten on grain so that the first would be ready to dress out by the eleventh of November, Ella's father's birthday. When the weather got cold enough, her mother would dress out half a dozen or more geese to hang in the smokehouse where they would keep for Thanksgiving, Christmas, and other special occasions.

She prepared the meat in several ways. Sometimes she would slice the breast and fry it like Canadian bacon, boiling the bony parts for soup. "The liver is nice. Nothing is as nice as goose liver fried in butter," Ella said. But the most common way of preparing was baking.

And baking a goose was what Pearl Thelma Massey wanted to do for the big Christmas dinner she always has at her house for her husband's family. Using her nephew's farm-raised goose, and following Ella's directions for dressing and baking, she added her own years of experience in cooking fowl to prepare her Christmas goose.

DRESSING THE GOOSE

Any age goose can be used, but the best for baking are those less than a year old.

Chop off the head in one clean stroke with an ax. Do not let the bird flop around afterward or the meat will get bruised. Hold the goose tightly for a few minutes until it stops struggling, then hold it by the legs with the neck down to let it bleed.

The easiest way to remove the feathers is to scald the bird, but if you wish to save the feathers for pillows, you should pick the goose dry, though dry picking is much harder. It is possible to save the wet feathers, but they have to be dried to store.

Since the feathers on a goose are very thick and full of oil that makes them

The Christmas goose.

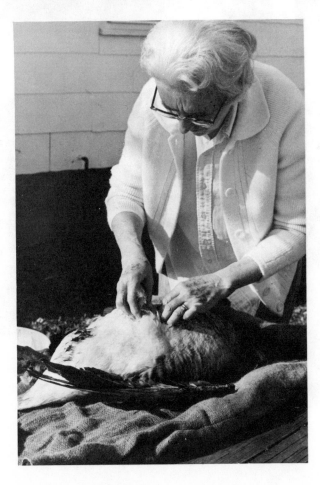

Pearl Thelma Massey
picks the soft down to use
in pillows.

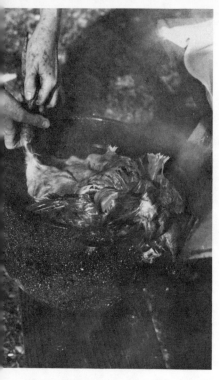

Scald bird in lots of steaming water to loosen the feathers.

Wrap steaming bird in heavy towel.

Remove the feathers leaving skin clean.

Singe to remove hair.

cling together, it is helpful to soak the bird in cold water before scalding. Soaking helps saturate the feathers and makes them easier to pluck. Some people soak the goose in water sudsy with detergent, which cuts the oil better and allows the water to penetrate to the skin.

After cold water has penetrated to the skin, dip the goose in scalding water, briefly but adequately, so that the hot water can loosen the feathers from the skin. Dip in neck first, and then feet first to be sure all parts are scalded.

Then wrap the bird immediately in a large bath towel or a sack heavy enough to hold in all the steam. Let the bird steam for fifteen to twenty minutes.

Remove the towel and pick all the feathers. This is the hardest part of dressing a goose but is important for a beautiful finished dish for the table.

When all feathers are removed, singe the bird to remove the hairs. A crumpled-up piece of newspaper set on fire is adequate. Run all sides of the bird quickly through the flame.

The goose is now prepared as you would any other fowl. To cut off the feet, bend them down and with a sharp knife cut through the skin and membranes at the joints. Discard the feet.

Wash the skin thoroughly with clean cold water to remove any feathers, soot from singeing, and other dirt. The skin should be soft and oily and a slightly yellowish white.

Now you are ready to remove the innards, or draw the goose. Pull back the skin on the throat, reach in, and pull out the craw or crop. Be careful not to squeeze it. Cut the esophagus leading to the intestines. Discard the craw.

Now go to the other end of the goose. Cut off the oil sack on top of the tail. Holding the tail up, cut a horizontal line just under the tail about two to three inches long. Be careful to cut close to the tail and not puncture the end of the intestinal tract. Cut another line parallel to that one under the anus, again making sure not to cut through the tract. Then cut around the opening of the anus. (Some people find scissors very helpful in making these cuts.) You should now have a square opening large enough to insert your hand. Reach in carefully and pull out the innards. Everything should come out together, as you already cut the connection at the neck when you took out the craw. Remove everything without piercing the intestines and lay this aside. You may have to reach in again to remove the liver, heart, and lungs (often called lights). Be sure everything in the cavity is removed.

Wash the bird carefully inside and out.

Now remove from the intestinal mass the heart, liver, and gizzard. Cut the arteries from the heart and squeeze out any blood. Wash and put it in a pan of water. Cut the gall (a long, greenish gland) from the liver. Be careful not to cut into it, for the gall will spread greenish fluid over the liver. Next separate the gizzard from the intestines. Hold it in your left hand so that one of the openings to the intestines is up and the other opening, about one third around the gizzard, is facing you. You will notice between the openings fatty

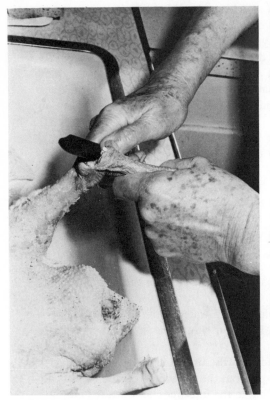

Cut off feet at the joint.

Cut under tail to remove the innards.

Cut open the gizzard between the two openings. Be careful not to cut the sack.

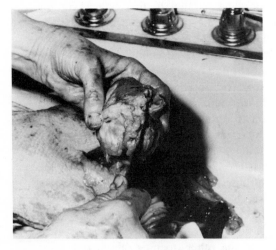

tissue covering a sort of rounded muscular tissue. With a knife cut straight in between the two openings (go the short way, not the long way around), through the gizzard muscle and through the first layer of membrane on the inside cavity. Do not puncture the covering of the inside sack, which holds the almost digested food. If you cut carefully, you can, with the fingers and thumbs of both hands, gently pull the gizzard apart the rest of the way, freeing the inside sack without breaking it. Discard the inside sack and finish cutting open the gizzard so it will lie flat. Trim off any extraneous membranes and wash well.

Put the liver and gizzard in the pan of water with the heart (these are the giblets) and discard the rest of the insides.

COOKING THE GOOSE

GIBLETS

Cook the giblets in salted water until tender, using a low heat. Save the broth for the dressing. Cut the giblets into small pieces and put aside for the gravy.

DRESSING

Ella's mother used apple dressing to stuff the goose, for she thought the apples blended best with the flavor of goose. Ella said her dressing was like regular dressing with apples diced in it. Pearl Thelma made her dressing as follows:

1 loaf stale (or toasted) bread	3 beaten eggs
3 cups diced apples	½ cup melted butter
1 cup chopped celery	Hot broth from giblets (or boiling
1 cup chopped raw onions	water)
Sage, salt, and pepper to taste	

Crumble or dice the bread. Mix in apples, celery, onions, and seasonings. Add eggs, melted butter, and broth or boiling water until you get a soupy consistency. Stuff this into the cavity of the goose and fasten the hole closed with clamps or sew with heavy cord. Put the excess dressing in flat pans and bake 1 hour at 350° until tender. This will make about two pans of extra dressing.

BAKED GOOSE

As you work with the goose meat you will notice how much fat there is in it before cooking. For that reason it is helpful to place the bird on a rack in the roasting pan so that, as it bakes and the fat cooks out, you can dip the fat out. Because the meat is so moist there is no need to baste. Bake in a covered pan at 375° until tender. Goose takes longer to bake than turkey; a 10-pound young goose might take about 3 hours. The cooking time depends on the size and age of the bird. When tender remove the cover, turn the heat up to 400°, and brown. The main difference between goose and other fowl is the excessive amount of fat, which should be dipped out as it accumulates.

GOOSE FAT

The fat from the goose is a beautiful translucent pale yellow color. An average-sized goose may yield as much as a pint. Let the settlings go to the bottom and chill. The fat is fine for cooking, or for making cakes and other foods which need a rich fat.

GIBLET GRAVY

After the goose is done, remove it from the pan. Pour off the fat, leaving about 6 tablespoons (depending on the amount of gravy needed). Mix about 3 tablespoons cornstarch in a small amount of water and beat until smooth, then add to the fat and mix well. Add water gradually, stirring until smooth (in proportions of 1 cup to 1 tablespoon cornstarch), and season to taste. Add diced giblets and stir gravy constantly until thick. Be sure to stir in all the browned drippings from the bottom of the pan for flavor. Six tablespoons of flour can be substituted for the cornstarch, but it gives the gravy a milky color. If preferred, the gravy can be made with milk. This recipe makes about 3 cups.

What's sauce for the goose is sauce for the gander, so why not cook your goose for Christmas?

3. THE MAN

If the center of the woman's world was the kitchen, the man's world was the outdoors. During each daylight hour he and his sons would be working in the barns, fields, pastures, or woods no matter what the season or the weather. At dawn—wearing long underwear, felt hat, heavy coat, and overshoes in the winter, or the ever present felt or straw hat and lighter clothes in the summer —he would leave the house to do his morning feeding and other chores about the barn lot. In the winter those chores—tending to all the animals, cutting and hauling wood, repairing fences and buildings, and chopping ice for stock water—sometimes took most of the day. Summer chores were easier and done as quickly as possible to get to the fields to plant or harvest the wheat, oats, corn, hay, or other crops.

During the growing season all family work revolved around the field work, for the crops were all-important. Their success determined how well the family lived, since they were the source of food and cash both directly and indi-

rectly. The corn and wheat were ground into meal and flour for family use; the grain along with the hay raised was fed to the cattle, poultry, and hogs which produced meat, milk, and eggs for the family. The crops, animals, and animal products that were produced over and above the family needs were sold, providing almost the only source of income for most families.

The never-ending work routine of the woman in the kitchen was matched outside by the man with his repeating seasonal routine. No matter how hot, windy, or dusty it was, the man had to plow his corn when it needed to be

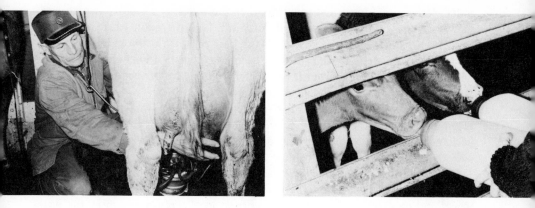

done. No matter how cold, windy, or icy, he had to take hay or grain to his animals daily. No matter how sick or tired he was, he had to milk the cows and chop firewood for the house. If he'd been in the fields cutting wheat since five o'clock in the morning, he still had to continue until eight-thirty or as long as he could see to swing the grain cradle or put hay in the loft, for the next day the threatened storm might ruin the rest of the crop. Even the relief from hand labor that modern machinery brought did not lessen the workday: tractors meant that he could plant more acres and the lights on the tractor meant he didn't need to stop at dusk.

When the man did have a slack time—as in the winter and various times when the crop was in and before it was time for harvest—he often took his recreation, hunting and fishing on his own or neighboring farms. That cost nothing and added variety to the meat the family lived on.

Just as the women thought nothing of their long hours and delighted in their families and their ability to keep them healthy and happy, the men, too, received great satisfaction. At nine o'clock on a cold snowy day in early December the man of the house could come inside his warm home, remove his

outer clothing and toast first one side, then the other by his stove, which was glowing with wood he'd grown and cut. Until late afternoon when he'd have to see to his stock again, he could relax, taking comfort in the knowledge that his family had a well-stocked smokehouse and cellar, that his barn was full of hay and grain sufficient to finish the winter, that his well-fed animals were all warm in their stalls, and his fences were good.

He could look forward to a relatively leisurely winter—maybe get in some gigging, play with the children, spend some time at the store and mill, and perhaps get around to making that quilting frame his wife had been wanting —and, for sure, make a new bed for the wagon.

Early the next spring the seasonal cycle would begin all over again. He would have to plant his oats, the garden, and corn, cut, bind, and thresh the wheat and oats, put up hay, plow the corn at least three times, mow the pasture, fill the silo, plant the wheat, gather the corn, and cut the winter wood. But in December, with all that just completed, next spring was a long time away.

On the Farm

Using a Grain Cradle

Until the early 1900s when the horse-drawn binder became widely used on the Ozarks river-bottom farms and larger fields, the hand grain cradle was used in harvesting grain crops for later threshing or feeding.

The people of the Ozarks were slow to adopt newer agricultural methods. Because of their isolation, smaller fields, and lack of money, some farmers didn't use binders until the 1930s, especially if they had only a few acres of wheat or oats which they raised for their own consumption. For the same reasons, the combine did not completely replace the threshing machine in the Ozarks until the late 1950s.

Many Ozark farmers like Elva Hough continued to use the hand cradle to harvest grain. Proficient in its use, he continued to use it occasionally until 1946 when he cut his last two acres of wheat with it. He still has the stronger of the two cradles his father and he bought back in 1901. To show us how it was used, Elvie planted a small patch of oats, got the old cradle out of storage, sharpened the blade, and on a hot July morning strode down the patch swinging the cradle, catching the grain, and throwing it in piles behind him so quickly we had to slow him down to understand what he was doing.

The cradle is a long-handled scythe with a built-on cradle consisting of four tapered fingers to catch the grain, and a thumb, the blade. Elvie's cradle, factory made and costing about five dollars, is called a "grapevine." The other cradle his father bought, a "turkey wing," was practically the same except that it was lighter. Both did the work, but if the wheat was heavy, the heavier grapevine was better to use.

The cradle did not take much maintenance. Elvie has had his for over seventy years, and, as he said, "That one there has been pretty rough treated just cutting patches of feed for cattle or hogs or whatever I was feeding." After cradling about a quarter of a mile, it may need sharpening, depending on the heaviness of the grain and its ripeness. Every cradler carried a whet rock in his pocket to sharpen the blade as needed.

Harvesting using the cradle was done several ways and depended on the

Elva Hough explains how
to sharpen a cradle blade.

size of the field and available cash for labor. Elvie explained that sometimes,
especially on small fields, families would cradle their own crop. He and his
cousin would cut, tie, and shock. They'd cut as much as they thought they
could finish, go back to tie it into bundles, then shock it. Elvie said, "What
it'd about average was four acres a day for two of us, and that's a pretty good
day's work."

If the fields were bigger, most small farmers traded work rather than pay
wages. Usually eight to ten neighbors, or as many as it took to complete the
job, would come to a farm, harvest the crop, then move to the next. By working for everyone else, each got his crop harvested.

Farmers who had especially large fields—usually those on the river bottoms—had to hire harvest crews. Elvie remembered, "I drawed a dollar and
a quarter a day for cradling. It was seventy-five cents for them that tied and
seventy-five cents for the ones that shocked."

With a crew harvesting, about five or six men with cradles would begin,

"They always cradled with their blades coming out of the grain."

The fingers of the cradle catch the grain, the heads all lying the same direction.

The grain falls into a neat bundle held in place by the curved rods. Grasping the grain in his left hand, Elvie throws it behind him onto the cut stubble.

"I'd go clean down the length of the field and turn around and come back the other side."

"Now let me pull these stalks out."

"Wrap them around the bundle like this."

"Catch between your finger and thumb. Then twist it. Go around and push it under."

"When we set them down, put two this way, and two over there. We leave six to eight standing."

"You put one across then turn another across like that. You got a double cap there and it won't rain into it. The wind don't blow them off and tear it up."

one following the other. The lead would lay off the land, usually the length of the field and as wide as they could finish in a day. The cradlers would cross the field swinging, catching the grain and dropping it on the ground, one strung out behind the other, circling the field in smaller circles each time around. Behind them would come a couple of binders or tiers who would pick up the piles of grain, tie them, and throw them in windrows for the shocker, who picked up the tied bundles to put in shocks. Sometimes, instead of being shocked, the bundles were hauled to be stored in huge stacks near the barn for easy feeding or later threshing.

Watching an expert like Elvie move easily down the field, cradling looks easy, but it takes practice, skill, and stamina. Holding the cradle with the right hand on the short lower handle and the left hand near the top of the long handle, the cradler walks down the center of the swath he intends to cut, usually seven feet wide. He swings the cradle from right to left, turning his body halfway around with the swing. The sharp blade cuts the grain about four inches from the ground, and the grain falls toward the handle onto the fingers with the heads away from the blade.

Elvie supports the cradle with his right arm and left leg while he grasps with his left hand the bundle of grain that has been held in place by the curved rods built in the cradle. As his body has been turned partly around following the swing of the cradle, he drops the grain on the stubble that he has just cut. He grabs the short handle again with his right hand, the long handle with his left, swivels his body forward again, takes a step and makes another cut.

Swing, grab the grain, drop it, step, swing, over and over in rhythm without pausing for the length of a field. Elvie says, "I'd go a quarter of a mile, then stop and rest, whet the cradle, it wouldn't take but a few strops, then turn around and be ready to go again."

To tie a bundle Elvie holds the grain under his right arm. He then pulls a few stalks of grain out and wraps them around the bundle. He catches the stalk ends between his finger and thumb, twisting them around and pushing the ends under to form the knot.

To shock the grain he sets the tied bundles upright against each other with the grain end up. He starts by leaning two bundles together to form the nucleus. Other bundles are added around these, two at a time opposite each other to balance the shock. Depending on the grain—how long it is and its weight—he sets six to eight upright. If the bundles are small, he would use eight or even ten to a shock. The bundles would have to sit usually a few weeks to cure and wait for the threshing machine, so the shock would need to be capped to keep the grain dry. He spreads out one bundle as much as possible without untying and lays it one way across the tops of the upright bundles. This makes an effective "roof" to shed the water. "You put another bundle on top of that and it'll stay there until September or October. I've seen them haul them out way up in October. But they're better the quicker you can thrash them after they get cured. You see, you got a double cap there, and it won't rain into it. The wind don't blow them off and tear it up, why it's there."

He was right. When we went back to make molasses in October, the shock he made for us was still standing and the grain was dry.

Steam on the Farm

Around the turn of the century a new source of power for the everyday farm tasks such as threshing, lumber sawing, rock crushing, gristmills, and many other jobs came into the Ozarks region to replace the horse. This new power that brought the highest level of productivity in the world to the farmer was steam.

In the 1890s the first steam engines began clouding the skies of the Ozarks with smoke belching from their smokestacks and scenting the air with the smell of burning wood or coal, boiling water, and hot lubricating oil. These early engines, called bull and tongue engines, had to be pulled by horses or

oxen to the job, and thus they did mostly stationary jobs like operating a sawmill, gristmill, or threshing.

Then in the late 1890s the first traction engines (one that can move under its own power) began rumbling on the farm. These engines were a blessing to the farmer, because, unlike the horse, they could work all day under a heavy load like threshing, and never tire. The steam engine worked more quickly, was more dependable, and was far more powerful than horses. The traction

A steam engine equipped with rollers.

Homer Hough threshing with steam in early 1900s.

engine brought more than just better work to the farm; it brought an excitement, a thrill that is very hard to describe. It was much the same as the earlier railroad locomotives. People would watch in utter amazement as the engine went about the tasks set for it.

The steam engineers were trained and skilled professionals, a breed of proud, strong, and very important men who loved their work. Ellis Wedge was one of those individuals and we asked him about the kind of engine he ran.

"My engine has done more work, I would imagine, than any other engine in the county. It was a 20 horse and weighed 12 tons and carried 160 pounds of pressure."

At the height of the steam era, over thirty companies were manufacturing more than 5,000 large engines a year, ranging from 6 to 150 horsepower and weighing up to 30 tons. Some had traction wheels up to six feet tall and two feet wide, made of steel so they would not crack under the strain of the terrain. Case, Oughtman-Taylor, Peerless, Reed, Avery, and Bellville were just a few of the companies that produced these metal giants. I asked Ellis just what was the best engine produced.

"Well now, that would be hard to say. It's a matter of opinion. But, if I were buying, I'd buy a Geiser-Peerless. You couldn't tear them up."

But were they more powerful than gasoline engines?

"For power, there is nothing that can compare to steam. Although, with a gasoline tractor, I can go out to work by myself, whereas with steam I needed three other men—a separator man, a water hauler, and a man to feed the bundles. But when you were threshing with steam, there was no missing or cutting out like gasoline tractors will do sometimes. When you started your engine in the morning, you knew you were going to have power all day. And the harder you pulled them, the better they liked it."

At the time Ellis was running his machine, there were only eight or ten engines in the county. This made him a very important man in the eyes of the farmers.

"Being a steam engineer was the finest life that ever was," he said.

Ellis was certainly right about it being a fine life. At this time, common labor was earning seventy-five cents to a dollar a day. But the steam engineer was earning about five dollars a day, which made him the envy of quite a few people.

One unusual thing about steam engines is the measurement of speed. Speed is not measured by miles an hour, for the best engine could only run "about two or three miles an hour down a hill with a good wind behind it," but by the revolutions per minute of the engine. The average speed of an engine was about 250 to 300 r.p.m.'s. The engines had governors to regulate the speed; if you wanted a faster speed, you only had to turn a screw on the governor and the speed was there. Some engines were equipped with expansion plates for high speeds of about 500 r.p.m.'s, though such a speed was impractical and hard on the engine.

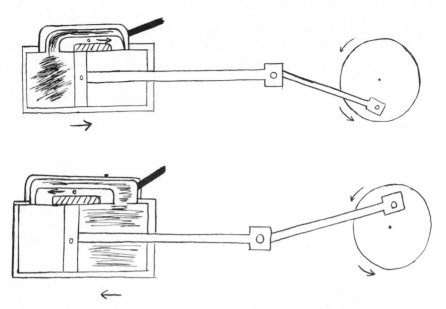

Piston action on one stroke of a steam engine. Unlike a gasoline engine, the steam engine has power pushing the piston both forward and backward.

The firebox on bull and tongue engines is small compared to firebox capacity on later engines.

This bull and tongue engine was one of the first in the county.

To operate a steam engine you need two things—fuel and water. The fuel goes in the firebox, and the boiler is filled with water. The fuel heats the water in the boiler to 212° F. at which point the water boils and changes into steam. The steam is kept enclosed so as to build up pressure, and under pressure it rises into the steam dome. When it reaches the proper amount of pressure, a valve is opened at the top of the steam dome and the steam pushes through a tube that leads to the cylinder. The steam enters the cylinder through a sliding valve that is hooked to the flywheel by a very small rod. The steam builds inside the cylinder and drives the piston back, pushing the connecting rod that turns the flywheel. The flywheel pushes the rod that slides the valve forward. Then steam enters behind the piston and pushes the piston forward. This pulls the connecting rod back, which in turn brings the flywheel around to complete the revolution. The exhaust exits by way of two valves at each end of the piston: as the piston is pushed forward, the force of the piston moving pushes the exhaust steam out of the cylinder; the same is true when the piston is being pulled back. A belt is attached to the flywheel to do the work of threshing or sawing lumber. The speed is controlled by simply regulating the amount of steam that enters the piston. In the event that too much pressure should build up in the boiler, a safety valve opens, but when it does, you lose all your steam, so good engineers would keep the safety valve from "blowing off." Occasionally something would go wrong with the safety valve and the steam engine would explode, the hot steam burning the engineer so badly that he died. Steam engines were not playthings.

The average day of the working steam engineer and engine began early. The engineer had to be at his engine at about five o'clock in the morning to build a fire in the firebox so he could have enough steam to put more water in the boiler. If the farmer was threshing, the engineer's job was to feed the fuel into the firebox and make sure everything was running smoothly on the engine. He also kept his eye on the gauges to make sure the steam didn't gain too much pressure. The water hauler took the water wagon to a pond or spring. He would lower a long hose into the water, then climb up on top of the wagon and start pumping the hand pump. He would pump 300 gallons of water into the wagon, then return to the engine. He would have to make four or five trips a day. The water hauler, if he was experienced, knew every pond, river, lake, or spring in the county. "Some ponds were so full of alkaline that in an hour you couldn't be a-threshing. If there were a bunch of geese in a pond, an engine would blow the water plumb out of it. I don't know why, but you cannot use that water.

"Now here's what my father told me about. Alkaline water will make an engine boil over. We called it foaming. It will jerk its water over in its cylinders. With water in your cylinders you can't do nothing, you have to keep them dry."

If alkaline water was left in the boiler it could rust the inside. So if you had alkaline water in your boiler you had to clean it by pumping clean water in it again. You repeated this process until the water in the water glass was clear.

Thus, the water hauler had to know not only where all the ponds were but where the best water was too. When Ellis worked near town he had to buy his water at fifteen cents for 300 gallons. During the average working day a steam engine could use as much as 1,500 gallons of water and burn up to a ton of coal or a cord of wood. The engine could thresh up to 1,000 bushels of wheat.

The engines ran very long days and sometimes into the night. But at the close of each day the engineer would cool it down by pumping the engine full of cold water. He had to take into account the fact that if a small fire was left in the engine he would lose quite a bit of water overnight. So he would fill it accordingly.

Ellis Wedge's father, Charley Wedge, was an engineer before him. Ellis grew up with the sight, sound, and smell of steam engines right outside his door, and he had a love for the engines that cannot be put into words. Some days Ellis would be sitting in school and he would hear the sound of a whistle. He would get up and run outside, because the whistle was on a steam engine and it was telling young Ellis that his father needed him to help.

As Ellis was growing up, there was no doubt in his mind what profession he would take up. When he was old enough he bought a steam engine and went into business in the county. Steam engines were in very big demand, and he worked on farms or in town and he worked on roads.

At the time, steam was the most economical, dependable, and hardest-working source of power known. But with the coming of gasoline and diesel engines, steam became impractical because it burned large amounts of fuel and required a number of men to operate the engine.

So we no longer hear the sound of the engine puffing, smell the burning wood, feel the heat generated by the boiling water, or feel the ground shake and rumble beneath our feet as did the farmers of the steam era. Nor do we hear the engineer shouting at his men, "Fire her up. There's work to be done."

Ellis Wedge graded roads with his steam engine.

Thrashing About the Ozarks

The yearly job of threshing grain has always been a co-operative effort of men swapping work in the fields and at the separator and women cooking for the men when the owner of the machines would pull into the neighborhood.

An early alternative to separating the grain from the straw by beating it out by hand was a small separator powered by a horse or mule on a treadmill. Although faster than hand, very little grain could be threshed in a day. Soon bigger, more efficient separators which required more power came into use. Ellis Wedge remembers his father telling about using ten horses for power to operate a separator.

The horses in five teams, one in front of the other, were hitched to a pole which turned gears and a tumbling rod attached to the cylinder shaft of the separator. The horses were handled by a man on a platform in the middle of the separator. The teams walked in circles, stepping over the tumbling rod.

Charley Wedge unloaded the first traction engine in the county in 1898. The arrival of the self-powered traction engines ushered in an era that lasted well into the 1930s; 1934 was the last year Ellis operated his steam engine to thresh. Though he much preferred steam engines, gasoline tractors could move faster from place to place; steam engines would only go about two to two and a half miles an hour. The four men it took to operate a steam engine and separator were reduced to two men for gasoline power. People stopped getting the wood needed for steam because gasoline was cheaper, only seven and a half cents a gallon in 1932, and diesel fuel only six cents.

In the early fifties people stopped threshing in this area altogether. Ellis explained that the government paid farmers not to raise wheat during the times of huge wheat surpluses, and the result was insufficient business to pay Ellis and others to operate the big machines. Farmers were put on wheat allotments based on a percentage of their usual acreage. The grain fields in the Ozarks were always small—usually eight-, ten-, or twenty-acre fields—and most of the grain raised was for the farmer's own consumption. With acreage further reduced, some to five acres or less, the cost of equipment to raise grain and the effort involved made it impractical. Most farmers quit raising grain altogether.

The ones who continued to raise grain tried using combines. Threshing machines had continued to operate in the Ozarks long after combines re-

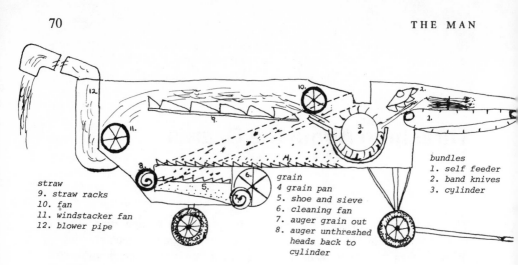

straw
9. straw racks
10. fan
11. windstacker fan
12. blower pipe

grain
4 grain pan
5. shoe and sieve
6. cleaning fan
7. auger grain out
8. auger unthreshed
   heads back to
   cylinder

bundles
1. self feeder
2. band knives
3. cylinder

Simplified cutaway view of the separator.

placed them on Western fields. Ellis tried combines but he said, "A combine will never be successful in this country. It is too damp here. Your grain won't dry out." The heads of grain must be completely dry to thresh. In the Ozarks the grain standing on the stalk would not be dry enough to combine until late in the day. The grain needed to be cut and shocked to dry out thoroughly. Today very little grain is raised in the Ozarks.

"If I was to thresh today," Ellis said, "I wouldn't know how to go out and thresh for people. I wouldn't know how to charge them to make any money at over sixty cents a gallon for gas. In 1934 I charged ten cents a bushel for wheat. Years before, my father did it two cents for oats and three cents for wheat. On a good day I'd thresh an average of a thousand bushels. I have threshed two thousand bushels a day beginning as soon as you could get in the fields and thresh as long as you could see. But I never even thought of threshing on Sunday. I only did it one time and Preacher Patterson said no man would ever go wrong with that I done that Sunday. After a long wet spell, we got to threshing at my place on Saturday. We lacked just a few wagons finishing on Saturday and, before a rain come up Sunday morning, I cleaned off those wagons."

The separators improved over the years. Before the self-feeder became standard equipment on separators, the bundles were fed in by hand, requiring four men—two working at a time and two to relieve them, for a man couldn't stand more than an hour at a time feeding grain into the machine. One man cut the band on the bundle and the other pulled the bundles onto the cylinders and spread out the straw.

Before the machine was equipped to weigh and tally the grain, which was released in half-bushel amounts, it took three or four men to operate the measuring and sacking of grain. The machine would auger out the grain in a little stream from the separator into the half-bushel measure. When this filled, the men slid it out and it tripped a tally box. The men then hand-sacked and loaded the grain. In later separators the grain fed into a weigher with a pair of scales which would automatically trip the tally. The machine kept track and dumped the grain into a wagon or sacks.

"One important thing in running the threshing machine," Ellis explained, "is keeping the people in good humor. One farmer would want to thresh right now and another'd want to thresh right now and I'd have to make a decision which place I went. A lot of people, they'd cook for us, you know, and some folks would try to figure out how to keep from cooking. Then sometimes we'd finish one place at eleven o'clock and dinner would be about ready and we'd go to another where they wasn't expecting us. But we couldn't sit around with hands hired and work to do while the weather was right. We'd move on."

Today the thrashing about the Ozarks is done only at special demonstrations and old threshers' conventions where old and young alike gather to remember or experience for the first time the excitement felt by all when someone yelled, "The threshers are coming."

A Homemade Water Jug

After working for hours pitching bundles on wagons in a dusty field, the Ozark farmer could ask for nothing better than a generous drink of cool spring or well water from the burlap-wrapped water jug. The Ozarks have an abundance of good water, but often it is located too far from the fields. Accustomed to drinking 52° water fresh from the spring or well, the thirsty farmer could not quench his thirst with lukewarm water.

Before thermos bottles and styrofoam ice chests were invented, farmers made their own insulated water jugs. They needed a jug, tow sack, needle, and heavy thread or cord.

The jug was a thick stone crock which itself offered some insulation. The small opening at the top made a handy spout to drink from and the handle was just right for the forefinger and thumb to grasp. The jug, raised to shoulder height and supported by the crooked arm, made a convenient drinking utensil.

After the sack is wrapped tightly around the jug, begin sewing at the neck.

Cut off any excess material.

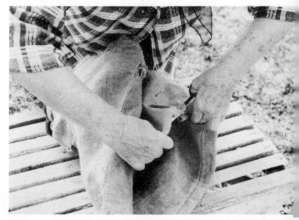

The covering could be any thick sturdy material that would soak up water, but usually a tow sack was used. Heavy thread was used to fasten the material around the jug. The cord was as durable as the material and sturdy enough to withstand all weather conditions. The needle had an eye large enough to thread the cord through it, and some people used a curved needle for easier sewing.

Most of the time, the man of the family made the covering for the jug. He wrapped the sack around the jug tightly. The more material he put around the more insulated it would be. Next, he sewed the material securely so it would not come apart. The tighter the sack was sewn the longer the water would stay cool. He usually began sewing around the neck of the jug and sewed down to the bottom. If made properly, the covering would last for about three years. For the finishing touch he often whittled down a fresh, clean corncob for the stopper.

When he put the water in the jug to take to the field, he would thoroughly wet the covering and run cool water inside the jug to cool it before he put the drinking water in. According to Julie Massie, who showed us how to cover a jug, the water would stay cool all afternoon. She said, "When we were young, we would have to go ever' so often if they were threshing or anything like that, and would have to go with these water jugs and take water to the men. That was our job. The men would work awhile, then take a big drink, then go back to working." If the man took his jug with him, he set it in the shade to protect it from the sun.

When the farmer finished his day's work, he would head back to the house with his empty water jug in hand.

Sew the sack securely with strong cord.

Wet the sack covering and use a corncob stopper.

Mules—"The Foundation of the World"

"They've made lots of machinery that replaced horses and mules and lots of it's good. But they've made nothing yet that would come up with a mule and a double shovel in a potato patch. They never made nothing yet and they never will."

Charley Brittain owns a tractor, but he rarely starts it on his farm. He prefers the two-mule power of his team to his many-horsepowered tractor, and he uses his team for everything from plowing his garden and putting out his corn to mowing his hay. "I don't have a baler or rake, or we'd use them for that too. I like to drive mules and, if you like to and don't, you're a fool. That's all there is to it."

Mules are beasts of burden, used mainly for working and occasionally for riding. They are of little use for almost anything else, and when mechanized power took over mules rapidly declined in numbers until now, even in Missouri, one has to search for people like Charley who still prefer them for work.

Mules have a long history. They originated in Asia Minor and were sent to Greece at least three thousand years ago. However, they were not used in great numbers in the United States until after the Civil War. Then farmers, miners, the army, and construction companies used them. They laid the pipelines and built the railroads, the power lines, and even the roads. "Mules are the foundation of the world," Charley asserts.

Since mules, both male and female, are sterile, they will not reproduce. They are a hybrid animal produced by crossing the horse and the ass. A mule is out of a mare (female horse) and a jack (male ass). If a jenny (female ass) is mated with a stallion (male horse), the offspring is called a hinny. Only an expert could distinguish a hinny from a mule because the only major difference is that hinnies are slightly narrower at the heel. However, when the two are worked, the mule is far less stubborn and works better, so the former mating is used most often.

Mules retain characteristics of both parents. From the jack the mule gets its braying voice, sure-footedness, endurance, long ears, thin limbs, and small feet. From the mare he gets his large well-shaped body, strong muscles,

"They've made nothing yet that would come up with a mule and a double shovel in a potato patch."

height, and shape of neck and croup. The size of the mule depends on the size of the mare used. Belgian and Percheron mares, or any big draft mare, raise the best mules because their colts are big—around 16 to 16½ hands (64 to 66 inches at the withers)—with big bones, big heads, big ears, and calm natures. A draft mare which weighs about 1,200 to 1,300 pounds will produce mule colts that will grow to 900 pounds. Saddle mares will raise smaller mule colts—about 15 hands (60 inches) or less—with thin bones, small feet, and more nervous natures. As a general rule, the bigger the mule, the easier he is to handle and the better he is to work.

Many people today use Shetland ponies to raise miniature mules about the size of the pony. Most raise the miniature mules as a hobby and use them in mule pulls or to pull wagons in parades or in show competition, but some, like Warren Shultz, use them to plow gardens for both himself and his neighbors.

Even though mules will not reproduce, they were used far more often than horses in the South. Their life span of thirty to thirty-five years is ten to fifteen more than a horse's, and they are more intelligent, surer-footed, and tougher. Charley thinks mules are the smartest animal there is. "A mule's not going to hurt himself. If they get hurt, somebody else was the cause of it. They never done it themselves. If a mule gets tangled up in his harness, he

Parts of the Harness

1. hames
2. tugs
3. jack strap
4. pole strap
5. breeching
6. hip strap
7. back band strap
8. back band
9. gag reins
10. nose piece
11. blind bridle
12. brow band
13. lines
14. lug strap
15. side straps

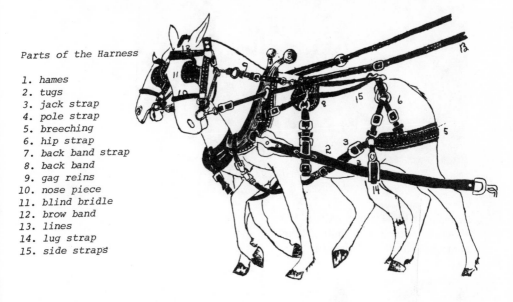

won't fight himself to death like some horses will. Before he'll do that, he'll lay down and sull and say, 'I'll be here when you come back.'"

A mule team, like a team of horses, will run away, but usually do so out of orneriness and won't hurt themselves. When horses run away, they run from fright and for dear life. Sometimes they won't quit until they tear all the harnesses off and will keep on running even into a fence or something solid, often hurting themselves. Waldo Davis once had a team of mules hitched with a saddle mare run away. "They run for over a mile, hung up down there in the river bottom in the fence. One mule outrun the others and circled them around and run them into the fence, hung them up. Well, we was quite a little while getting down there. Them mules was a-standing still as they could and this mare was a-kicking and pulling and trying to get loose. The mules was just standing there still as a cat stood. Now that's just the difference between a mule and a horse."

Mules can stand heat better than horses. Their ability to do a third more work on a third less food on a hot day made them popular in the South. When a horse gets hot, he starts to fret, and gets hotter. If he is worked long enough, the heat will kill the horse. But a mule starts coasting when he gets hot, becoming lazier to save himself. When he comes to the end of a row, he will take enough time turning around so that by the time he does so he has his wind back and can work longer.

The mule's small feet are good for working in gardens because they won't trample the plants. They will not stumble and, unlike a horse who will wind, will pull straight. They resist disease better than horses and they will not eat too much and founder. Also, they will not fight among themselves as horses will.

A team of small mules pulls a
thousand pounds at a mule-pulling
contest at Stoutland, Missouri.

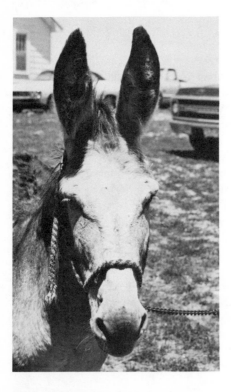

George Washington is credited with
beginning the raising of jacks in the
United States when Lafayette
gave him a gift of a jack and two
jennies.

Today some coon hunters use
mules because of their
sure-footedness and their ability to
jump as high as six feet without a
running start. Here one tests his
ability at a mule show. The rider
dismounts at the fence and crosses.
Then, holding the reins, he
encourages the mule to jump
flat-footed over the fence.

A pulling horse will outpull a mule, though, because a horse will use all the strength he has. A mule won't. He will use just what it takes to pull a load and not a pound more. If the load is too heavy, he will not try too hard to move it. The horse will keep on trying even if the load is impossibly heavy.

Mules do everything the easy way, including learning. They are easier to break than horses; mules may put up more fight at first, but they give up quicker. Once a mule learns something, he never forgets it.

The first step in breaking a mule is to know at least a little more than the mule. At two years (before they get too strong) most people start by teaming the young mule with a broken mule or horse. Waldo Davis, who has broken over three hundred mules and handled over two thousand, says, to break a mule, "You just catch them and tie them up and put the harness on them. Hook them by one that's broken and push it around to your plow. Get it still enough to get it hooked and get behind it and start out a-working till you wear it down. The broke one has to kind of handle it, though. When you say, 'Whoa,' the broke stock will tell the other one he has to stop. You just work them till you wear them down. Some of them last all day and some of them don't last over a half a day. You work them till they are pretty tired, till you can't get them to go as a rule. Just as a rule when they get about two thirds of the way tired, they'll stop. Whenever they get tired that-a-way, pull the lines to work them bits. You can say, 'Whoa,' and get them stopped. Then say, 'Get up,' and whip them a little or your old one will start. Say, 'Get up,' and they will go just a little ways, and then say, 'Whoa,' and the old one will stop. They'll learn that in twenty minutes' time, a lot of them. In three or four days you can handle it in field work, but you couldn't on the road."

Waldo used a harness he called a "W" on the last mules he broke. The "W" teaches young mules what "Whoa" means. To hook up a "W," harness the young mule with a leather strap around each front ankle and a steel ring fastened to the strap on the inside of each foot. Run the rope down the inside of the front leg, through the ring on the ankle, back up to a ring where the pole strap joins the collar, down to the ring on the other ankle, and back up to the ring on the hames on the other side. The two ends of the rope go back to the driver and are held like lines.

Once the mule starts moving (getting the mule moving may be a small problem) say, "Whoa," and pull on the rope. The rope causes the mule to fall to his knees. Waldo says, "He may jump up a little bit to start off. When you pull that again and say, 'Whoa,' about the third time when he hears you, he'll know what 'Whoa' is. That really works. First time I tried it I had a pair of sorrel mules here. They was big mules. We worked about two hours getting them around. One of them here, she'd fight and bite. And we even put them "Ws" on them mules before we harnessed them. We turned that one mule loose down there in the driveway and she started out there and I hollered, 'Whoa,' and she was going with such a force that she went right over on her back. She just turned a flip-flop. I ran around in behind her and she got up and started again. I hollered, 'Whoa,' and I think I throwed her about nine or ten times. After a while we harnessed her and didn't even tie her up. She knew what 'Whoa' was. She'd start to move—just flinch. Now she had her feet on the ground, you see. She was afraid a little bit to move. We put the pair of them on a wagon out there in a horse lot, and we started up this country road up here, crossed a low-water bridge and down onto the highway, drove them up to my brother's. When we got back home, those

mules was broke. I picked corn with them the next day. That's just how quick they're broke."

Mules are one-man animals and prefer the person who works them to anyone else. If they are sold, or a new person starts working them, they will get used to the new person in time, but at first they get homesick, and, if given the opportunity, will come home. Charley Brittain told us about a pair of mules he once owned.

"I sold a guy a pair of mules down in Arkansas. I had the mules five years and broke them and he bought them. He come up here on Saturday and got them. He hauled them all the way to Jonesboro, Arkansas, in a horse trailer and they can't see out, only just what little they can see in front. Anyway, he called me on Tuesday and said, 'The mules ain't eat a bite nor drunk a drop of water since they've been here. What am I going to do with them?' I said, 'You better leave them in the barn. They'll leave if you ever turn them out. They're homesick. That's what's the matter with them. They're homesick.' He said, 'If they don't eat by tomorrow, I'm going to turn them out.' I said, 'I bet you five dollars they'll leave if you do.' They never had gone through a fence. I mean they wouldn't go through a fence. Anyway, he turned them out Wednesday night and when he got up Thursday morning they was gone.

They just pawed his gate down and left. You know where he found them? Over the other side of Fort Leonard Wood. They made it to right there. And I went over and caught them. He couldn't even catch them. He found them on Monday right there. And they had come all that way from down there on their own back to there [about two hundred miles]. They got the instinct to know where home is. If he'd left them alone, they'd made her in that day, too."

Although mules have almost disappeared from use, as long as there are people like Charley Brittain around, there'll always be mules.

"A mule'll learn more in the barn than a horse will out working because he'll stand around and figure it out. I like them better'n horses. I'd rather work them. Yes, I'll tell you, if there's anyone who likes mules better'n me, I don't know how he stands it."

Fuget Garrison's mules take him home after an afternoon of fixing fences.

"Them Ponies Ain't Got No Reverse"

Roy Gage also prefers a team to a tractor, but his team is Shetland ponies. They help him supply wood to his neighbors, hauling it in the little pony-sized wagon he built for them.

Buster, can't you be quiet for a minute? Whoa, Ginger, you can scratch your leg tomorrow.

I guess I'm foolish, but I've loved these here horses more than a new car.

Anna May [his sister] don't like it too much. She won't ride with me but then that don't make no difference. I just get out on Sundays and ride around

"I guess I'm foolish, but I've loved these here ponies more than a new car."

this way for a pastime. I just like it. I guess I'm kinda too much of an old-timer, I don't know why, but I just like things like that.

I trained these ponies, and it took, oh, I'd say about all summer. This year I broke this little sorrel horse at work this spring. I had a time with him in the watermelon patch a while back. Oh, my goodness! It was the first time he'd been worked in the garden, and he turned around there and cut the aw-fulest shine you ever seen in your life, and I couldn't hold him or do anything with him, and I couldn't whip him. You can't whip him 'cause he just goes to pieces whenever you do. I don't like to be whipped myself either, so I guess he don't.

I tell you I think people ought to have more horses than a lot of other stuff they've got. So many of these little ole horses and ponies are taken off to be killed and make dog feed out of them. You know, I'm afraid that's gonna be bad on Judgment Day for people like that. I don't believe in that. I think people ought to have a little more love in their heart than to act like that.

Take these ponies here. They're nothing extra. There's better ponies than these, but I would not sell them to be killed at no price. I'm a very poor person, but you couldn't pile up enough gold there in front of me to take these ponies and kill them. You know a horse back in older days, that's the only way people had of making a living. Now I know we was poor folks. We hauled ties from here to Lebanon, cut cord wood, stave bolts, and everything else to make a living. If we hadn't had a horse we couldn't of done it. We might of went hungry otherwise, but we didn't.

Now that there wagon, I made that all by myself. I made every bit of it. Everything but the wheels and axle. The rest of it I made. Everything!

I used to make a lot of stuff like this. It's just born in me, I reckon, to do stuff like that. It's just sort of like music. Now if that ain't born in you, you just as well not start in 'cause you've got to have it there. Hard to learn. Now my folks were all musicians, every one of them, but I can't play nothing but a radio and it's got to be in pretty good shape or I can't do that.

I didn't have no pattern on this here wagon whatever. I just made it out of my head. I ruint a lot of stuff getting it made, too. I did. I'd say I ruint 'bout as much timber as I got in the wagon.

I worked in the house a-doing that. I didn't work steady on it all the time, you know, just worked a little on her every day to pass away the time. I worked even till midnight sometimes. I'm just kinda guessing but I think it took 'bout three weeks to make. I used just common hand tools, that's all. Just my handsaw, hammer, and drawknife.

I made the wagon bed out of pine but the rest of it's made out of white oak. It's just the right size for a rank of wood. A rank, it don't make no load at all. It don't pull them [the ponies]. I believe I could pull two rank of wood with them. That little mare can do it almost by herself. She's got more life in her than I have. I guess I just ain't as young as I used to be.

Old-time Horse Cures

When horses were depended upon for transportation and many jobs around the farm their health was of vital concern. Farmers often had to depend on their own remedies to cure their horses' ailments, for even when a town happened to have a veterinarian, money was too tight and precious to spend on a horse when a home remedy would do. Many of these remedies are still used today.

To make an all-purpose ointment called "White Liniment," combine ¼ pint salty meat grease, ½ pint turpentine, ½ pint kerosene, 1 pint vinegar, 1 pint apple cider, a handful of salt, and 3 or 4 egg whites. This can be used for cuts, bruises, and just about everything.

Kerosene and turpentine, two of the most widely used ingredients in home remedies for horses, are used by themselves on cuts. After applying either one of these, put salty meat grease on the wound to keep the hair around it from turning white.

Another remedy for cuts, especially those from metal, is the application of a mixture of ground goldenseal root mixed with lard. The herb pulls out the pus and the lard keeps the wound soft. Pine tar is also good for cuts.

For swellings on a horse's leg, mix all the salt that will dissolve into apple cider vinegar, and apply this mixture to the swollen area. The salt draws out the water.

Another remedy for swelling is to apply a wet, hot poultice of dried comfrey mixed with lard. Leave it on for an hour or two. Reheat the poultice and reapply. The swelling will soon disappear.

Before the days of insect repellent, people kept flies away from horses by soaking a rag with coal oil and attaching it to the throat latch that held the bridle on. Some people tied a little bush to the throat latch, and the horse's movements would swing the bush to scare away the flies.

To treat a horse for distemper, burn old leather under his nose. This keeps his nose from clogging and prevents choking.

For heaves (or a cough) smear the horse's tongue with pine tar.

Fistula, a boil-like sore from an ill-fitting collar, can ruin a horse. To cure this, put powdered alum on the sore area.

Horses would often get growths like corns on their hoofs when they were worked hard. To rid the horse of these, lift up the hoof and pour spirits of turpentine on it, then set the turpentine on fire. The heat will heal it and keep the hoof from becoming sore.

To relieve the horse of gas, make him jump logs. If he lies down he will likely die.

If a horse hurts his eye (as when hit by a twig), throw table salt in it.

These old-time cures were frequently used but just as many veterinarians disagree on the worth of modern treatments, so many of the people we talked with disagree on the worth of the home remedies they shared with us.

Tractors Are My Hobby

Like many other changes in the Ozarks, the change from mule and horse power to tractor power was slow. Most farmers agreed, "A tractor'll never replace a team on these rocky hills." But not all ignored the tractor's potential. Gene Chambers and his father used tractors for pulling and plowing their river-bottom farms back in 1920.

I want you to see that picture there. That's where I want to start. You ever see a tractor like that one in that picture? That's where I started right there. Only thing was, that's not the first tractor I had like it. I had two of them. That's the second, but there wasn't any difference in the two Fordsons. The first was a 1916 model—this was a 1927.

I well remember when that was taken. My sister come down to the field there and took that picture. The old tractor was almost wore out then, wasn't pulling worth a dime, and I was so disgusted I coulda blowed it in two if I'd had something to have done it with. The last few years I used the thing it wasn't much of a tractor. It was wore out too bad. But I drove her whenever she'd do her stuff and I thought that was the finest tractor I ever drove in my life.

Gene Chambers on a 1927 model Fordson tractor. Photo taken in 1935.

I started service work on them things when I was ten. Them things was my hobby. It would make me mad when they would call for dinner. I'd be in a field driving one. I wanted to drive and they'd holler dinnertime. I'd get so aggravated sometimes I wouldn't go for a while. I was just that anxious to drive. At nights—there wasn't no lights—I'd tie an old kerosene lamp on the front of the radiator and stay till they'd come to get me.

I was eight years old when Dad brought out our first tractor on this place. That was in 1920 and it was the first tractor that ever entered this neighborhood. By the time I was ten I was a-driving it all over the country working it and by the time I was fifteen I was everywhere servicing them. I've not seen the inside of one of them things for thirty-five years, but I still think I could take one apart and overhaul it just like I did then. I don't think I forgot a thing.

It's just one horse. That's all it is. No power take-off shaft or nothing. Right under the wheel was the throttle. You would run that with your hand. There was no governor on them. You just set there and, if it needed a little more, you'd pull down a little further and pushed her up to shut her off. And Lord, I've fed them things! I thought that a pretty job setting up there working that lever once in a while.

Now that model run on kerosene. Those old lads back in that day and time were cheaper to operate. I think we give six or eight cents a gallon for kerosene. The gasoline was about fifteen, sixteen cents a gallon back then, and it wouldn't burn any more gallons of kerosene than it would gas and it just cost you that much less. You started them on gasoline and warmed them

Gene Chambers.

"Gas tanks were in two sections, one for gas and one for kerosene."

4"   to intake
            manifold.

3"

from carburetor..   2 inches
                           thick.

"The manifold looked like a molasses trough."

"The radiator held ten gallons of water, and boiled from sunup till sundown."

up a little bit and then switched them over to kerosene and take on off. It just wasn't possible to start it on kerosene; you just as well talk to a stump as try to crank it on kerosene. Kerosene wouldn't explode until it got warm. It wouldn't vaporize into a gas form.

This tractor had two tanks. It had a little auxiliary tank built in the back—one with a cap for gas and one in the middle for kerosene. This little gas tank held just a gallon or so built down inside of it, and down below it had a two way faucet. Turn it one way for gas to drain down in the carburetor and flip it back the other way to the big tank to let the kerosene come in there.

But you had to crank on the gas and you had to let her get warmed up in this heating manifold. The manifold was built so that the kerosene made a long trip through it to heat that fuel up so that it would ignite. It just kept the kerosene in there till it got hot. The gas and kerosene both went through the same thing in that particular model.

I remember it had a big flat place on the side of the manifold big as my hand. It was held on there by four screws. The manifold looked like a molasses trough. They made it that way so that the fuel would start cooking up at one end, and by the time it got down to the far end it was hot enough. That's the way that lad was made. Carbon would form in there after a while and stop them troughs up and then you had to take that plate off and gouge that carbon out of there. I've done that about ten thousand times in my life.

Diesel or kerosene will make more carbon than gasoline because gasoline will come nearest to making a hundred per cent burn than they will. Carbon and stuff like this is just unburnt fuel. These lads sure had a bad habit of stopping up in that heating manifold. They'd get to when you'd pull that throttle out, that lad would just set there and just barely move and wouldn't do nothing. Then you'd have to clean them out.

But as big as that motor was, it should have had much more power than it had. It had a four-inch bore and a five-inch stroke. Well, a lot of these motors today ain't got any more than that. But its compression ratio and the ignition system and the timing system it had, it just didn't develop the power that they do nowadays.

Another thing that was crude about this tractor was there wasn't no water pump on them on the cooling system. The radiator held ten gallons of water and boiled from daylight to dark when you was plowing. I carried a bucket right on that radiator. The radiator would boil down and I'd put a bucket of water in it every two hours. Today the tractors I've got hold ten quarts of water. They may clog up with dirt or dust, but they just won't boil. So you see the change which has kept them from boiling is this cooling system, not the amount of water. The only way the water could move in those old models was just through nature. Hot water has the nature and tendency to rise and cold water goes the other way. So it had a top hose come out off this cylinder head. That pushed the hot water up in the top of the radiator and it fell down into the radiator where it was cooled by the fan. Then the cold water went back through the motor block. That was the only circulation it had. It had to get hot before it would even try to circulate. Heat's what done it. Tractors today have got a water pump that starts that water a-rolling just the minute that you crank the motor. That tractor was built before a water pump was ever thought of.

These Fordsons had a two-inch flat belt on them for a fan belt and the bottom pulley was just a smooth-face pulley. Since there wasn't anything to hold it on, it was easy to slip that flat belt 'cause all they had was that tension on them—not like a later V belt that wedges in a pulley. When it starts to pulling itself, it goes to wedging a little tighter. It pulls from the sides and these old ones pull from the bottom—just the bottom flat side of them.

"The Fordson had a fixed spark and a hand throttle, and was a honey to shift."

That one had a four-blade fan in it, but they didn't have as much speed on that fan as they do nowadays and didn't cause as much air. They just didn't have much of a cooling system on them.

Now this motor here, all it had in there for a cylinder liner was just the block, and when that block wore out, you had to rebore them. They'd bore that hole in that block a little bigger to straighten it up and dress it up and then put a bigger piston in there. Nowadays the cylinder has a liner in there. You just pull that liner out of there and throw it down and put another one in there and a new piston in and you're right back to standard piston again. That's why we get better service now than we did out of those. When those old ones once wore out, there wasn't one feller out of fifty that would rebore one. You just as well talk to them about pulling a tree as to tell them you want to have a motor rebored.

Now the old clutch, when it got hot, it'd release pretty good in the summertime, but if you had to drive it out of the shed in the spring of the year, you just had to get on that old lever and ride her in there—jerk it in there. I'd just shut the throttle down as low as I could get it to idle and just grab that lever and give it a jerk into low gear. It'd take off just as soon as you jobbed her into low gear. I'd just set there with my foot on the clutch and head her uphill where I could give it a load and just hold that clutch down—pull the throttle open and just let her go until she took a notion she couldn't pull it. She'd release itself that way.

It had a foot clutch, but it was a right-hand clutch instead of left. You pedaled with your right foot. It didn't have any brake pedal on it.

This engine had an oil disc clutch in it with about sixteen or seventeen discs—a whole ring of them clutch plates, what they call male and female plates. There'd be one of one kind and one of the other. Each one had notches on them. One notch fit on bolts and that held the flywheel onto the crankshaft, and the other plate had the notches on the outside that fit in the notch on the clutch housing. When you separated them plates that released your clutch, and when you squeezed them together she took off.

And she was a honey to shift. When it was cold them plates just would not turn loose and stop that transmission. You'd just have to jerk it in gear when it was cold. And the other side of that story, you just couldn't hardly wear that clutch out, running in oil like that. Modern clutches are dry and will operate much better and release better than this one did.

This old tractor had a fixed spark. You had to move a lever to change the advancement of that spark. Nowadays the spark is automatic. As the motor varies the speed, it changes that itself—it feeds the spark like it feeds the gas. The spark is as essential as the gas. But these old ones, they just didn't do her. They had a little ole lever back here on the dash. You pushed her down and retired the spark and then cranked her out in front. Then you raised that lever back up where it'd run pretty good and take off. Everything was just as crude as could be and nothing automatic. No battery, no starter, no generator, no nothing on them.

Ever'thing in this motor run in oil, flywheel and all. It held two gallon of oil. They don't do that any more. And that was another drawback to the power on this tractor. That big ole flywheel was running all the time and that just was a load to pull that wheel through that oil. It had all them magnets on that flywheel and set just right close to a big field coil clear around there. That made the fire of the ignition which come out on the left-hand side. We had a pole screwed in there on this field coil—brought the fire out over there. And them magnets was double set just as thick as they could be built all the way around the flywheel. They was a-paddling in that flywheel all the time. They had a little oil line at the top of that flywheel and the flywheel throwed oil in this line and it drained right back down at the front end in a bunch of troughs. It rolled it down them troughs and picked up the oil and slung it up to the pistons and the main bearings. That's the way to lubricate it. A complete splash oil system was all they had. So you lost several horsepower right there in that flywheel pulling it in oil.

They was constructed with the final drive in the back end. The differential in them was just like a tap on a bolt. In other words, it was threads. It would run one way and that had to be driven by the motor. When you went to turn those back wheels, it would run backwards and just simply wouldn't hardly turn. That's why it was so hard to drag. It was only a firebox in there and it just melted that transmission out of there just about as fast as you could put them in it.

Nowadays tractors all have ring gears and pinions which is just two cogs running agin one another. There's very little friction to a straight cog. But this old worm drive is just like threads on a bolt. It just kept twisting that worm—in other words, running that nut right down in the bolt all the time— just friction and nothing else. While riding it, I burnt the calf of my legs when I was leaning over agin the side of that transmission till there'd be long blisters. It'd get that hot way down here in this case and that transmission.

The transmission was full of ball bearings—they was very crude constructed. And it would just jar them bearings till they separated and come apart, and then the ball would go a-riding and grabbing on it and just bust that bearing all to pieces. And there you'd set. You'd just drop that transmission out of gear. My pickup wouldn't carry all the bearings I've put in them lads in my time.

Same way was with the front wheels. They had Timken bearings. They was the same bearings we use today, but they was steel and they wouldn't stay in there 'cause it was too rough a-riding for them. Nowadays you might hear of a tractor losing a front wheel bearing once in a lifetime and you might never hear of it at all. If it is properly greased, it would last as long as the tractor. But they wouldn't do it. If it lasted two years you was lucky as you could be.

Every spring I had to go around—the country was full of them—that I wore myself out at putting bearings in them lads. Every year gears and bearings always out. If they'd been transferred to rubber wheels like they have nowadays ninety per cent of that trouble would have been eliminated. They just shook them to pieces.

There just wasn't any brake on them. The only thing to stop them was that worm-drive differential. It would just stop the tractor when you throwed it out of gear.

These old tractors wouldn't go very fast. They plowed in second gear. About three mile an hour was top speed for plowing. In high gear they'd run about twenty mile an hour, but you couldn't do nothing in that gear. You couldn't hardly stand it on that steel wheel. It wouldn't pull anything on it. Three-speed transmissions was all they had—that's another change that's been brought on down the line—three forward gears, one reverse. As time rolled on they stepped them up to four forward and now they've got them as high as twelve gears. To me, I think that is a bunch of nonsense 'cause you don't need that many gears. But they've got them.

This here old baby had an awful fast high gear. It would run twenty to twenty-five miles an hour. But there wasn't a place in the state of Missouri you could use it only right out in a soft field. You couldn't pull nothing with it. On them kind of steel wheels you couldn't get out on the road and use high at all—jar you to pieces. Just out of the question. I don't know why they put it in there so fast, but they did.

And the low gear was still worse than second. It was down there about two mile an hour, I imagine. It was too slow for anything to work in it, but I've pulled in it lots of times when I'd get in a rough place.

The wheels were steel and the back wheels had twelve-inch lugs four inches deep. It was just like riding a bucking bronc all the time. Oh, in a soft field it wasn't so bad but in plowing, when you'd jump off the end of the furrow, it was just like hitting a stump. There wasn't no give to it. And those lugs would tear up the ground awful bad around over the place. That was a wonderful improvement when they got rid of that wheel, but the idea of putting them lugs on there was for extra traction.

You look at them old lugs, you'd think there wouldn't be any way in the world to stick that wheel. It just looks like it'd pull anything in the world, but

"Riding the tractor was like trying
to stay on a bucking bronco."
(The rod is wired over the lugs to
protect the garage floors.)

"The front wheels, made of iron,
would cut the ground up."

it wouldn't pull fifty per cent of what a rubber tire will pull. That don't sound
right but that's the truth.

When tractors began to come in here with rubber, farmers would buy it on
the front wheels 'cause it would steer and ride a little better up there. They
thought that was just fine. But they wouldn't have it on the back 'cause there
wasn't no traction. That was the idea. I know a number of tractors that come
through this country built that way—rubber in front and steel behind so
they'd have plenty of traction. They were going right square agin theirselves
and didn't know it.

I bought another tractor after I got rid of the first one. There wasn't no
steel wheel to it—just rubber. Well, I thought I'd be into it, for I thought it
wouldn't pull my hat off my head with that rubber in a lot of places. ('Course
they won't pull it in mud, nor lugs won't either.) But they'll do just as much
in mud as this will. And anywhere else it would skin it all to pieces. You
might be plowing sod where there was grass. One wheel runs up on land and
on a wet morning rubber might slip more than lugs would for a little while till
the grass dried off a little bit—that's all the advantage I can see for lugs.

The seat didn't help the jarring much. Oh, it had a little spring to it, but it
took a much heavier man than I was to get much benefit of that 'cause it was
a pretty stout spring. I'd keep a pad in the seat all the time. But I was young
back in that day and time, and I just loved to set in that seat. As long as I
could set up there, I never got tired. I didn't pay any attention to it. I'd stay

"The spring didn't help cushion the jarring much. It took a heavy man to benefit from this suspension system."

all day and half the night. Now I've got lights on both of my tractors and I could plow any night I wanted to, but I can see where the house is at about two hours before the sun goes down now. I don't need them lights any more.

This old baby was just for pulling. They did have them so you could put a belt pulley on it. You took a plate off on the side and put her in there. But it wasn't standard equipment. It was extra. You could pull a wood saw and stuff like that and that's about all.

Those tractors lasted . . . oh, I'd say if you drove one of them ten years you was just as lucky as you could be, and you wouldn't do that without a lot of expense on it a-tearing out this and that and the other.

That lad in the picture had several owners in its time, but I got the best of her. I wore her out. She wasn't worth much but I did get a hundred dollars out of the sucker. I was glad to see it leave 'cause ever' time I went to the field, I had to pretty near overhaul it. It was about wore out 'cause it was getting up there. It was built in '27 and that was '47 when I sold it, so you see it was twenty years old.

But those tractors did a lot of work if you knew how to handle them. They'd come out of some pretty rough places, could pull a pretty big load, if you used your head. You'd get her down there in a low gear and give her just as little a throttle as you could move it with, she'd go out of there. But if you jerked her up there in second gear and pulled that throttle open she'd-a been over on top of you in a minute. And it's true today. The tractors you got today will do the same thing if you don't watch yourself.

I remember the story about those tractors rearing up. When they brought us our first tractor Dad's brother asked the salesman, he said, "Is that story true about them tractors being bad to fall over backwards and kill a man?" "Well," he said, "yes, they'll rear up and fall over backwards, but," he said, "they're the only tractor on the market that has enough power to raise theirself." 'Course that was wrong. They wasn't loaded with power. But he said, "When Henry Ford built that tractor he expected the brains to be in the driver's head and not the damn seat!" That's the very words he used. I was eight years old when he said that and I never did forget that story when I begin to driving the thing, and I've had them lads in every shape in the world —some of the darnedest places and pulling them with all they'd pull.

Back then that tractor cost, oh, I'd say six or seven hundred dollars and that one was built in 1927. I really don't know. Something like that—might have been a thousand, but I doubt it very much. Back when that tractor was built that was the finest thing in the world. That's all they knew. That's all they had.

Tractors were slow to come into the Ozarks because farmers thought they'd never be any good in the hills and the farms were all small. They used tractors like horses, just to pull. Farmers didn't want a big tractor. They wanted maneuverability with a smaller tractor.

Nowadays the trend is every man is trying to get a bigger one than the other feller's got. There's two points that's caused it.

These tractor pulls all over the country is one thing that started it. Every man's trying to get one they can outpull the rest with. Another thing, they've added about four farms into one. Most ever'body has—and they've got to have—those bigger-capacity tractors to be able to operate their farms.

Nowadays you just have about three days in spring to plow a hundred acres. If you don't get them plowed in them three days, you don't plow. That sounds funny, but that's the weather that's causing that. We don't have the weather we used to have when I was a boy. I can remember plowing the corn with a team for thirty days at a time and never be knocked out of the field. We plowed all over this country—four head of mules or six or eight head of mules—and plowed and plowed till I couldn't sit down in a chair. Might lose one half a day in a month. Well, nowadays if you get in a week's plowing, you're going to be lucky. It'll rain you out so that you don't get in the field.

Now them tractors back then if they plowed four, not over five, acres a day you was lucky, 'cause you had to put in so much time cleaning plugs or fixing the coil on it or something would go wrong that would delay you. Also they didn't have a lot of speed. They only pulled two twelve-inch plows. It just didn't cover a lot of territory. What I'm telling here was with tractors with twelve or fifteen horsepower. This old Fordson only had one horse.

Back then on the average in this country there were a lot of small fields. But a lot of times most of us would have out, I guess, thirty-five or forty acres on an average. Sometimes maybe a little more than that. We used the tractor to break the ground—just a plow and disc was all the equipment with the tractor. We plowed corn with mules.

Back in my childhood days, whatever you owned was in corn every year, just about. That's all we raised, practically. Don't anyone raise any corn any more. It's all hay. That day and time the old-time farmers like my neighbor over there, I've heard him tell his son many a time—he'd have out about twenty-five acres of corn—he'd say to him, "You ain't got out no corn crop. You better go out and plow up another field and put out some more corn."

Corn's got so expensive, but in that day and time that's all they had. That's all they knew about and that's all they fed ever'thing they had—cattle and hog feed and make silage out of it. There's a lot of hard work to corn any way you go to try to take care of it. I don't care what you do, if you silo it or pick it or what you do with it, it is real hard work. And that's what got the matter nowadays. We don't have that work and manpower on the farm any more and that's why they quit raising corn.

We used to silo with twenty-five or thirty men. Now three or four does the same job—machinery is what does it. My young neighbor over here is the only one in this neighborhood that silos any more and I expect he's got thirty thousand dollars in equipment, just for siloing alone.

Last spring he plowed up a hundred and fifty acres on all his places and put it in corn, and I'll swear he plowed that, by George, before I could hardly get my breakfast eat. Just in a week's time and that sucker was done. Beats anything I ever seen. One day I seen him in that big bottom field. He just took around it. And, boy, I went up the ridge the second day and he had her upside down, just turned over—the whole works—fifty acres of it.

Now if I had to plow it with this tractor, I'd be thirty days a-plowing it— been lucky to get it plowed in thirty days, for I'd had to overhauled it four or five times before I got it done.

Nobody would have that tractor today if it was brand new. Wouldn't be nothing to it and nobody'd be interested in it because it wouldn't do what they wanted it to do compared to tractors now. But I thought back then that that tractor was just the best job in the world and it was just a natural-born hobby for me. It still is.

Barbed Wire

Barbed wire did not play as significant a role in the Ozarks as it did on the Western plains. The topography of the area did not lend itself to large cattle ranges, and thus families would often homestead only forty, eighty, or maybe a hundred and sixty acres. They farmed the open areas and the cleared creek and river bottoms or hollows for their own needs, using the rougher timbered areas for pasture for their small herds of stock. Instead of putting a fence around all their land, they fenced in their gardens and cultivated fields, allowing the stock to roam free on their land, their neighbors' land, railroad land, or any other unfenced land. In some southern Missouri counties this was still the case until quite recently.

Early fences were made with a great deal of labor from material at hand, which in the Ozarks was split-rail fences or occasionally rock fences. The timber cleared off the fields was cut into rail lengths and split to make the necessary enclosure. Rocks carried from the field after every plowing would gradually form a fence, though usually not one adequate enough to turn stock.

However, not all the Ozark farms were wooded. There were regions of

Charlie McMicken shows *Bittersweet* staff members his fence made with several kinds of old wire.

open prairies requiring farmers to haul logs several miles. The untreated rails would rot, fall down, or be torn down easily by stock. So when barbed wire became available, the Ozark farmer made good use of it, though its widespread use was later here than in other areas of the United States.

Wire was used for fencing in England as early as 1840, but woven and barbed wire was not developed until after 1860. The first patent for barbed wire in the United States was granted in 1867, though it was not until 1874 that Joseph Glidden of De Kalb, Illinois, invented a machine to manufacture it that barbed wire became usable to any great extent.

Barbed wire today is made of two longitudinal wires twisted together to form a cable. Spaced at regular intervals are wire barbs wound around either one or both of the cables. The barbs are made from round, half-round, or flat wire, cut diagonally at the end to make a sharper point. There are either two or four points depending on whether the barbs are formed of one wire or two. The barbs are about one inch from tip to tip. The wire is from 12½- to 16-gauge wire with the barbs of slightly heavier gauge. The wire is galvanized for resistance to corrosion.

In the early days of experimentation there were many kinds of barbed wire and hundreds of patents. Some wires were single-strand 9-gauge oval or flat wires with serrated edges. Many of them broke easily under the pressure of cattle and the contraction and expansion in cold and hot weather. The Glidden wire with two strands twisted together permitted contraction and expansion and was strong enough to hold cattle without harming them.

The first of the barbed wire that came out around 1853 was a vicious, razor-sharp wire without barbs, which today is called blind wire. The idea was to turn stock. The animals did not know anything about the wire and when they ran into or through the fences they cut themselves to pieces.

Farmers therefore had to fix the wire so that their animals could see it. They twisted wooden blocks, metal strips, tin plates, balls, anything they could devise into the wire to warn the stock that the fence was there. The blocks let the animal see the fence was there before discovering it by running into it. These warning devices were sometimes added at the factory or were put on by the rancher or farmer himself.

The warning devices gained many nicknames through the years of use. Such names are "barbed-wire signals," "indicators," "warning strips," "warn-

Boone's Round Guard Block (1884). Sheet metal insert holds the round guard block to other wire.

Dodge's Spur Wheel (1881). The six-point metal barb rolls when grazed.

ing plates," and "cattle protectors." After the stock became used to the presence of the barbed-wire fence, these warning devices lost their importance and were no longer used.

A fencing wire that was used to keep stock from being injured was the Dodge's Spur Wheel. It was a visual wire, but if an animal leaned against it, the wheel would roll with him. The ends of the wheel would prick him just a little, but not hurt him.

Many different gimmicks were used to give barbed wire a "see-ability" without the use of warning devices. Wire was developed with large plate barbs or, more commonly, twisted wires with evenly spaced barbs, such as Riter's Visible Wire with Barbs.

The wire that won out over all other variations, and is still bought and used today almost as it was when it was originally made, is the Glidden wire. It was developed by J. F. Glidden, who would make the barbs by twisting them around something a little larger than the wire. He then sent a man up on a windmill with two strands of greased wire and had another man on the ground holding the other ends. The man up on the windmill put the barb on a wire and let it slide down. The man at the bottom put a twist or two in it. Another barb would be put on to slide down the greased wire and the two strands twisted again.

Glidden experimented with putting the twist of the wire on with a grindstone and a coffee mill before he invented a machine to produce it. His invention is basically the same as that used today to manufacture barbed wire. Two cable wires are fed through the machine longitudinally. Wire for the two-point barbs feeds into the machine at right angles from the side, going into a spinner which twists them around the cables. Cut-off knives cut the barbs to the desired length and point. The machine moves the cable to the proper distance and twists on another barb.

The Frisco railroad was instrumental in introducing barbed wire into the Ozarks. The railroad used variations of Buckthorn wire to fence their right of way to keep roaming livestock from straying onto the tracks. Farmers recognized the value of the wire quietly demonstrating its efficiency all along the miles of the railroad which cut through the region. Gradually the fenced-in places of those who could afford it were made of wire and today one still sees fences of Buckthorn wire throughout the Ozarks.

Riter's Visual (1893). A two-strand wire with loose and tight twists in the wire.

Allis Buckthorn (1881). A metal strip with reinforcing core.

Some men and women interested in preserving evidences of the past which have had an influence on our history enjoy collecting different kinds of barbed wire, cataloguing and labeling them, and trading with other collectors. Charlie McMicken has collected over eight hundred different kinds, walking miles along the Frisco right of way and in areas back from the tracks.

Charlie explained, "You see, the Frisco was probably the first to use barbed wire to fence here in this country. They had a fence on each side of the tracks. Now when a county road was built alongside, they did not need a fence there any more, and they gave it to any farmer to use or throw away. I have found six wires that I am sure the Frisco has used as part of their right-of-way fence, and the reason I feel that is because I have found them either as part of the fence or close by. Some of the wires are used more frequently than others. There is one wire I have found as much as twelve miles away from the tracks where the farmer threw it out. On a farm along or close to the railroad you might find any kind of wire."

We asked Charlie where else would be a good place to find old barbed wire in the Ozarks. He said, "The place to find good barbed wire is in the prairie country rather than in the Ozarks, but if you become serious as a collector, you can get off away from the railroads and hunt in the prairie sections of the Ozarks. If it was five miles back to the woods from where they lived the people just didn't go and make rails. They bought wire and made fence. The

Charlie has collected over 800 different kinds of barbed wire.

people that lived in the woods did not have money enough—the further in the woods the less money they had—and they were the ones who used rails. The farther you got from the woods, the better land and the more affluent they were. Look around any old field. To find the fence on an old field, go around the field out maybe four or five feet or maybe ten or fifteen feet. If you hunt hard enough you'll find evidence of a fence somewhere around the field.

"You should also look along old roads that people had to use to get from their house to the main road or to the railroad, especially if they were in back of another house."

When Charlie finds wire worth collecting, he gets all he can of it and trades off what he doesn't need for his collection.

Often when old wire was replaced, it was rolled up and thrown away. When the collector finds the old fields, he looks for rolls of the discarded wire hanging on trees or fence posts. He also searches overgrown or rocky corners, nearby junk heaps, sink holes, and ditches.

The wire is cut into eighteen-inch lengths for mounting, storing, or trading. A collector can have dozens of variations of one patent. He may find wires with unusual situations, irregularities, or splices which make the strand of wire valuable as a collector's item or show the stages in the development of wire. The irregularities can be factory errors, like barbs bunched together, wire not twisted correctly, or other mistakes in manufacturing. The splices are where the wire was broken or cut, then spliced together at the factory. If the wire has an irregularity or splice, that defect is placed in the middle of the length of wire for display purposes.

The chart on the next page illustrates a few of the varieties that Charlie Mc has found in the Ozarks.

An Ozark corner post.

CRANDEL'S LINK OUT-
SIDE SPLICED VARIATION
Spliced at center to
form two-point barb.
Variation of patent.

GREGG'S SNAKE WIRE
First wire patented,
Nov.18, 1890,
by Samuel H. Gregg.

GLIDDEN'S BARB,
THREE STRAND VARIA-
TION
Wire barb with two
points.
Variation of patent

LOOP AND HITCH
ORNAMENTAL FENCING
Looping edge strands.
Inventor unknown.

FORD'S STRAIGHT-CUT
RIBBON
Cutout barb points
along one edge.
Patented Jan. 13,
1885, by Franklin D.
Ford.

KILMER'S WINDOW STRIP
Sheet metal with tri-
angular openings. Pat-
ented May 12, 1885, by
Irving A. and Melvin
D. Kilmer.

BABER'S TACK RAIL
Sheet metal strip
with tack barbs.
April 18, 1882.
George C. Baber.

DOERR'S ELECTRIC
FENCE WIRE
Two-point wire barb.
Patented Oct.20,
1959, by Raymond S.
Doerr.

CENTER-CORE METALLIC
Strip has center
core for reinforce-
ment. Made but
never patented.

STUBBE'S SMALL
FORMEE CROSS
Eight-point sheet
metal barb plate
with two-strand
wire. Patented Oct.
23, 1883, by John
Stubbe.

GREGG'S BARBED
SNAKE WIRE
Single-strand wire
with two-point barb.

GLIDDEN'S BARB
COMMON VARIATION
Two-point barb with
two-strand wire.
Variation of patent.

ELLWOOD'S THREE-
STRAND PARALLEL AND
TIED REVERSE
Four-point wire barb
with three parallel
single-wire strands.
Patented Jan. 31,
1882, by Abram Ellwood.

GLIDDEN'S BARB
PAIRED BARBS
Two wire barbs with
three strand wire.
Variation of patent.

Fox Trotting
through the Ozarks

A Missouri fox trotter? Well, the fox trot is a dance, so a Missouri fox trotter must be a person from Missouri that dances the fox trot. Almost right, but not quite. It's not a person but a horse—one that originated in the Ozarks of southern Missouri and northern Arkansas and that moves with all the grace, style, rhythm, and action of a dancer.

The fox trot gait that makes this horse move like a dancer is a syncopated

Russell Moore's Yankee's Golden Sensation was the 1973 world champion senior mare.

two-beat gait. The horse walks with his front feet and trots with his hind feet. The name comes from the fox, which leaves only two tracks. Its hind foot steps in the track left by the front one. The old-time fox trotting horse also traveled in a straight line, "capping his tracks," hence the name.

The fox trotting horse is a relatively new breed. When the first settlers came to the Ozarks from Kentucky and Tennessee a hundred and fifty years ago, they brought their own five-gaited and plantation horses. However, the settlers soon found that the high-spirited five-gaited horse did not work as well in the more rugged Ozarks as they did in the East. They were easy riding horses, but they weren't the sturdy, sure-footed, even-tempered horse the Ozark hills demanded to look after the cattle and hogs that roamed free in the woods.

So the settlers started crossing their stock with Morgan and Arabian stock to make them more sure-footed and better-natured. In the 1930s a lot of mustang mares were shipped into the Ozarks and some of them were bred to fox trotting horses. "It's a pretty mixed-up breed," Quentin Middleton explained.

Many of the Ozark people had small forty-acre farms and could not afford to own a work team as well as two or three riding horses, so the fox trotter was also bred to fill the need for an all-purpose horse. Most were used to make a living for the settler, plowing fields all day and furnishing transportation at night and Sundays to church and social gatherings.

Ewin "Rusty" McClure remembers, "When we weren't riding them, we did whatever work there was to do with them. We tried not to pull them on a load, tried not to wagon them too much. I always thought it made them stiff in the shoulders. We'd plow with them, harrow with them, drag with them. We used to ride and work them of a day and ride them fox hunting of a night."

Quentin Middleton put in, "I've worked them at anything a horse can be worked to from a double shovel on up. I've even used them in the log woods. We worked them. And if we had any time and our horses wasn't too tired, Dad let us ride them on weekends. When I was a kid, I worked them more than I rode them."

And James Hufft added, "They're just a hillbilly universal horse."

Today the hillbilly horse finds himself quite far from the Ozarks and quite at home in forty-eight states and in several countries including Canada, Mexico, and Australia, proving his breeding by his ability to travel long distances. He is no longer only hillbilly; the fox trotter is the universal horse.

Like most breeds of horses, fox trotters are now used mainly for pleasure and are frequently seen at trail rides. They have been back-yard horses, ridden, driven, and used for roping. Martha Jo Willard found fox trotters scarce when she moved her horse to Virginia, but she found a new sport for fox trotters—jumping. "Dorie [her horse] has jumped four feet, but I feel more comfortable at three to three and a half feet," she said. "His take-off and landing are good."

Mr. President, owned by James Hufft, was grand champion horse of the Model Stake Class at the 1971 Missouri Fox Trotters Horse Breeders Association Show and Celebration, Ava, Missouri.

Many people still work fox trotters, especially for cattle, and they still are used during the day and ridden at night. C. H. "Dutch" Snyder said, "An ole fox trotting horse, you can run cattle with them, you can use them on your place, or you can take them to a show. I've run cattle with my horse, then take them to a show of a night and show them and win, too."

Quentin Middleton added, "If I had a real good show horse, I sure wouldn't run him after cattle. Some people do, I know. But I wouldn't care a bit to take my show horse and break him to plow my garden."

Some fox trotters earn their keep in other ways. The Kansas City sheriff's posse uses them to direct traffic at ball games and for shore patrol duty and they are used at the Missouri State Fair to guard the grounds. In recent years the U. S. Forest Service, after trying several other breeds of horses, found fox trotters the best all-around horse for the job. R. N. Riding, Forest Supervisor, Big Horn National Forest, Sheridan, Wyoming, wrote:

"Fox trotters now travel over approximately fifteen million acres of National Forest land. We have used them for riding sheep ranges, cattle ranges, checking wilderness areas, checking deer, elk and moose hunters and check-

The tough yet beautiful, smooth-gaited fox trotter is ideal for trail rides.

ing on back area camps. We have used them on fires varying from two acres in size to six thousand acres in size. Some of these horses have been packed. Most have been ridden; but whatever job we need to do horseback we have found these horses ideally suited for our purposes. Their gentleness, intelligence, great toughness, and capacity to go on after most horses are tired have made them a very valuable management tool for a great number of rangers in the National Forest system of the Rocky Mountains."

When the original settlers bred the fox trotters, they were concerned not only with versatility and endurance but also with the beauty of the animal. Ideally, the horses would stand around fifteen hands to fifteen hands two inches (a hand is four inches measured from the withers to the ground), and though they are all colors, blacks, sorrels, palominos, bays, and red and blue roans are the most popular, with white markings desirable. The head should be carried not quite straight with the front legs, and should be medium sized with a high rolling forehead. The nose should be slightly forward, and the ears small, alert, and straight. The horse needs good bright eyes set wide apart. The neck should have a slight crest with a smooth-flowing line evenly muscled to allow freedom for the horse to work his head. The horse has to

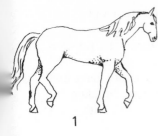
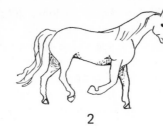

1   2   3

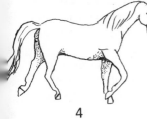
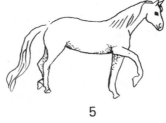
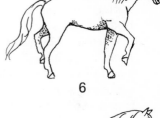

4   5   6

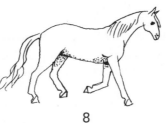
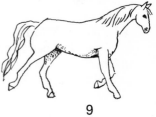

7   8   9

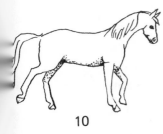
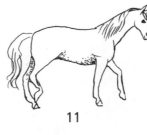
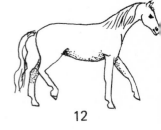

10   11   12

The diagrams illustrate the fox trotting gait.

have a deep sloping shoulder to be able to work the front end. The body should be medium in length, not as short as the quarter horse or as long as an American saddle horse. To give an easier ride, the fox trotter should be cut up in the flank with a good long hip and the hind legs should not be quite as straight as they are in the quarter horse. To develop their reach and stride they need long pastern joints and a long slim foot with heels on front and back cut reasonably low. The tail should be long, full-flowing, natural, and set fairly high. The mane, too, is full and free.

The fox trotter is a three-gaited horse which does a flat foot walk, fox trot, and canter. The walk is fast and square. The horse's legs should be well under his body and not pacing or swinging from side to side. The hind foot oversteps the front foot anywhere from four to eight inches. Nodding his head and flopping his ears in time with the feet, the horse walks with spirit and grace.

The fox trot, walking with the front legs and trotting with the hind, is a relaxed syncopated two-beat gait with a one-two, one-two rhythm. The horse travels at a speed of four to eight miles an hour. The legs move diagonally; starting with the left front leg, the sequence is left front, right rear, right front and left rear.

When the Missouri Fox Trotting Horse Breed Association was formed in 1948, many horses would fox trot but not reach up far enough with their hind feet to cap or disfigure their tracks. Today many fox trotters are being crossbred with Tennessee walking horses, giving them more stride behind. Now many fox trotters actually overstep the track left by the front foot.

The easy ride of the fox trot comes from the horse's shifting of his weight as he moves. When he picks up his front foot, his weight is across his back and loins. Just before he slides his hind foot in place, he shifts his weight to his chest and withers, leaving the hind foot weightless. This eliminates the bounce and jar associated with a trot or jog trot.

The whole body of the horse has to work in rhythm with his feet to do the fox trot. To give the most comfortable ride, the horse has to work his head and neck. The head nods in rhythm, rising when the front foot steps and falling when the hind foot does.

How to hold the reins to ride a fox trotter.

The horse's rhythm is definitely a part of the fox trot and is what sets the fox trot apart from other gaits. All fox trotters have some means of keeping time. Some flop their ears, others pop their teeth. The tail gracefully swishes and bobs in time with the feet. Like all good dancers, the fox trotter performs with a relaxed grace and seeming ease that belie the complexity of the movement.

The third gait, the canter, is not used until the horse is three years old, but like the fox trot and the walk, it is a natural gait. The canter is rhythmical and slow, like riding a rocking chair. It is a little higher than a quarter horse lope, but not as high as the walking horse canter. As with the walk and fox trot, the horse canters with ease.

THE SNYDER-BROKE HORSE

No matter what you begin to talk to Dutch Snyder about, somehow the conversation always swings around to horses. Dutch has trained fox trotters for years, likes horses, and doesn't mind talking about them.

I remember this mare I broke for a young boy. He was about ten and he had a real pretty little sorrel mare. He was proud of her as anything. Any time anyone would say anything about the mare or brag on her, he would say, "Yup, she's Snyder-broke."

Oh my, I tell you what, I've rode horses for about sixty years. And now I've trained them for years and years. I don't know how long it has been. I guess I've trained horses for twenty-six, -seven years. And I used to break and ride all my own horses and mules. Well, I've worked at it all my life. I bought my first horse when I was ten years old. Give thirty-five dollars for it

"You've got to be smarter than your horse."—C. H. "Dutch" Snyder.

and the feller I worked for give me fifty cents a day and my dinner and he paid for my horse and I worked it out when I was ten years old.

It was just a little fox trotting mare. She was pretty. Her name was Old Beauty. I never will forget her. But if I've ever been off of mules or horses ever since I was ten years old, I don't know it.

I used to show walking horses. I used to ride them all the time. And then I started in a-breaking out quarter horses and Appaloosies. They got too rough for me as I got older and I started in on these ole fox trotting horses. I've rode them ever since they ever started.

I like fox trotting horses best. They ain't as much trouble. You don't put in as much time with them, and it don't take as much riding [to break them]. You don't have to take care of them like you do these walking horses. Now walking horses you got to keep them shod so-so. You can't turn them out, they jerk them old heavy shoes off. And these fox trotting horses ain't no trouble. You see if you want to, just turn one out and ride it and go right on. A quarter horse is the same way only I just got where I didn't like to ride them, just too rough riding unless you just let them jog along about like a snail'll go. But an ole fox trotting horse, you can run cattle with them, you can use them on your place, or you can take them to a show. You can do any way you want to with them and they're just not near as much trouble.

You can start riding a fox trotter all the way from seventeen months on up to two years. I'd rather start them at two, or just before they get two. They're easier broke and they're not set in their ways. But it depends on your horses. Some horses is more developed and you can start them quicker than you can others. You take them where they ain't developed good nor been took good care of—you can't do that. You're liable to hurt them. You've got to know about what a young horse can stand when you start in. If you don't, you better leave it alone. That's all there is to it.

The first thing in training a horse is to learn it to mind. That's easy done for me. I just show them what I want them to do. After I show them and they understand what I want them to do, I make them do it. Just like you would a kid. You got to learn them what "whoa" is and all that stuff and then you just start from there on out just like you would anything else.

Once a horse is halter broke, I sometimes put the saddle and bridle on them and let them stand in the stall and I tie their head a certain way and do that for a few days straight, and sometimes I just put the saddle and bridle on them, turn them out in the lot, let them fight it and get used to it. Half the time, if they're gentle and all, I just get them in and go to riding them, like I'm doing this horse here. Depends on the horse.

Sometimes I use an older horse to help break a young one. When I'm riding outside, I generally have some boy to ride the young one and I do the leading, the horse and all.

General rule, I use just a regular limber bit [snaffle bit]. You see, they can fight it and it don't hurt their mouth. Sometimes I ride them according to whether I can handle them or not. If they're pretty hard to handle, I ride them with a regular bit on.

I generally flat foot them first. Get them set in their flat foot good. Then just go from there. You can tell by your horse how soon you can go to fox trotting. But that flat foot is the main thing you ought to learn them first. I've rode lots of horses and I hardly ever ride two that breaks out alike.

You have to wait until the horse is three before cantering him. Sometimes you go try to canter a two-year-old 'fore you get him set in his gait, you'll get him where you push him up a little, he'll quit fox trotting. It confuses them.

I like to take good care of the horses before they're ready to ride. You can let them run out clear up to they're a yearling. They ought to run out. Then when they are a yearling and you're going to ride them about that fall, you ought to bring them in and take good care of them and grow them.

You got to be smarter than your horse. Horses are pretty smart. I tell you horses is really smarter than people really give them credit to be. The horse is smarter than two thirds of the people. Now that's the truth, if I ever told it. They're smart enough to know how to not let them break them. And they're smart enough to know what to do when they're doing it. My experience is, if you ain't smarter than the horse, you're pretty well blowed up.

But maybe even more important than that, you've got to love horses. If you don't like them, and like to fool with them, you just better leave them alone. Now, that's the whole thing in a nutshell. You've got to love the animal when you start in. I'm a horse lover. I have been all my life. My dad always took care of his horses and he loved them and I guess I took back after him.

SHOEING THE FOX TROTTER

To find out how to shoe the fox trotter, we talked to Keith Mizer one afternoon while he shod a mare named Honey. When asked why he started shoeing, Keith replied, "Lack of sense, I think!" Actually, Keith had a quarter horse mare that needed shoes and Lloyd Bell, the only farrier in the area, was ill. He lent Keith his tools and told him to shoe the mare. "I just started in. It was a terrible-looking mess when I got done with it."

For three and a half years Keith shod horses under Lloyd Bell's supervision. "He [Mr. Bell] told me that if I wanted to learn how to shoe he'd teach me to shoe fox trotting horses because that's what he'd been shoeing for thirty-five to forty years. When he started out, he drove shoes on for ten cents a shoe. Of course, you know, I get a bit more than that now.

"Anyway, I let quarter horses go and went on to fox trotting horses. I started out just part time. It got bigger and bigger and bigger until now I not only shoe full time but have my own training barn. And I think I have two of the best trainers around—Iva Lou and Rick [his wife and son].

"Usually, you start shoeing when the horse is a two-year-old. Sometimes yearlings are shod, but only when you're going to show them in model classes and their feet are worn down or are in poor condition.

Keith Mizer specializes in shoeing fox trotters.

Horseshoeing tools.

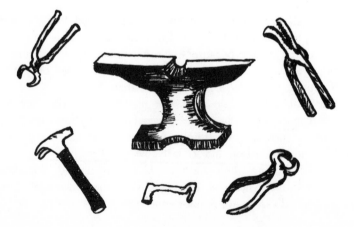

"I like to ride the two-year-old several times before shoeing him. In fact, it's best not to shoe him until his feet begin to wear. And if he gets a little tender-footed, he will stay on the ground better and won't hop or jump around or act up as much. The first time you shoe a horse, you should use a flat plate.

"The average horse, you cut the front hoof shorter than the back. The front toe is three and a half inches and the back toe is four inches long. You set both front and back feet on a fifty-degree angle. The angle you use runs from your pastern joint to the tip of the foot. Look at Honey here. Stand her square, look down her shoulder right here and keep this same slope from her shoulder to the tip of her toe and you have a perfect slope for shoeing. Usually, a cowboy shoe—a shoe with a little toe and heel—is used. That's what we're using here on Honey.

"That's your average horse. But different horses have different problems just like people, and the way the horse is shod can make all the difference in a champion horse and a mediocre one. So I like to watch a horse travel before I shoe. Then I can shoe for his way of going.

"If the horse has trouble walking, I use a weighted shoe such as the Boston toe weight. This'll get his shoulders working. However, you've got to be careful using weight because some horses will become too trotty with too much weight. Used to, people would take a horse and run a lot of weight on them. I've had people have me put on shoes that weigh two pounds or more. But now the Missouri Fox Trotting Horse Breed Association has prohibited that and judges can disqualify a horse for too much weight, so you should only use regulation shoes on fox trotters. Your Boston toe weight is about the

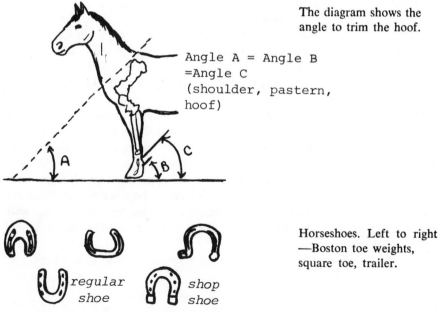

The diagram shows the angle to trim the hoof.

Angle A = Angle B
=Angle C
(shoulder, pastern, hoof)

regular shoe

shop shoe

Horseshoes. Left to right
—Boston toe weights, square toe, trailer.

heaviest regulation shoe and weighs one pound, the cowboy shoe thirteen ounces and a flat plate only nine ounces.

"The fox trotter has a lot of Tennessee walking horse in his background so a lot of them will do a running walk naturally. To break up the running walk, set both the front and back hoof on a fifty-two-degree angle and use a weighted toe in front. You can do the same thing if the horse is pacey.

"But if the horse is trotty, set the hoof on a forty-five-degree angle behind and use a flat plate. In front, set a forty-seven-degree angle and leave more toe. I like a flat plate in front, too, but some people use a cowboy shoe. Sometimes you can let a trotty horse go barefoot in front and get tender so he'll reach more and stay on the ground better and settle into the fox trot.

"Some horses need more action in their front end at a walk or fox trot to be working good. On them, I leave the front toe longer than three and a half inches. And if he needs more action in back, leave the back toe longer than four inches."

The hammer ringing on the anvil interrupted conversation while Keith shaped the shoe to fit Honey's foot. After checking the fit, Keith continued talking while driving the nails.

"If you've got a short-gaited horse and you want him to reach out more with his back feet, you lower the front heels and leave the toe longer so you have a forty-five-degree angle and use a weighted toe. On the back feet, set on a fifty-degree angle and use a cowboy shoe.

"A lot of horses will interfere or strike hock [the hind foot hits the front foot during the stride]. On them cut the front very short and leave a longer toe behind to make him break his back end.

"If a horse wings or paddles [instead of bringing his front feet straight forward during his stride, the horse throws his feet to the outside] and it's not in his knee, you can straighten him by lowering the hoof about one fourth inch lower on the outside than the inside. Weight the inside to bring the foot over straight. You can use what you call a square-toed shoe on them but I've had more success just cutting low on the outside and weighting the inside.

"Pigeon-toed horses or horses that toe in should be trimmed shorter on the inside. Horses that toe out are trimmed on the outside. The way you set your shoe can really help straighten the hoof, too.

"Some horses are special problems because they have been foundered or they have dry or cracked hoofs. The best thing you can do about founder is to prevent it. It's caused by anything that upsets the circulation because the hoof can't sweat to get rid of excess heat. Stomach contents, concussion, overwork, spoiled hay or grain, lush grass, hard use immediately after trimming long feet, letting a hot horse drink or wade in cold water—all these can cause founder. If your horse should founder, then trim the affected hoof wall. If you need to, you can build up the hoof with acrylic. This lets the hoof grow and function normally.

"Cracked hoofs can be stopped by filing across the crack. If you keep your horse in a stall, you should watch for and prevent dry, brittle hoofs. This is easy to do by simply applying a hoof conditioner every two or three days."

Honey finally decided she had stood still long enough and just as Keith bent over to pick up her hind foot she began a little jig dance. Keith was expecting something like that from her, and he quickly straightened her out with a healthy swat on her backside.

"That's really nothing at all for a horse to behave like that," Keith said. "You should see some horses when I try to shoe them. Ruth, there, had two I'll never forget. One mare was as gentle as a lamb with her front feet and the very devil when you tried to do anything at all with her hind feet. We had all kinds of fun with her. I can tell you, I'm glad Ruth only rode her one year so I didn't have to shoe her very much.

"Another one of Ruth's horses was a yearling past, almost ready to start riding. Anyway, Ruth bought a new saddle from me, so we put it on him to see how it would look. We were out in the field and it was really muddy. Since I'd have to shoe the horse soon, I decided to pick up his feet and check them out. I picked up his front foot and he promptly laid down in the mud. With Ruth's new saddle on! I don't know who had the best expression—me holding a horse's foot in the air and the rest of him stretched out on his side on the ground, or Ruth when she saw her new saddle down in all that mud!"

Keith had finished with Honey and stood back to check his job. "Bring her back in about six weeks. That's about how often a fox trotter needs to be shod to keep them in their gears and doing their best. And after show season is over, during the winter when you're not going to ride Honey much, you should pull her shoes off and just let her run barefooted."

Keith was sweating a little and we noted that shoeing was hard work. Keith agreed. "I have spent as high as three hours on one horse and have shod them in as little as twenty-five minutes. You'll average spending an hour and a half to two hours on it. One thing you never want to do is really hurry on a horse when you're shoeing it because if your horse hasn't got good feet, you haven't got much of a horse.

"One summer out in Bonner Springs, Kansas, I shod twenty-two horses in one day. I started one morning about six o'clock and it was quarter to eleven that night when I got done. But that's the last, and I'll never do that again. Just on an average, I'll usually do five, maybe six horses a day."

Intrigued by the nails used to shoe horses, we wondered if they hurt the horses. "They've got what you call a wall in the horse's foot and they've got a white line. As long as you stay outside that white line you're okay. But if you get inside that white line, then you're into the sole of the foot that's filled with just real tiny nerves and stuff, and you're in trouble. But shoeing, just like anything else that has to do with horses, you've got to know the horse and just use a little common sense, and you're all right."

COME SHOW WITH ME

You've never been to a horse show? There's one tonight I'm taking Chocolate Drop to. Why don't you come with us and you can help us get ready, too.

Chocolate is getting a bit woolly, so you hold her while I give her a haircut. I need to trim her bridle path, ear, nose whiskers, fetlocks, and hairline above the hoofs so she will look neater and trimmer.

Okay, now tie her under the maple tree so we can give her a bath with a garden hose, shampoo, and creme rinse. I've been using strawberry-scented shampoo. I think apple is Chocolate's favorite, but they were out of it last time I bought some.

The hardest part about the bath is doing her tail. Watch her. I bet as soon as I get it wet and sudsy, Chocolate will swish it across my face.

Would you put the feed in the trailer? I've got the saddle and bridle and my good saddle blanket. I sure hope we tied Chocolate so that she can't lie down in the dirt! We don't have time for another bath. Here, take the hay while I put her cooler on so we can load her and go.

Usually Chocolate's really good about loading and unloading and riding in the trailer, but one night we got home from a show about two in the morning and Chocolate was in a hurry to get out. Before I could unfasten the tail guard, she started backing out and ended up wedged half in and half out, un-

Russell Moore adds the finishing touches to his mare just before his showing.

able to move. We finally had to saw through the chain tail guard to get her out!

Well, here we are. I need to get Chocolate ready and warm up in the ring before the show starts, so why don't you brush her and I'll comb out her mane and tail. Don't let me forget to put the insect repellent on her, or she'll be stomping at flies when she should be standing quietly in line.

Okay, now saddle her. Doesn't this bright yellow saddle blanket look good on Chocolate? That and the yellow brow band really stand out on her color.

Once my cousin went to a show with me. She had been showing three-gaited horses in the East, mainly Connecticut. Anyway, she was amazed at the people who show fox trotters, how friendly and how helpful they are, even with people they constantly show against. Most of the conversation is joking and advice. You'll probably hear someone say, "This time I'm going to come out ahead of you!" and be answered with, "On that two-cent plug?" What they tell me all the time is, "Kick her up and hold her back. You're not going to make it like that tonight! Kick her up and hold her back." I'm still not sure how to kick a horse up and hold him back even yet. A young horse will be straightened out with a healthy swat and a "That'll learn ya, dern ya!" or someone might ask, "Have you got an extra blanket? Would you believe it? I've been showing for years and forgot mine!" One always appears with understanding smiles.

Quentin Middleton has worked fox trotters all his life, and now trains them for the show ring. Here he rides Zane's Queen of Hearts. (Photo courtesy of *The Missouri Fox Trotter*)

The show's starting now. Let's go watch awhile. Chocolate will be okay tied to the trailer. All I have left to do is to put the yellow ribbons in her mane, brush out my own mane, and put my ribbons in. If I put Chocolate's in now, she'll chew on them so I'll do it just before her class.

I'd like to see my friend show her horse in the model class. In a model class, the horses are shown at halter and judged strictly on conformation. The horses are led at a walk usually once around the ring, then lined up so the judges can get a good look at them. The horses stand just about square. Notice those out there are not stretched; they stand quietly.

The next class is the two-year-old fox trot classes. The horses will come in to the right at a fox trot. Watch. Almost every horse is stepping right in time with the music. The organist tonight is good, but notice how the horses keep with the beat. The two-year-olds don't canter. They are shown at a walk and a fox trot both ways of the ring. The usual judging standards for them are fifty per cent on the fox trot and twenty-five per cent each on the walk and conformation. In the three-year-old class—Chocolate's class—the fox trot mares class and the fox trot studs and geldings class, the horses canter and are judged forty per cent on fox trot, twenty per cent each on walk and canter, and twenty per cent on conformation.

The announcer is doing a good job tonight. You know, though, I think the horses like winning even more than the riders. Chocolate always knows when she wins and usually acts pretty pleased with herself. Maybe it's the apple I give her she likes, but I think she likes winning, too.

Looks like the judge has just about made up his mind on this class so I better get Chocolate. We're in the next class. You stay here and watch. I just need you for two things. Let me know if we're on the right lead when we canter, and wish us good luck.

Winning a trophy at the American Fox Trot Horse Breed Association Show makes the years of breeding, care, and training all worthwhile to Ruth Massey.

In the Village

Each family needed many material things they couldn't raise or make, so people depended on some businesses and trades in town. The general store and post office in every community would trade the farmer's products for the goods he needed. The blacksmith shop—complete with forge, tools, material, and a smith—would handle and fashion metal. Many towns also had a mill. There wasn't much need to go farther to supply all that was needed to support the family.

Crackers, Coal Oil, and Conversation— The Country Store

Most people have visited a modern shopping mall. While they walk in air-conditioned or centrally heated comfort, they have an opportunity to explore everything from large department stores to specialty shops which sell an endless variety of products. Strolling through the shops, they may comment that the shopping center is a modern innovation. As far as the architecture, heating and cooling, and interior design are concerned, they are right; but as for the endless variety of products under one roof, that's not as new as they might imagine.

In the old general or country store of the past one could certainly find an infinite number of things in one spot—groceries, dry goods, ammunition, hardware, feed for livestock, even a post office. If you never had the opportu-

nity to visit one of these fast vanishing phenomena of country living, come
along with us and see what a general store was really like according to storekeepers of the past and those still in business.

Stores were located wherever they could most profitably serve the most
people. They opened at crossroads, along frequently traveled roads, and
other natural gathering places. Since villages were ten to fifteen miles apart
each community needed a store of its own to serve its own population. People couldn't travel long distances once or twice a week to patronize a store in
another community.

Some stores had humble beginnings: the Caffeyville store was originally
started to sell ice water to travelers driving along new highway 66 in the early
1920s. When new roads and highways were constructed, someone invariably
opened a store to serve the travelers and the nearby community.

Such good locations also attracted other businesses. Often such important
businesses as the mill, blacksmith shop, and post office were near the general
store.

The post office was quite often in the same building as the country store. A
small corner of the store was usually set aside to accommodate a stamp window and a series of shelves with cubbyholes for local letters and papers. Although another person could be employed to serve as postmaster, most com-

Though not many country stores still have their own post offices, the one at
Phillipsburg, Missouri, is still in business.

A typical country store.

munities were so small that the storekeeper served as postmaster. This made the storekeeper's life a busy one, hopping from the store to the mill, to the post office, and back.

Stores would differ in their exteriors, ranging from wooden to stone to tar paper. Most of them were two stories, and the second story housed either a lodge hall, where town meetings and festivities took place, or the owner's living quarters. Most stores had porches in front that would run the full width of the building with chairs and benches set out so customers would have a place to stop and rest and, of course, visit.

The front door was usually wooden with a screen door before it. In the summer only the screen door would be used. Windows were usually regular pane windows that would lift up and down to let in cool breezes or keep out the cold air. The doors and windows of the store were like those of a regular house rather than like the automatic doors and plate-glass windows found in a supermarket today.

Although the exterior of each store differed, the interiors had the same basic floor plan. The floors were usually made of rough gray boards worn in spots by the steady traffic of customers. Ceilings were fairly high in order to accommodate hanging lanterns, hats, and other household items.

The shelves where the groceries and other supplies were stocked ran down both sides of the room. They reached almost to the ceiling and were situated

General stores were popular with the men and boys during the slack winter months.

to be seen easily by a customer as he walked in the door. The shelves were divided into compartments of different shapes and sizes to house the variety of goods. A walking space lay between the wall shelves and the glass cases, or counters, that were placed parallel to them. Showcases held candy, tobacco, or dry goods. Crackers and pickle barrels sat close to the long counters. Scales, sales pads, and the cash register were placed on top of the counters.

Many stores had an open space in the central area of the room where a potbellied stove with chairs placed around it was located. This was a favorite gathering spot on cold winter days for those who wanted to visit a spell and warm up before venturing back outside.

Since there was no electricity in the early country stores, kerosene lamps were widely used as were gas and carbide lanterns. All had to be cleaned and refilled often. The lights were placed on the walls close to counters and work areas throughout the store for greatest efficiency. When electricity arrived during the thirties and forties, the country store installed hanging lights—a single bulb on the end of a cord.

Phone service became available in some of the rural areas about 1910. The crank-type party-line telephone was an important addition to the store. The store telephone was used mainly for calling in orders to the wholesale sup-

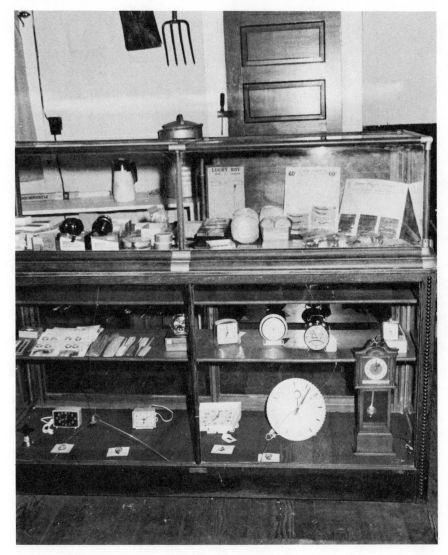

A typical glass showcase used in most country stores.

pliers in larger towns. A person would call the exchange to ask for a number and a different line and the operator would call it. Eavesdropping was a common pastime. Since people knew their neighbor's ring, all they had to do was pick up the phone receiver and listen.

With a comfortable building and the convenience of lamps and the crank phones, things were a little easier for the storekeeper. The foundation was set. Next the storekeeper faced the chore of stocking the store and then maintaining his business.

The well-stocked store at Drynob in 1909.

CRACKERS AND COAL OIL

It was the storekeeper's responsibility to find a supplier for his business, but even after finding one such as the Wholesale House in Lebanon, he was not assured of any deliveries. The stock needed at country stores had to be ordered from town and picked up by the storekeeper himself.

The frequency of trips varied from store to store. For some the rough and rugged journey into town would mean a full day's ride. Others located farther away would drive their teams to town, make their orders, spend the night, and return home the following day. In cases such as this, the stores would stock up more heavily and not go to the supplier quite as often.

In later years thriving country stores had to increase their number of trips to two a week, and then to every day to supply the demands of their loyal customers. The old International trucks with the solid tires made the journeys much easier for storekeepers to keep up with the increased need for trips and were often given nicknames such as "Princess" and "Old Blaze."

The Wholesale House in Lebanon supplied groceries to many country stores in the surrounding area. It started its business in 1909, employing a minimum of twelve to fifteen people—all men except the female book-keepers. One of the many bookkeeping jobs was to keep track of the gasoline, mileage, and expense of the trucks, which only made deliveries in town.

The Wholesale House sold groceries and some dry goods. A display of grocery items was set up in the front of the store for buyers to consult when purchasing. All orders taken in both wholesale houses and the country stores were written by hand. As transportation and roads became better, the territory the wholesale business sold to extended farther in all directions until they were supplying groceries for stores a hundred miles away.

With the improving conditions salesmen—called "drummers"—of a variety of products found it profitable to visit country stores. Dry goods and shoe drummers came every four to six months while hardware drummers made yearly rounds to all the country stores along their routes. At first the drummer made his rounds in a hack which resembled a buggy with a truck bed which was filled with trunks containing samples.

Other salesmen rode trains, getting off at certain points to take orders. They would mail the orders back to the companies, where they were filled as soon as they arrived. The goods were shipped back to the stores by train and left at depots to be picked up by the storekeepers. Deliveries were very efficient, often arriving on freight cars the next day. Merchants were happy about rapid deliveries but a little annoyed at the growing number of salesmen. As Loren Alloway commented, "There used to be a salesman every time you turned around. You couldn't wait on a customer, for a salesman."

Country store owners were still making trips to the wholesale houses for groceries when drastic changes began taking place—chain stores and supermarkets arrived with their own suppliers. Local business decreased so that the Wholesale House in Lebanon had to close after sixty years. Since several smaller stores still depended on the Lebanon Wholesale House to stock their stores, when it went out of business, some of them were forced to close because they had no other grocery supplier. The few remaining country stores that found other suppliers and still have enough business today have their deliveries made directly in company trucks, and salesmen call to take orders by phone.

At Russ, Missouri, several salesmen call each week. Five milk trucks, two fruit trucks, a hardware truck, a cookie truck, an ice cream truck, several bread trucks, "and pop men galore," stop each week to supply grocery needs.

The country stores did business with all as they were usually the only store in the area, and so had to carry all the stock their customers needed, from groceries to ammunition, from clothing to feed for livestock. They also tried to stock some variety of brands to satisfy the demands for favorites. There were no frozen foods until refrigeration became possible, but there was always a good supply of non-perishables.

Since groceries were packaged in bulk, everything had to be weighed out. The first items a customer wanted were coffee and flour, if they didn't bring their own wheat to be ground. Flour was weighed out of a hundred- or fifty-pound sack and toasted coffee beans were in sacks or barrels of a hundred to a hundred and fifty pounds. Because coffee wasn't ground, coffee grinders or mills were found in almost every home. Roasted coffee beans could also be ground in the larger store mills after it was purchased. The other staples on the customer's list included sugar, salt, and rice.

There were few fresh fruits or vegetables in the store because of spoilage and lack of demand—most people grew their own. One exception was bananas. Big tall baskets containing stalks of bananas were brought in and opened at the store. Merchants would hang the stalks up and, according to Charlie Southard, "If someone wanted a quarter's worth of bananas, you took a crooked knife and cut off a bunch and weighed it up." Dried fruits were also found. Dried peaches from California were among the favorites, as were dried apples, raisins, and prunes.

The meat section consisted mostly of salted, cured, and smoked pork because beef had to be refrigerated. Slab bacon and side meat along with smoked jowl and fatback were the most prominent. The fatback was used in a manner similar to bologna today. Canned salmon or other fish was sold, too. The meat section wasn't very important because most families butchered their own meat, usually hogs. Country stores very seldom bought home-butchered meats, but Adley Fulford told us the Oakland store once bought a home-butchered hog.

"One of our neighbors came up and asked if we would buy some home-cured bacon. My brother-in-law and partner, Gordon Elmore, said, 'Yes, I'll buy it.' So in a few days he came in a wagon with six huge sides of bacon off of a four- or five-hundred-pound hog. And Gordon bought it for fourteen cents a pound. Then while we were unloading it, the mailman asked where the bacon came from and how much we wanted to sell it for. Gordon said fifteen cents a pound. The mailman bought it all. We had to cut each side in two to fit them into a rumble seat on the back of his Chevrolet car."

The Oakland store had a contract for four or five years with a lawyer in St. Louis to furnish him with one hundred and twenty-five dressed turkeys every Christmas. They would hand-dress and put the turkeys in barrels and ship them to St. Louis by railway express. The lawyer would give these turkeys to his clients for Christmas.

There were two kinds of cheeses sold in country stores, cheddar and longhorn. Cheddar, shaped like a grindstone, came in fifty-pound round lugs with a thick wax coating on the outside to protect it. It was cut and measured with a notched knife. Longhorn cheese came in long tubes eight inches across, with six tubes in a wooden box to be sliced with a butcher knife and then weighed. For the men who stayed around all day, a dime's worth of cheese and a few crackers from the cracker barrels made a pretty good meal.

Pickles were stored in barrels where they could be had for the asking. Vinegar also came in barrels and was sold by the quart. People brought their own vinegar jugs to fill. Customers pumped the vinegar out of the barrels

Cheese came in round wooden lugs. The storekeeper cut off hunks for his customers.

The storekeeper would serve his customers right out of the barrels.

from built-in pumps, or used the wooden spigots inserted in the barrel to drain the vinegar.

To sweeten things in life there has always been candy. But the candy was not like that we have today. Adley Fulford said, "There wasn't such a thing as a candy bar then. It was either stick or mixed candy or the chocolate drops." Old-fashioned chocolate drops came in fifty-pound wooden buckets about fourteen inches at the top and twelve inches at the bottom. The drops were packed layer over layer all the way around the inside of the buckets. Adley also remembered, "My brother-in-law opened a barrel of that candy with a young man there that said he could eat the entire top row, which was the largest. My brother-in-law said, 'If you eat it all at one time, I'll just give them to you.' And he did! And then the young man said, 'I can eat the next row,' which he did. He must have eaten at least two pounds!"

As progress came, so did soda pop. When the country store first started selling pop it was kept in an ice-filled tub and cost three cents a bottle.

Soda was and still is enjoyed by all members of the family, but for the men's taste there was tobacco. There were several tobaccos to smoke and several to chew, and the stores sold cigars for five cents. Plugs of chewing tobacco sold for a dime each. The plug tobacco was sweetened with fruit juices to make it stick together. A special tobacco cutter of iron with a hinged knife cut the plugs. Horseshoe, Natural Leaf, and Star were the favorite brands of flat and of plug tobacco. The Horseshoe brand had a little picture of a horse-

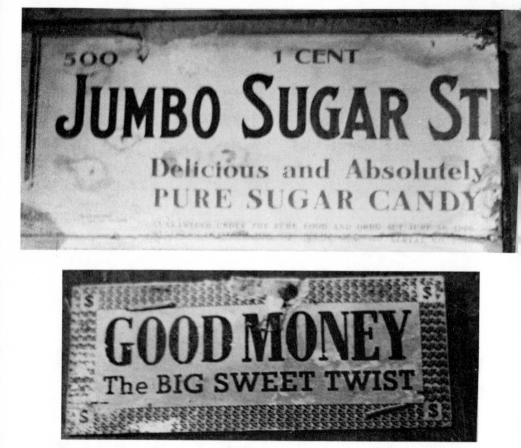

Old signs still decorate the walls of abandoned country stores.

shoe on it that could be redeemed in cash like our trading stamps today—the Oakland store got its cash register by doing so.

Pipe smokers used a twist tobacco that could be crumbled easily. Twist tobacco came in bulk, 144 twists in a box. Brands were varied, ranging from Prince Albert or Velvet to Advertiser and Country Gentleman. "And it was real he-man tobacco, that twist was," Adley Fulford explained. "It was the kind that would knock your hat off if you weren't used to it. The plug would set you on your heels." Strong flavor was what the men wanted. A popular billboard tobacco advertisement bragged, "It ain't toothache, it's Climax."

In addition to food, the store stocked ready-made overalls, dress shirts, and work shirts for men, but didn't carry ready-made clothes for women because they made everything for themselves. Women bought their sewing notions and dress material at the store, choosing from calico, gingham, broadcloth, corduroy, or woolen materials of different types.

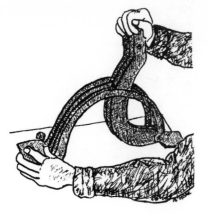

Tobacco came in long strips, and had to be cut into plugs with a hinged tobacco cutter.

International Shoes from St. Louis was one of the first brands of shoes the stores stocked. Millinery corners in the stores were popular. Many of the hats came in on consignment from other towns and could be returned if not sold. Eppah Humphreys remembers the fun the young folks had trying on hats whether they bought any or not. As soon as a new box of hats came in, so did the girls.

Dry goods changed with the seasons. In wintertime scarves, hoods, and caps took the place of summer hats. Heavy winter underwear, socks, and felt boots were common apparel purchased by farmers. The boots, made of pressed felt half an inch thick covered with a rubber overshoe, were popular because they kept the farmer's feet warm and dry.

Because there were no hardware stores, storekeepers always kept on hand everyday repair and building items such as nails, wire, staples, plow points for the old walking plows, and rolled asphalt roofing. Harnesses, shoes, and horseshoe nails were necessary for farmers. Since farm equipment changed rapidly, the stores had little choice but to follow, carrying more tractor parts and less equipment for horses. Until the stores had to have licenses, they sold ammunition, and for the kitchen there were cooking utensils.

Several stores carried patent medicines for people and livestock. The children enjoyed the small books or rhymes that accompanied many of the medicines such as Castoria for babies that read, "Castoria Dick . . . or Little Dick Green, Finest baby you've ever seen." The veterinary products were for ailments of chickens, horses, cattle, sheep, and other animals. Stores made forty per cent of the total price on each bottle of patent medicine.

Although many farmers grew their own grain and had it ground at the mill, stores kept livestock grain and feed in stock for farmers who needed it. Generally wheat, oats, and corn were the basic feeds. In the early 1930s corn could be bought for fifteen to twenty cents a bushel and wheat from thirty to thirty-five cents a bushel. There were few mixed feeds before the Depression but later mixed feeds became more widely used. Livestock salt came in fifty-

Each store owned
platform scales to weigh
and package bulk feed.

pound blocks and sold for thirty to thirty-five cents a block during the Depression years.

Gasoline shortages weren't heard of years ago because gas was rarely used. Kerosene, or coal oil, was always in demand because it was one of the major sources of light for many years. Houses had kerosene lamps and kerosene stoves for cooking. Motor oil was sold for oiling machinery. Hand-pumped gasoline pumps were installed when the advancement of power machinery created the demand for gasoline.

The country stores carried all the necessary products but because of the wide diversity of items were unable to stock as many different brands of one item as the stores do today. However, they offered a service one doesn't find frequently today. If a customer needed something not in stock, or some specialized part for farm machinery, the storekeeper got it for him.

"YOU WORKED FROM SUN TO SUN"

To stock, care for, and sell so many different types of commodities necessitated a great deal of work. "You worked from sun to sun. Any time the sun caught you in bed, you were sleeping too late," John Hill explained. The store opened anywhere from six to seven-thirty in the morning. Sweeping out the store and tidying up were done before the customers began to arrive. In the winter wood would have to be carried in and a fire built in the stove.

Not many customers would arrive very early in the morning since there would be chores to take care of on the farm before trading could be done.

Around eight o'clock the customers would begin to arrive to purchase their groceries and household items. Crowds usually dissipated around noon, although some farmers in need of plow points or hardware would stop by the store to purchase their supplies before returning home to dinner from the fields.

Usually there was enough help in the store so that the clerks could take turns eating lunch. The back part of the store, the storeroom, served as a kitchen if there was not enough time to go home to eat and return within an hour.

The afternoon hours were the busiest at the store. Since chores were done and the noon meal was over, housewives would come to the store to trade.

Closing hours were indefinite. Sometimes the store stayed open until all the customers stopped coming, but generally seven or eight was closing time. Eppah Humphreys said, "Most of the customers didn't come after six o'clock. In the summertime they might come later than that, but in the winter they seldom did." She also remembers when she and her father would have to go back to the store after supper to work. "Sometimes we'd open boxes and mark prices, and it would be ten or eleven before we got back to the house. A lot of times we'd get ready to go someplace on Sundays, but we'd have to go to the store and get something for somebody. That used to make me so provoked because we'd get all ready to go to Sunday school and then they'd make us late. They'd come at night and call my father back to the store sometimes, too, if they wanted something. It's quite different now."

Running the store was usually a family affair. One store might be run by the same family for several generations. As soon as a son or daughter married, they would be taken into the business. When their parents could no longer operate the store, they would take over and keep the business alive until their children could inherit it from them.

Almost every storekeeper's son or daughter worked in the store while they were young, usually starting at age ten or twelve. At first they would probably be assigned odd jobs such as sweeping out the store or dusting the counters, then they would graduate to helping the customer by weighing groceries, testing cream, and casing eggs. There were never many workers in the store and usually two or three people were all that were needed.

Running the country store took a lot of time and hard work. Even bookkeeping was a chore. Since there were no adding machines, handwritten accounts of business transactions were kept on a sales pad. Close watch also had to be kept on the store's merchandise. If the store was running low on groceries, hardware, or dry goods, the merchant would have to make a trip into town to order more. Once in awhile when the pressures of running the store began to take their toll, the men of the family would have to take off to go fishing or hunting. The ladies of the family would then have to "mind the store."

When food was packaged in bulk, the storekeeper or one of his clerks would weigh it out for the customers. Flour, coffee, sugar, dried beans, and other staples were weighed and packaged in burlap sacks or paper pokes; meat and cheese were cut and wrapped; candy was weighed and put in small sacks; tobacco was cut into plugs. If dry goods were needed, material was measured and cut from a bolt of cloth and then thread and buttons chosen to match.

For high shelves and hidden items nothing came in handier than a fetching stick—a stick with a long handle and a forked end. With it the merchant could reach the item he needed without having to climb a ladder.

Customers would usually give the clerk a list or tell him themselves what items they needed. The storekeeper would get the first item, package it and weigh it, bring it to the counter, and then get the next item on the customer's list. This would continue until the order was done and the customer was ready to pay for his purchases.

If the customer paid in cash for his groceries, the money would be put in a cash register. The cash register, unlike those of today, only had a drawer for money and did not add up the purchases. Other storekeepers who did not have cash registers wrapped their money up and stashed it under the counter or kept it in a cigar box. Farmers who could not pay cash for their groceries until they took their produce or livestock to market, or until harvest time, put the total on a bill to pay when they had the money.

Loren Alloway remembers when people would pay for groceries with scrip. When workers shoveled coal or worked on the railroad, they would be given scrip—small pieces of paper like trading stamps with a place for their names on them—instead of receiving cash wages. The store would accept these in payment for their groceries just like food stamps today. The storekeeper would then send the scrip to Jefferson City and would receive money in return.

Those customers who did not have enough money to pay for their groceries would trade eggs, livestock, grain, or furs in return for their groceries, hardware, and dry goods. The storekeeper had to be sure that his trade was a good one: if livestock was traded, it was often an old cow that kicked hard or one gone dry.

Farmers could also sell their eggs for five cents a dozen. It was a common sight to see some of the store employees counting eggs and putting them in egg cases that held thirty dozen. As a young worker, Eppah Humphreys had to fill a fresh case for each customer selling the eggs. Her father couldn't risk a miscount with a customer's produce. Later Eppah had to replace the empty slots of one case with the partially filled ones of another.

The store also bought cream and butter. The storekeepers often tested the cream for butterfat content themselves by using a machine that held test tubes full of cream. They added acid, and then stirred and shook the cream. The butterfat content was indicated after mixing in a few other ingredients.

Some of the country stores didn't buy cream because they weren't set up for the testing, but would buy the butter that farmers made. The butter was put in a fifty-pound lard stand all mixed together, some of it salty and some old-smelling. The store would never turn butter down, though Eppah commented, "I know I never would have wanted it on my biscuits."

After the lard containers were full, they would be cleaned and taken into town to sell to the produce house along with other dairy products. Often the butter was several days old and the cream had soured days before it reached the produce house, but both were easily sold. The produce house would process the cream into cheese. This left whey. Farmers bought the whey from the creamery to feed their pigs, completing a cycle of selling and buying between farmer and merchant.

Besides trading livestock and dairy products, furs were also a big market item many years ago. Furs and hides also brought spending money for young boys. They would set traps or go hunting in the wintertime when animal pelts were the best. If they caught a rabbit, they would remove the intestines and clean the animal, but they did not skin it. The men or boys would tie the feet of the animals together, then bind the animals all together on a string or leather strap to throw over their shoulders to carry to the store. Rabbits were not the only animals trapped: other valuable furs and hides came from possum, skunk, coon, mink, and fox. Wild game such as quail and turkey were also traded. Sometimes the hides would bring ten or fifteen cents each. Others brought only a nickel.

The mailman from Richland used to pick up furs from one store when he was on his route and take them into Richland to resell or dispose of later. Most stores sent most of the furs to St. Louis to one of the fur companies there. The hides were never kept long because of the foul smell.

Thus the country store served not only as a place to buy but also as a place to trade and to sell farm produce.

The country store would never have been a successful venture if it had not been for many faithful customers. Most of the store's business was from local townspeople and farmers. As roads began to improve, however, travelers would also patronize the store. On Saturdays one could always find friends and neighbors shopping at the store. Women would exchange gossip while their eggs were being counted, their cream tested, and staples weighed. Men would often visit while pondering over what feed, hardware, or other farm necessities they needed. Some customers were so loyal to their old store that even after they moved away from the area they would still purchase particular items from that store. A man from the Russ area who moved to Idaho in later years still had his favorite tobacco sent to him from Russ store.

Since going to the store took quite a bit of the day, many families would regard the trip as a family outing. Transportation to and from the store was varied in the early days. Some chose a stout wagon drawn by a team of horses. Others preferred to travel horseback and those who lived near the store would walk. For some the going was a little harder when they had to cross a creek or river to get to the store. There were very few bridges in those days, so they had to ford the creek by wading across or using a small boat.

As transportation improved, first horses and buggies, then cars and small

A potbellied stove, chairs, and a checkerboard were standard furnishings of almost every store.

pickups appeared on the road to the country store. But as Wilma McMahan recalls, there were still some women who had to walk a mile or more home from the store with a twenty-five-pound sack of flour on one shoulder and a burlap sack of groceries on the other.

While for most people a trip to the store did not usually last all day, it frequently did for the older men of the community. They, along with the loafers, or bums, as they were called, would stay at the store almost all day. They would have a dinner of cheese and crackers and resume telling tales, playing checkers, and other games around the potbellied stove. Adley Fulford said, "There've been lots of checker games played and a world of big fish killed, and lots and lots of 'coon races in and around the store in the wintertime."

Eppah Humphreys remembers the champion marble player at Russ store. "There was one old man, Mr. Howard Stoval. He loved to play marbles. He carried his marbles around in his pocket and he'd get anybody to play marbles with him, a game that had five marbles, one in each corner and one in the middle. If you knocked the middle one out, you won. But if you knocked the others out, they counted so many points. They had to get all of them out before they could win that game. And he just loved to be the first

The Topaz store, which now serves as a work shop, was once an elegant country store with long glass counters, built-in flour bins, and even a second-floor balcony with dressing rooms, a millinery, and ready-made clothes.

one to have done it. He'd say, 'I got a middler.' He was pretty good at it, too."

Whether it was to trade or just to sit all day and pass the time, the country store was the place to go, even providing a special meeting place in many communities.

Fourth of July picnics were among the biggest events of the year. People would often meet on the lawn of the store or a field nearby to enjoy the day's festivities. Some picnics would take place at a nearby river. In any case the get-together would be a happy one. There would be sack races, carrot-, potato-, or egg-on-the-spoon races, horseshoe games, or baseball games. An abundance of food was always on hand, including lemonade, cake and home-made ice cream, and watermelon. These were all regarded as summertime treats. There was not a variety of fireworks, but usually someone, especially little boys, had firecrackers.

Baseball games were played in a field next to the Russ store almost every Saturday in the summertime. There would always be a big crowd at the store if there was a game. Customers would expect the merchant to have their eggs counted, cream tested, and groceries weighed and waiting for them as soon as the game was over.

A special Christmas event at the Russ store each year was the turkey shoot. Different men would take turns buying turkeys each year. Whoever could hit the bull's eye would win a turkey for his Christmas dinner.

For the Christmas season stores would stock special items. Christmas gifts were special in those days since families did not have a lot of money to spend. There were usually dolls for girls and toy cars for boys. Storybooks, Bibles, and candy were also popular gifts with young people. Not all gifts were toys, though. Most families purchased some practical items such as caps, scarves, mittens, boots, or shoes along with a few toys and candy.

When there weren't any holidays to celebrate, meetings often took place at the store. If there weren't any family quarters on the second floor of the store, there was often a lodge hall where people could gather. The community would hold elections, community debates, and pie suppers in the hall. Sometimes these gatherings turned out to be as much fun as holiday celebrations.

Although there were a lot of good times, there were times of trouble, too. The war years brought many problems to the stores. During World War II, one problem was the rationing of sugar and gasoline. A hundred pounds of sugar that before the war cost a dollar cost five dollars during the shortage. Meat would come in by the barrelful from Kansas City. People from miles around would wait to get their meat before it ran out. Ration stamps were almost as valuable as money during the war.

Because of improving times, rapid improvement of highways, and plentiful gasoline, the country store was often passed by after the war. Though trucking made the storekeeper's job of stocking his store easier, it also made it easier for his customers to go to larger markets to trade. Many small stores were forced to close.

Those stores like Russ, Falcon, and Brownfield that still continue their independent tradition of serving their community have changed with the times. Refrigeration has made it possible for country stores to stock many types of fresh meats, fruits, and vegetables; owners no longer weigh out staples but, just like the supermarkets, offer packaged foods in various sizes ready to use. Customers serve themselves if they want to and pay with money—there is no longer any trading with produce.

Times have changed, and perhaps it's easier now for both the grocer and the customer to do business, yet there are still people who remember, and long for, the "good old days" when a hundred pounds of sugar cost just a dollar.

Milling

The many water mills which operated in the Ozarks from early settlement until about the 1930s were a perfect example of the link between power, utility, fellowship, and beauty. The numerous hill streams provided power to turn the great wheels and turbines which converted a raw agricultural product into a fine quality food. The businesses and mills became natural gathering places for the area people to fish, picnic, dance, visit, or throw horseshoes under the valley's shade trees in the summer; places to swap tales or play checkers around a potbellied stove in the winter. Mills often became community centers where the Ozarkers could exchange new ideas, different methods, and even the local gossip. People from as far as twenty miles away would come with their stories and news. If the community had a square dance, you could bet it would be near the mill.

The mill served the community by dispensing news. Often there was a bulletin board where notices, announcements, and advertisements were posted. Some mills like Zanoni were official polling places even as late as 1972.

Often many other businesses, such as a general store and post office—often operated by the miller and his family—sprang up near the mill. There might even be a barbershop as there was at Topaz. Sometimes there were black-smith shops as at Orla, and their successors, gas stations. The excess power from the mills often ran other machines like sawmills, rock crushers, and cotton gins.

Going to the mill in times past would have been a greater thrill to the youngsters than a trip to St. Louis would be today. It provided the latest news, commodities, and services: At Zanoni Mill "indoor plumbing" was available: the inside privies made use of the fast-running stream below.

WATER POWER

Water mills abounded in the Ozarks and the power came from either springs or rivers. Each had its own advantages.

Springs were a relatively sure source of water. Those large enough to furnish power were usually unaffected by dry spells, and the flow of water from the spring was swift enough to provide ample power.

Although rivers offered a wider choice of location for the mill, they had some disadvantages that did not affect springs. Sometimes a river would not flow fast enough to provide the necessary power. The gradient, the number of feet per mile that the river dropped, had to be sufficient to ensure a swift current to turn the mill wheel. The general gradients of three Ozark rivers—the Niangua, the Osage Fork of the Gasconade, and the North Fork of the White River—range from 4.6 to 7.5, and these rivers had many mills built on them. Other disadvantages were floods, which might (and in many instances did) damage the mill or wash it away, and dry spells, which reduced the flow of water and thus the power available to operate the mill.

Water power was put to other uses besides operating mills. At Zanoni Mill, water diverted from the flume provided a water system for the neighboring farm. At many locations (including Zanoni and Alley Spring) generators run by water power supplied electricity for nearby rural areas before the REA came into being. Cotton gins, clothing and overall factories, sawmills and rock crushers were other businesses that utilized water power.

There were several ways of directing water to the wheels that harnessed the force of the water, and the tub mill, overshot wheel, undershot wheel, and turbine were all used in the Ozarks. Of these, the tub mill was the least common as well as the simplest. It consisted of a lever-type device with a water box at one end of a pole and a heavy pounding stone at the other. Water from the flume would pour into the box, and when the box was full, the weight of the water caused it to lower and empty. On the other end, the weight of the pounding stone would then bring that end down and pound the grain. The water box would fill again and the process would repeat endlessly.

The overshot and undershot wheels were used on older mills before the

A tub mill in operation.

turbine came into use. The overshot wheel employed a stream of water falling on top of the wheel to turn it; the undershot used water flowing under it. The turbines were completely submerged in water.

The tub mill and the overshot wheel required a flume to harness the water. A sort of elevated canal, the flume was used to transport the water from a higher source down to the wheel. Flumes were constructed of wood and later of concrete and supported by standards which were also made of wood or concrete.

A dam was almost a necessity for an undershot wheel. The dam restricted and controlled the flow of the river, directing the water by raceways to the wheel, thus giving the wheel more power. Originally dams were weighted down so they would not wash away; later dams were constructed of concrete.

Turbines used dams that directed the water to the forebay where the turbine was located. At Topaz there was an interesting arrangement whereby the dammed-up spring water was carried by a flume to fall into a larger boiler flume in which the turbine was submerged. This arrangement, utilizing only a small amount of falling water, provided a great deal of power.

When the mill was not in use the flow of water could be shut off to reduce wear on the wheel. This was done by means of gates located in the flume or the raceway, which led to the big wheel. In like manner there was provision for cutting off the water leading to the forebay. The miller used these gates to control the flow of water, reducing or increasing the speed of the wheel, which in turn reduced or increased the speed at which the mill operated.

The major differences between the overshot and undershot wheels were the manner in which water was brought to the wheel—whether from above or below—and the direction in which the wheel turned. The weight of the water pouring across the top of the overshot wheel turned it clockwise, while the current underneath the undershot wheel turned it counterclockwise.

There were also other differences. The overshot wheel gave up to twice as

An elevated flume from a spring at Zanoni Mill.

The dam (background) diverts the water through the raceway (right) to turn the turbine at Dawt Mill.

A mill dam of logs at Bennett Spring.

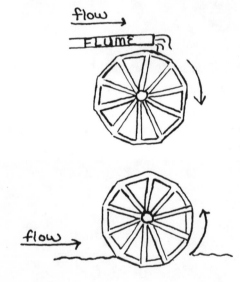

The overshot wheel (above) and undershot wheel (below).

much power with the same amount of water because falling water has more power than running water, and the weight of the water caught in the wheel caused it to turn faster. The construction of the two differed. The overshot wheel consisted of little buckets to catch the falling water, while the undershot might be nothing more than paddles which the current would catch.

It was the turbine, however, that found most favor with mill builders. The larger three-story buildings equipped with the newer roller mills required more power than could be supplied by the older wheels. The turbine, invented in the 1830s by a Frenchman named Fourneyron and perfected by several Americans, provided the necessary power, plus many other advantages. It is still used today to convert water power into hydroelectricity.

There were many differences between the turbine and other types of wheels. Where the older upright wheels were placed on a horizontal axis, the turbine was on its side with a vertical axis. The wheels were large and bulky, but the turbine was compact. The wheels were constructed of fragile wood, but the turbine was made of durable metal. The turbine could also utilize a higher head water (height from wheel to source). But the turbine's biggest advantage was its great efficiency. On the older wheels, water could strike only one bucket or paddle at a time but in the turbine water struck all the buckets at once.

The turning part of the turbine was set inside an immovable cast-iron outer casing, around the bottom of which were many openings or fins. These fins directed the flowing water into the buckets of the turning brass wheel. For every bucket there was an opening, so water continuously struck each bucket. This arrangement was so efficient that Orla Mill used only one of its two turbines.

Care had to be taken, though, to see that the turbine did not become clogged with debris. Jim Smith, present miller at Alley Spring Mill, told us, "The current is so swift it'll carry a big rock right in there. The other week I had a log—about six inches in diameter and about six feet long—hung there. I got that log loose and to show how much power the water has, it went through the spillway, took a nose dive and stayed under at least a minute. Finally it came up way downstream. It came up with such force about half of the log was straight up in the air before it fell over.

"The turbine catches everything that goes through if you don't have some protection. We had a beaver spend the winter with us. He cut down most of the small bushes up by the spring. All the fine limbs he cut off floated into the

The spring at Zanoni Mill comes out of the side of the hill. The dam holds the water while the flume directs it to the overshot wheel.

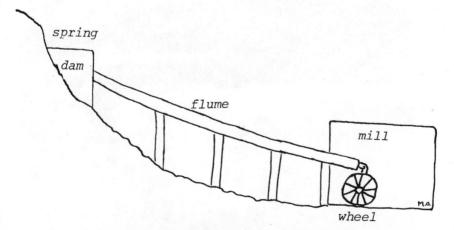

turbine. Oh, I had an awful job getting all that out of there. It took me two or three hours to get the limbs and rocks out so the turbine would turn."

The turning wheel also caused the axis to spin. At the end of the axis was a gear, which matched the one on the main drive shaft. The drive shaft gear usually had wooden teeth, which were quieter and easier to replace than metal ones.

When the gears meshed, the main drive turned. There were several pulleys on the shaft—which usually ran the length of the basement floor or under the building—which connected by leather belts to other pulleys on different floors. Holes were cut in the floor for the belts to run through. For example, if the main drive shaft was in the basement, the belt connecting it with the first floor would turn a shaft on the first floor, which would be connected to a shaft on the second floor by means of another belt. In this arrangement, the system for grinding wheat was either fully on or fully off. Corn was on a separate system.

An unused turbine.

The turbine disassembled. Note the fins and the water-catching buckets.

A wooden-toothed gear from a drive shaft.

The pulleys on the main drive shaft in the basement of Topaz Mill are connected to belts that drive the shafts on each floor. Note the rough oak lumber and the wooden chute for transporting grains or flour.

Another way for power to reach the mill is exemplified by Greer Mill. The water wheel was located in a valley and, by a system involving a steel cable and pulleys, the power was transferred to the mill, about a quarter mile up the hill.

CORN TO MEAL

The Ozark farmer raised his own corn and wheat to be ground into flour and meal. Almost all the miller's trade was local people who brought their grain for grinding. Those who lived some distance away would bring a load just a few times a year, but those who lived closer came whenever they needed to. Jim Smith remembers, "I was carrying grain to a gristmill when I just started to school. Each year we shucked the ear and would shell off by hand the bad part of the grain on the end of the ear. If it had a bad part we'd shell that off and sack it all up. Dad would put it on a horse, tie it on the saddle, and I'd ride the horse to the mill. The mill was—oh, three miles up the river and the old miller would unload the corn for me and tell me what day to come back and I'd go back and he'd load it up for me.

"We used to go to the mill about once every two months. It would depend on the size of the family. I was one of six children. If I wanted to stay to wait and the miller wasn't busy when I'd go there, in about an hour or so he'd have me sacked up and ready to go back. It'd usually take about two or three sacks of corn—that would be on the cob. That would actually be about a hundred pounds of grain. He could grind it all in about a couple hours."

John O'Neal shows the stone burrs from Topaz used for grinding corn to meal. The best burrs came from France, and cost as much as a thousand dollars in 1851.

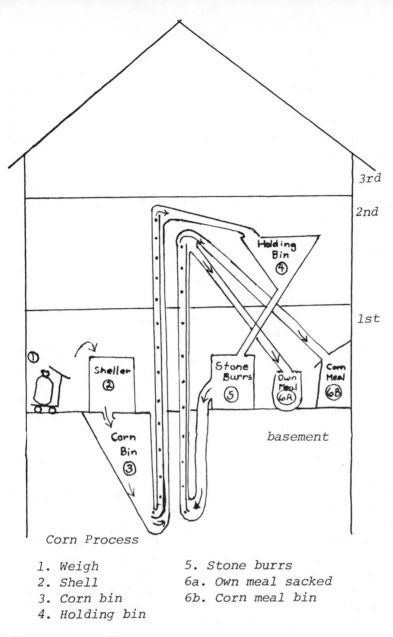

3rd

2nd

Holding
Bin
④

1st

①

Sheller
②

Stone
Burrs
⑤

Own
Meal
⑥A

Corn
Meal
⑥B

Corn
Bin
③

basement

Corn Process

1. Weigh
2. Shell
3. Corn bin
4. Holding bin

5. Stone burrs
6a. Own meal sacked
6b. Corn meal bin

The process of grinding corn.

The corn would be put into shellers which removed the grain from the cob. They poured the whole ears of corn in the top. The machine would beat the grain off the cob and the shaker would shake the grain to separate it and blow the trash outside. It cleaned the grain at the same time.

On the first floor under the holding bin were the big stone burrs. The burrs were large flat circular granite stones, one set above the other. One stone was stationary, the other rotated. A valve released the right amount of corn through a chute into the center of the burrs. As the grain fell into the center, the rotating stones would catch the kernel and crush it. Centrifugal force would carry the grain through the grooves to the outside of the stone where the grooves became smaller, grinding the grain finer and finer. The amount of power coming to the burrs had to be regulated correctly. If they turned too fast, the corn was burned. The finished corn meal collected on the outside of the burrs, fell through chutes to the basement, and was carried by elevators to the the second floor. From there it fell by gravity into the corn meal bin on the first floor. If the customer wanted his own meal back, the miller would pull a lever to open a valve which directed the meal into another chute. Otherwise the meal went into a big holding bin.

Throughout the Ozarks corn bread was probably eaten more often than biscuits or light bread made from flour. This was especially true in the hillier areas. Jim continued, "There wasn't a lot of wheat grown around Alley Spring. The flour mill didn't do too good. Everyone raised corn. Everybody had a team of horses or mules to cultivate with and a plow, but they all didn't have what it took to raise wheat and they didn't have enough land. Everyone raised corn and everybody ate corn bread. And most of the old-timers liked the white corn. A lot used Boone County White and Hickory Cane [King] Corn. I know several old-timers still saving their seed and using this Boone County White Corn."

Many people were particular about their corn meal and wanted only the meal from their own corn. They'd think that others' corn might have some rotten kernels or wouldn't be as good as their own. They would wait for the miller to grind their turn of corn. For those not so particular, the miller would weigh their corn and exchange their corn for so much meal.

When the farmer brought his sacks of corn to the mill, the miller would weigh them on the platform scales near the door and determine his toll. The toll would be a certain percentage of the grain, usually from ten to twenty per cent, though it depended quite a bit on the times. The miller could grind his share into flour or meal to sell to those who did not raise their own, or he could sell or trade the grain.

A toll chart was tacked on the wall. The miller would keep his part and would then weigh out how much flour or meal, how much shorts and bran the farmer would get according to the chart.

WHEAT TO FLOUR

Originally wheat was also ground on stone burrs. In that manner the finished product was whole wheat, for the burrs provided no way of separating the bran and wheat germ. The process was similar to that of grinding corn meal. The mill buildings did not need to be large or have much machinery, just two burrs, two holding bins, and two storage bins. Early mills were one-story sheds without elevators. The water power was needed only to turn the burrs.

People had to sift their own meal to remove coarse hulls and parts from the kernel. Today mills like Dawt, Hodgson's, and Alley Spring, which grind corn for sale, have a shaker system to sift out the coarse particles after the meal comes from the burrs.

When the process of using metal rollers became widespread in the Ozarks in the 1880s and '90s, the mills built new tall, imposing-looking wooden structures to accommodate the machinery and chutes needed in order to meet the demand for white patent flour.

In the prairie regions of the Ozarks and in the river-bottom farms, most farmers raised wheat as well as corn for their own use. Along some of the rivers flowing through more populated farming areas like the Osage Fork of the Gasconade, there were operating mills every ten to fifteen miles. Their number can be easily attested to by the frequent use of the word "mill" still used in referring to bridges and fords, though the mill has long gone.

The flour mills operated profitably until the 1920s and '30s when many found it impossible to compete with the mass production of industrial flour mills using the more desirable hard wheat imported from the Western plains.

The mill at Topaz, though it has not operated for years, has all its machinery still intact. The process already described for corn and the following process for wheat were used there as explained by Joe O'Neal, the present owner. These processes might be typical of mills built at this time.

The farmer would bring his sacks of wheat to the mill and, after being weighed and the miller's toll taken, the grain was dumped through the trap door at the entrance into a storage bin in the basement.

From there elevators carried the wheat to the third floor from which it fell by gravity to the cleaner on the second floor. The cleaner caused the wheat to go through a series of screens and blowing action. The dust and light stuff would be blown out the side of the mill. The heavier, undesirable trash, cheat, and other impurities would go to a trash bin on the first floor.

The partially cleaned wheat would then fall through chutes to the basement to be picked up by another set of elevators and taken to the third floor where it would once again fall back down to the second floor. This time it would go through the smutter, which removed the fine dust and smut and the fine burr on the kernel.

Then the grain descended through chutes and up elevators and back to the first floor to the grinders. There were three grinders with two sets of rollers in each. The corrugated teeth on the first set were pretty coarse. The next was a little finer and the next more so. The last three sets of rollers were smooth. Each roller was set with a little more tension, making the grain a little finer each time it came through a set of rollers. The rollers just mashed the grain. One roller rolled faster than the other, thus giving a grinding effect. Each time the grain came through a set of rollers it would fall to the basement through the chutes from each machine, be taken up to the third floor by elevators, and fall back to the second floor, this time to the shaker.

Steel rollers used in making white patent flour.

These three flour mills at Alley Spring Mill were seldom used. Most people nearby grew corn.

The many screens in the shaker separated the grain and flour and then channeled it to the next step. When the shaker ran, the whole building shook.

The shaker was a big piece of equipment with many chutes entering from above and leaving through the floor below. Its purpose was to separate the crushed grain according to size. The shaker had many different-sized screens which separated the grain to suit the fineness for each of the six pairs of rollers. The shaker also removed the bran. When the shaker was in motion the whole building shook.

The grain separated according to size again fell through different chutes to the basement. It returned through the elevators to the third floor and moved down to the next process. If the wheat was still too coarse for flour, it went to a finer roller and continued the process until it was fine enough.

The finest portion from the shaker went to the silk bolts on the second floor. This machine had a long cylinder with a fine silk screen covering it. The flour was on the inside. A brush would brush against the outside of the screen as the cylinder turned, sweeping off the flour. This flour would drop down into a trough where the wooden auger would push the flour into the chute. This in turn would take it down to the basement and then up through elevators to the flour bin on the second floor. Directly under the bin on the first floor was the place the flour was sacked by opening a lever and letting flour fall out.

The by-product left inside the cylinder was the shorts. They would work their way by means of another wooden auger to a chute that took them directly to the shorts bin on the first floor. Old-timers say that the shorts from the water mills were almost like a low-grade flour. The shorts contained

Silk screen covered the cylinder where the finished flour was brushed off before going to the flour bin. Millers had trouble with mice who ate the silk.

Close-up of elevator cups.

wheat germ, which was objectionable in baking; however, they contained much of the food value of the grain.

Coming from the shaker was another by-product of flour called bran—the outer covering of the kernel. The bran went into the bran duster, a small piece of machinery beside the shaker which brushed the flour off in order to salvage as much as possible. Cleaned of all flour, the bran fell directly into the bran bin next to the shorts bin on the first floor. The flour retrieved by the duster was taken by elevators back to the shaker and grinders. The elevators were a series of moving vertical belts on which were fastened at regular intervals small dipper cups about the size of a cupped hand. These cups scooped up the grain and carried it up to the top of the elevators on the top floor. As the belt moved to the top and started down again, its motion would pitch the grain or flour just enough so that it would go into the chute, where it would fall by gravity. Topaz Mill has ten pairs of elevators for wheat and two pairs for corn.

The buildings had to be tall to make effective use of gravity. Everything moved on vertical belts, being carried up by power and falling by gravity. Therefore the machinery was located on different floors to best utilize the space and power.

The basement was the storage area for wheat and corn and the bottom of the ten sets of elevators. The third or top floor was used only as a place for the tops of the elevators. On the first floor raw products were unloaded and finished products (flour, meal, shorts, bran) were stored or loaded, and here the actual grinding took place. The second floor was a working floor where the cleaner, smutter, shaker, bran duster, and silk bolt were located.

After the flour or meal was ground, it was sacked in fifty- or hundred-pound sacks. The bran sacks were burlap, but the flour and meal sacks were close-woven white sacks. People kept their own sacks and would wash and care for them carefully. If a mouse chewed a hole in one, the women would sew it up neatly. Women made clothes and tea towels from empty sacks.

As with any endeavor, there was a certain amount of risk in operating a mill. A building full of moving belts and pulleys was dangerous even though the machinery did not move fast. Usually the workmen were all family—sons or brothers of the miller—who were cognizant of the mill's power and danger.

Another ever present danger was fire in the highly inflammable atmosphere of flour dust in wooden buildings. For that reason mills were not heated and

were uncomfortable in winter, necessitating frequent trips to the adjacent store or barbershop for warmth.

The decline of business at the water mills came with the invention and wide use of the automobile, which gave easier access to markets to purchase flour and bread, and with the importation of bleached, hard wheat flour made from wheat grown on the Western plains.

Most people preferred this new type of flour for baking to the off-white, soft wheat flour traditionally produced at water mills throughout the Ozarks. It was nicer to make breads out of the store-bought hard wheat flour because

The process for milling wheat was much more complicated than for corn.

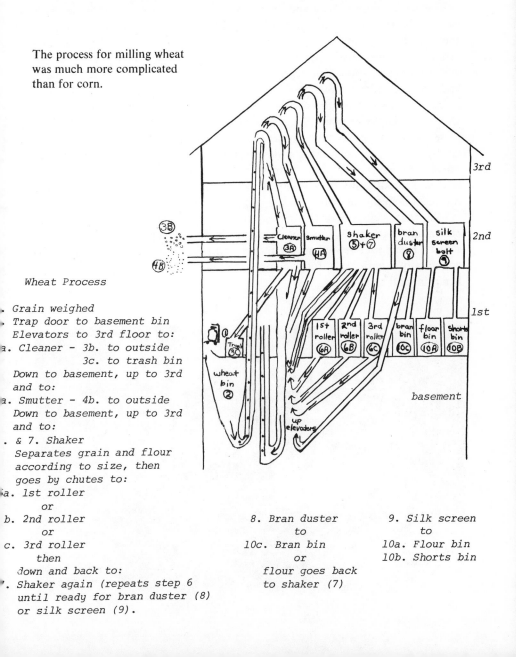

Wheat Process

. Grain weighed
. Trap door to basement bin
  Elevators to 3rd floor to:
a. Cleaner - 3b. to outside
            3c. to trash bin
  Down to basement, up to 3rd
  and to:
a. Smutter - 4b. to outside
  Down to basement, up to 3rd
  and to:
. & 7. Shaker
  Separates grain and flour
  according to size, then
  goes by chutes to:
a. 1st roller
      or
b. 2nd roller
      or
c. 3rd roller
      then
  down and back to:
. Shaker again (repeats step 6
  until ready for bran duster (8)
  or silk screen (9).

8. Bran duster
      to
10c. Bran bin
      or
  flour goes back
  to shaker (7)

9. Silk screen
      to
10a. Flour bin
10b. Shorts bin

they would rise better and had a lighter texture. Also the whiter color of the flour made the product more desirable than the duller unbleached flour from the mills.

The wheat kernel is made up of three main parts. The endosperm cells, which account for eighty-five per cent of the total kernel, are the part that is used in white flour. It consists largely of starch, protein, and cellulose oil walls with some sugar. The other two parts are the bran, or outer coat, and the embryo, or wheat germ. These two parts contain most of the vitamin and mineral content of the grain.

The removal of the bran and the wheat germ from the embryo, the heat action of the rollers in grinding the flour, and the bleaching process all cause the loss of many nutrients in white patent flour. Because of this loss the government has instituted regulations to enrich the flour partially back to the wheat's original state. But even the enriched flour does not have as much food value as whole wheat.

In comparison with the earlier stone-ground whole wheat flour, both the Ozark and imported white flours had a definite nutritional loss. Whole wheat flour ground on stone burrs consisted of the whole wheat kernel. White patent flour consisted only of the endosperm, with most of the bran and germ removed. However, the white flour ground in water mills, not being quite so refined and not going through the bleaching process, probably retained more nutrients than the imported flour.

Like the blacksmith who supplied the tools necessary for an agricultural community as well as some of its comforts and ornaments, the miller provided a basic need as well as a refinement to country living. He processed the community's basic raw food commodity into a product which furnished healthful and tasty eating.

Blacksmithing

Under a spreading chestnut-tree
    The village smithy stands;
The smith, a mighty man is he,
    With large and sinewy hands;
And the muscles of his brawny arms
    Are strong as iron bands.

His hair is crisp, and black, and long,
    His face is like the tan;
His brow is wet with honest sweat,
    He earns whate'er he can,
And looks the whole world in the face,
    For he owes not any man.

Week in, week out, from morn till night,
    You can hear his bellows blow;
You can hear him swing his heavy sledge
    With measured beat and slow,
Like a sexton ringing the village bell,
    When the evening sun is low.

      —HENRY WADSWORTH LONGFELLOW

Fred Manes has been a blacksmith all his life, as his father and grandfather before him.

The beginning of this famous poem depicts a highly honorable man who practices a somewhat glamorous trade. During the middle 1800s when Longfellow wrote this poem, the blacksmith was an esteemed man and his trade was indeed respected.

Many people nowadays would never believe that blacksmiths like Longfellow's still exist, but there are a few. The reason there are not more is not so much because blacksmithing is an intolerable trade as because one man working with his hands is no match for mass production.

Blacksmiths are a special breed—men with uncommon talents who create with metal. A good blacksmith has to be intelligent, but not necessarily educated, for he learns by doing, usually through apprenticeship. Often blacksmiths are sons of blacksmiths.

From colonial times until the late 1800s the blacksmith was considered one of the most, if not *the* most, essential members in the community and was heavily depended upon. The most important duty of any village blacksmith was to supply the tools on which civilization depended—tools for building, for crafts, for farming, and for war. Blacksmiths were necessary to keeping horses and mules shod and to keep anything made of metal in repair and functioning. The housewife depended as much on the blacksmith as anyone for kitchen wares and cooking utensils made of metal.

To understand the importance of the blacksmith, one must bear in mind that the essentials for building any structure or piece of equipment could not be acquired at the local hardware store. Hinges, door latches, and window latches were handmade by the village blacksmith.

Blacksmithing requires imagination and visualization. As is true of any art, there are those who are exceptionally skillful, and those who are not. Those

The blacksmith shop at Oakland, Missouri, in 1910.

Charley Smith and Red Jennings in the blacksmith shop in Lebanon around 1912.

who were not good were called "botchers" and had to go way back in the hills to get any work.

Most of the few blacksmiths who still practice today do it as a hobby or a sideline, depending upon some other source for the large part of their incomes. However, Fred Manes still depends on blacksmithing as his source of income, and he has practiced his art for over sixty years on the same corner of the main street of Richland, Missouri, where his father operated before he did.

A blacksmith shop is an interesting and intriguing place. One of the first things we noticed when we visited Fred Manes's shop was the activity, the excitement of the blazing fire and flying sparks, and the refreshing atmosphere of seeming disarray which welcomed the passer-by to stop a moment. For this reason loafers are probably as traditional in a blacksmith shop as is the anvil. We later learned that the same men came to the shop every day, just passing the time while Fred worked at the forge. Fred does not mind having the loafers around; in fact, he says he would work himself to death if there wasn't anyone around to stop and talk to.

Children of all ages drop in the shop from time to time and Fred enjoys having them around as well. To a child there is probably nothing more intriguing than a blacksmith shop. What could be more fascinating to a young person's eyes than the smoke rolling from the fire, the red-hot metal shaping under the hammer, turning from red to iron blue, and the hot metal sizzling

Even today men and boys like to loaf in a blacksmith shop.

when thrust in water? Just as fascinating are the interesting junk and old tools hanging on the walls. For the little girls, Fred shapes rings out of spoon handles. "You make them a ring, you've about won them over," he says.

Fred's shop is typical of any old-time blacksmith shop—the only difference being that Fred has some electrically powered tools not available to earlier blacksmiths. One side of his shop is scattered with bar stock and scrap metal. In the middle of the wall is the forge with the anvil standing about three or four feet in front of it. The bellows is built into the forge. On the opposite side of the building from the forge is a workbench where Fred does various things, such as fitting ax heads and cutting wooden handles to fit. Under this bench Fred keeps his supply of various kinds of handles for axes and hoes. The area between the forge and the workbench is usually occupied by the loafers sitting in chairs Fred keeps around the shop for them.

As you walk into his shop you will see in the left corner a cluttered desk where Fred keeps his records. The desk, bought from a butcher, is over a hundred years old.

The walls of the shop, blackened over the years from the smoke, are used for hanging various tools. The floor is heavily cluttered with all sorts of metal ranging from scrap horseshoes to bar stock. Fred leaves everything on the floor so he will know where to look to find it. The floor is anything but clean

The forge is the most essential item in a blacksmith's shop.

and is probably not swept very often, for cleanliness is one thing a blacksmith does not have to worry about in the shop. The shop is continually filled with smoke from the forge and thus the double doors on three walls are kept open most of the time.

Like all craftsmen, the blacksmith needs tools, but he has the unique ability to make his own. Every blacksmith probably has a few tools like no other tools anywhere else in the world—the smith's own tools for his individual methods. But some basic essential tools are found in every shop; among these are the forge and bellows, anvil and slack tub and hand tools like the hardy, fuller, hammer and tongs, punch and chisel.

The forge, no matter what size, is the all-important fire container to heat the metal to the right temperature for working with it. Forges are usually at least thirty inches high and about two to three feet square. The hearth also varies in size but is usually proportioned to the overall dimension. It is made of brick and can cause metal to reach white-hot temperatures in a few minutes. Directly over the forge is a hood connected to a chimney which carries the smoke out. The most common fuel is coal. Fred estimates that he uses anywhere from seventy-five to a hundred pounds of coal each day. Every forge is accompanied by an air pipe connected to a bellows which keeps a steady flow of air blowing up through the fire to keep it burning and also to make the fire hotter.

There are various types of bellows, but they all work on the same principle. If you have ever seen a fireplace bellows, you have seen a miniature form of the blacksmith's bellows. The hand-powered bellows were made of wood and leather with valves, pipes, and levers.

The simpler single-chambered bellows was made of two boards of the same shape, usually teardrop, attached to each other with leather to make an airtight chamber. When the boards were separated, they created a vacuum which filled the chamber with air through a hole located on one of the boards. A valve in this hole opened automatically from the pull of the vacuum and allowed the air to enter. Pressing the boards together created a pressure which closed the air valve and forced the air out of the chamber through a blowpipe where the boards were hinged together. This pipe carried the air under the fire and blew it up through the fire. The single-chambered bellows was replaced after the invention of the double-chambered bellows and has not been used for many years.

The more efficient double-chambered bellows was made of two airtight chambers instead of one. This bellows created a steady flow of air—the single chamber produced air in spurts—and kept a hotter and steadier temperature. The double-chambered bellows was made of three teardrop-shaped boards about three or four feet long. In addition to the top board and the bottom board, there was a middle board which separated the two chambers. The leather was tacked around these boards to make two airtight chambers. The lower and middle boards each had air valves. The bellows was mounted on uprights, a chain attached to the bottom board and to a lever located above the bellows. The upper board rested on top of the middle board and the lower board fell by its own weight. The lever was used to raise the lower board, forcing air through the air valve in the middle board, inflating the upper chamber, and sending air through the blowpipe to the hearth. The lever was released, the lower board again fell, and the lower chamber inflated with air. At the same time the upper board fell, forcing the middle valve shut and blowing more air through the pipe. A weight was usually placed on the top board to increase pressure. Pumping the lever at a steady pace maintained a constant flow of air.

Fred Manes no longer uses a bellows, for an electric air pump supplies his air. He simply turns a lever near his hearth when he needs more air. Before electric air pumps were available, blacksmiths had to have assistants to pump the bellows while working at the forge. Without an assistant he would have to pump until the fire was hot enough to work with and then work until it was no longer hot enough.

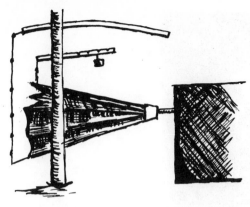

A hand-operated bellows.

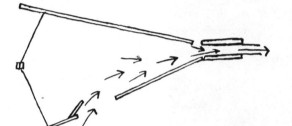

A single-chambered bellows.

A double-chambered bellows.

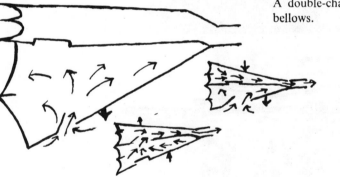

On the top of Fred's forge are scattered hand tools of various sorts, such as tongs and pokers, which are used in conjunction with the forge.

The anvil has probably been associated with blacksmith shops ever since their beginning. It is a basic tool of the blacksmith and is located near the forge. Fred simply pivots from his forge to reach his anvil. The typical size of the anvil used by most smiths ranges from one hundred to two or three hundred pounds. Care must be taken not to chip the anvil, for in spite of its great weight it is not indestructible.

A cross section of a log bigger in diameter than the base of the anvil is

The hammer and anvil are essential tools to the blacksmith.

The parts of the anvil.

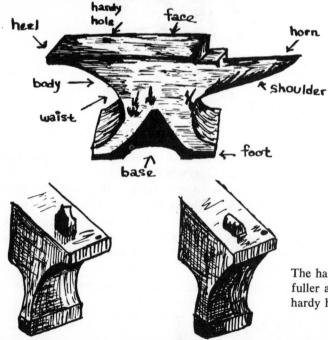

heel

handy hole

face

horn

body

shoulder

waist

base

foot

The hardy (left) and fuller are placed in the hardy hole of the anvil.

The slack tub is used to cool and temper the hot metal.

used to support Fred's anvil. The log raises the anvil to a comfortable working level several inches below the waist. Tools are hung by nails on this log for quick access. The log has a hollow place in it where Fred puts lard. He inserts the point of the punch through a hole in the log, covering it with grease to make punching easier.

Another of the basic necessities in a blacksmith shop is the slack tub, a large tub or barrel filled with water. The slack tub is used to cool the iron rapidly so that it may be handled, but more important, dipping very hot metal into cool water tempers it—makes it harder and stronger. In Fred's shop the rim of the slack tub is used for storing horseshoes.

There is an abundance of hand tools that play an important part in the art of blacksmithing. The three basic tools used with the forge are the rake, shovel, and poker. The rake is used to smooth the coals over the fire. The small shovel is used to arrange the coal and to pack it. The poker is a blunt-pointed rod about one fourth of an inch in diameter and about three feet long. Fred explained, "I use it to keep my fire going and to dig down if there's a clinker gets in the bottom of my forge. You dig it out 'cause that's where your sulphur out of your coal gathers in those clinkers that get in the bottom of your fire. A piece of sulphur as big as a pinhead will keep a place as big as your hand from welding. We don't get good coal now like we used to. We just have to take whatever we can get. The real blacksmith coal is mined in the East. It is a deep-mine coal—no sulphur in it. You can work all day and maybe get a clinker as big as your hand in the bottom of your forge."

The next group of tools is used with the anvil. Most of the anvil tools are similar in that they have a square shank design which fits snugly into the hardy hole located on the face of the heel of the anvil.

Probably the most important anvil tool is the hardy, from which the name for the hardy hole was derived. It is a chisel used for cutting bar stock. Bar stock is a long strip or bar of metal about ten to fifteen feet in length used for many things including making horseshoes. There are two different kinds of hardies, as is true of many of the anvil tools: those made for working with the metal while it is hot and those for working with the metal when it is cold.

Another anvil tool which closely resembles the hardy is the fuller, which differs from the hardy in that it has a rounded edge instead of a sharp one. The fuller is used for making a piece of metal thinner or for flattening it out. Metal is pounded against the fuller and then smoothed with a hammer.

The hammer is one of the most frequently used tools in the blacksmith shop, and in most shops there are many different sizes and shapes of hammers, usually made of steel and iron. The most commonly used is the four-pound cross-peen hammer. A four-pound hammer, according to Fred, is the most practical, being light enough for the smith to work with it all day, and heavy enough to do the job. Many other types of hammers are used, most of them having a specific use, such as the chisel-maker and file-maker hammers. Most hammers are hard-faced, but some are soft-faced for doing repair work where the hard-faced hammer would mar the surface.

The blacksmith tongs vaguely resemble a big pair of pliers. They are used to hold the hot metal while working with it at the forge and anvil. They work on the same principle as do household pliers and are usually about two feet long. The jaws form a circle with the lips holding the metal. Straight-lipped tongs are the most commonly used, but for various shapes of metal there are tongs with various types of lips. Fred makes his own tongs. "I never buy a pair of tongs. I forged out every pair."

Punches and chisels are simple tools, but nevertheless very important to blacksmithing. Punches were used instead of drills before electrical drills became available. Even today they are important for other uses. Punching is done by holding the punch of the desired size with the pointed end against the hot metal. The punch is driven through the hot metal with a hammer, leaving a perfectly round hole.

Some punches are equipped with handles for safety. The ones that do not have handles are usually about two feet long, for punching is almost always done when the metal is hot. The handles are crude, because they do not have

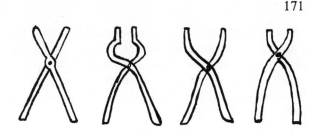

Tongs come in various shapes and sizes.

The cross-peen
hammer.

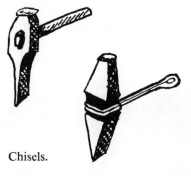

Punches.   Chisels.

to be shaped to hold the punch. Punch sizes range from one fourth inch to one and one half inches.

There are two kinds of hardy chisels, the hot and the cold chisel. Cold chisels have short shanks, and the hot chisels, since they are used with hot metal, have long shanks or handles like the punches. The width of chisels ranges from one half inch to two inches.

Fred still has in his shop some tools which used to be essential but which he rarely uses any more. He explained some of them to us. Swages were made in almost every imaginable shape and size, and were used for such things as making bolts, tools, various shapes of rods, and many other items. A swage is a mold, more or less. "That was used when those old steam engines had to have bolts—you couldn't buy them. We could make all the bolts they used. All these little places here had a hammer the same that matched all these and you put whatever you're making down in that and take a sledge hammer and drive it in here for the square shoulders next to the head. You make your bolt the size you want it. It was a wonderful tool in its day and I still use it, but it's kinda going out." Swage blocks are usually about three inches thick and about twenty inches square. Today there is little if any use for swage blocks because bolts and tools are abundant in hardware stores.

The traveler is a six-inch iron wheel equipped with a handle. The wheel turns freely. A traveler can be used to measure the diameter of something.

"You measure the outside of a wagon wheel and the inside of a tire with that. That's the only way you used to be able to measure it. There's your starting place on this marker. You go around the wheel with it and when you get back to where you started you move this to mark each round. This would be the exact measurement of the wheel. But now'days that's all over. That used to be about all we done."

It used to be common to see an iron cast cone standing about three feet tall as it rested on its base on the floor with the point of the cone up. "That also was used back in the days of building wagons," Fred explained. "This is a thing we used to use to bend the wagon tire with, curl it around, weld it up and put it on. That's called a mandrel. See how it tapers? That was made to make a hub band—a band that went around the hub of a wagon. We'd drop them down over that and cure them up."

The swage block was used to make bolts and nuts in any size needed.

The traveler used to be the only way to measure the diameter of such things as wagon wheels.

The mandrel was used to shape round objects such as hub bands.

The trip hammer was once powered by water.

The trip hammer seemed to stand out among all the other tools in Fred's shop, perhaps because it was the loudest thing in the shop. This piece of equipment used to be powered by water but now is electrical. The trip hammer consists of a large hammer head that pounds rapidly against a plate. It is operated by a foot pedal and is used for heavy metal work which requires a lot of hard pounding.

The blacksmith may not be a match for mass production, but mass production may not be a match for the quality and durability of the blacksmith's work. A good example of this is welding. "I don't think there ever was a weld that would equal a forge weld," Fred said. "It's the best weld there is." The process is relatively simple. In order to weld two rods together, both rods are stuck into the forge, burying one end of each rod under the coals until red hot. The hot ends are dipped in sand to make the weld hold. The two hot ends are then pounded together with a hammer on the anvil until the metal is too cool to work with and then it is put back in the fire. This is repeated until the two are fused together, making the joint as strong as the rest of the rod.

When we asked Fred if any young man ever came in to work with him, he replied, "No, it's too hard work. Once in a while some young fella comes in and he'll work at the electric welder. I try to get him to go over there to the forge, but that sweat over there makes him sick . . . he can't stand the smell of sweat. They won't stay with it. I ought to have two young men in here to do all the work."

Some black walnut crackers Fred designed.

"What will happen to your shop when you quit?"

"It'll close down. That will be the end of it."

Fred comes from a long line of blacksmiths. His father was a smith and his grandfather before that. He probably knows as much about blacksmithing as any man in the country, as he has been practicing it continually for over sixty years. Most of the work Fred does is making and shaping horseshoes, making his self-designed black walnut crackers, sharpening picks and hoes, welding, and general repair work of metal farm tools. At the age of eighty-one he has no intention of retiring—yet. He often tells his loafers that he is going to keep blacksmithing until he is a hundred years old, then go to farming for a year. If he doesn't like farming, he will come back to the shop.

One customer told us, "He's the best I've seen, and I've been all over the world."

"I'm as Regular as a
Goose A-going Barefoot"

A VISIT WITH FRED MANES

Howdy. Are you some of my Lebanon boys? Come on in and join my
loafers. I'm glad to have young fellas here. I was raised in this shop. My dad
had a shop on the corner of these two lots here for years and years. My
granddad had a shop here. I believe he was discharged from the Civil War in
1860 something. I've got his discharge. And he come here and put up a
blacksmith shop. That was the first blacksmith shop here in Richland with
the same name.

I've been in the shop all my life. I was in here when I was just a little bitty kid. I could put a horseshoe on a horse when I was seven years old. They had to be gentle, but I could do 'er . . . but I'll have to give 'er up one of these days. When you get up pert' near a hundred years old as I have, it's about time to quit.

When I was sixteen years old one time in Lebanon, I proved I could shoe more horses than two bigger men. They were big fellas and they made fun of me, you know. I just laughed and went in to shoe horses. There was three big men and I just weighed one hundred and thirty-five pounds. The fast man is supposed to be at the head of the list, and I went in there, and why, hell-fire, I could just go all around them. I know the first night we was there—I think that day I shod twenty-five, and I remember when the day's work was over and we took off our aprons and set our boxes out of the way, one fella said to the big boys, he said, "What do you think of the kid a-shoeing horses now?" One of them said, "Why, he's the fastest little son of a gun I've ever saw."

I was twenty-five when I went in business for myself. I hired out to shoe horses when I was fifteen. I built this shop building in 1925 by myself.

I'll tell you, boys, you make just as much as you want to make if you want to work hard enough. I'm satisfied now if I make—oh, maybe ten dollars one day and twenty the next and some days eighteen, twenty, twenty-five. And if I don't feel good, sometimes I don't make more than five. You make just

"I'm glad Saturday night I don't have to come back, but Monday morning I'm ready again."

what you want to—how you feel. I have made 'er here. I've made enough to
get as good a farm as there is in this part of the country and get 'er covered
with black cows.

But it wasn't easy. Sometimes it was hard going for my customers to pay
anything. I had to go to California during the Depression to make some
money. The bottom was out of everything and I'd been blacksmithing here. It
hit other places before it did here. The first year we begin to feel it here, I
wasn't afraid. I wasn't afraid of my customers. I done their work for them
and charged it to them. But by the next year there wasn't a thing. They
couldn't pay nothing. I shod their horses all through summer and fall when
they wanted to do hauling. I had a big pile of old shoes that I'd took off and
I'd tell them, "Now you can't use them barefooted. You gather you up some
old shoes and I've got a bunch of them." I fit them and I shod, I bet, a hundred horses for those old poor boys on these ridge farms. Didn't even charge
it to them. Didn't make no record of them 'cause they couldn't have paid it to
save their lives.

But one winter here during that—it was in '35—farmers had brought me
in corn and hogs. I had twenty-five hogs and plenty of corn. One old carpenter was here and he hadn't had a job for a year. He just couldn't get a dime's
worth of work to do. One day he came down and told me, he said, "Fred,
I'm going up to your house and kill a hog and dress him. We've got to have
something to eat." And he did. He'd kill one and give me half of it. And
sometimes he'd go up there and kill three or four and we'd just pass it around
to people with big families. We killed ever'one of them.

Boy, that was tough going. A fella that never went through that, he doesn't
know what hard picking is. I've come here to the shop many a week during
that Depression and not make two dollars. People didn't have it and they
couldn't get it.

So I went to California to get me a job. I left here December 13, 1936, and
come back in '38. I got a good job there in the oil fields and paid up what I
owed here and bought me twenty-five cows when I got back. When I left
here, I think me and my wife and boy left here in an old Model A. The best I
remember, I had about eighty dollars. We took off. But I went to work just as
quick as I got there. I'd work at the oil fields five days a week. Then I'd come
to town and the blacksmith there in that town, he had mules and horses scattered over the country that he'd go out and shoe. I went out with him quite a
while. Then I went out on my own on Saturday and Sunday. I'd go out to
those ranches and shoe their horses and sharpen their plows. I made more on
Saturday and Sunday than I did the days I was working in the oil fields. Boy,
she was tough going then.

I've been here ever since. I'm going to stay here as long as I can stand up
to use the hammer. I wouldn't quit this shop—I could make it all right without it. I wouldn't quit here if they offered me a thousand dollars a month
pension. This is my life right here. I'm always glad Saturday night I don't
have to come back the next morning, but Monday morning I'm ready again.

I work just the same in the wintertime with a three-foot snow on. I'll close that door and come in here. I make something that'll bring me anywhere from twelve to fifteen to twenty-five dollars a day. I make a walnut cracker—twenty-five bucks. I may not get my money until next summer, but I'd better be a-doing that as setting on my ass.

Last year I made a hundred steeple pullers—you know, that you take a hammer and drive it in to pull the steeple out? I made a hundred of them and put them in a box there. I was out, oh, by the first of July. It didn't amount to much but it was fifty dollars' worth. I made them in the winter when there wasn't nothing else to do.

You know, it's a fact that you will rust out quicker than you'll wear out. You sit on your ass and don't do nothing, it will get you a whole lot quicker than working ever' day. You'll rust out. It takes a long time to wear a man out. You just keep bucking.

Boys, come over here. There's the art in blacksmithing right there—that forge. I built this one in 1925. Before that I had one that turned with a crank. I used one with a long arm when I was a kid. I've stood on a box—the bellows would be as high as pert' near to the ceiling—and I've stood up on a box with a rope fastened onto it and pumped the thing. It wasn't a steady blast. It was just a "shwish, shwish." I don't see how they blacksmithed with it.

With this forge you can make anything if you just want to bad enough. Back in wartime I made many a piece for a tractor they couldn't order. Many and many a piece. But you can make anything they bring you if you want to and will try.

To learn how to use the forge you got to know quite a little bit about steel —what a piece of steel is. You can burn an inch rod in two in just a little bit there. It just takes a few minutes for it to get hot as a hen laying a goose egg. Why, I can burn that horseshoe up there. You have to watch that fire there or you'll get it too hot and then it's no good. Just get it hot enough that it'll melt together. You can tell when it's hot enough by just working at it long enough. You just know when to wait.

I'm used to working at a fire like this. Now I can't work fifteen minutes out in the sun though I can work by that fire all day. When you're around a fire, you can take it in here, but you go out and work in the sun and it turns your damper down.

I'm doing all the work in here now myself that three men used to do 'cause it was all done the hard way. We didn't have no grinders, no power. Had to turn the drill by hand.

I don't shoe horses any more. I just make the shoes. Used to, if a horse had a crippled foot, I'd take care of it. I'd repair it and make a shoe to fit it. I'd cut into a foot, open them if there was anything wrong with a shoe. I quit that when I was seventy-five years old.

I still make shoes. Some days when I work at it all day, I get twenty-five, thirty pairs made. I had to quit making walking shoes, though. Orders came in from Jeff City and Columbia and everywhere else more than I could make in six months. So I just don't try. I just make enough for my son's horses.

If the Humane Society would see what some people today fix up and put on horses, they'd tote them down. A horse came to our barn shod with a part pressing in on the toe of the foot on both feet. It lamed him. It's a crime to butcher a horse up that way.

I make walnut crackers if I've got time. It takes about five or six hours to make one of them things. If you get them off the least bit they won't crack walnuts. You take black walnuts when there's moisture in them. When the walnut's bone dry, well, the kernel's bone dry. But if you'll crack them when there's a little moisture in them, you can get them out in quarters and halves all the time, 'cause it just shoves that hull away from them. I made them one winter—I made a whole bunch of them, and good gosh, they didn't last no time.

Another thing I make a lot right now are those horseshoe-nail rings and spoon rings. I have a rush on them pert' near ever' year. This time it's pitiful the nice fancy spoons I cut off and make rings out of them. I've got a whole sackful. Now they're wanting me to take a longer-handled spoon and make bracelets out of them—flatten the spoon out. I dread that.

I've made rings all this week. I make them for kids, the young gals around that's fell for these. I make lots of them. Don't get nothing for it, but I make them anyway. If you want to have friends when you get old, make them out of kids and you'll win. But if you're ever mean to a kid, the little ones, they never forget it. I learned better than that by experience of my own when I was a kid. When people run over you when you're a kid, it's hard to forget. You can forgive a person for something, but boy, to forget it, that's hard to do. Now I've got a good bunch of customers and I like them ever' one. If I didn't, I'd be out on the farm.

You boys cold? Come over here by the fire. I have to keep a good fire here. My boys would quit coming down to visit me. I couldn't take that. That stove, it's been here for about eighteen years, I guess. I'll put a fire in it because I have a bunch of loafers in here. I can stay warm at that forge a-hammering. If it wasn't for the boys coming down here to loaf, lots of times I wouldn't even build a fire in it. But I'm lucky about my wood for down here. The chief of police here in town—he's a big old husky and he's got him a chain saw and a truck and he'd rather get out in the woods and work as anything. Last winter he piled, oh, about six big old truckloads of wood right out there.

I see you're looking at my mouse house. Some people made that in St. Charles, Missouri. They knew about my mice and they sent me that. My name is on it. I don't know if you can see it any more or not. Fred's Mouse House. I . . . I like my mice.

I feed them maybe, oh . . . a hundred and fifty pound a winter of walnuts. They'll eat walnuts. You can crack them pecans or English walnuts and lay them down there but they'll eat the black walnuts first. I'll tell you one thing,

"I like my mice. As long as they can't learn to open my safe or chew the horn off my anvil, why, they're all right."

I've saw the time here in the wintertime that I'd come up here and go to cracking walnuts, maybe there'd be fifty mice come right here to eat at my feet. They'd hear this walnut cracker starting and they knew what it was. I can poke a walnut kernel in one of them holes and they'll take it out of my fingers. I've got enough mice to carry a gallon of cracked walnuts away in ten minutes. Real cold weather I have lots of them.

I make it easy for the mice to get in. I cut a hole out in the wall back there so they can get under the floor and then in the wintertime I've got a hole cut there by my anvil and they can go under and out here or run in there. I like my mice. As long as they can't learn to open my safe or chew the horn off my anvil, why, they're all right. They can't cause no trouble. Produce boys up here ever' once in a while will send me down a pack of d-CON. They think I'll feed it to them but I don't.

The only trouble I have is cats can get in here. Women all over this end of town raises hell with me for running off their cats. I've told these people that if I ever caught one of my mice a-hurting one of their cats, then I'd let them fight it out. Till they do, I'm going to defend my mice.

I use a bean flipper to keep the cats away. I haven't practiced it lately, but when I'm in tune, you set five dimes out there and let me set five dimes and we take a shot apiece and I'll get the most of your dimes, I'll guarantee you, with the bean flipper from twenty foot. See that can sitting down there, down the road there? There was a boy mowing that yard one day and I bet a fella two dollars and a half I could bust his gallon gas can with it. He had a big glass jar. He bet me two dollars and a half I couldn't bust it with a bean flipper. And I busted it.

Then one day the police judge was going across the tracks home. I got right there at the door with my bean flipper. He was in his shirt sleeves and I cut in on him—took him in the back. He said it knocked him to his knees, but it didn't. It set him afire and he thought somebody'd took a shot at him. He went uptown and got the other law and come down here and hunted all over hell for somebody who took a shot at him. I didn't tell this, of course, for a while. He asked me if I saw anybody down here. "Yeah, I saw a fellow going up over agin the track there a while ago pretty fast." They tried their damnedest to catch somebody with a rifle or something that shot him. He never did know what happened. The other marshal did. I told the other marshal.

You have to go? You boys come down any time you want to. Come down and work the fire a little bit. Come back any time you want. I'll be here. I'm as regular as a goose a-going barefoot.

4. THE NEIGHBORHOOD

The woman's world did not end in the kitchen, nor the man's in the fields or shops. Nor did the well-being and love of the family absorb all their energies. In these tightly knit, homogeneous communities everyone knew everyone else for several miles—where most grew up, married, and died within the same general area—and one was related to many of those people.

The school playmates, the fishing buddies, the future spouses, the midwives and doctors, the teachers and the preachers, and the neighbors who came during time of joy or trouble were all part of the neighborhood.

A Diamond in the Rough

On a beautiful early spring day we stood beside Bear Creek in Taney County, some of us wading in the icy water and climbing on the big rocks. Behind us was a country road squeezed between the creek and the foliage-covered limestone bluffs. Just up the road, built against the hill marking the edge of the creek bottom, was the one-story home where we had just enjoyed a farm dinner in the company of Ella Dunn and her companion Ruth Branstetter.

We had been drawn naturally to the creek which had played such a part in Ella's life. We stood there silently enjoying the unusual warmth, listening to the birds and the noise of the water rushing over the rocks worn smooth over countless years.

Did you ever think of it, that that's why we are here? We're a diamond in the rough, and when the Lord rolls us around here enough that we're polished, He'll take us home.

For the last fifty years Ella has lived by this creek. Married at fourteen, she and her husband moved back and forth from Taney County to Colorado, Kansas City, and Arkansas in their early years of marriage before settling here where the creek has played a dominant role in their lives.

In the spring when the rains come, why, the creek fills up until it covers my field. One time it just lacked an inch going into my door. Water was all in my cellar and out to the barn. It has never got in the house yet, but it's got up around it. I never put down wall-to-wall carpet. I never put any fine furniture in, for I never knew when I'd have to go up the hill. We used to have a bed in this old shed up on the hill. Sometimes I'm bottled up in here for a couple of days. But the water runs down fast.

Most of the time the creek was useful to Ella and her husband. They used the rich creek-bottom land for raising vegetables and for truck farming, and the creek to irrigate their fields and garden.

My husband had been raised in Colorado, so he knew how to irrigate. So we came over here to this farm to raise fresh vegetables for the Taneycomo Hotel at Rockaway Beach. We got a centrifugal pump and Fairbanks-Morris engine. He made a flume and pumped water from the creek and we irrigated all this land—halfway to where you see the timber. Since the creek ran all summer, we diverted the water with these flumes and we made ditches through the garden by our stuff to run this water clear through. And boy, it was a full-time job. We had to follow those ditches all the time because the moles would cut a hole and we'd lose the water. We had to keep it going.

As soon as we took off one crop, we put in another. We fertilized well. And every other day we went to the Beach [Rockaway Beach] with another load of vegetables. We took the very top—first-class stuff. Anything that was not well developed and number one we laid it out and took good care of it. When I got back home, that left was all trimmed up and washed and cut up to make vegetable stew. We had a canner and capper and canned in No. 2 cans. We bought them by the thousand. We sold by the case. All the stuff that wasn't Number One to go on the market we canned at home—tomatoes, cabbage and carrots, celery and okra—everything you would use in stew. We had a standing demand for them all the time.

But we stayed with it and made good. The children all married off and left. My husband and I continued until he had a stroke—fell off the hay wagon and broke his hip and had a compound break in his ankle. He soon died of a heart condition and that stopped our gardening.

I got rid of these charley horses in my legs wading in this cold water. My brother had a little dog and he had me keep it while he was in the hospital. Children would play in this creek in the summer—the dog would hear them and go to them and I'd have to wade the creek and hunt him. Every night my legs would just draw in knots and my feet would draw in. And when I got to wading in this cold water, I didn't have any of that. Now I can't wade, but I still bathe my legs in cold water.

We walked across the culvert which was built in recent years to span the hollow coming from behind her barn. We were standing just where the hollow way empties into the creek.

This used to be a good fishing hole. See, the creek is all filling up and someday we may not have any water here.

As she looked at the shallow water that once was deep she remembered an incident there.

I think if you're going to tell somebody you're going to do something, you should do it. That's my motto. One day I was sitting here fishing with my neighbor, Rose Baimer. She hadn't caught a thing and I caught a water bucket full of perch and goggle-eye. "Oh," I said, "I wish I could just catch a real big one. If I do, I'll give it to you." Well, I hadn't more than said that until I caught a big one—the largest fish I ever caught in Bear Creek. It was a big one—a bass. I never did catch one that big there before. And she said, "Now what are you going to do?" I said, "I'm going to give it to you. I told you I would." She said, "You're better than I am. I wouldn't give anything like that away." But I made the promise, and I live with myself. So I was glad to do it.

We walked up the short drive to her buildings. She showed us the brooder house where she and her husband used to raise baby chicks.

"This string's too short. The mice ate it off, but they would pull down on this string and this dumbull'd put your hair up on top."

The floor is heated, and we would raise two hundred without losing a chick. It's just a place for junk now.

She pulled out an old nail keg.

We had so many tourists coming in here at night and parking in the driveway back when Rockaway was full. So we made us a dumbull. We scared them out.

You never heard of a dumbull? It's a nail keg with a groundhog hide stretched on it like a drum. And there's a little hole in the middle of it and a button and a long string—a trotline about ten foot long. You rosin the string. You pull on that string—reach way out—with a glove on, you pull the rosin down and you can make it roar. My goodness, it will scare the dead and put your hair up on top. It sounds weird—like, well, like a mad bull. That is where it got its name.

It was first created here in the hills. You know people used to make a living hunting skins, hunting animals for fur. Young men went hunting nights and sold fur. They sort of had a territory of their own to hunt in around their own places at home. Sometimes an outsider would infringe on their right— come in maybe with better dogs and catch their fur. So they decided to invent something good. They really intended to scare the hunter with the dumbull, but it scared the dogs out of the hills too. They went home. So if they didn't want them to hunt, they just went out and pulled down on that dumbull and they went home. The dogs wouldn't come back any more at night. I know my own dog jumped over my chicken wire fence and came to the door.

It sure scared them when we pulled on that string. We had some boys that were so lazy they couldn't play ball with the rest of them. And the other boys needed them to play. They'd just go set in the shade. They was so lazy they wouldn't work and they wouldn't even play. So my son Bill and his friends Walter Cummings, Clifford Palmer, and Cecil Weatherman made it up to see if they could get them to at least run once. It wasn't because they were sick. They were strong and healthy—just lazy. So my husband and son had made a dumbull and my son said, "Well, we'll just see if we can get the Baker boys to move for once." And he said, "Now, Mother, if I don't come home tonight, don't think anything about it. I may go home with Clifford for the night."

He intended to come home, but he didn't want me to know he was going to scare these boys. So they got on this bluff right around the bend. Walter said he'd walk with the Bakers to see if they got scared enough to run. He wanted to see them run.

When the boys turned that thing loose to bellowing, I want to tell you those boys run! It scared them to death, and Walter, he fell down in the road a-laughing.

Well, the Bakers ran in here and they was just scared to death. They said there was a wild beast down there and had got Walter down. They said, "He couldn't get away. He just couldn't go any farther and fell in the road, but we got here." They said, "If you'll just let us come in here and lay down on the floor."

I said, "Well, come on in. But it's more 'n likely someone scaring you."

And they said, "No, it ain't. No one could make that kind of a racket."

I went outside and listened and I heard Walter laughing. I said, "Why, he's not hurt. I hear him laughing."

"No, he's just a-taking on. That animal's got him." And they said, "We're just scared to death. We're afraid to go on home." They were full-grown men, both of them.

I said, "No, it's someone trying to scare you. Go on home."

Well, I talked to them until I got them to go down to the culvert on the way toward home, and bless Pat, them boys pulled down on the dumbull again.

And here the Bakers come back. And they said, "Just let us come in, Mrs. Dunn, and lay on the floor. We just can't go another step and you're just going to have to let us lay on the floor."

I said, "Well, come on in and you can go to bed in Bill's bed because I don't think he's coming home." Well, honest to goodness, I didn't know if he was coming home, and here he comes with the other boy carrying the dumbull. Well, I run out to meet them. When I heard them talking and laughing fit to kill, I knew what they'd done. So they went out to the shop and hid the dumbull before they come in.

I said, "The Baker boys are in here in your bed. You just scared them to death."

Bill said, "Heck, Mother, I never done anything mean in my life that didn't backfire."

I had to make him and Clifford a bed down instead of the Bakers.

But the next week they couldn't get the Bakers to work or move. They'd rented my brother's place up Bear Creek. They wouldn't work and my brother had let them have the mules to farm with and they wouldn't work or let him have the mules back. So the bunch of boys from down at Walnut Shade went up where they lived with the dumbull and they turned it loose. The cattle all went to bawling and running and the bells were jingling on the cattle. It sounded like the Mexican army had moved in.

The next day the old man went to my brother. He said, "Charley, you can have them mules back and your place, too. We are leaving out. We ain't staying where they got sich animals as you have here. We never hearn tell of sich a noise."

Ella was always busy. In addition to taking care of her family, she filled up her time with writing, painting, and making jewelry from shells, as well as working by the side of her husband in the truck patch and any place else she could. Side by side in 1908 they built their first house, a two-room box house.

In most all our young life I was my husband's helper, you might say. He'd get up on the building and tell me how much he wanted sawed off of a board. I'd measure it and cut it off and hand it up.

I always had my little nose in everything, trying to find out what made them perk. I wanted to know about everything. I guess that's why I have the knowledge I do of the things that went on. Because I always wanted to see the why and the how.

I was always just a little scrawny, sickly child. When I was seven I had St. Vitus' dance. They had to hand-feed me for three months and I chilled fairly often for the next year.

We didn't have toys. I never had a doll except an old rag doll. I used to whittle out animals and things with a pocket knife and make little horses and dolls out of corn cobs and things of that sort. We also built houses and animals out of clay mud. But we always found something to do when we ran out of work around the house.

I didn't study as hard as I should in school. I loved my geography, reading, writing, and spelling—that was it. I was good in addition, but I never got beyond multiplication. After my husband died I learned to subtract quite a bit. I had to when I was filling out my light cards. I made a few mistakes.

We didn't have grades, we had readers. You just went from one reader to the next. I got to the fourth. When you went to the fifth reader you had your geography, arithmetic, English, reading, history, and physiology. And if you completed that you could go down to the county courthouse at Forsyth and if you passed the county examination, they would give you a certificate—a privilege to apply and get a school to teach. You could teach a country school then. You was a graduate when you completed the fifth reader.

But like I said, I just got to the fourth reader and I was out one day a week to do the washing because my mother had inflammatory rheumatism. Her knees were so swollen she could hardly walk—carried one on a chair part of the time. I was the only girl big enough to help my mother. My older sister worked away. She worked out all the time for a dollar a week to buy our dresses. We bought calico and muslin at five cents a yard. She'd get ten yards of calico and would bring it home for Mother and her and I. And Mother'd make it up. In the winter Mother spun and wove and made our clothes from wool sheared from sheep. My younger sisters were small—five years between me and the next youngest sister. Then there was about eleven years between me and my oldest sister. So I grew up, you might say, alone—just with the five boys.

I was fourteen when I got married. I married on January 18, 1905. My husband was twenty-one the seventeenth of January, and I was fifteen the twenty-fourth of February. I ought of been home being spanked and washing the dishes.

He stayed one summer and tried farming on a little farm over north of Forsyth. But he'd never been on a farm—never seen a stalk of corn growing till he was seventeen. He said, "We're going west where I can make some money. Fifty cents a day is not enough." So we went to Colorado.

My husband's uncle and aunt ran a hotel in Lake City, Colorado. I started washing dishes and my husband helped in cooking, room care, and odd jobs, such as going down Elk Creek for the milk and butter every other day. That paid our board until he was called to the Golden Fleece Mine up above Lake City beyond Lake San Cristoval. The snow was so deep up the mountain, navigation was all done after midnight on snowshoes, and everyone carried a long pole to use as a guide and safety to not get buried in the deep snow.

He went to this mine as cook. He had a boy flunky to help him. He was paid fifty dollars a month. We saved enough to buy the eighty acres over near Powersite Dam for two hundred dollars where we built the two-room box house.

As he seldom came down the mountain to town, I was very lonesome for my own people. I got acquainted with seven or eight of the girls my age in this small mining town. Some one of them would visit me most every day. My education was so limited. They enjoyed my backwoods hillbilly talk.

Every night everybody went to the post office at nine o'clock when the mail train came in from Salida. I was anxious to hear from my people in Missouri. So all the girls I had met would be there with me and had fun razzing me. Of course, my hillbilly language was new to them. They got a lot of fun at my expense. I called a sack a poke, salad was "sallet," isn't was "hent." It was all very amusing to them.

One evening when two of the usual old miners stood listening and waiting, one of the girls came up to me and says, "Ellie, they sure have lots of fools in Missouri, don't they?"

I fired back, "Yes, they are scattered about, but they don't gather up by the half dozen in the post office like they do here."

Well, the two old miners slapped their hands and said to the girl, "You asked for it and you got it. Maybe you'll behave yourself now." I didn't suppose I'd said anything. I was just that green, but they were my friends—good friends after that—and they never razzed me any more.

I went home to the house—it was a small, cheaply built house—the kitchen door had a latch on the inside where you could lock it, but not on the outside. When I got home I heard some stumping in the house and I was scared to death. I didn't know what to do. I had my revolver in the dresser drawer—I was good with that—and I had my flashlight on my dresser, so I slipped in the front door. I put the key in the lock and turned it real easy. I slipped to the kitchen door ready to shoot somebody—I didn't know who. I expected somebody was there, and I got real brave.

But when I got to the kitchen door, there was a big old burro standing there eating all my vegetables, my meal and everything in the house. He'd eat up everything I had. He'd eat the labels off the cans in the coal house, and backing out of it, he backed into the kitchen door and busted the knob off of it. Well, I took the broom and I sure did brush him out. I guess I'd just a-shot him, but I couldn't drag him off. So that was just one day's hardships. There were many more. I was ready to come home.

So when my husband came down off the mountain he put me on the train and I came home alone. And then in August he came back to my father's place and our first little boy was born—seventy years ago the sixth day of September. He stayed and worked building mills to crush the ore from rock at Webb City and Duenweg, Missouri, and then he went to work for a doctor at Forsyth. Fifty cents a day from sunup until after sundown. He said, "We can't put up with this. We'll never get anywhere." So we went back to Colorado but after about six months we came back to Missouri. My husband told my father, "Well, I took your daughter out of the hills, but I can't take the hills out of her."

One of the jobs I had was in Rockaway Beach. I took care of cottages and I cooked three years in the hotel. I had a lot of experiences when I was taking care of the cottages. I had to see that everything was in shape and see if they had linens and all that stuff. I had fourteen cottages to look after.

Many times you run across people of all kinds of character—of every description. Some of them are real nice and others are not. One couple came to me and waited until I was in company with other people—I don't know whether they had any money or not—but they come up to me and took my hand and put a dime in my hand and shut it and said, "We want you to have this because you've been so sweet to us. We want to show our appreciation."

I could tell it was just a small piece of money. I didn't want their money. I just opened my hand up and said, "You just keep it. I was poor too one time before I went to work here!"

Was I mean? But just such experiences as that helps give you an education.

I had a lot of experiences while I was a midwife. I didn't start because I wanted to. I was really pushed into it. See, my mother had been a midwife for forty years, so I guess I was born to be, but she fell and broke her hip and was on crutches. Just after she fell she went out by Forsyth to deliver a child—she stood on her crutch and delivered the baby and took care of it—and when she come home, she said to me, "I don't intend to deliver any more kids. It's up to you."

Well, I didn't take to it very agreeable. I didn't think I wanted any of it. Mother said, "You're more like I am than the other girls, so you'll have to do it." So she told me I had to take over. I said I couldn't. But finally I got caught in with a case and had to do it. And it was made to order, I suppose, because I got through it so nicely, I said, "Well, if it is this easy, I'll go ahead with it." I did. And in a short time the word got out that Ella was delivering babies. And it went like wildfire and sometimes I went twice a night, sometimes twins, or a breech birth and sometimes a premature baby. And I, of course, didn't know enough about it—I tried to save one or two, but if there'd been a hospital . . . there wasn't any here then.

When my husband had his leg and hip broken, a nurse came down through here to have a look at him and after she was through she questioned my knowledge in child delivery—like a teacher's examination. She said the government would school me if I would go. She remarked that I had made the best rating of any midwife on the list on her travel. And I said, "I can't leave my home."

So after he got well enough, I asked my doctor at Forsyth what he thought about me taking training and he said, "If you've got a lot of money you want to get rid of, why, you go on." But he said, "You won't learn as much as you know. You've had the actual experience and that's more than you'll learn when you get there." But I don't know. I never felt like I knew that much.

But this nurse in St. Louis sent me the certificate book—birth register—and silver nitrate for the eyes and a lot of literature to give to these mothers for prenatal care. She thought everybody came to me and asked about delivering them, you know, which they didn't all do. Very few of them did. When they was ready to deliver, they sent for me. Women back then was more timid of talking of things like that. You didn't know much about it till it happened.

I hardly ever had a doctor with any of my cases. When I had a doctor I did not deliver or register the births in my book. The doctor did. I just registered when I delivered the baby alone. Just me and the mother and daddy, a grandmother, or a neighbor.

I never had a telephone so people just had to come after me. In the latter years of the thirties there were telephones in the country, but I didn't have one here until three or four years before my husband died.

I only delivered one baby after Skaggs hospital was built over here in '49. I told them it was just as easy to take them to the hospital as it was to come to me.

Another thing I can tell you that you probably don't realize or know is that today it's not as easy to deliver babies as it was then. Then women walked a lot. They didn't set so much and ride in cars. That makes a big difference. They got enough exercise and nowadays they don't. They eat fatty foods and they don't restrict their diet as they should.

I had to restrict them on beans sometimes. They ate too many dried beans. That makes a hardheaded baby. So I would cut them down and give them a diet that would make childbirth more easy and I'd give them a schedule on their daily habits.

And you know another thing I drilled them on was their daily thought. That has a big influence over the child. The mind is developing as well as the body and if you want a good child, if you want a child to be industrious and work and not sleep all the time, keep a busy mind. But keep your mind on the good of life. Not anything that's contrary.

I've tried that out. I've tested that on different women. And if you'd talk to them today, they would tell you it would make a big difference—what you are thinking and what you do when you carry your child.

If I was to talk to young women today, I would stress very deeply that they should keep a good thought in their heads all the way through if they ever intended to be a mother. And then it's not hard when you begin to train a little one after it comes to you. It's not so hard to go ahead training because it's already instilled in its little mind. So I think that is very, very essential and I've proved it out.

Life is very different now from what it was when Ella grew up and raised her family. Technology, good roads, and tourists have greatly changed the living conditions of the people and their geographical surroundings.

I've seen what the tourist trade has done with this area. It's good for the country. And people live better. They live without working so hard, but I think we had a better world without it.

The progress has been wonderful. We have good roads and good schools, and young people can make money better ways than beating it out of the soil and hunting pelts and raising tobacco like in the early days. But there's also a lot of bad things that we can't do anything about that came in with progress. I think it really tore up home living a lot. Just to put it straight to you, I think it's broke up an awful lot of homes—progressive living—brought dissatisfaction in many homes.

I'm glad to see women have the opportunity of making the same amount of money a man makes, but I'm not quite an advocator and believer for women's liberation. We've got a lot of well-educated women who don't let it go to their head, but some it tears up their homes and they don't ever care for home life again. "I can make my own. I don't need anybody," they'll say. It creates a sort of selfishness, I guess you'd call it. But as a whole, back when women depended more on their husband and their home, their home life was better, their children's life was better. But they didn't have as much.

I've seen marriages drift away. I've seen the broken homes—the lack of interest in the home. Now when a mother goes out to work and just leaves the children, maybe they're big enough to go ahead with things in the home— maybe they're not. And the dad don't care so much either. Children are turned loose when they're too young to go on their own. They buy them a car. They don't have the judgment to be turned loose quite so young.

My mother said, "I gave my life for my children." I felt the same way. If it was to do over, I'd spend more time with them than I did. I taught them to work. You know, that's a good thing for them—self-reliance. I don't think children have to do enough this day and time to really know what it means to make a home. It takes a lot of strength. But I wouldn't want them to do like I had to do.

Progress has taken a lot of the hardships out of life that people like Ella had to cope with. But back in her day she could always count on family and friends to help out in case of trouble.

I think there's a lot less neighborliness. People don't like to get out and visit. They'd rather watch television. You know television used in the right way would be a blessing to the world, but as it is, I think it is a detriment. I set and watch it for pastime a lot. I don't read my Bible as much as I used to, either. Neighbors are another thing you neglect when you've got television and other things like picture shows and cars to go in. We had time back then for our neighbors. Now then we don't have time any more. You can see the change, can't you?

My life has been a fulfilling one. I've met many people and seen many things. My eyes are failing me badly now, but if I reach the place to where I'm unable to read or piece quilt blocks, then I hope my children will raise me some cotton. I can at least keep busy picking out the seed. I've picked out enough seeds and made the bats for several quilts and quilted them. We used to raise cotton back home, you know, so it wouldn't be a new trick I was trying out. When we moved here to the creek and began raising vegetables, I raised cotton right along with them, but just enough for my family. I also use cotton balls for my stroke patients to get them to use their hands.

There's been a lot of hard work on this place since we settled down here fifty years ago. I've been here ever since. I'll stay as long as I can.

"Next time you come, come eat with me. I always have something to eat. I may not be fancy. I always tell everybody the latchstring is out and always welcome for them to come in."

"Sometimes I Let It Age Ten or Fifteen Minutes"

Beside another rushing Ozark stream we visited with another friend who has made good use of his creek but in a quite different way. This Ozarkian has used the cold water in his business of making whiskey.

"Now they's three different kinds of whiskey. They's white mule, they's moonshine, and they's white lightning. Now your white mule, that's when you've got your still way to hell back in the woods. You have to ride your old mule back in there and carry your sugar in and your whiskey out. Now moonshine, that's when you set up at night and make it. White lightning, that's when you come right out in the open like we do right here and make it in the daytime."

The twinkle in his bright blue eyes and his friendly smile denoted a touch of humor. Art Patterson, the man who makes whiskey at Alley Spring, often comments about his working for the government.

"I used to work against them and now I'm working fer them. When they came to hire me, I said, 'It looks like a foolish idea, you people trying to hire me as many years as you've been a-running me.' They said, 'We've just decided we can hire you cheaper'n we can hire two revenue men to be after you all the time!'"

The smoke that came from his pipe seemed to complement his overalls, old army hat, and rolled-up shirt sleeves. His bright eyes, ruddy cheeks, and calloused hands showed years of hard work around the still, making good whiskey while watching for "revenuers."

"I had sold my still to the government five years ago for a hundred and fifty dollars. That's what I give for it new, and then after using it all them years—I'd say I got my money's worth. Now what started this all. They put the word out they wanted to buy a still to set up in the Old Red Mill for people to see. I had that one and didn't figure on ever using it again, so I sold it to them. They left it set over there about two weeks and they got up the idea they'd like to have whiskey made here. So they come to me to ask if I'd take a job if they could get a permit to make here. I told them I would for enough money. They wanted to know what I wanted and I told them, hell, I was

The smoke from Art Patterson's pipe often keeps company with the smoke from the fire under his still.

skilled labor. I thought I ought to have five dollars an hour. They said they just couldn't pay that. All they wanted was for a demonstration. I said, 'Hell, if that's all you want it there for, I'll just work for nothing.' That kind of tickled them. Then I said, 'Provided you give me what I run through.' So that put them to talking again. Then they came up with a pretty good price and I took it."

Many people confuse the making of whiskey and the selling of it. We asked Art what the difference between a moonshiner and a bootlegger was.

"Your moonshiner, he's the man that makes it. And your bootlegger, he's the man that peddles it out and sells it."

Making and peddling whiskey violates eleven federal laws. The revenuers were always looking for the moonshiners. Art told us what he and his brother did to keep intruding revenuers away.

"I've operated a whiskey still ever since I was seventeen. I used to work for my brother before that. I got fifty cents a day till I learned how to operate, then I just bought me a still of my own. I wasn't making a lot of money at fifty cents a day. While we were working we had somebody sitting on the hill-side with a good .30-.30 most of the time. You go to barking the trees around them boys and they ain't going to stay put. They're going to move on. 'Course, they was always two of us working. One was sitting up on a hillside watching, while the other was working. We seen a stranger coming, we found out what his business was and sent him on his way.

"They'd come down there and try to fool us. They'd come there as hog buyers or cattle buyers or land buyers or something. We just didn't have none of that kind of stuff to sell, so we didn't fool with them and let them go.

"I never did use the .30-.30. I seen my brother put two boys on the go one time. I guess they was revenue men because they had caught some boys just over the river from us where they had another still. The revenue men come in there and got them boys. But, hell, we had twelve barrels of mash setting up and we couldn't tear down and run. We had to stay. So I told my brother, 'Hell, they'll be back.' He said, 'Well, if they do we'll just have to move them. We can't move.'

"So the next day they was back across the river walking around over the hillside a-looking for some more whiskey, for they knew there was more around. My brother decided he'd just move them. And he did. He had his gun. I told him, 'Hell, don't kill one for it, for we'll have more law in here than we'll know what to do about.' He said, 'I ain't a-going to kill one unless he breaks his neck a-running.' He got up there on that hill and got to barking the trees around them. They took off and never did come back."

Although Art and his brother took every advantage not to be caught, there was one time that being caught couldn't be avoided.

"By God, they come to the house and got my brother out of bed. They didn't come to the still and get us when we was a-working. He lived in one place and I lived in another. They'd been sitting on the hill watching us with field glasses. So we goes home and he goes to bed and I went on to my house. They come to his house and got him out of bed, but he never would tell on me. That was back in '35. They took him and went over to the still. We was in a cave at that time. They took the two stills and him and headed for Cape Girardeau. I went down the next day and got him out on bond and they had his trial. They fined him a hundred dollars and ninety days in jail. I told him I was taking the hard part of it. I paid the fine and he just had to lay out the jail sentence!"

Art thinks there was probably more whiskey made during prohibition (1920–33) than ever before. During that period it was illegal to make or sell whiskey even if it was for strictly personal use. Today it is illegal to own a still. In spite of the ban on whiskey, there's always been a lively market, even during the Depression. In the Ozarks the drought of 1934 and '36 hurt people more than the Depression because most people raised their living on farms. Those who lived on the poor upland farms that wouldn't raise anything in the dry years had no way of making a living, or even growing enough to eat. With families to support, some turned to making whiskey.

"We worked hard. It was the way we made our living. We sold to anybody that had money. We hauled most of our whiskey to St. Louis. We had a man that come down hunting and fishing and we got to selling him a little bit of whiskey. He'd take five gallon back with him every time he was down. Finally he told us, 'Now, boys, if you folks'll haul it into St. Louis, I'll handle sixty gallons every two weeks.' Well, we had an old Studebaker car with a rumble seat in the back. We just took that seat out and threw it away. Three twenty-gallon kegs set in there just right. We'd put them in there and lock that down and go to St. Louis. The man had a bakery shop up there and he had a garage under it. We'd just drive up there, drive under the garage, and unload our whiskey, then we'd get our other barrels and come on back. 'Course, he give us a dollar extra on the gallon for delivering it into the city, which was a lot of money at that time. We sold it for three dollars a gallon down here where they took it from the keg. We made lots of good money. There was always a market for whiskey.

"People used to leave the moonshiners alone. Everyone minded his own business. People didn't want to cause you no trouble or nothing. They was trying to make a living and we was trying to make a living, so they'd just leave us alone."

The raids and arrests of many moonshiners indicate the strictness of some government officials. In the period between 1935 and 1973, at least 5,741 stills were seized by federal authorities in Missouri and Arkansas alone. The illegal making of whiskey used to be a much bigger problem than it is now. Over 2,000 of those stills were seized between 1935 and 1939. However, the punishments then were not as severe. Now the sentence is up to three years in prison. Some revenuers were mean and insulting. Grover Ballard told this story:

"There was a feller who killed a United States marshal when they first made this liquor and put a revenue on it. The revenue man was pretty mean and a lot of folks here didn't believe in all this regulation. They thought you could make all the whiskey you wanted, all you had to have was a bushel of corn to get you a gallon of whiskey.

"Well, this feller bought a still but never put it up, and whenever the government found it out, they put the revenuers on it. The feller was gone one day and he had a wild bunch of kids. These two revenue men come to his house—I guess they was smart ducks—and they asked where he was at. The kids told them their daddy was gone. They asked them when he'd come back and the wife told them she didn't know about what time that would be. So they took out these handcuffs and showed them to the kids and told them they'd have them on their daddy afore night. Then his wife got them some dinner and they made fun of the food. They left and went over to the neighbors. Of course, the feller come home, and it made him so damn mad, he just walked over there, throwed the door open, and said, "Halt, you son of a b———. I'll shoot you!" and killed one of the revenuers right there on the floor. And this other one, he run up the stairs. I seen this stairway.

Dad had told me all this when I was a boy, you see, so I went down there and hit was still there. I looked at it.

"The next day the feller give a boy five dollars to pilot him around through the woods to Linn Creek. There wasn't no railroads up here then and the revenuers come up here on them boats, or I guess they'd of killed him. Of course, the revenuers got after him and of course everybody was fer him. There wasn't no transportation like it is now. No telephones or nothing, so they brought a bunch of dogs down there—bloodhounds. And by God, they put them bloodhounds on that feller's track. He knowed that river, he lived right there on it, the Big Niangua. There's a big sycamore there that was holler, and it had washed up and was in the water. There was a big holler place in it where it stuck out of the water only you couldn't tell it. I don't know this to be a fact, but I guess it was so, they told it. The feller dived in under there. Then he crawled in there up to where he'd get air. They said them bloodhounds swum all around that. The revenuers thought he'd went down the river in a boat. Never did get him. No, they never did get him."

Although some revenuers were strict and hard-nosed, some were lenient. Here's a portion of some letters sent to a government official informing him of moonshining activity.

Hello Mr. Charlie Gray,

Will drop you a few lines to let you know, you are not doing your job in Jump Off, you can't even walk around the lakes out here unless you fine a stile. You let old J. D. McBee get away from you once, but I am going to give you the facts and if somthing ant done about the whiskey making in Jump Off I will let the head man know just how you run office.

Your friend
of Jump Off

Mr. Grey

There is a 55 or 56 model green ford car with liter top hauling whiskey through here one or two nites a week around 10pm.

A blond woman from Manchester either driving or is in the car. She is Edith Hodges & is boot legging in a white house a block behind the Fifth Wheel Rest in Manchester.

The license no is 41-4447 They go some where in White City & Get the load she and some man from Coffee Co.

The local law here wont try & catch them & we, the citizens are tired of it.

Art told us about a co-operative sheriff of his county. "I tell you there just wasn't very many people that lived around up there. It was wild country and everybody knew we was making whiskey, but they knowed we had a good rig, that we wasn't gonna poison nobody, that we were gonna make everybody happy, so they just let us go. Why, we had a sheriff down here at that time who knowed we was making whiskey, but hell, we'd give him five gallon a month. He wouldn't bother us. A bunch of good women would go down there and tell him we were making whiskey up there on the river. Well, he'd send us word, then he'd get four or five deputies down there and they'd come up there and, hell, nothing around. Then they'd come back and tell them, 'You was mistaken. There wasn't nobody making whiskey up there.' In two or three days we'd slip him a five-gallon keg. Come election time, we'd put out a lot of whiskey to get him elected again."

We heard of another man who made whiskey during the Depression. The revenuers came driving a car up the old dirt road looking for his house. They met him on the road and asked him, "We're looking for a man named Johnson. Do you know where he lives?" Johnson said he did, got in the car with them, and took them to his house. His wife was making a gooseberry pie and she greeted the men. She fed them pie and coffee while they visited. The still was upstairs. The revenuers asked Johnson if he made whiskey. On getting a negative answer the men left. They didn't think anyone that nice could be making moonshine!

Another time different officials came. This time Johnson had his still under the house. The trap door to get there was hidden by the iron cookstove that sat over it. Johnson had to move the stove to get to the still. He also kept some of the jars and supplies upstairs above the stove. There was a movable piece of ceiling above the stove to get to the jars. A revenuer saw that and stepped up to feel around with his hand. He didn't get up high enough to look in. The jars were back far enough so that he didn't feel them.

Standing by his still every day that it doesn't rain, all Art has to do is tend his fire occasionally, keep his pipe lit, and spin yarns.

"A good sister come down and told me it was a sin to make whiskey on Sunday. She said it should all be dumped in the river. Hell, I agreed with her. She went back up to the church, and do you know the first song she wanted to sing? 'Shall We Gather at the River.'

"One time there was an ant here when I was emptying the jug and he got a taste. He ran out of here and jumped on a snake and nearly choked it to death.

"Another time a squirrel got some of it. There was a tree with a knot on it just over there. That squirrel tried to run up it backwards. You ought to've seen that.

"We run the whiskey out into a gallon fruit jar. That's how I got this ridge across my nose—from drinking out of a fruit jar. When I used to make moonshine, I could always tell who drunk by the ridge across his nose. One time when I was in town I saw a man with a ridge across his nose and I asked him if he'd like to buy some good whiskey. He said he was a preacher and when I asked him about the ridge on his nose, he said he had just left his glasses at home.

"We have a barrel there. You can stoop over and smell the whiskey. There was an old gal the other day who stooped over smelling it and a damn butterfly flew in there. He got a little billful of that whiskey. He got to wobbling around as he leaves there and that gal stooped over to smell and that butterfly got up her dress tail and liked to tickled her to death.

"When I used to be a moonshiner, I had a batch ready to run off, but my hay needed to be put up. I went up to the still and I slipped a pint in my hip pocket. Every time I passed a tumblebug I give him a little drink. You know when I got back to the barn that night them tumblebugs had rolled every bit of that hay right down to the barn.

"Drink about half a pint of this whiskey and get bit by a snake and, hell, it'll be dead in thirty minutes."

To the other employees at Alley Spring, Art is jokingly known as "our dirty old man," but he makes excellent corn whiskey. Although we don't suggest you try this recipe, here are his directions.

"To make corn whiskey you need fifty pounds of corn chops, fifty pounds of sugar, and one package of yeast. You put this in a fifty-five-gallon wooden white oak barrel with forty gallons of water.

"You don't use much yeast, just a little bit to start it. That's just to rush up the process more. Now when it's right hot weather you really don't have to use the yeast. It'll go ahead and make without it. But when it's cool you need

Since it takes three days to ferment the corn, Art keeps three barrels going to have one ready each day.

the yeast to start it fermenting, then your grain and sugar'll pick it up. It'll work about three days, working that grain to the top while it's fermenting. When it gets all the alcyhol worked out of your sugar and grain, it'll quit working and the grain will all go to the bottom. Then it's ready to run through the still."

To keep the mash warm enough in the winter for it to ferment, Art and many other moonshiners used caves that kept an even temperature as well as providing running water and a hiding place. Sometimes the barrels were buried in sawdust for warmth. The fermented mash is like home brew. Some people like it and drink it without distilling out the alcohol.

To distill the alcohol, "You just dip the water offen your grain and you pour it in the cooker. You seal the top of the lid up there tight so you won't lose none of the steam. You seal it with dough—just flour and water—smear it around there and then, as the cooker heats up, it cooks that dough. Then if you get right drunk and need something to eat, why, you can jerk yourself off a piece of that dough and eat it.

"We most generally put a rag around the lid there first, then smear that dough on the rag and cook it there. When you get ready to take it off, you clip that rag and peel it right off. That is also used as a safety valve. When we first started making whiskey we used clay mud on top that formed a hard seal. Heck, once we blowed up the still over it. This dough, if you get too much fire, the pressure'll raise that and release the steam. It'll break the seal.

"Whiskey is the steam off the water in the cooker. The alcyhol is in the water—worked out of your grain and sugar. What you've got to do is put that in your still and make your alcyhol boil at a lower temperature than your water.

"We used to try to get ten or fifteen gallons of whiskey a day. It all depended on how dry our customers got. If we wanted to put in two shifts, we could cook out two batches a day. But it takes about eight hours to cook one batch through by the time you fire up and everything. If we needed more whiskey, why, we'd just dump that, put in another batch, and start in again. That put us up in the night, for someone had to stay to keep the fire.

"You build a fire under the cooker and keep it just right. If you let it get too much fire and go to boiling, your whiskey would look like muddy water —not clear like this. That's where you get your rotgut whiskey from. They say the still is puking when you got too much fire. It gets steam from water as well as from the alcyhol going through the worm.

"We use white oak wood. There's not no smoke in white oak if you take the bark off. You can have a fire and see no smoke at all, just heat a-coming up. You see, you make it back there in the woods, and you didn't want a lot of smoke coming up, for the revenue men might find you.

"Now when it heats up right, the alcyhol comes out of your water. It comes to the top as steam. The steam then goes down a copper tubing there that is thirty-five feet long, wound inside the barrel. That copper tube is called the worm. We keep cool water running over the worm so that as your hot steam

"The dough acts as a sealer so the steam from the alcyhol can't escape through the cracks. You can't make whiskey in the rain because the cool rain against the hot metal creates a vacuum in the still and causes it to cave in."

Art uses white oak wood because it creates very little smoke. Smoke was a dead giveaway to revenuers that moonshiners were in the woods.

Alcohol steam escapes from the still through the copper tubing "worm." As it travels down the worm and is cooled by the water, it condenses to liquid which is caught in gallon fruit jars. Art said, "You take a drink of that and you'll love your mother-in-law."

comes down through it your cold water condenses your steam back into liquid and that is your whiskey. Mine is 120 proof.

"Back when you was making out in the woods, there'd be a spring a-coming out here and 'course your holler runs downhill. You'd set your still below that spring, make a lead trough to bring the water down to the top of the barrel. Then let the water fill the barrel and run on out.

"There's about thirty gallons of water left in the still after the alcyhol was boiled out. When it quits running out at the bottom of the worm you'll know you're done with it. Just turn a faucet on the bottom of the still and run your water out.

"You can use your mash in the barrels three times to get alcyhol. Just add more water, sugar, and yeast and it'll take off again. Yellow corn makes the best whiskey. It has more alcyhol in it than white corn. When I get through with the grain, I take it home and feed the hogs—it just makes them happy. The other day I took a barrel up there and poured some in their trough. Them hogs, they just tore in and went to eating that. I went to the house and ate supper. When I come back out there they was so happy—I had an old male hog there, too. He had one of them gilts on his knee a-sitting out there a-trotting and whistling to her. But seriously, the grain's good for them.

Equipment for making moonshine includes three white oak barrels full of mash, the still or cooker, and the metal barrel that contains the worm. All metal used in making whiskey must be of copper—the alcohol in the mash will eat away any other metal, resulting in lead poisoning for those who drink it. A paddle is needed to stir the mash to aid fermentation.

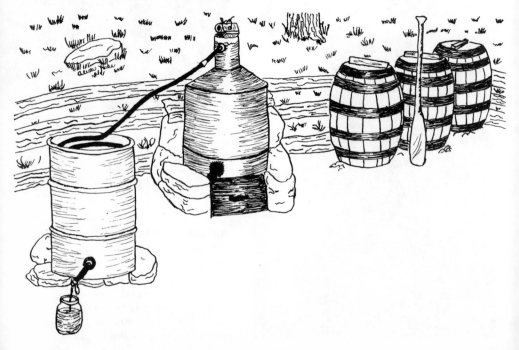

Yeah. They get to feeling mighty good. There's not a lot of alcyhol in that corn and they ain't a lot of food value to it either. But they still like it. It's soaked up, you know."

The equipment used in making whiskey should be all copper to prevent lead poisoning. Many people died or were paralyzed because the still, worm, and other metal parts weren't copper. Art thinks one reason the government started putting so many restrictions on whiskey making was because of the danger of poisoning.

"People used to make whiskey when they didn't have money to buy copper. They'd set up an old cream can or something and there was a lot of people who got killed and paralyzed and went blind over that lead poisoning. You've got to have everything copper if you're making whiskey. Alcyhol will pick up lead out of any kind of metal besides copper. Get everything copper, then you're safe."

Except for the copper still which he bought in 1921, the rest of the equipment is made or easily procured. The copper tubing comes in rolls and is wound to fit inside the metal drum. White oak whiskey barrels hold the fermenting mash and a glass fruit jar catches the whiskey as it comes out of the worm in spurts.

"Old-timers used to drink it as it came out, but whiskey should age from six months to seven or eight years. Hell, sometimes I let it age ten or fifteen minutes."

This Speech of Ours

One of the subtle changes in the modern Ozark way of life is the change in speech. This speech of ours is a mixture of Southern and Midland dialects, with characteristics of its own. The original settlers from the isolated rural regions of the southern Appalachian Mountains came from stock descended generations earlier from rural England and Scotland and were also semi-isolated in the Ozarks. Away from the mainstream of westward movement and the American melting pot of cultures for at least a hundred years, their descendants retained many characteristics of Elizabethan and older forms of English grammar, pronunciation, and vocabulary long after these forms were discarded elsewhere. It is still possible to hear old-timers say "hit" for "it," "et" for "ate," "rid" for "rode," and pronouncing wrestle/wrastle/, shut/shet/, and help/holp/. All these forms were once "correct" English.

The archaic English helps make an interesting dialect, and when combined with the country humor and imagination of the people, it became one of the most colorful in the United States. No longer isolated, the Ozarks speech is rapidly becoming standardized, but if an outsider listens closely, he still may hear the following terms and phrases.

Anti-goggling (crooked): He went anti-goggling across the field.

Big windy (tall tale): He sure can tell some big windies.

Bate (big quantity): He ate a whole bate of potatoes.

Own cousin (first cousin): She's my own cousin.

Double cousins (children of two brothers who married two sisters—cousins on both parents' sides)

Dilitary (lazy): He's the most dilitary person I've seen.

Do things up in brown rags (nice): My aunt really does things up in brown rags.

Down in the back (ailing): My father has been down in his back all week.

Ear bobs (earrings): I lost one of my ear bobs.

Evening (any time after 2 P.M.): Why don't you come by this evening about three-thirty?

Far piece (long way): It's a far piece up the road.

Flour gravy (thickened gravy): After the chicken was done, Mother would always make flour gravy from the grease left in the frying pan.

Gentleman cow, brute, male animal (bull): My grandmother never used the word "bull." She always said "gentleman cow."

Get your ears lowered (haircut): I see you've got your ears lowered.

Gussied up (dressed up): She got all gussied up for company.

Hoof it (walk): I missed my ride and had to hoof it home.

Hornswaggle (cheat): He could sure hornswaggle you out of anything.

Ink pen, tooth dentist, church house (redundant words): I left my ink pen at the tooth dentist in my hurry to get to the church house.

Jump the broomstick (get married): I hear tell Lucy and Bill jumped the broomstick.

Lolly-gagging (loafing): She was just lolly-gagging around.

Mess (serving): We always look forward to a mess of greens in springtime.

Mippety-nip (equal sharing): We all pitched in mippety-nip.

Narrow between the eyes (can't be trusted): Don't ask him. He's narrow between the eyes.

Norate (make public by word of mouth): Just as well put it in the paper as tell Aunt Marthie, because she norates everything.

On-common (not usual): It was on-common good.

Passel (large number): He had a passel of kids.

Perkative (laxative): Sassafras tea makes a good perkative.

Pindling (weakling): She was a pindling child.

Play pretties (baby's toys): The baby lost his play pretty.

Proud (glad): I'm sure proud you could come.

Redd up (clean up): All the family had to help redd up the house for company.

Right smart (large amount): The house is a right smart piece from here.

Slaunchways (sideways or catty-cornered): The snake moved slaunchways across the yard and under the shed.

Snot rag (handkerchief): Use your snot rag.

Split the blanket (dissolve a marriage): I heard Sam and Alice split the blanket.

Study (think): He stood there and studied for a minute before he answered.

Swamp measles (dirty): The boys always seemed to have a case of swamp measles.

Take up books (begin studying): We took up books after the morning prayer.

Tetch (a little bit): He has just a tetch of rheumatiz.

Tetched (crazy), *Mite* (little): After the old man's wife died, everyone thought he was a mite tetched after being alone so long.

Takes after (resembles): He takes after his father.

Whenever (when): Whenever you leave, come get me.

Whip stitch (brief interval): My cousin visits me every whip stitch.

Work brittle (willing to work hard): She's more work brittle than I am.

Young'uns (children): You young'uns mind your manners.
You'uns (you all): You'uns come see us soon.

PRONUNCIATION

Mass media and education are major factors causing the Ozark speech, like other regional dialects, to disappear. The standard pronunciation and usage in motion pictures, radio, and television has had a leveling effect on all regional dialects. Schools also have a decided leveling effect on dialects. Native teachers now have advanced college degrees and many non-native teachers speak standard American English. Most teachers would be astonished if one of their pupils said, "I wouldn't use them/plau'wers/pliers to fix that/cam'ry/camera," and would try to "correct" the pronunciation and usage, even sometimes ridiculing the dialect.

However, many people are studying and preserving regional dialects because of the variety and interest they add to English. We think that different dialects are fascinating to hear, even though these differences sometimes lead to misunderstandings. One family, new to the Ozarks, received a phone call about giving their daughter a ride home.

"Are you'uns going to pick up your daughter?"

"No, Ewings aren't. We had planned to pick her up ourselves."

"Well, she said you'uns would pick her up."

"I don't know. There wasn't any plan about them doing it."

Another person at a drugstore counter wanted to make sure she was drinking from the right glass.

"Is this/yur'n/ your'n?"

"No, that's Coke."

Here are a few commonly used pronunciations found in the Ozarks:

Add *a* before a verb—a-shinin', a-rainin', a-skeered.
Change /ī/, long *i,* to the /ä/ sound in "car"—/fär/ fire, /tär/ tire, /wär/ wire, /här/ hire.
Add *h* sound on "it" and "overalls"—hit, overhalls.
Leave off endings—/pry/ prize.
Leave off beginning vowel sounds—/magine/ imagine, /lows/ allows.
/ĕ/, short *e* vowel sound is changed to /ĭ/, short *i*—/kĭttle/ kettle, /gĭt/ get, /pĭn/ pen.
Words ending in "ow" get the "er" sound—/holler/, /beller/, /feller/, /winder/, /yeller/.
Words ending in /à/ or /ə/ often pronounced /ē/—alfalfa alfalf/ē/, idea id/ē/, soda sod/ē/, Martha Marth/ē/.

Some individual words are pronounced among the Ozarkians as:

/agin/against
/argy/argue

/cheer/chair
/die' van/divan (meaning couch)
/dreen/drain
/fig' ger/figure
/fur' in ers/foreigners
/keer/care
/lack/like
/nar'ə/narrow
/new' mon ie/pneumonia
/pert' neer/pretty near
/pie' anna/piano
/rench/rinse
/sum' ers/somewheres
/thrashin'/threshing
/whur/where

Most of the differences in pronunciation are found in the vowel sounds. This characteristic tempted one newcomer to quip, "The Ozark people have dialectal constipation. They need a vowel movement."

PLURALS

Some words considered plural such as "molasses" and "cheese" use plural verbs and pronouns—(Them molasses run all over my plate so I can't catch them with my bread. Them cheese sure are good). Others add an *s* to the word and use as any plural—hairs (I washed my hairs), cabbages (I put out more cabbages this year than common), gravels (Dump them gravels in the mud hole), and baking powders (My mother never measured the baking powders when she made biscuits).

COMPARISONS

Our favorites of this speech of ours are the colorful, humorous, and imaginative figures of speech which are basically rural and nature-oriented. The similes and metaphors that make up the older and newly coined sayings sprinkled throughout the speech are vivid and descriptive. To say, "He looks like he's been chewing tobaccy and spitting agin the wind," certainly gives a more accurate picture than, "He's a mess." Expressions such as, "Well, if that don't beat a hen a-pecking," or "If that wouldn't take the warts off a toad," add vim, vigor, and laughter. If you listen closely you just might catch some unusual sayings.

To emphasize an insult, an exasperated person might say—

You're not worth a milk bucket under a bull.
You're worthless as tits on a boar.
I'll slap you bald-headed.

Don't look at me with those hog eyes.
If you don't straighten up, I'll cut your water off and take your meter out.
You ain't fitting to associate with the hogs.
What's time to a hog [when someone is late]?
You're so crooked you couldn't sleep in a round house.
If you ever become a bigger liar, you'll have to put on weight.
You don't have sense enough to pound sand in a rathole.
I'll turn you every way but loose [to a struggling child].
If you had a brain, you'd have it in your hand a-playing with it.

Even though some expressions are quite comical, there are those a person would rather not hear, that could be deflating to his ego. A person would much rather hear, "He's as handy as a pocket in a shirt," than—

He's so awkward he couldn't lead geese to water with a double rein.
If he didn't have so much turned under, he'd be taller on top.
I'll dance at your wedding in a pig trough.
She's as ugly as a mud fence after a rain.
He's so ugly he has to sneak up on a glass of water to get a drink.
He's so ugly he has to slap himself to sleep.
He's still wet behind the ears [immature and inexperienced].
She's so bowlegged she couldn't pen a pig in a ditch.
He could talk your arm off, then curse you for being crippled.
She could talk the leg off a chair.
Her tongue wags at both ends.
She was so scared her eyes stuck out so far you could knock them off without touching her head.
His eyes stuck out so far you could rope them with a grapevine.
Her hair is as fine as frog's hair.
He's as tight as a frog's hind end.
She's heavier than a ton of lard in a molasses can.
He's mad enough to chew splinters.
He has no more chance than a grasshopper in a chicken house.
Get your hat before the sun cooks the sour water in your head.
Two heads are better than one even if one is a sheep's head.
She's one of the old blue hen's chicks [She's a character].

Interesting comparisons add to our speech, such as she "walks like an old hen with an egg broken inside her," and—

Big enough to go bear hunting with a switch.
No bigger than a minute.
So big you couldn't throw a fly line around her.
Black as the ace of spades.
Busy as a stump-tailed cow in fly time.
Busier than a one-armed paper hanger.
Busier than a two-tailed cat.

So cluttered you could lose a threshing machine in the drawer.
Comfortable as a snake's belly in an old wagon rut.
Contented as cows in a corn patch.
Cold as a well digger's hind end.
Colder than a witch's breast in a brass bra on a freezing day in January.
Colder than an old maid in December.
Cooler than the center of a cucumber.
Dry as a powder house [thirsty].
Duller than a widder woman's ax.
So dull it wouldn't cut hot butter.
Freckled as a turkey egg.
Full as a tick.
So full you could crack a tick on his belly.
Green as a gourd.
Grinning like a skunk eating cabbage.
Happy as a hog in a wallow.
Happier than a dog in a meat-packing house.
Just a hoot and a holler down the hill.
Hot as loving in August.
Hot as a billy goat in a pepper patch.
Hungry enough to eat buzzard's bait.
Jumpier than a truckload of starving kangaroos.
Last as long as a paper shirt in a bear fight.
Too lazy to say sooey if the hogs was eating him up.
Long as a month of Sundays.
So low I'd have to have a stepladder to kick a duck in the hiney.
Low as a snake's belly in a wagon rut.
Lower than a dog's belly.
Nervous as a porcupine in a balloon factory.
Nervous as a June bride in a feather bed.
So poor he couldn't buy hay for a nightmare.
The ground is so poor they couldn't raise a row with a pitchfork.
Redder than a turkey's rump in pokeberry time.
Country so rough if you got sick and the weather's bad, they'd just have to
   let you die and haul you out when it faired up.
Skinny as a plucked chicken.
Slick as a wax snake on a marble floor.
Slick as snot on a doorknob.
Slow as the seven-year itch, seven years behind scratching.
Kitchen so small you can't cuss a cat without getting hair in your mouth.
Steady as a wart on a toad.
Strong enough to stink a dog off a gut wagon.
Thick as fiddlers in hell.
Glasses thicker than fruit jars.
So tight he'd skin a flea for its tallow.

That hen was so tough you couldn't stick a fork in her gravy.

Useless as a hog with a side saddle.

Walk like you had a cob between your legs.

There are expressions to fit every occasion, whether it calls for comments on life like, "The squeaky hinge gets the grease," or advice like, "You don't need that any more than a tomcat needs a marriage license," or—

Every tub must stand on its own bottom.

Poor people have poor ways.

There never was a lane so long that it didn't have a turning.

There's more than one way to kill a cat than by choking him on hot butter.

What crawls under your belly lands on your back.

That's life. If it isn't chickens, it's feathers.

I wish I was a rich man's dog and my owner didn't have any cattle [a life of ease].

When it comes to eating chicken, I'm the tall hog at the trough.

I'll be there if nothing breaks or comes untwisted.

I can't turn off the work like I used to.

I finished the job by main strength and awkwardness.

He'd complain even if you hanged him with a brand-new rope.

He's got the world by the tail with a downhill pull.

He takes to you like a hog after persimmons.

He's got money enough to burn a wet mule.

His eyes are too big for his stomach [took too much food on his plate].

She doesn't care if school keeps or not [uninterested in anything].

They eat high on the hog [eat well].

He didn't know me from Adam's off ox.

She sews with a hot needle and a galloping thread.

Thank you till you're better paid.

Quit hollering down the rain barrel [useless talking].

Don't start chopping till you've treed the coon [don't jump to conclusions].

You couldn't beat that with a switch [when congratulating someone].

You've got the saw by the wrong tree [telling a story wrong].

Call a spade a spade and dig with it.

That went over like a lead balloon.

It'll be a cold day in July when that happens [unlikely].

There'll be many a wet and dry day before . . . [a long time].

Where hoot owls roost with the chickens and women cut wood [very backwoods].

We use or have heard all these expressions. Really. We'd lie to you only if we couldn't tell you the truth several different ways.

Keeping Company...

Courting, sparking, keeping company, dating. No matter what words we use to describe this important time in our lives, the purpose, a hundred years ago as today, has not changed. It is the desire of each of us to choose a companion and build a home and life together.

During the past seventy-five years the process of courting a girl has changed greatly from what it used to be. The advent of the automobile shortened distances and made it possible to travel as far as necessary to date a girl, whereas earlier dating was restricted to as far as one could walk or ride horseback. More boys and girls attend high school and college today than before, and often meet one another there. The "electronic age" has fostered more pastimes for courting couples than our grandparents would have dreamed about. And most important, today's parents are much more lenient than yesterday's, giving the couples more freedom.

Until the age of fourteen to sixteen, boys usually showed very little interest in girls. In the one-room country school romance was seldom carried on because, after eighth grade, most boys and girls stopped going to school and devoted their full time to farming or housework. There were some couples who met at school, or were childhood sweethearts, and carried on courtship clear through to marriage, but they were the exception—not the rule.

Farming and housework were both hard, always needed to be done, and left little time for pleasure. As Ila Lamkins told us, "Just about most of the time was work and no play. We had to work if we ate. And everybody wanted to eat."

But farm life did leave room for *some* entertainment. Social gatherings were well publicized, and people caught up on their work to be sure not to miss these gatherings. A picnic, school, or church social was an excellent chance to meet girls and boys from surrounding farms.

"Everybody looked forward to the Fourth of July picnic," Ila said. "Then you saw people from other communities. Your parents would give you a quarter, you'd take off to the picnic, and you'd see people from other districts."

The Fourth of July picnic was a big event held every summer. The men would build a brush arbor. They would dig ice from the previous winter out of its sawdust storage and wash it off before putting it into tubs for lemonade or using it to make ice cream. Each sold for a nickel. People would meet there to enjoy themselves until the evening chores at home called them back.

Girls would often make a special effort to attend a pie supper at a church or school, where the chance to meet boys was always good.

"About the only place you went you walked," Ila said. "You went to a pie supper with a beautifully decorated pie and had hopes of some young man buying your pie. He'd buy your pie and want to walk you home."

A good place to meet girls was at church. Boys would line up outside the church door and, as the girl walked out the door, a boy would ask her if he might walk her home. This placed the boy in an awkward position, for if the girl refused he faced embarrassment from his peers. Also, it took a lot of nerve to ask a girl for a walk with her parents, especially her father, standing nearby.

Dorothy McMicken remembers, "If we went to church together, we would sit beside each other. Otherwise we'd just go in and set down. Well, when we'd go out usually there's another girl with me. Then those boys would be lined up outside the door and they'd ask every girl that come out. The boys probably got quite a kick out of it. We could turn them down as fast as we wanted to if we didn't want to keep company with them. If we did, we walked home and stood at the gate a little while and that was that."

Young people also met at neighborhood parties. With the help of a willing parent, an afternoon could be set aside for a party, either Valentine's Day, Halloween, Christmas, birthday, or merely a get-together for the young people. Ashford and Ella Hough related their experiences. Ella told us, "We first met at a Valentine party. My older sister had a party for all the young people in the neighborhood. We had made paper valentines and cut them into halves. Then everybody would pick a valentine and match it with the other half to find your partner. I matched with Ashford. We also made our own refreshments—didn't have anything store-bought—and popped corn for popcorn balls."

"Now all of the games were good, clean fun," Ashford continued, "nothing rank or raw about them. It was all a nice clean sport and we all enjoyed ourselves and just had a good time. We played wink-em. The way you played, you lined chairs in a circle and a girl set in each chair with a boy behind her. One boy across the circle behind an empty chair would wink at a girl, and if her boy didn't grab her before she got out of her chair, he'd lose her. Now her sister had a big husky boy behind her, and he was as bashful as could be. So when she jumped, he grabbed at her and tore her waist off. She headed up the stairs right away!"

In many communities dancing parties were not acceptable gatherings for young women. Myrtle Hough said, "Then society sort of looked on dancing as an evil. We had play parties and had all kinds of play games and kissing games. But when I grew up, I went to some square dance parties, but I had to be careful because people sort of looked on it as evil—or girls that danced.

The boys weren't misjudged very much, but the majority of elderly people didn't like to think about their young ladies dancing. But it is lots of fun."

Ella said, "I'd have got a whipping if I'd have gone to a dance. The reason mostly was there were fairly rough crowds at dances. Really, they didn't hardly have any dances out in our neighborhood. Adjoining neighborhoods maybe, we heard about them, but our folks told us we weren't going. We were raised strict. We tried to mind the best we could. I guess sometimes we misbehaved. We couldn't get very far away from home in those days."

But in other neighborhoods where the dancing was held in homes by parents and the whiskey-toting crowd was excluded, young people would meet at dances. Dorothy met her husband at a dance at his parents' home. "In wintertime, and that was when most of the dances were held, I would go to my sister's, for my brother-in-law was a fiddler and I knew he would go—he and his wife. My folks never objected to me going up there and I went with them. And if I went with them, then I came back the same way. Sometimes we went to dances and Charles came and got me."

Having met a girl, the boy was sorely pressed to find time to court. Sunday afforded the best time, as families always set time off to attend church and Sunday school and visit neighbors, so only necessary chores and cooking were done. "Lots of times the young people didn't have any place to go, so they took their dates to church and Sunday school. And they would have singings and other such things," Ashford said.

Once at church, the boy usually sat beside the girl if he had accompanied her that day. Otherwise, the girls sat in one group and the boys in another until they became acquainted after church was over. But church occurred only once a month in most districts, and once a month was hardly enough. Sunday afternoon, boys would visit their young ladies at their homes.

"Why, they'd come to your house on Sunday afternoon and you just set around, either in the parlor or the kitchen, and visit until usually when the man of the house began to wind the clock, why, they always knew it was time to take off. You sat at home and did your sparking," Ila told us.

"He always come Sunday afternoons," Myrtle said. "But usually he would come in the morning and we'd walk down to Sunday school and we'd walk back. Then he'd go home and eat his dinner and then he'd come back in the afternoon. And of course now, you have to stop and think. There was just a crowd of young folks there all the time."

Brother Patterson remembers, "We weren't a social bunch. We didn't attend dances and parties. We'd go to picnics and county fairs. We'd have more fun there than anywhere. But the last year we planned for our wedding and then we planned how we was going to set up housekeeping and we learned what each liked. She tried to fix just what I wanted for breakfast. And after a while I learned to take just what she set in front of me. You grow into that, you know. You know each other."

Getting together often had still more limiting factors. Bad weather, poor roads, and long distances hampered visits. Dorothy lived in a place that was particularly hard to get to. "He would come on Sunday and Wednesday nights if the roads were passable. It was about six miles from here, but the roads were bad in the wintertime. It was just old flat ridge land and the bottom would just drop out. Now it was hard for a horse to pull through that. We'd go to Sunday school on horseback and them horses would just pull their feet out of that ole mud. You couldn't think about going over it in a Model T in the wintertime a large part of the time, so we figured on going horseback, if we could get there on horseback. Sometimes he just could get through with his Model T, if it was frozen up enough so he could. So we'd see each other Saturday night, Sunday, and Wednesday. It was just come to my house unless there was something to do like come to a dance or party or something like that. Of course there were revivals and things like that to do, too."

There remained the problem of getting the approval of the parents. A parent's yes or no was final and arguing usually resulted in even stiffer treatment.

"I was the only girl in my family," Mary Moore said. "I had three brothers and, if you had a daddy as cranky as mine, you wouldn't do no walking with a boy."

Until the family got to know the young man better, the couple would sometimes see each other without their knowledge. "Sometimes I'd get to walk home with her from church," Ashford said. "We got along pretty good that way. Of course, back to start with, she had a pretty wise old mother. She didn't know what a good fellow I was, so we just wasn't open and aboveboard. I have a few times turned home before I got quite all the way there with her. But they finally got to know me. During that period of time, why, we seen one another most every week. Once in a while we'd fail, but most every week we'd have a little chat sometime and that was about seven and a half or eight years before we got married.

"She wasn't sure, see. It wasn't that easy for me to wait that long, but her being younger, why, it was a little harder for her to make up her mind. No, she was raised in a family that was going, doing things in a big way in that day and age, and she went on to school after she got through with grade school. She went to Springfield and got an education and then she taught school.

"And we were up and going. We had to work at home to keep things going and we had to study at school to get our lessons, you see. So we were a busy bunch. But we enjoyed life. We got together, had parties and things of that sort. And we lived good lives. In fact, there was nothing much wild going on back in those days. It was pretty well civilized. The people were pretty well under control and they controlled their children pretty good. Of course, now and then there'd be one get out of step."

Dating away from home was mostly restricted by age. Girls especially were seldom allowed to date alone until sixteen or eighteen. A brother or other family member often accompanied the daughter as a chaperon. Instead, boys and girls would gather together in a big group and all would go out at the same time. Boys and girls paired off in couples, each with his or her special partner.

In spite of these restrictions, all the people we visited remembered what good times they had. Myrtle said, "I think every generation has its own fun. I can't think of any more fun to have than we all had as we were growing up and as we were dating. It was a lot of fun in those days, just the same as it's fun for young people today."

Lois Beard said, "We had lots of fun and we walked from my house to church and back—and we always had barrels of fun. There was, of course, things that were not so pleasant in dating in that day, but we had fun as much as you have today."

"Let me tell you it was fun," Elvie said. "We just had a lot of fun, but we didn't cover the whole state of Missouri or Laclede County a-running around. Lebanon was a long ways [twenty miles]."

Myrtle continued, "We had no way of going—only in a wagon or in a buggy. The Hough family had a buggy, but there were three boys they had to share it with, so most times one boy would get it one Sunday, another boy get it the next Sunday. But there wasn't many places to go in a buggy, only to town. We didn't do that. Elvie one time even before we were engaged took a wagonload of young folks to Lebanon to the fair. And we all had a ball. Just a dirt road here to town in a big old farm wagon."

The couples stayed out until the affairs were over, usually no later than nine or ten o'clock, as it was always necessary to get up early the next morning. After the night's date, the boy walked the girl to the gate where they had to part company. After a few last words, anywhere from a minute to half an hour, and a good night kiss, they separated until later.

If not out courting, then the group would congregate at someone's house to pass the time just being together, playing ball games, croquet, or singing.

"When we had a group together on Sunday afternoon we played croquet in the summertime," Lois said. "We sat around the old organ or the old piano in the wintertime a lot. We had lots of group singing. And we had ball games. The boys used to have cob fights—you know, throw corncobs at each other. The girls would be at the house getting popcorn or homemade candy ready and the boys would get out and have a cob fight. Never did have one but someone got their pants tore off them. They'd start to jump a fence or start running around the barn and get hung up on a nail somewhere. And when they came in someone had to hunt up a pair of britches."

Very few people owned cars in the Ozarks until the 1920s, so the only two methods of transportation were either on foot or by horses. "I walked many miles," Ashford said. "That's what made me so strong. I got in good exercise, see. And I built up a good healthy man out of me."

Horseback riding was one of the activities left open to courting couples. They often took advantage of it providing that they had the horses. Sometimes they rode work horses or even mules bareback if saddle horses were not available.

"We would go horseback riding," Ila said. "Most of the time they'd come after you to go somewhere on a horse. The girl would ride in the saddle and the boy friend would ride behind. If they had a real nice saddle horse back then, it was as if you have a new Lincoln car now. And if you had a fat horse, it was really something."

Most of the women we talked with rode astride in special divided riding skirts. Mary, being a few years older than the others, said "I rode sidesaddle. It was red velvet on top and good leather in it. You know, we didn't have many places to go and, when we was going together, there wasn't much to it. I went a-horseback. I had a nice saddle and a riding skirt. I rode many a horse."

Myrtle had a near-serious accident while riding horseback on a date. "I'll tell you one thing that was really funny. There was about six or eight couples of us going to the McBride church. A revival meeting was going on, so we all went horseback. Everybody had their own horse. Elvie brought me a horse to ride. I rode straddle saddle. There was a road went back behind our farm down this way and straight to McBride church, which is about three miles from here. And as my horse went under a limb, it caught me right by my neck here and I just went back off of the horse clear off on the ground! But we had fun that night. They all accused Elvie of trying to break my neck!"

Occasionally a buggy or hack was obtainable and the use of one was thought to be a royal treat, especially in winter when the cold weather was offset by a heavy lap robe. Also, it was "necessary" to sit closer together to stay warm, making winter a favorable time to court.

Elva and Myrtle Hough in 1916 at the time of their courtship.

Courting in a buggy had its advantages. No one was in a hurry and the horses knew the way home.

"We went in a buggy and, you know, we couldn't set four in a seat," Lois said. "I was always the little one that always had to set on someone's lap. It was much more fun than a car. And the team was always gentle. You just tied the lines together and threw them over the dashboard. We wasn't in a hurry to get someplace and it wasn't taking a lot of expense." The best thing about a horse was that he knew the way home, freeing both the driver's hands!

Winter, and the snow, brought sports and other dating opportunities. With the work at home done, the group would build a big bonfire and the young people skated on frozen ponds, pausing from time to time to warm up before continuing. They sledded on snowy hillsides on handmade wooden sleds, built snowmen, and had snowball fights.

Whether horseback riding, wrapped up on a buggy ride, or sledding, the young people wished to look their best. Their appearance was just as important then as now. Even without the many beauty aids we have now, girls and boys still managed to primp up for the date. Girls used hair wavers and curling irons, which were heated by placing them in the chimney of a kerosene lamp until they were "hot enough to fry spit." Any hotter would burn the hair. Then the girls applied them to their hair to get the right wave or curl. If curling irons were not at hand, girls would cut tin strips from a tin can, roll paper around them to protect the hair, and then roll hair around

Girls often used a waving iron (top) or curling iron (bottom) to curl their hair.

Diana Foreman demonstrates the use of the waver while the curler heats in the lamp chimney.

that. It was difficult to sleep with these in the hair, but they achieved the wanted effect. The girls, wanting their shoes to be clean and shiny for church, often walked barefoot to church, putting on their shoes just before getting there.

Since face powder and rouge were scarce, girls often bought a chalk powder to use as a foundation. Another cosmetic was made from the leaves of the wild tansy plant. Girls endeavored to keep their faces and arms white and wanted to remove or cover up a tan. The tansy leaves, which are large and fernlike, were crushed and mixed with buttermilk, then applied to the face and arms, bleaching the skin white.

Boys didn't fix up as much as the ladies, but every boy had his hair cut and combed in a certain way. Both usually dressed in their "Sunday best," a suit or dress saved for special occasions.

The age of courtship varied greatly, for girls from fifteen to twenty, for boys anywhere from sixteen to twenty-two. Many times boys would be several years older than the girls, and parents were reluctant to trust a daughter with an "older" boy. Again, it fell upon the boy to impress her parents favorably. With the very few opportunities open for courting, it sometimes took months or even years to please parents.

After the couple began serious courting, they had to make very sure they were right for each other. Marriage was a very serious thing, and divorce was scorned almost as a sin. Therefore many couples dated from six months to a year.

"When you were picking your partner you didn't have many to choose from," Ila said. "It wasn't like it is now. And you didn't take as long as they do now. I think it was more serious than now. And you had to kinda spark the old folks, too. Because you always had to ask the parents for permission. I guess now there's not much of that goes on."

The young man first had to ask the girl to marry him and did not always ask simply, "Will you marry me?"

Myrtle said, "Now he never asked me outright to marry him. The first time he said anything he asked me if I wanted to peel tomatoes for him the rest of his life. You see, he likes tomatoes real well. Then later on at Christmas he gave me a birthstone ring. When he gave it to me he said, 'Now, when you promise to marry me, I'll replace this with a diamond.' That was the second time he ever did say anything about marriage. He didn't say, 'Will you marry me?' he said, 'I'll replace this with a diamond when you promise to marry me.' "

Lois told us that she and her future husband were in a buggy. "Cole said, 'Why don't you marry me?' And I said, 'Oh, I'm too young. Dad and Mother wouldn't let me marry now.' I was about seventeen. He said, 'Oh, you tell them I'm going to commit suicide.' And just as that was said, a neighbor stepped out from behind a tree. He'd heard every word of it. We was going right along top of the hill above his house and he'd come up a side road and stepped out from behind that tree. Now we weren't in a car. We were in a buggy and he could hear it all!"

If the boy was successful in asking the girl, his next task was to ask her parents. Again, this was a very awkward situation, for the boy was never quite sure how the parents felt.

"We had already decided we were getting married," Brother Patterson said, "but we still had to ask her parents. She was afraid to ask them, but I said we should just go ahead. The only problem with us getting married was that she was the organist at the Methodist Church and I was a young Baptist preacher. And I figured there might be some trouble since the Methodists would be losing their organ player. And while we were talking, her mother came in and I knew she suspected something. She said, 'You kids are kind of staying late tonight, aren't you?' And she—my wife—said, 'Mother, we're talking about getting married and we were just wondering what Dad's going to say.' Well, she told us to go ask him and we might be surprised. So I went on out to talk to her father, who was milking since it was evening. Anyway, I engaged him in a conversation until I run out of things to say. I finally asked him if he had any objections to me marrying his daughter. Well, he stopped milking, and he looked up at me and said, no, he didn't mind if we got married, and he said he had been expecting it. Well, I was so happy when I left I jumped over the rail fence in the yard."

After the young man was successful in winning the heart of his girl and gaining the blessing of her parents, there was still more to do. Before they could take their place as a new family in the community they had yet to take the final step—marriage.

Getting Hitched

When a team of horses were hitched to a wagon or plow, they knew they were expected to share equally in the responsibility of pulling the load. Though used humorously, the expression "getting hitched"—meaning married—is nevertheless an appropriate metaphor. Marriage meant that the young man and woman were binding themselves together to share in the load of a lifetime of responsibilities and labor to build a home, raise a family, and do their part in the community.

Carrying the comparison with the horses still further, they had been trained since early childhood so that they were ready and eager to take their places in the adult community.

WEDDING PREPARATIONS

Until recently the now prevalent tradition of the bride wearing white at the ceremony was seldom practiced in this area. Usually the bride would choose her favorite color or the color that was most attractive for her. The dresses were also practical because they were worn not only at the wedding but also to church and other dress-up socials.

Dorothy McMicken told us about the determination it took to shop for a special dress in a small rural town. "I wanted blue and blue was what I was going to have. I could find everything but blue, so I looked at Richland and Crocker. They kept showing me dresses and I said blue. And sure enough I got a pale blue, long-sleeved dress the length they wore them."

Although dresses were available at town stores in the early 1900s, buying them was a luxury most could not afford. Nor did many consider it. Most women chose to make or have someone make their wedding dresses.

Mary Moore was married in "a dress that was brown. It was really mixed as much blue as it was brown, trimmed in white silk. It was clear down to the bottom. It touched the floor in the back. They didn't wear none of them trains then in them days. Nothing like that. But they wore them down—clear down. My mother made it. We bought the material and she made it in a couple of days and then done her other work, too. There wasn't a lot of fancy work to it."

"My dress was a light blue taffeta," Lois Beard said. "It was beautiful. Of course, it had to be made. I never had a store-bought dress at that time. Mother didn't want to make it. She was not too good a hand to sew, she didn't think, so I rode horseback with my material down to my good friends Jim and Frances Davis. Frances was a good hand to sew. I stayed all day and she made my wedding dress. Now I'd say the length of it was about one half-way between my knee and ankle. It had a waistline cut separate and there was a panel of shadowed lace about eighteen inches wide on either side that flowed loose from the waistline. The shadowed lace was embroidered around the bottom. Then a tie belt tied in a bow in the back and the sleeves were sheer.

"Cole's suit was blue with a little bitty pin stripe. We had no flowers, not even a corsage nor boutonniere. We didn't dream of such a thing as going to town to buy flowers. It didn't enter our minds."

The man wore a suit, usually brown or blue. Mary said, "There wasn't no matching or nothing like that done. People didn't have money to do things like they do now."

"I wore a brown lady's suit and high-topped shoes," Myrtle Hough said. "It was brown, sort of brown and probably more of a beige than a brown, but it was brown tones. And a white blouse and a little cap that matched the suit. And white kid gloves. Elvie really was fixed up. He had a blue serge suit. He really looked nice."

Showers were not commonly given to the bride. "Of course we didn't have a shower," Lois said. "Back fifty-two years ago you never heard of a shower. But we had a few wedding presents—just a few. We had a kerosene lamp given to us. We didn't have any towels or sheets given us. I know we didn't have many things given to us—a dish or two, but no sets of dishes, no big elaborate things—a teakettle."

"I don't think anyone got invitations, so they wasn't expected to give," Dorothy said. "But if there was someone in the family like aunts or Charles's sister, she liked to do fancy work and she give us pillow slips and embroidered sheets. And the aunt gave us a bedspread and we got a dresser scarf and just things like that from close relatives and close friends. But as far as them being told so they felt like they should do it, why, they didn't.

"Sometimes I've heard a cow was given to a daughter when she got married, but it wasn't always done. Probably a farmer that was a little above average was the one that did that."

TYING THE KNOT

After the preparations were complete the ceremony would take place. There was no typical Ozark wedding, for they varied with tastes and community. Large church weddings such as we have today were virtually unheard of in rural areas. More often the couples were married in the pastor's home, their parents' home, or in the courthouse.

"Usually country folks got married then on Sunday or Saturday nights, usually around in the home," Brother Patterson said. "The minister, relatives, and everybody would go in. But in the towns and the larger places, occasionally there would be a church wedding."

"Charles and I were married at the pastor's home in Crocker," Dorothy said. "My brother was here from St. Louis, he and his girl friend [later his wife]. They wanted to be at the wedding, so we got married on Wednesday night at eight o'clock. We were without a church house at that time as a tornado had blown it away, but I doubt if we would have been married in the church. Usually marriages were performed either in the pastor's house or the pastor came to their house."

Ashford and Ella Hough were married in their pastor's home, but it wasn't as convenient. "I was twenty-two and he was twenty-eight when we got married," Ella said, "so we weren't kids any more. We went to Springfield and had our pastor marry us in his home."

"We sneaked off!" Ashford teased. "Our pastor lived in Springfield, see. He had different churches he came to. Lebanon was one of his churches as was our little church in the country. He maybe preached different churches, but he preached here once a month."

"Our pastors would come down Saturday and be there Sunday and Sunday night," Ella explained. "Then go back Monday. They'd stay around with members of the church—different ones would invite them to come stay with them. The churches couldn't support a minister full time. They would come once a month and preach."

"We had half a dozen different preachers during that period of time—lived in Springfield," Ashford explained. "We didn't have many of our native preachers that preached in our church during those times we're talking about. It was mostly Springfield preachers that belonged to the conference, and time for conference annual meet was when they'd assign pastors to churches they were supposed to take care of. It works all right, but a preacher can't do you much good just coming down, preach, and go back. He doesn't have a chance to know who he's preaching to.

"We could do mean things and he wouldn't know about it. Now if he was living here, he'd catch up with us. That's the trouble with preachers today. They kind of keep checking on us! But we both were active in church before we were married. We were raised that way. We didn't fight it, we liked it—to be part of it. And since we got married we, of course, think more of one another and we try harder to live together. In fact, I had such a hard time getting married the first time, I don't want to take another chance."

Lois and Cole chose to have the preacher come to her father's home to perform the service. "The older four in our family married in a little over a year. I was the youngest of the four. We were about worn out with marriages, but I was the only one in the family that had a home wedding. My dad was always proud of that. He thought I had honored him by being married in the home he had provided. And I've always been proud that I did that."

Brother Patterson said, "I was married in the home of my wife's parents.

There's one oddity about it. She was the organist in the Methodist Church. And I was involved in the Baptist Sunday school in two different places. So usually the bridegroom leaves it up to the bride to select a pastor to perform the ceremony. She wanted her pastor to do it and I'm glad of it. He hesitated because he knew he was going to lose an organist and I was gaining one. So he protested the wedding. He didn't want us to get married!"

The county courthouse was also a fitting place for the entire service. The couple could get the license and the services of a minister for under five dollars.

"Our wedding was rather simple," Myrtle said. "Elvie came after me on Saturday morning and we went to town and we were married in the courthouse by the pastor of the First Methodist Church. And you could buy your license there. It cost two dollars to buy a license and two dollars for the preacher. I was scared stiff. I didn't know what was happening. Elvie walked in and give them two dollars and told them our names and our ages. I don't remember exactly what else he did. I was walking on air at that time. The recorder of deeds and his wife were friends of ours, so they stood up with us. None of our families were there."

The Lamkins also went before the judge. "You didn't see these big weddings like you go through now, because you did well to get a wedding dress," Ila said. "Most people—I said most people—went before a judge because I guess it was more simple. Most of the friends I know did. You'd go to the courthouse. You'd go get your license and go in to the judge, you had two witnesses and the judge would marry you. Then you'd go back home and live with your folks for about a year until you got able to get you a place to go to. We didn't have a new house waiting for us then."

Some women had engagement and wedding rings, but there was no general practice. Most usually had a plain gold wedding band. Mary had a solid gold ring. Only in recent times have the man and wife both had rings. Though Brother Patterson has performed many marriages, he doesn't much care for double-ring ceremonies. "Now I tell you one thing, it'll be a long time till I get used to the double-ring ceremony. It's divided. First is, 'I take thee, June, to be my lawful wife,' and then she says, 'I take thee to be my lawful wedded husband.' And then they take their vows in that ceremonial. When that's over we enter the double-ring ceremony. The bridesmaid has the bride's ring and she gives it to me. And then I make that remark about the emblem and the significance of its bond being endless. And then I give it to her and she puts it on his finger and repeats after me, 'With this ring I thee wed in the name of the Father, Son, and Holy Ghost.' It's the bridegroom that has her ring and then he give it to the other man and he gives it to the groom—no, gives it to her and she—I don't know! But it was quite a ceremony.

"After the ceremony, later on when we were associated with churches and church weddings, we had receptions, but usually it was in the home in most cases. The family and relatives and the neighbors would come in and they'd have a pretty good feast. Then the ceremony after. But the reception and entertainments and things like that, back in those days of small towns and rural communities, wasn't much known about."

The people of German descent had some different customs. Emma Niewald remembers her wedding day.

"Our wedding day was on Sunday morning, December 11, 1910. We had a wonderful nice day. Our attendants are still living and August's brother Walter is now pastor of that same little church.

"Another brother, Emil, was the one we chose to do the inviting. He was given the list of the relatives, friends, and neighbors he was to invite. He wore his best dress hat and then went out to do the inviting. All those that he invited would give him a ribbon, and either they or he would pin it to his hat. He had quite a number of ribbons by the time all the people were invited and they were many colors and lengths. He then wore this hat on our wedding day with the ribbons. His horse also had a few ribbons on its bridle.

Emma and August Niewald on their wedding day.

"I believe we were the first couple to be married in our church, Freedom Lutheran Church. They would always have it in the homes, but August wanted to be married before the altar. The pastor walked down the aisle, then August and I, and then my cousin Dora, bridesmaid, and Walter, best man, came last. We walked in side by side, two and two. There were chairs set up in front of the altar where we sat all during the regular church service. The pastor based his sermon on the Wedding at Cana. Then, after the sermon, the wedding ceremony followed in German. The congregation sang the hymn, 'With the Lord Begin Thy Task, Jesus Will Direct It.'

"After the service all the invited guests went to my home, which was located about a two-mile journey near the Gasconade River. Emil riding his horse took the lead. We were all in buggies, wagons, or horseback. There were no cars.

"When we reached my home there was a nice dinner waiting for all of us. My parents had butchered a hog on Friday and a number of chickens. The hams were cooked in the big black kettle outside the evening before and were they good! The cake had been baked in a tube pan and then put on a nice cake stand.

"The next evening the choir was scheduled to practice for the Christmas season. After the practice they surprised us with a shivaree at Emil's home. A good crowd had gathered to make a lot of noise. Our relatives had made a lot of pies and cakes for all to enjoy."

The marriage in the older days was a very solid bond—in many ways stronger than today's. The vow "till death do us part" was almost always kept sacred. "It really was a disgrace for people who were divorced back in those days," Ila said. "I think people were more serious in those days. I think life was harder and they were serious about who they married and they were taught that when they married that was until death. That was one thing that was taught to me—to be very careful because when I married that was unto death. We really didn't have a whole lot of choice, but again we were careful."

"It seems like we have more divorce now than we did back then," Dorothy said. "I think there is more independence on the woman's part any more. She can work and she can make her way. Back then it was expected that the man work. The man provided. And now the woman is equal. Now she can say, 'Oh well, I don't have to take anything off of him because I can make my way.' I believe that's it. Like myself now, if I had been dissatisfied with Charles, I just wonder what I would have done. I didn't know a thing about working away from home. Now I just wonder what I would have done except go back to my parents. But if I was young now, I'd do just like others do, perhaps. And most all of them has got good education now and they can go ahead and get a job if they're not happily married."

Long after the knot of marriage was tied, the strength of the bonds still endures. "Now she's been dead fifteen years," Brother Patterson said. "I don't know, but my daughters when they come home notice that many of the articles, particularly in the kitchen and around the place, is just like she left them. This divan was just like that and so was the desk. Many things. She had a certain place in the cupboard in there for one thing and I keep it that way. You know we were together forty-eight years after we married. And you get used to somebody that long."

AFTER THE WEDDING

After the wedding there wasn't very often a honeymoon. "Our honeymoon started about five o'clock that evening," Brother Patterson continued. "We got in the buggy and thought we was going on a trip. I mean just drive around the country for two or three hours—that's about as far as our plans went. We didn't make Niagara Falls or New York City or any long trips, because the travel conveniences weren't what they are now. We traveled perhaps a mile and a half and the old horse was fighting nit flies and horseflies so I couldn't turn the lines loose, and I said, 'Oh shucks, let's go home.' So we went down to the little house where we had fixed up to set up housekeeping. I went about my chores the next morning and she went about putting things straight and fixing up her house. That's all the honeymoon we had, but you know, that was because of circumstances and finances and motor traveling. We hadn't thought about those other places. We just grew up there in those communities where the church was about the only thing in the social connections."

Instead of a honeymoon more often the family had a large dinner for the newlyweds right after the ceremony. Lois related, "They had a supper for us —Mother and Dad did—real nice, elegant at that day and time. But there was no show, fanfare, or nothing fancy like we have today.

"We were married at my father's home on Sunday afternoon at four o'clock. We had the supper at six. We spent the night there at my dad's. And the next morning we got up it was snowing and was cold as the blazes. We got in the buggy and went to his parents for the infare dinner. That was the one, like for instance when they have a wedding rehearsal, the parents of the groom has a supper or something for the wedding party. That's in the same order as the infare dinner, only the cousins and neighbors or who all is invited come in and the women help fix an old hen and noddles, dumplings or a baked chicken or something. They helped the parents prepare the dinner. And they have that big feed for the groom and his bride in their home."

After the dinner, depending on the circumstances, the couple would spend the night with their parents or in their new home. Dorothy said, "I don't recall anybody going on a honeymoon. Usually they didn't have any more than they needed to set up housekeeping with and I know that was the way with my sister that lived a half a mile from me. She and her husband got married the twenty-fourth of December and they went in a buggy up to the Christian preacher just about a mile from our home to get married. And she kept saying as she put up the Christmas decorations, 'I've got to quit.' She had her

hair all done up in curlers. She said, 'I'm going to have to quit after a while,
for I'm getting married.' She kept telling us and we didn't believe she meant
it. But sure enough she did, and she had beaded a beautiful dress for her
wedding. Put in so much work on that beaded dress. So they had to go up
there in a buggy, and the snow, I guess, was clear up there by the step of the
buggy. They went to his folks that night.

"Then the next night they set at the table and figured out how much everything was going to cost. They put down the necessary things to go to
housekeeping with. And it's surprising how many things it would take. It cost
quite a little bit back then to start out. They started out with as little as they
could possibly get by on. They could add to it as they went along."

Lois recalls the first home she and Cole moved into. "We had about fifty-
two dollars and a half worth of furnishings for that house. We had a dresser
in the front room with two beds and we had six chairs that went with the
dining table we'd bought. He bought the dining table at a sale and paid two
dollars and a half for it! And a little four-cap cookstove. Did you ever see
one? It was a little bitty narrow thing that sets up on legs with a little oven
door on either side. It's cute. But anyway, that's the kind of stove I had and
it set up on bricks, it was so short. He'd made a cook table and I had a set of
plates and a set of teacups and saucers and one platter. Then we got a milk
bucket or two and a milk strainer and a crock to put our milk in.

"We had everything pretty handy for a beginner's life. There wasn't much
in that little house—bare floors painted brown. The beds were in the front
room, for that's all the room we had. Just a bed on either side. They were
iron—I still have them—with a round post that went all the way over with
little gold spots on them. I had made bedspreads just alike and appliquéd
them all the way around out of unbleached muslin. And they had a pillow
sham that went across. And I had maybe a couple pictures on the wall that
he had bought. And the old log house was papered with building paper that
was tacked on and then we put the wallpaper on that. We had a few pots and
pans. We got along.

"We had plenty of meat hanging in the smokehouse and fruit upstairs by
the flue where it would keep warm in the wintertime. It was a pretty good
way to start out. Not too many people had anything any better."

SHIVAREE

Even after the marriage vows and settling in their new home, no couple felt
they were completely married until they had been officially greeted with a
shivaree. A few nights after the marriage their neighbors and friends, banging
pots and pans and firing shotguns, would startle them out of bed.

"Oh, they done everything that could be done," Mary said. "But then, I'll
tell you what they didn't do. They never tore up nothing. But you'd think
they was going to. They did it just because you was friends. If one failed to

have a shivaree it was someone wasn't very well thought of. If they didn't have no shivaree made it kind of bad."

Lois and Cole had a big shivaree. "Oh, my goodness, yes, we had a shivaree. But they shivareed us before we got in our own home. They shivareed us the second night after we were married. They picked up over a hundred shotguns shells in the yard the next morning.

"People did it just to bug you. It was just as normal to shivaree a new married couple then as it is for them to go on a honeymoon now. That was just your greeting in the community. And you better have your candy and cigars ready, too, because you sure got to go to the pond. They'd put you in the creek or the pond or something.

"But we had two or three boxes of candy and a box of cigars ready and we just had a good time when that group came into the house. Why, my goodness, the house was so crowded you couldn't see.

"They had circle saws. Did you ever see a circle saw? A saw that's about so big around with teeth all the way around it and they'd take it off of the saw rig and someone carries it on a pole and beats it from both sides. It rings just like two or three bells being rung. It makes a terrible noise. They had all kinds of horns like fox horns. They had them a-blowing from every corner and all that beating and a-pounding and someone hitting the house. Oh, it sounded like they were going to tear the place down.

"We knew it was a-coming," Lois continued, "because we always knew they always did that. I'd been in a few shivarees, but I don't care for them really. I really like a greeting all right when new people move into the neighborhood or a marriage, but I don't like all that noise. It just seems like it's carrying it too far. I'd rather just go down and sit down in a yard and sing awhile. I like that so much better than shivarees because I have seen a few dangerous things at a shivaree. I've seen them shoot the corner of the house through and I have known a few people getting hurt. I sort of have a fear on it. So I'll stay away from a shivaree."

No couple was immune to a shivaree because of age. Brother Patterson told us of one incident. "I'll tell you there were lots of them back then there in those hills. Shivarees were peculiar to certain communities and they shivareed any age.

"My father married a couple one time that was past fifty, maybe sixty. We all got our washtubs and dinner bells and cowbells and horns. One of the boys brought an old shotgun. He'd shoot it in the air, you know. We gathered at their house, and they didn't know we were coming. We slipped around and surrounded the house—just a two-room building. And when the racket started, that lady let out a yell you could have heard—well, it was like a wildcat down in the swamp. But he came out and tried to get us to leave, but of course in that case we had to go through the whole rigamarole. Somebody got a rail and we grabbed him by the arm, put him astraddle of the rail, and hauled him around the house. That old lady, I felt so sorry for her. She was standing in the door just a-crying. She thought we was going to kill her hubby."

Myrtle and Elvie's shivaree was very unusual. "Oh, I was teaching school," Myrtle recalled. "We were having a pie supper when the young folks in the neighborhood decided they were going to shivaree us. And they really did take that house down! They just shot guns and done everything you could think of. They rang bells and yelled and shouted round about the school-house. Nearly broke the pie supper up. We were having a program—a good program. I had about sixty pupils in the school. It was a night. So these friends of ours and the neighborhood and everybody else you could think of and where I'd taught school for three or four years, they all just really gave us a shivaree. They really got a little bit too rough. We couldn't treat them because the directors of the school didn't like it for making noise at the schoolhouse. They got angry and got out and arrested some of the boys and made them pay a fine for disturbing the peace. Nobody meant anything by it, but you know how young folks are."

It must have been quite a scare to an Eastern bride not accustomed to the ways of her new community. That factor certainly added to the fun and enjoyment of the neighbors participating. Elvie had helped in many shivarees at home. "We'd just get a crowd together and organize. Ones would bring certain things to make racket with—shotguns and bells and horns, them big old saws, circular saws you cut wood with. Couple of fellows'd carry it, put a stick through the eye, you know. They'd carry it and a couple people behind would just pound that thing. Then they'd treat cigars and candy. If they didn't treat you it was just too bad. Take him to the closest mudhole and put him in it. Some of them did ride him on a rail. They just really put him on a rail. Someone would hold him up on one side of it. One man holding on each end of the rail and the one on the rail jumping around. Oh, they wouldn't carry them too far, just to introduce them to it."

"You can imagine how uncomfortable it'd be, someone carrying you half a mile on nothing but a rail," Myrtle added. "They didn't do anything to the bride. Just the groom. They left the bride a-weeping and a-wailing, afraid they was going to kill him.

"I remember when a couple lived down in the little house on the creek," Myrtle continued. "We shivareed them one night. But they weren't expecting it and they didn't have any treat for us. But they wasn't too many of us. There's about a dozen and a half or two dozen of us. And we just made . . . bells, guns, horns. We didn't do anything to the groom that time. We just felt sorry for him and let him go back in the house, for it was a cold, cold night. Snow was on the ground. That would probably have made him sick if they'd took him out and dumped him or rolled him in the snow."

BEGINNING A NEW LIFE

Though shivarees were fun for most, they were also the neighborhood's way of welcoming the new couple into the community and wishing them well. The new couple immediately got down to the serious business of setting up housekeeping, making a living, and learning to live together.

Girls often had hope chests of linens and bedding, but right away they worked together setting up for housekeeping. Dorothy found out early the kind of man she'd married. "I never had a shower, or a hope chest, either. I had some things in a trunk. The day after we were moved in—we lived with his folks—I went home and got my trunk. We started back over here and we had three flat tires in that old Model T. Every time he had to unload to get the car tools to fix that flat. That's when I knew Charles was pretty wonderful. He never said one bad word."

"We didn't have showers," Myrtle said. "So you young folks can be so thankful. In this day and time we always give our young folks showers. We just began to buy. I had what we now call a hope chest. It was just a big old trunk. I had it full of this and that and the other—linens and so on. But that's all we had."

Like the McMickens, the Lamkins also stayed with his parents for a while. "There wasn't jobs then," Ila said. "Only farm jobs back in the country. And what you usually did, why, you just farmed, and pretty soon you'd maybe get a house somewhere, and you'd work somewhere on a farm. My goodness, and about the first time you was able to afford a cow and some pigs you thought you was really doing good. It was very simple compared to what it is now."

Some couples were fortunate enough to have a place of their own to move to. Ashford said, "We was living on a farm. I had a farm at the time and we were farmers. But we were broke most of the time and she taught school two years to give us something to eat! Back in those days we didn't have lots of money. But we lived good and she was a good cook. I was really a fair provider. I batched for two years on this farm before we were married, so you can see why I was beginning to get anxious. We had a house to live in. It was on the farm when I got it. It was just a place to live, is what you'd call it. An humble home."

But all agreed life was good. "Nobody knew anything different" is the comment we heard constantly when talking about earlier times. Everyone had the necessary shelter, no one went hungry, and they had love for each other, supported by the security of their relatives and neighbors all around them.

When Myrtle asked us, "Aren't you glad you're living in this day and time?" Danny, her grandson, answered hesitantly and without much conviction, "I guess."

Ketchin' Babies

When hospitals were non-existent in the hills, when mothers had their babies at home, and when doctors arrived late or were not available, expectant mothers and their nervous husbands knew they could depend on the local granny woman or midwife, who knew just what to do because she specialized in ketchin'—delivering—babies.

DOCTORS

In the early 1900s and before, it was very hard for expectant mothers to get to a doctor's office, and thus it was much easier for the doctors who had the best horses or the first cars to go to the homes, where the mothers and babies would be cared for by the family or friends.

The doctor often traveled by horseback, using pintos because they could stand almost anything and they were fast, too. Some preferred fox trotters because of their comfortable mile-eating gait. It was less tiring for the doctor to ride in a vehicle like a buckboard wagon pulled by a team of horses. If he could afford it, the doctor sometimes had a driver and a man who could care for one team of horses while the others were out, for confinement cases often meant he was gone all night. Belle Farthing, the widow of a doctor who began practicing in the early 1900s at Ozark, Missouri, told us, "His conveyance to practice was a buckboard and a horse blind in one eye."

If the doctor had enough money he would have a more comfortable horse-drawn buggy. The best buggies were closed in with curtains that buttoned on the side, but even these curtains were unable to keep out chilling winter winds.

Often the family could not pay the doctor in cash, though people were generous about giving food and other items he needed. Belle told us, "Oh, they didn't pay very good then. They were always good to bring to us what they had. If they had potatoes or sorghum or hams, they'd help out that way. I believe people even then tried to do the very best they could. They knew they had to have a doctor and they wanted to be as good to him as they possibly could so that he'd come again. One couple began saving pennies to pay the doctor for delivering a baby. One day he went to their home and when he came home he handed me a wrapped half-gallon jar of pennies. It took us two or three days to get those counted and wrapped. It was twenty dollars. The only way we got along was by being frugal."

Infection and death were constant threats to mothers and babies. The death rate was higher than now both in and out of hospitals: More women died after birth in the unsanitary, poorly staffed and operated hospitals that did exist than died in their homes. As roads improved and automobiles became more widely used, some doctors managed their own small hospitals where they could care for more patients. Gradually civic hospitals staffed with trained people working in sanitary conditions were built in some of the larger towns and cities in the Ozarks. But it was not until the 1930s and '40s that women in the Ozarks used hospitals for delivering babies as a matter of course.

GRANNY WOMEN AND MIDWIVES

Women who wished to have their babies at home or were confinement cases were handled by doctors with the help of neighborhood women or by the midwives themselves.

Doctors and mothers all found the midwife very helpful. Country doctors rarely had nurses to help them, so they relied on this woman, and the expectant mother trusted her experienced friend and knew that she was in good hands, even if the doctor could not make it in time. The woman would take care of the baby after it was born while the doctor took care of the mother.

Though it is difficult to distinguish between them, the women who helped out might be classified in three ways: neighborhood women who had a natural talent and willingness to help in any sort of sickness, including confinement cases, but had no special training; granny women who specialized only in ketchin' babies, and gained their knowledge by experience; and midwives, who also specialized in baby delivery, but received some special training from doctors or schooling. The terms "granny woman" and "midwife," however, are often synonymous.

Every community had such women. Annie Fike married into a family where the women were midwives, so because of her family connections and her own willingness to help out if needed, she helped women in her community when their time was close at hand. She recalled helping with several births. "I never was any place where we didn't have a good doctor. Usually we had two or three ladies who knew what they were doing. It was their job to take the baby and wash it and dress it."

Anna Wormsley was inspired to become a nurse because of her admiration for her great-aunt Annie Roper, who helped her neighbors any time she could. Anna wrote us suggesting we feature these women who dedicated their lives to nursing others. She wrote, "I was very young when Aunt Annie Roper did this kind of work. One of her last cases was the birth of my little brother in 1938. There was lots of preparation months before his birth with all the handmade baby things that was called the layette. There were dozens of diapers, little shirts, gowns, dresses, rompers, crocheted sweaters, bootees, and caps. I remember something in the layette that is not used now—they were made of flannel and were called bellybands and had to be very snugly kept around the baby's middle for about the first month to prevent an umbilical hernia.

"Aunt Annie came to stay with us about a week before the 'stork' was due. As with all of her other confinement cases she sort of took charge of the household until the mother was finished with the delivery and able to be up and around again. Mama hadn't been allowed to do heavy lifting for months, and she was not supposed to put her hands in cold water, for that would dry up her milk. She was supposed to be calm and serene so that the baby would not be marked and would be a good healthy baby. On that day that they knew the baby was going to arrive, my brother and I were sent over to Aunt Lola's, but we knew that there was lots of hustle and bustle about something. In those days all of the things connected with childbirth were kept big secrets. When a woman was 'in the family way,' nobody knew about it except very close family and intimate friends. And as soon as she started to 'show' the expectant mother went into seclusion in her home and was not seen in public until after the baby was born.

"That must have been quite an exciting day for my parents, for baby brother decided not to wait for the doctor to arrive. He was about an hour old when old 'Doc' Farthing of Ozark got there. He examined the baby and pronounced him fit. Of course, Aunt Annie had handled the delivery, as I am sure she had done other times before, for sometimes babies do get in a hurry to be born, even now. I learned after I became a registered nurse that she had even been prepared, just in case, with a supply of linen thread with which to tie the umbilical cord and a pair of clean silver scissors with which to cut it. She also knew just how to take care of the mother."

Much of the time these women were not paid, or were given produce in payment. Annie Roper's sister-in-law, Gertrude Roper, said, "They would pay her some, but most of it was just give and take. You do for me this time and I'll do for you the next time. Sometimes she would be paid in foodstuff, garden fruit, or material for a new dress."

Annie Fike said, "I wasn't worth enough to think about paying me for anything. I just done it because they asked me. It made me proud."

Some families did not want a doctor in attendance at all. They believed that only another woman should deliver a baby. Other families could not afford a doctor or could not get one in time. In these cases they called on granny women or midwives who handled the complete delivery themselves.

Granny women had no particular technical background. Some could not even write. Their job was to go to the home, deliver the baby, care for him and the mother, care for the other children, cook for the family, do the washing, make the beds, and do all the other household chores while the mother was recuperating, a period of from nine to ten days.

The granny woman had to be a good organizer. Her own home and family had to make out by themselves while she was gone, so she would always have food prepared ahead of time for them, a cellar full of canned food, and everything in shape to be able to leave at a moment's notice. Her family was proud of her skill and grateful for the extra income she brought home. This was one of the few ways a married woman could earn outside income.

Today, though, it is illegal in the United States for a granny woman to deliver a baby for pay. In Missouri certification for granny midwives was abolished in 1958.

Women with special training are known as midwives. Mabel Stephens worked as a midwife under the supervision of doctors. She told us how she thought midwives were probably named. "The 'mid' meant midnight 'cause you'd have to be up all times of the night." She told us of a time when the doctor didn't arrive in time to deliver her own grandbaby. "The doctor came and said, 'I'll be back at nine o'clock.' My daughter had been sick about three days then. I said, 'It's not going to be that long.' 'Oh,' he said, 'it will.' I said, 'Oh no, it won't! Now, you don't wait till nine o'clock to come back here.' He said, 'Yeah, I'll be back at nine o'clock.' Seven o'clock the baby arrived!"

Midwives were trained by doctors or at schools. Their duties were much the same as the granny women with the same pay. Some were paid three dollars and some five, depending on the family they were helping and the economy. In the past the woman who wanted to become a midwife worked under a doctor who took her into homes where babies were expected. She could see him work and learn the techniques and knowledge she needed to work on her own. When the doctor thought she was ready, he would rely on her to deliver babies unassisted, and she could start her own practice. A few midwives had some nurse's training in schools.

Doctors claim the care provided by granny women and midwives was sometimes dangerous. Midwives did not have very effective tools, scales, or anesthesia, and could not transfuse blood. A breech birth usually meant trouble. Some babies bled to death because the natal cord was cut too short. Often the conditions of the birth were not sterile and sometimes caused infection or death for the baby or the mother. Prenatal care of the mother was usually lacking, for the midwife was not called until the time of birth. In addition, doctors also objected to many of the superstitions and home practices of the uneducated granny women.

Some believed that if you put an ax under the bed of the woman in labor, it would cut the pain. Some thought that the woman should not have a bath right after giving birth for several days. Various teas were prepared for the mother and baby. Pepper teas would induce labor pains and catnip tea would quiet the baby. We heard of another tea made of the white off the dropping of chickens which was used to quiet a baby. Another story told of using urine to wash out the mouths of babies who had sore mouths and throats. A dangerous practice was that of putting cow dung on the natal cord: it was thought to be a good dressing to stop bleeding, but often caused tetanus.

MOTHERS

The mothers had a hard time preparing for and having babies. Few practiced birth control then and it must have been frightening to a new wife to know she would probably have eight or ten children. Many girls reached their wedding nights with very little knowledge of reproduction. Just before marriage the mother would tell her daughter she could expect to have a child every two years until she was forty! So when she did become pregnant, knowing a helping neighbor was always near must have been a comfort to her. Annie Fike told us of a rather recent time when a neighbor meant a lot because outside help was cut off. "It was an awful stormy night. The creek was up. The husband had tried to go to Lebanon and couldn't cross the creek. He finally went to Grovespring after Doc Hough. But he was too late. I had the baby in its crib and asleep when he come. I didn't want to leave until Doc looked at the baby. So he went and examined it and said it was just all right. So he was."

Home conditions were not always the best for an expectant mother. Belle Farthing explained, "I would feel awfully sorry for lots of those people where they were having babies, because that was the best they could do. Sometimes you would go and see that some women had tried so hard to make preparations. Some of them didn't. They'd just let it come on with no preparation whatever. And the homes so often were just two rooms, so many of them with a lean-to maybe.

"But the thing I have thought of as much as anything—we had a case one night and I went with my husband. He wanted me to go to dress the babies, because he felt like I knew what to do with those children. They had two grown girls. The mother and this one girl had gowns that were made out of unbleached muslin, made gathered onto a yoke. They were clear down to the floor. The girl had on one and the mother had on one. The mother's baby was born. She had a hemorrhage and her gown had to be changed. She wasn't going to change it at first when the gown got so soiled, but she called the oldest girl in and said, 'Give me your gown, honey.' The girl took hers off and let her have it. It was pitiful, really."

In the winter the cold was a threat to women giving birth. Belle told of a time when a husband tried to keep his wife warm while she was in labor. "One night we went to a case. It was cold and the woman was in the bed, back in the corner of the room. The man was trying so hard to keep the room warm that he put too much wood in his old King heater. The room was lined or papered with heavy paper and it came up right around the flue and it got afire. And oh, he grabbed buckets of water and threw the water, and some of it would land on the woman."

Before her time was up the woman usually made preparations to keep things as sterile as possible. Some women had things all ready for the doctor or midwife. Clean sheets and extra cloths were sterilized in a hot oven for five minutes, or by running a very hot iron over them. They then covered the mattress or bed tick with several layers of newspaper and put the sterile sheet over that. The clean cloths were wrapped in newspaper and then stacked together. The cloths were made from clean rags, towels, or pillowcases.

All of the instruments used were boiled in a pan of water on the stove. When it was time for the baby to be born the midwife or doctor asked for a pan of boiling water. They would let it cool, then wash their hands in it so they would be clean. Dr. Ruth said, "The midwives usually got some clean towels or clean rags ready to use around the bed and they'd see to it the mother had a hot foot bath and her feet were clean."

After the baby was born the woman enjoyed a period of confinement, called lying-in. Everyone thought this quiet time was necessary to allow the organs to go back in place. The woman was kept very quiet in bed and not allowed to do any work for nine or ten days. The importance of lying flat in bed is evident even in some of the practices. Usually a feather bed is turned every day to fluff up feathers for more comfort, but granny women would not allow the feather bed of a new mother to be turned for ten days. Many times this period was the only vacation a mother ever had. Myrtle Hough still thinks that was a good idea. "I've had six babies and I stayed in bed every day until the tenth day. I got along fine. I think maybe that's the reason I'm so strong."

BABIES

As soon as the baby was born the midwife cut the natal cord. Annie Fike, remembering what she did on that stormy night before the doctor got there, said, "We read up what to do before the doctor comes. It said to wait two hours after a baby was born and if the doctor doesn't get there to not wait any longer to tie the natal cord. So we fixed the cord, got us some crochet thread, and made a string. Then we scalded the scissors and the thread, cut and tied the cord. We tied it first seven inches from the baby's body, then tied it again two inches back towards the body and then cut between the ties. That would leave a little stub on the cord. Then we would take a piece of cloth and burn it on the stove—scorch it. We'd cut a hole in it and put it over the cord, then put cotton on the cloth, then put the band over that. That held the cord in place, they claimed. We'd do that just at birth. If it got irritated, we'd do it again."

The baby was then given a bath. Myrtle recalls her one experience when a midwife delivered one of her children before the doctor could get there. "When she brought the baby back to bed, why, its little face was just so yellow and I said, " 'What have you done to my baby?' She said, 'Oh, we washed it in egg.' She had whipped up an egg and had washed the baby in an egg. And I said, 'Oh, please take her back and clean her off.' So she did. She said the egg would make my baby's skin soft."

After the bath the baby was dressed. Usually the mother had prepared the clothes before and had made long gowns out of soft material or used garments. But first the natal band was put on the baby. Myrtle had a band her husband and all of her babies had worn. It was made from white cotton and went on like a little shirt. Most bands were about three inches wide and long enough to reach around the baby to tie or pin in place. These bands were worn until the cord dropped off and healed, which was in about three weeks.

Diapers were homemade out of cotton twill, outing or cotton flannel, and muslin. Some were made out of old shirttails or skirts, or any material available. Mothers would have anywhere from a half dozen to two dozen diapers. Diapers did not always stay white. Washing was difficult and many times the busy mother dried the wet diaper and put it back on the baby without washing.

The diaper was a square piece of material folded into a triangle. The three ends were pinned together in the middle front of the baby with one big pin. Without rubber pants or other clothing to hold them in place—boys and girls alike wore long dresses until toilet trained—the diaper would often fall down. Gertrude Roper remembers, "They slipped down. I can remember, oh, way back, seeing those little diapers drop down and the children would be walking around playing and the diapers would trip them, come clear down around their feet."

Then as now there were many ways of doing things. Some women were very particular about the baby's clothes and washed and boiled them in a big black kettle outside or on the stove. They hung them outside in the sunshine and ironed them with a good hot iron, even ironing each diaper carefully.

The nutrition of the baby depended entirely on the health of the mother. Nursing used to be the only way of feeding a baby for the first year or two. Gertrude told us, "Women nursed their babies so much longer than now. It wasn't anything to see a child three years old run up and nurse. The mother would be sitting there at the picnic, and away he would go. People were taught to nurse their babies until after the second summer because there was always a diarrhea here. You had to nurse them through the second summer, until their teeth started to develop, so they could eat. Children were not fed scarcely anything at all. I marvel at the way they even stood up under it all." Women also believed that as long as they nursed a child they would not become pregnant again.

An unusual bellyband for a
newborn baby made in the form of
a vest.

If the mother of the baby didn't have enough milk or died, there wasn't much to do unless there was a wet nurse available. The wet nurse was a woman who had had a baby and produced enough milk to feed two children.

If a wet nurse was not available, the baby was fed diluted cow's milk. Before bottles and nipples, the mother dipped a cloth in the milk and the baby would suck it out. This was very unsatisfactory and could hardly nourish a baby. The same method was used with sugar water to appease the baby. These cloths became known as sugar tits—old-fashioned pacifiers. Babies were weaned by feeding them some milk in a spoon. Gradually they were fed solid food such as thick gravy, mashed potatoes, and other soft foods until they could eat the food at the table.

The doctors, midwives, granny women, and neighborhood women all worked toward the same goals: helping people who were sick and caring for mothers and new babies. They did everything they could to assure a safe delivery and a healthy child.

Dr. Ruth

"Oh, my goodness, she brought my daughter into the world fifty-nine years ago, and I knew her long before that," exclaimed one of Dr. Ruth Seever's patients, answering our questions about her. Dr. Ruth is a ninety-four-year-old "female" doctor still practicing at Osceola, Missouri. Another of her patients said, "I think she knows more about things than anyone in medicine today. They just give you a shot and some pills and see if it does you any good. She really knows your case. I ain't never took anything yet that hasn't done me good."

When we first walked through the door we weren't sure if we were at the right place. There was no office smell, no crowded waiting room filled with disgruntled people because the doctor is running late, no nurse in a white

uniform asking questions without looking up to see who you are. Instead there were four small comfortable rooms. The first one could be called a waiting room, but there was no window to announce you were there; Dr. Ruth would come out to you. The examination room was very small, with a cot and an easy chair. Next was her office with her desk, and medical books in an antique bookcase along with her files. Beyond that was a room containing rows of medicines. Instead of the crisp voice of a nurse calling out the name of the next patient, Dr. Ruth came shaking our hands and inviting us to come in, almost as though it was her own home rather than a doctor's office.

Around the waiting room were plaques on the wall which showed us Dr. Ruth's personality and interests. One in particular which interested us was an arrangement of buttons. Dr. Ruth told us she saves all kinds of buttons and then makes a plaque out of them. While we were there a woman called to ask how to fix her tray and what to put on it to take it to the state button show.

In the inner room we were surprised to see a brand-new riding lawn mower squeezed between her desk and the medicine room. Dr. Ruth explained, laughing, that it was stored temporarily in her office because that was the only door large enough to get it through. She explained that she has been in charge of the cemetery for years. When the city did not keep it treed and mowed, the women of the community formed a cemetery association. The first man they hired mowed it by hand for twenty cents an hour. Now they have purchased the riding lawn mower.

Dr. Ruth is part of the community. She not only has been in charge of the cemetery but was also on the school board. She was president for about thirty-four years and has her fifty-year pin, which President Truman's sister gave to her in a ceremony. She was also a secretary of the county Democratic Committee for about forty years. If the community ever needed a chairman for any organization, they could almost always count on Dr. Ruth.

Being paid for her services wasn't her main concern: she wanted to help. While we were there a patient brought her some eggs. "She has been the doc-

Dr. Ruth still receives produce from her patients. These eggs were given her while we were there.

tor that an average citizen could rely on and she didn't charge so much that you couldn't pay it. She's really marvelous. I just don't know how in the world she does what she does at her age."

Dr. Ruth likes to tell the story of a young woman who was in labor one Sunday afternoon. Someone sent for Dr. Ruth. When she got there the husband was lying on the floor drunk, sleeping off a Saturday night fight. Dr. Ruth delivered the baby and fixed up the man so he could go back to work on Monday. A few months later Dr. Ruth met him on the street and asked him if he didn't think it was about time he paid her for the nice baby boy she delivered. He pulled out fifty cents and said that was all the kid was worth.

One would think she would get very impatient with people coming in day after day for over seventy years with the same old complaints. But Dr. Ruth doesn't seem to tire. She has treated the same families for three or four generations and looks as if she could for another generation. When a patient comes through the door, Dr. Ruth immediately jumps up to see to him. She finds out what he needs and goes to the medicine room for the drugs. She then sits down to write out the directions, and takes time to visit a few minutes before going on with her work.

Although her way of life has changed—she now drives a new car—some things have not. An old-fashioned stove still heats the office, and her hair is still short, not because of any hair fashion but because it is easy to care for. She still has the old-fashioned characteristic of modesty. She doesn't really think she has done anything worth our attention and was surprised that we thought she was remarkable to be so useful and active, outliving most of her patients.

A VISIT WITH DR. RUTH

My patients die off and leave me. You see, people, I have served my day, really—since 1906. I think it will be seventy-one years in June since I made my first call. Most of the doctors are dead long before this time.

I doubt if I'll ever retire. What would be the use? People would still come and want to know things. And you just as well have a little medicine on hand to give to them. I have some of these people who come to me that are third and fourth generations of the family, and they say, "Oh, don't, don't close your office. Don't close your office." Well now, what are you going to do? You've got the ability and you've got the materials at hand to aid these folks. And I don't know what I'd do if I retired. I never lived on schedule. Never worked by appointments. I just take people as they come. Once in a while somebody comes in so sick I want to get them back here to lay on the lounge.

Sometimes people used to walk to see me in the snow when they didn't have rubber footwear. They wrapped their feet in gunny sacks tied with strings. That kept them from slipping on the ice and protected their shoes somewhat from the snow if they weren't out too long. Denim coats and overalls. Blue shirts for the men, calico dresses for the women long enough to drag in the dust sometimes. I still have one or two of the older women that come to town in their sunbonnets and their aprons. You know, a full apron tied around the waist. No, I can't retire.

We were wondering when you first decided you wanted to become a doctor.

Now that was in the summer of 1902.

How old were you?

Are you a good mathematician? I was born in 1883.

What made you want to become a doctor?

Well, my father was a doctor and had five girls. The four older ones had all turned him down. The first girl became a teacher. The second one married her college professor, and the third one was going to study medicine, but she met a young medical student. One day she said, "Father, I'm not going to be a doctor but a doctor's wife." And so she married. Then my next sister, the fourth one, just had no use for sick people. She just said, "No, I'm not going to take care of sick people."

I was seven years younger and when I was through high school I applied for a little country school out here. The board didn't give it to me because they said I wouldn't be equal to handling the big rough boys. I weighed about a hundred pounds and was just a little over five feet tall. They kind of apologized to my father for not giving me the school, but they said they were just afraid I couldn't handle the big boys. Maybe I couldn't, I don't know. So then my father said, "Well, you have to do something, and if you'll go to school and study medicine for me, I'll see you through if you make me one promise. You mustn't stop in the middle of it and get married. Now the day you get your license to practice, you can get married if you want to, but you must finish it if you begin it." I began it and I finished it and here I am.

Did you ever get married?

No, I never had the time. It takes time to get married.

Wasn't it unusual for a woman to want to be a doctor back then?

Yes.

Did you have any problem going through medical school?

Nothing, except it took a lot of hard work. I'm often asked if I met discrimination in the classroom and I never did. When you looked at the faces of those men, they were nearly all straightforward and honest.

Were there any other girls in your class besides you?

Nor directly in my class, but there was one just younger and one older.

How many people were in your class?

When we started there were forty-eight and when we finished there were six in my graduating class.

What was your first call like?

Well, we got home on the three-thirty train and at four-thirty I was gone on my first call. It was an elderly woman who had rheumatism. The joints were all swollen.

Were you scared?

I don't think I've ever known what it's meant to be really scared with any-body day or night. I've gone all over this country and on the darkest nights of the world by myself and I've never been really frightened. I'm just not a scaredy-cat.

Weren't you afraid somebody might rob you?

I didn't have anything for them to steal. There had been some robberies around in the country, and I know my father was a little fearful sometimes that he might be held up. I had been out southwest of town on a confinement case one Saturday night. About three o'clock in the morning I started home and, instead of driving my own two horses that could have outrun anything, I had a little team from the livery stable. I had these little horses I drove every once in a while when mine were tired. You couldn't hurry them for your life. They just wouldn't hurry. So about three o'clock in the morning I started home on a bright moonlight early Sunday morning. As I started to go up a hill, I came upon a little creek bottom. A couple of young men rode their horses right in the middle of the road that I had to travel. And right by a monstrously large oak tree that shaded that road, they rode into the shadow and stopped. One man got off of his horse and I thought they were going to rob me. I didn't have any money with me. But I did have my watch pinned on me. So I unpinned it and slipped it down with my arm between the seat without letting them see a motion of my arm. There was nothing to do but ride on. As I came pretty close to them, this one man that was on foot stepped right out in the middle of the road. I just let the horses walk right up to him, and he turned around and looked at the other young man on the horse and said, "Oh, it's nobody but Dr. Ruth." Now I think they were prob-ably just a couple of young fellows that enjoyed getting their companions a little scared. But they certainly didn't bother me. They both waved their hands when I went by. That's the only time that I ever thought that I was going to be robbed.

I had a big dog, part bulldog and part bird dog. He was my bodyguard and it was his delight to go with the team. I never saw him back away from any-thing except once. One night I was driving out east here and came up from a creek bottom and started up a hill when one of the horses began to snort. I supposed that maybe there was a snake in the road. She hated snakes and we had lots of them here around the creek bottoms. So I spoke encouragingly to her. Then the dog stopped beside the buggy and bristled his neck and I knew something was wrong, but I didn't know what. I called the dog to get up in the buggy. And as we drove on by, there were three big timber wolves down by the side of the road. But they didn't bother us at all. But that's what had frightened the horses and the dog. That's the only time I ever knew him to back down on anything.

He was a big dog. He weighed around sixty pounds. In those days doctors carried little medicine bags with medicine bottles in them. The dog carried my medicine case. He had to hold his head up to keep it from dragging on the rough places. So I started walking down the street here going home in the evening. There was a dogfight out in the middle of the road. He walked out to it, set his medicine case down, and settled the dogs. He came trotting back to me, you know, kind of proud of what he had done. There were a couple of men standing in front of the store. One of them turned to the other and said, "I always knew that dog would drop that case someday." Of course, I was ready for him to come back to me, and when he got back I said, "Cub, where's your medicine case? Go get it." And he walked out and picked it up and brought it home.

One of the worst troubles he had was carrying the mail for me. He was thirsty, and instead of going across the bridge, he went down into the water to get him a drink. He had to drop his mouthful of mail and, of course, the current carried it off downstream. He was terribly distressed. It took him quite a little bit to retrieve all of that. But he got it, every piece, and brought it back out.

Another night I went out on a confinement case. There were two women and three men. The men were all three drunk. It was stormy and cold. I'd tied the horses under a big cedar tree and, when I found I was going to have to stay all night, I said to the men. "I wish you'd go out and unhook the horses and put them in the stable to get them in out of this cold storm. So they all three went out and were gone for a little while. Pretty soon one of them came back and said, "You know, I'm just kinda ashamed of myself to be afraid of a dog, but that there dog of yours won't let us touch those horses. If you'll just call the dog in the house, we'll take care of the horses."

I had a tanned hide off of a black Angus cow, great big thing lined with felt. It was my buggy rug to keep me warm. I'd always take it in the house and let the dog lie down on it. So he slept inside the house on that rug the rest of the night, for I didn't start home that time until daylight. He was a very faithful animal.

At first did men hesitate coming to you because you are a woman?

You might say I stepped into my father's shoes. My father and mother came from Iowa in '81 and settled here. Father started his office on this corner with a lawyer. They had a front reception room and each had their consultation room. I began practicing in the same building. When he died his patients kept coming to me. Sometimes I have five or six men in here a day when I won't have but one or two women. It just depends on who needs something.

Being a woman, I'm sure you handled a lot of maternity cases. Do you have any idea how many babies you did help deliver?

I quit keeping track of them after World War II and at that time it was 2,999. I've not done so much of that work lately because so many folk like to go to the hospital.

Have you had many babies named after you?

There's a lot of little Ruths over the country. I delivered a baby girl out east of town. The mother wanted to name her Ruth but she had an older son. He said, "Oh, Mother, I don't think I would name her Ruth." The mother said, "Why not? Don't you think it would be nice naming her after Dr. Ruth?" He said, "Just think how many other babies are going to be named Ruth." So they named it Margaret Ruth.

Do you sometimes have to go on house calls and stay there overnight?

Yes, and I slept all sorts of places. On top of the grand piano, on a feather bed, under the dining-room table, on a straw tick in the corner of the room. I've traveled almost all ways. In the wintertime when we had sleet and snow, we had what we called ice shoes put on the horses. These iron horseshoes would have spikes welded to them so that when they put their foot down they didn't slip on the ice. And I've gone as far as I could in my buggy. Usually the high school boy that would be staying with us to go to high school would drive me a distance, or one of my sisters. And then somebody'd maybe meet me and carry me across the water where there was no bridge and no other way to get through. Then from the other side of the creek I had to walk to the house.

One time I came back off of those night calls and the man carried me to the other side of the creek and set me and my bags down and he went on home. I had to walk on into town. And oh, I was so tired. I'd been up all night and ended with a breech delivery and I was worn out, so I thought, to cut a little distance, I'd cut catty-cornered across a field, not follow the road around. I laid down and rolled under the wire fence. It felt so good to stretch out on that snow, and the sun was pretty and warm. I thought, I believe I could just lie right here and go to sleep. And then I thought, well, it's awfully cold; if I do I might freeze. I'd rather get up and go on in home. I was only three fourths of a mile from home then but when I did get home I had frosted my toes and both my hands. That was about as bad an exposure as I ever had.

Another time I was called in the night to come across the river where there was no bridge. I drove my horses out from town here about two miles, wakened the people at the house, and told the man what I wanted. I said, "Mr. Glassen, I want to be set across the river. And I'll probably be gone all night and I want you, when you come back from setting me across the river, to put my horses in your stable." He said, "All right. I'll dress and be out there in a minute." It was one of the blackest nights I was ever out. That man took me down the riverbank and skipping 'cross that old swollen river landed me right across in the opening on the other side. How he measured his distance and knew just how many strokes to give I pondered about it. But he was a fisherman and knew the river. Then on the other side the man met me and carried my bags about half a mile. When I came back the next day, he harnessed my horses for me to come back in home.

But another time when I left my team at his place I was taken up the river in a boat. I had to go about a mile and a half up the river in a skiff. I found a baby with spinal meningitis. There was ice in the river then. It was beading up. And the only way to get that baby back to town where I could take care of it was back down the river. So I put the little thing on a pillow, wrapped it all up in a blanket, and got back in the boat. The man guided the boat down the river while I held onto a paddle and pushed the pieces of ice away when they were about to hit us on the side. That, I think, was the hardest trip I ever did make.

My horses' names were Alice and Topsy. They were full-blooded full-sister Hambletonians, best driving team in this part of the country at least. Topsy was rawboned and high-headed, just always up and ready to go. Alice was round and roly. Sometimes she protested. She might have to be urged a little bit, but you never had to urge Topsy.

Sometimes I would ride horseback in places where a buggy wouldn't go, but I never rode horseback by choice. I don't like riding, but I could ride. We always had four horses and I could ride any one of mine. We used to go down here and cross the bridge [down the street about one block]. Then we went down the river bottom till we came to a good-sized creek. For years and years there was no bridge there and, if the water was up, you couldn't put your buggy there without getting the buggy bed wet. I've ridden that road on horseback many a time.

Did you get a car as soon as they were available?

I had my first car in 1917, a Model T. Oh, I cranked on the old thing so much till my arms were black and blue.

Have there ever been any epidemics, like smallpox?

Yes, I've been through two bad epidemics of smallpox. I've bathed people and changed their bedding when their own folks were afraid to touch them. But I always kept vaccinated and I never had it. And, of course, we used to have epidemics of scarlet fever. It's been about wiped out. I think I've disinfected every schoolhouse in the country and some of the homes. We don't pay too much attention to chicken pox and measles. And the flu hits us to some extent most every winter. We had quite a little of it this winter and a number of deaths among the elderly people.

When you first started practicing medicine did a lot of the people around here have their own home remedies and cures?

We're right in the edge of the Ozarks, you know. Oh, back in the Depression when money was scarce, I just learned to use a lot of them.

Children used to always go barefoot in the summer and boys especially would develop what we called stone bruises. Ever hear of stone bruises? Big abscesses would form from them. Green mullein leaves make one of the finest poultices you can use on a stone bruise. Just cut the green leaves, wash them first to get the dust and dirt off, and mash them into a pulp. Put them right on.

Would you use those yourself when you treated people?

Yes, I sometimes had to show people how to do it the first time . . . and bread and milk poultice.

What would you use that for?

Anything that you'd want to poultice. A boil or a bruise to take the soreness out . . . and fat meat. The fat meat was used as a poultice to draw.

"What's the use of retiring? My patients would still come to me for help."

"I think times will get better, a lot better. People live longer and don't have to go to the poor farm."

You get a little infection started and that will draw all of the pus and the poison out and start it to bleeding good blood. Then the good blood heals it. The white of an egg was used for the same thing. It's been so long since I've heard these, I've almost forgot what we did use.

In the Depression days would people hesitate to call you because they couldn't pay?

They'd call for information lots of times, but some of them hesitated to ask for drugs. However, I don't think I lost much in the Depression, because when you sum human nature up the majority of the people do have a little honor and good in them. And if they couldn't pay the money, they paid in produce. Sometimes I got a cord of wood. One time I got a whole great big gunny sack full of cabbage to make my kraut. Maybe a dressed chicken. You know the country will produce your living if you'll just let it.

We used to have what was called collection agencies. I think there's still some operating around the country. But they used to go to the individual doctors and ask for our outstanding bills to collect them for us. They didn't believe me when I told them I had collected over ninety-five per cent of all the bills that I had put on the book.

If you could would you go back in time—relive your life? If you could change, would you still be a doctor?

Yes, if I could do it in times past. I would not want to begin and start out now because of all the government restrictions. But if the circumstances were the same as when I started out, I'd be the same thing over.

Old-time Cures

Have a sore throat? Then try taking a big swallow of rendered skunk oil. Though this may sound a little strange, skunk oil was actually used by families who did not have a doctor to treat their illnesses. Many of the home remedies used generations ago seemed worse than the sickness, but they are often still used.

Many remedies employed plants, either cultivated for the purpose or found growing wild.

Chew the bark of a slippery elm tree for a *SORE THROAT,* it will take the soreness right out.

To take away an *ITCH,* dig a quantity of poke roots. Boil for the potion and bathe in it. This is sometimes called liquid fire.

For *COLD* or *FEVER,* get some peppermint from a stream, put it in a glass, and pour cold water over it. Drink the liquid.

There were several teas used for *COLDS.* Take the bark off a big wild cherry tree and boil it in water. Take a couple tablespoons of the liquid with some sugar to make it easier to drink. Tea made from the stalk of the horehound was also used.

Make a poultice by chopping up some onions in small pieces and put them on a cloth. Put the cloth on your chest and it will help to get rid of a *COLD.*

A common spring tonic was a tea made from the sassafras root, which is dug early in February before the sap comes up. Boil the cleaned roots in water and drink the liquid. Many people today love the taste of this and boil the roots or bark any time of the year. Root beer began as the flavor of sassafras. The drink was to *THIN YOUR BLOOD,* a polite way of saying to clean out the intestinal tract.

Two or three applications of sassafras oil will destroy both *HEAD LICE* and their *EGGS.* Just rub the oil over the infected parts.

Another plant that grows in the region is pennyroyal, an aromatic plant of the mint family. It was used for *COLDS,* or crushed, then dusted or wiped on the arms and legs to keep off *CHIGGERS* and *SEED TICKS* when berry picking.

Ada Tooker gave her daughter, Elizabeth Fishwick, mullein syrup for a bad *COUGH*. Elizabeth said, "It really works. The stuff tasted so bad that I was afraid to cough."

To make mullein cough syrup, take fresh mullein leaves into a warm room and let them wilt. Put them in a pan and cover with a large amount of water. Set this on the back of the stove and let simmer for two to three days. Strain the liquid, then add sugar for a thick syrup. Let the mixture cool down until very thick. Take one teaspoonful every four hours.

Tea made from hot water and corn silk will cure *BED-WETTING* in children.

Vinegar alone or used in combination with a variety of things seemed to be almost as important in the medicine chest as in the kitchen.

Mix two teaspoons vinegar and two teaspoons honey in a glass of water and drink at each meal for *ARTHRITIS*.

If you have trouble *SLEEPING,* mix three teaspoons of vinegar and one cup of honey. Take two teaspoonfuls before going to bed.

Cider, vinegar, and honey mixed together is also good for a *COUGH*.

For a *SPRAINED ANKLE,* soak two brown paper bags in apple cider vinegar and apply it hot to the ankle. This reduces the swelling and relieves pain.

For *PNEUMONIA,* take six large onions, chop fine, put in a pan over the fire, and add enough corn meal and vinegar to make a paste. Stir thoroughly and let simmer for about ten minutes. Then put the mixture in two cotton bags and apply to the chest as hot as can be borne. As soon as one cools, apply the one which has been kept hot in a steamer. Keep changing, making fresh poultices from time to time.

If you have *CORNS,* quarter an onion and soak it in a strong vinegar until pickled. Bind a fresh slice of the pickled onion to the corn for three nights to remove the soreness and the corn. Another remedy is to work equal parts of beef tallow, sugar, and ordinary kitchen soap into a salve. Bind on corns with a small piece of adhesive tape.

To treat *POISON IVY,* add two balls blueing, two teaspoons white vinegar, and two teaspoons baking soda to a pint of water. Mix and apply to affected part often.

Add one tablespoon vinegar and one tablespoon turpentine to a beaten egg yolk and apply for *LAMENESS*.

For *FOOD POISONING* drink one teaspoon vinegar in a glass of water every five minutes.

Take two teaspoons vinegar and two teaspoons honey in a glass of water at each meal for *HIGH BLOOD PRESSURE*.

If you have *TARTAR ON YOUR TEETH,* put a teaspoon of vinegar in a glass of water and sip slowly.

For *RINGWORM,* apply vinegar six times a day directly on infected area.

Take two teaspoons vinegar in a glass of water for *NOSEBLEED*.

If you have a *SORE THROAT,* gargle with a teaspoon of vinegar in a glass of water every hour. As soreness goes away gargle every two hours.

Other readily available sources of medicines were animals and insects.

Spread papers out and lay a person suffering from *SHINGLES* down on them. Chop off a black hen's head and let the blood run all over the person.

For *FROSTBITE,* kill a young rabbit and cut it open. While the blood is still warm, place the area that is frostbitten into the carcass and let it become thoroughly bathed in the blood.

A mouse's head tied around a baby's neck will prevent several *ILLNESSES.*

Take the fat of the skunk and render it for the oil. Rub the oil all over your chest for a *COLD.* This holds in the heat. It doesn't smell as bad as the scent of a skunk, but it still smells pretty bad.

Oil rendered from the fat of skunks is good for the *CROUP,* also.

Take two teaspoons honey at each meal to relieve *CRAMPS IN THE LEGS.*

If you have *SINUS,* chew a piece of honeycomb about the size of a piece of gum for about fifteen minutes every few hours for a week, or take two teaspoons of honey at each meal.

If you find it hard to *BREATHE,* take a tablespoon of honey to clear your breathing tract.

For a *COUGH* squeeze two lemons and mix with two tablespoons of honey. Drink the mixture. Or take a lick of salt.

For an *EARACHE* find the little black beetle that lives in rotten logs and break it in two. There is one drop of liquid in it. Put that in the ear and it will stop aching.

A small piece of fat meat bound on a *BOIL* will soon draw it to a head.

Turpentine and kerosene were also helpful in many cures.

Put two or three drops of turpentine on sugar and swallow slowly for a *COLD, STOMACH-ACHE,* or *SORE THROAT.*

Pour turpentine over a *SNAKE BITE* to draw out the poison.

Put lard and turpentine all over—even under your arms and the bottom of your feet. Go to bed and cover up. This builds up a good sweat and cures a *COLD* in no time.

To help stop *BLEEDING,* mix turpentine and sugar and put on a cut.

If you have *WARTS,* mix two parts of mutton suet and one part of turpentine and apply to wart every other night.

For a *CHEST COLD* heat together turpentine, coal oil, and grease. When it is hot, dip a cloth (preferably wool) in the mixture and pin it on the inside of your clothing. This should relieve you of your chest cold. Your friends may not like the smell, but it will do the job.

Straight turpentine put on *CUTS* and *SCRAPES* helps them to heal and keeps out infection.

Rub kerosene on ankles, legs, and arms to keep off *CHIGGERS*.

Kerosene also makes a splendid *DISINFECTANT*. It keeps the wound or inflammation from festering and prevents lockjaw.

Other commonly used products which were bought in the general stores or drugstores were whiskey, asafetida, iodine, tobacco, and household ingredients like salt, soda, and flour.

People nearly always kept a little bottle of whiskey in the back of the medicine chest in case of *SNAKE BITE,* whether they used it for anything else or not.

Put a nickel's worth (1900s value) of rock candy, which is just pure crystallized sugar, in a pint of whiskey. This is good for *COLDS*.

To prevent a winter *COLD,* mothers would put asafetida in a cloth bag and tie it around a child's neck with a string. Asafetida is a very strong-smelling plant. The bad smell that was given off was supposed to keep away the germs. For best results it should be kept moist. The child would stick it in his mouth occasionally, then let it dangle down.

For *SORE THROAT,* swab the throat with iodine.

Add equal parts of salt, sugar, and soda together, about one teaspoon each, and mix in a glass of water. Gargle this and sniff it up your nose for relief of a *COLD*.

A teaspoon of sugar taken by itself is the best thing for *HICCOUGHS*.

A teaspoon of sugar with a few drops of turpentine will get rid of *PINWORMS*. Another remedy was a strong tea made from quassia chips injected into the rectum.

For *WARTS* rub either castor oil or stump water on the wart.

For *POISON IVY,* mix copperas with water. It takes just two applications. The mixture burns but does the job fast.

Put chewing tobacco juice straight from your mouth on *CUTS, SORES, RINGWORMS, BEE STINGS, BURNS, BLISTERS,* and *BOILS*. It draws out the infection.

Chew tobacco to kill malaria in *MALARIA FEVER*.

For *ASTHMA,* make a strong solution of saltpeter. Saturate pieces of blotting paper in this and dry. When an attack is felt, burn a piece of paper and inhale the smoke.

Take molasses and sulphur to *CLEAN THE BLOOD* of all impurities.

For a *SORE* put Crisco on the raw place and keep it oily so it doesn't form a scab.

Also for a *SORE,* mix a small amount of sulphur in grease, enough to make a paste, and apply. This also works for an *ITCH*.

For *BURNS,* make a paste of flour and water as quickly as possible and spread over the area. Also honey rubbed directly on a burn will keep it from blistering. Vanilla extract will take away soreness and prevent blistering.

For *BOILS, NAIL WOUNDS,* or *INFLAMMATION* of any kind, make a poultice by stirring buttermilk and flour to a very thick batter. Cover a cloth with this and bind to inflamed area.

Drink a glass of warm water with a half teaspoon of salt dissolved in it every morning before breakfast for a splendid *TONIC.*

Take one tablespoon of corn oil at each meal for *HAY FEVER.*

If you *STEP ON A NAIL,* bind a poultice of bread soaked in milk to the wound to draw out any infection.

There's a Sweet, Sweet Spirit in This Place

Surrounding any place of worship is a sweet calming spirit that touches all that comes in contact with it. To all who come to hear God's word, this peace is held in reverence. There is another unique atmosphere you may find in churches, but to do so you must travel several miles away from town to visit one of the country churches that dot the Ozark countryside. Away from the hustle and bustle of the city, they hold a wonderful peacefulness—a peacefulness reflected by the members as well as the churches. Even though we were strangers, we were warmly welcomed when we visited these churches and interviewed members. Everyone made a point of saying, "Come back soon."

The Lutheran Church at Morgan, Missouri, with its stone foundation, one-room frame building, and bell tower, is typical of hundreds of churches in the area.

The doors of these churches are always open for any passer-by. The only reason the door is ever locked is that the church no longer holds services. As members die or move their membership to bigger churches in towns, ministers are hard to find because the membership is too small to support them. It is sad to see a sturdy old church still standing but without a pastor and congregation to make it complete.

The beginning of a church is the first step in its life. When a group of a certain faith lived in the community, those few families would begin to hold services. Some held services in one of the homes. Some churches were started by brush arbor meetings, services held outdoors in the shade of a frame-and-bough structure constructed for the event. Some started in a log schoolhouse or the upstairs of an old store building. Eventually, most had enough membership to build a church.

When the people built the church houses, they built them to last. The people themselves got the materials that were native to the Ozarks and did all the construction: because rocks were so plentiful, many churches used them for foundations.

Most churches had just one room with a small vestibule or entryway. If the church grew and could afford it, other rooms were added later. Many a church had a bell tower on top of the vestibule; the bell called the members to worship and at times announced community news such as weddings and funerals. When a member of Morgan Lutheran Church died, the bell was tolled during the funeral once for each year of the person's life.

Seats in the church were sawed out of native oak lumber and a stove in the middle of the aisle was used for heat. Lighting was provided by reflector lights hung on the side walls. These lamps had a sheet of metal behind the flame that reflected the light into the center of the church. The pulpit, usually handmade by one of the church members, was small, with a rostrum.

Members often donated their time, efforts, and materials when building a new church. At Cross Roads Church a chart telling exactly what each person did, how much he paid, and where the materials were bought still hangs in the church.

After the church was built, members who lived nearby would donate their time as caretakers. They would sweep and clean the church, light the stove during winter, and see that the lamps were filled. Members were not encouraged to stay long after church so the lights could be blown out to save kerosene.

Many churches—Half Way Baptist, Friendship, Eureka, Blackfoot—were named after the community they were in. Others were named after geographical features of the area such as Fairview, White Oak Pond, Sunny View, and Little Vine. Biblical names—Mount Zion, Mount Pisgah, Antioch, Emmanuel Chapel—were given to others. Some were named after the people who donated the land the churches were built on, like Shaddy Chapel and Bramhall. Many times a cemetery existed before the church, so the church was named after the cemetery, as McBride and Hough Chapel were. Occa-

Abo Church in 1910.

sionally the church was named after an unusual happening. The men of one community were building a school and wondering what they could call it. One man said, "You know, wasn't it over in that thicket where Uncle Pete killed that bear?" So they named the school, the church, and the cemetery Bear Thicket. Another church, Happy Hill, got its name when one elderly lady of the church who had been faithful for years was asked to name the new church set on top of a hill with a view of all the countryside. She said, "Praise the Lord, we'll call it Happy Hill."

Larger communities, if they were at all able, would have a full-time minister who resided in or near enough to the town that he was able to preach every Sunday. The smaller communities were satisfied if a traveling preacher could work it into his schedule to visit them once a month. This man of God might start walking from his home early Friday to get to the church by Saturday. Services would usually start at eleven o'clock that morning and last for an hour and a half. Three other services, Saturday night, Sunday morning, and Sunday night, were held following this. Four meetings each month were all that a church could expect from a preacher who might have to walk twenty-five miles to reach the church.

Each weekend the traveling preacher would be in a different community. He was always traveling, never really having a true home, making the rounds to all who wanted to hear the gospel. These men were well liked and known

Fairview Methodist Church.

Happy Home Cumberland Presbyterian Church.

Plato Christian Church.

by all. Often they would get free rides if they met someone else traveling their way. Nobody tried to rob them during their travels, for it was known the preachers would have no money.

Preachers weren't given a guaranteed amount of money at a specific time. They accepted what was given and praised the Lord for it. Having another job was unavoidable, especially during hard times. December would usually be the lowest month because of bad weather and holidays, while during the summer months people gave more because they had more to give when farms were producing. Gifts such as a hog or other food were always welcomed by a preacher, especially one with a family to support.

One year Curtis Wilson preached at a small church with one hundred members for just $9.00. Part of the $9.00 was a $5.00 pig a man gave him. Another year he was paid $2.00 in August, $1.00 in September, 40¢ in October, 10¢ in December, 62¢ in January, 20¢ in February, 85¢ in May, and $2.00 in July. At the end of the year he had earned $8.98.

There is a story of one church that needed a new minister around 1895. When a man came to try for the job, he told the congregation that first Sunday morning, "I think we should have a fair understanding before I start. I'll pastor the church for a dollar a month, twelve dollars for the year." One of the elders stood up and said, "Before I help pay that, I'll do the preaching myself." The young preacher got on his horse and rode away.

Today most preachers have a full education at a seminary, but years ago men who were called into God's ministry trained themselves by reading the Bible. Making the decision to enter the ministry was hard. It meant having two jobs and still not much money, and, for traveling preachers, being away from home and family a great deal of the time or not even having a true home. For this reason, they might fight the call to become a preacher for a

Bear Thicket Methodist Church.

Phillipsburg Christian Church.

Rader
Lutheran Church.

Curtis Wilson, Walter Bugher, Nelson Reid, Bob Reid, and M. E. Brashur, ordained ministers of the gospel, in the 1940s at Cross Roads Church.

long time, then pray for guidance. One man who heard the call was troubled about what he should do. He started walking and praying for guidance. He noticed that the road he was on forked off two ways. He prayed that if he walked down the right side he would be a preacher and if he walked down the left he wouldn't. He started walking to the right side. He's preached ever since that time.

The first service was held on Saturday when the preacher arrived. The order of the service was left up to the preacher. Free Will Baptists would read the minutes from the last service held, then pray. A song followed and everyone extended the right hand of fellowship. Singing was a great part of the services because it got the people in the mood to worship. The services might be started with three or four songs. If the church didn't have books, only songs everyone knew were sung. Since most churches were small, there were no special choirs. Everyone sang. Pump organs were first used, then pianos. Sometimes the song leader would use a handmade Do-stick—similar to a baton with little whittled slots. Some song leaders were asked by other churches to come and lead the singing. "Uncle" Elmer Hilton, one of the finest bass singers in the county, was asked many times to sing as a special at other churches. Uncle Elmer's hands would get so shaky and his book would shake so that he couldn't read his music. Since he didn't know the music by heart, he would get lost pretty quickly and would hand the book and Do-stick over to another person to take over as he joined the congregation singing.

> "O praise the Lord, sing to the Lord a new song.
> Sing His praise in the assembly of the faithful."

After the singing, the preachers gave their message. They made walls shake getting the word across to the congregation. Children knew to be at their quietest. Adults listened well so they were able to follow what they heard being preached. Only the stentorian voice of the minister rang over the hillside.

One pew, called the Amen Corner, was reserved for the deacons of the church. Deacons were the most trusted men of the church. They handled things when the pastor was absent, and were chosen by the congregation just as the preacher was. The first question asked them was, "Do you have two living women?" If they did, that was as far as they got. When made a deacon, one was a deacon for life, or as long as one maintained sound doctrine. Usually there were four in the church.

During communion, the deacons would pass the one communal cup. Only if the church was financially well off could there be a cup for each member.

The offering plate was passed every meeting. One church was lucky to have an offering bag with a long handle so the men could stand in the aisle and pass it side to side. That way, no one had to get up to pass the plate. The bag was beautiful—lined with velvet and hung with tassels—and the church was very proud of this invention.

At least once every month in the summer many churches would hold a

Children's Day at Hazelgreen Methodist Church in 1929 called for a basket dinner.

basket dinner outside under the large shade trees that surround country churches. After lunch there might be a singing session. The children would play games of horseshoes and tag while their parents cleaned up the grounds to get ready for the evening services.

Christmas was a special time and each church had a special program to present. Morgan Lutheran Church had a community program. They decorated a large tree with lighted candles. Two men stood beside the tree holding a fishing pole with a wet rag tied on the end, so if one of the candles made the least drip they could put it out before the tree caught fire. One Christmas a big ice storm made it impossible for many to come to the program, but one man ice-shod two teams of mules and loaded a wagon with everybody who wanted to go to the event. Sawdust was spread on the ground so people wouldn't slip, and that Christmas was cherished by all who were able to attend.

Every church would need to be revived; and most revivals were held in the fall, usually in late August when the crops were laid by and farm families were not so busy. The revivals would last about two weeks, and there were two services daily; the elders said the one in the daytime warmed the church up for the second service that night.

After the revival was completed, there would be a great number of anxious converts ready to be baptized in the river. If it was winter and the creeks were frozen, they just broke the ice and went right in. There might be up to fifty people ready to be baptized. Curtis Wilson once baptized a six-year-old boy. He was holding a baptismal service in the river and the boy was in the crowd of watchers. All of a sudden the boy dashed into the water. The little boy's parents were against baptizing him and so were a few members of the church because they thought he was too young. However, his grandfather said to baptize him, so Curtis did. He talked to the boy, now a man, not long ago. He still sings and goes to church and has never doubted his faith or even been dissatisfied with it. The oldest person Curtis ever baptized was eighty-seven years old.

Sometimes people would do things the church didn't approve. A church trial would be held in which the person was asked if he was sorry for his misdeed. If not, he would be denied fellowship and be excluded from church membership. One member was denied fellowship for going to a dance, another was excluded because he traded dogs on Sunday. One man traded horses on Sunday. The church asked him if he was sorry. Not until he found out he made a bad trade, he replied. He was excluded.

The churches in this hill country hold many wonderful memories for all who have been to them, even though members move or churches close. One woman who has moved from the Ozarks comes back every summer on her vacation to visit the country church she grew up in. She visits the preacher, then goes to the church to play the piano and relive young memories.

Evangelist Dale Hufft, at Antioch Baptist Church in August 1940, baptizes at Long Ford on the Osage Fork River.

Voices filled with the excitement of a remembered revival service or eyes filled with tears of sweet memories reach out from these hill churches and touch those who hear about the past. A feeling of awe that can't be explained surrounds each individual, past and present, who comes in contact with the power these churches possess. Everyone from the preacher to the smallest child, from the member of a church no longer existing to a young person hearing about it, falls under the spell that exists only in a country church-house where—

I will lift up mine eyes unto the hills, from whence cometh my help.

SWEET, SWEET SPIRIT

There's a sweet, sweet spirit in this place,
And I know that it's the Spirit of the Lord;
There are sweet expressions on each face,
And I know they feel the presence of the Lord.

Sweet Holy Spirit,
Sweet heavenly dove,
Stay right here with us
Filling us with your love.
And for these blessings
We lift our hearts in praise:
Without a doubt we'll know that we have been revived
When we shall leave this place.

DORIS AKERS

Gone but Not Forgotten

A Little Time on Earth He Spent
Till God for Him His Angel Sent

This verse, chipped out years ago on a limestone head marker in a country graveyard, seems to express the Ozark people's acceptance of the shortness of life and its natural end. It states simply the strength of their Christian belief in God's concern for each and His plan for a better life.

This philosophy was evident in all the people we talked with about death and burial customs. They spoke of their own experiences and those told them by their parents from as far back as the Civil War to the early 1940s when most people used the services of hospitals and funeral homes.

When death occurred, there were a number of things which were done in a very different way from today, but they all agreed that death used to be taken more naturally as part of the life cycle. Children then were not excluded from the funeral activities and were taught a more natural approach to death. People did not hesitate to show their emotions, and the neighbors always showed their concern by helping the family in many ways.

In the late 1800s and early 1900s a larger number of infants and young children died because medicine was not as advanced, because hygiene conditions were often poor, and because there were not many doctors.

Childhood diseases such as measles or chicken pox could be fatal then. Common causes of death for adults were pneumonia, typhoid fever, and ruptured appendix, which the people called "dread colic." Childbirth was often fatal for both mother and child.

A visit to any cemetery shows rows of little markers inscribed with dates of death one or two years apart of children in the family who lived only a few days or years—often followed closely by a bigger stone for the mother.

Families experienced death often. The death occurred in the home, usually from sickness, and the family and close neighbors handled all the details of the sickness, death, preparation for the burial, the funeral, and the burial. Death's reality could not be avoided or lessened by removing the dying person to hospitals and funeral homes.

Charlie McMicken told us, "If a person became real sick, a doctor would be called. Around the turn of the century, a doctor was expected to make house calls at any time, day or night, three hundred and sixty-five days a year, and to any place within driving distance with a horse and buggy. There were a few automobiles at that time, but roads were so poor that they weren't used much out in the country." If a person was very sick, the doctor might stay several hours.

Mary Moore remembered being called one winter in the night to help with a lady who died. "You know, people then wasn't able much to get to doctors. And maybe they'd have a doctor today and maybe it'd be a week before they had a doctor any more. They didn't have no money. They couldn't have a doctor."

If someone was very sick or died, the news spread fast. In the early 1900s there were country telephone lines—party lines—with ten to fifteen neighbors on a line. When anyone called, everyone on the line heard the ring and listened. Charlie Mc remembered, "If the phone rang of a night, believe me, everyone was up and listening to find out who was sick, because we knew it was sickness if someone rang the one long ring for the operator at night." It wasn't being nosy. Most considered it their obligation to know so they could help.

Neighbors would come to help the family take care of the ill and to stand by in case of death. The neighbors and friends would take turns sitting up with the sick at night and helping to give medicines. It was desirable, if possible, for a near relative to be present at time of death.

Relatives who lived far away were notified of the death by letters. Sometimes people sent the news in a black-edged envelope. The postmaster would know that it contained news of a death and immediately send someone with the letter to the home.

When somebody died, the neighbors brought in food. Dorothy McMicken said, "Neighbors were nice to the people. They wanted to do things. The women cooked for the family to relieve them of the burden of the daily chores which at a time like that were too heavy." Others did anything they could to help. Myrtle Hough remembered, "They come as quick as they can get there. They all gather in, bring food and do anything they can. I know when my father died—we didn't have heated rooms then—a neighbor came early morning a little after daylight, and he cut wood nearly till noon for heating purposes. They'd come to work for you and do all the chores."

Today death and caring for the dead seem to be remote or divorced from the family life, with death occurring in hospitals and the dead cared for by professionals. Ella Hough said, "You shouldn't have to die alone. Folks should be with their family when they die and they should see death. You don't even see your folks die now, everything's changed so. Being together brings the family closer."

Most rural people in the Ozarks did not use the services of undertakers and embalming until the 1920s. Before that there were no undertakers to be had. Even buying a casket meant a long trip to town and back.

The first use of embalming in the rural areas of the Ozarks entailed someone bringing the equipment to the home and caring for the body there. Sometimes these men were connected to a funeral home, but often they were not. Helen Beard recalled a man who embalmed a lot. "You just called him and he came to the home. He came into the bedroom and was practically all day—eight to ten hours—embalming. He worked by himself and he really would do a good job."

In the thirties when the funeral parlors took over this function, trips to the home were discouraged for it was obviously more efficient to embalm in their laboratories. By then there was adequate transportation and more money, so bodies were taken to the funeral parlors to be embalmed, then returned to the home to lie in state.

Before this service was available, the neighbors did what was necessary. There was always someone in the neighborhood with experience who could be called on to care for the body.

The funeral was often the next day. If not treated, bodies begin to turn black and mortification sets in; therefore, they were buried as soon as it was possible to dig the grave and make the coffin.

If it was possible, some people waited to the third day before burial in respect to the Christian tradition of Jesus' burial.

PREPARATIONS FOR BURIAL

As soon as possible after death, the body would be prepared, or laid out. Women would lay out women and men lay out men.

The room where the death occurred was first cleaned. All the bedding was removed, and it was washed or burned. Helen Beard said, "They hardly ever let anyone else use it. Usually they burned the ticks, for they were made of straw or shucks. They would get some boards put across chair backs or propped up in some other way. The furniture would be rearranged to make that possible. That might mean taking out the bed entirely." Since in some one- or two-room homes this was not possible, the living and the dead shared the room until burial.

Those preparing the body started by taking off the nightgown and washing the body from head to toe with soap and water. After death the kidneys and bowels relax, so a sheet was wrapped around the body like a diaper.

Something was put on the eyes to keep them closed, usually quarters, which were often kept by the family as keepsakes. It is an old but false belief that a person's eyes can be closed just after he has died and they will stay closed. In fact they must be held closed until the body is cold. A cloth had to be tied around the chin and up over the top of the head to hold the mouth until the body was cold and set.

The body could then be dressed. Some older people had their burying clothes laid back. Usually the best dress or suit was used, but if there wasn't anything suitable, sometimes neighbor women would quickly make a dress. As long as the clothes were clean, they did not have to be new. The women had panties, an undershirt, a chemise (pronounced chimmy), and a petticoat, then the dress and stockings. Men had underwear, a shirt, tie, and suit. Older people often wanted shoes or house slippers on.

The hair was washed and combed the way the individual wore it. Make-up was not used until bodies were embalmed.

Some families left jewelry like rings on their dead. We also heard of several ladies who had a hat or a cap laid back especially for their burials, and cases where favorite belongings like a scrapbook and violin were buried with their owners.

After the person was dressed, he was laid out on the cooling board, a board sufficiently long which was laid on the backs of a couple of chairs and covered with a white sheet. In some cases a pillow was put under the head, but people were generally not supposed to do so because the pillow prevented the body from cooling as fast.

Wet soda cloths were put on the face and hands to help preserve the skin color and texture. The people who sat up with the body would wring out cloths every so often to put on the face. These cloths were kept in place except when someone was viewing the body.

After the body cooled, it was placed in the coffin, covered with a sheet, and lay in state until the funeral.

Neighbors and friends came to view the body in the darkened room. In those days, many people did not hesitate to show their emotions. They would cry and moan, fall to their knees, and pray aloud. The house was often crowded with people ready to help, coming to sympathize with the family, or to view the dead. The children were not excluded from this. They usually played just as normal, but were quieted if they became too noisy.

Meanwhile someone had to make the coffin or buy the casket, as it was called if purchased from a store. In most cases the coffin was homemade, and varied from a simple pine or rough oak box to beautifully crafted walnut coffins lined with black satin cloth for older people or white for a child or young person. The sides sometimes had cotton fill and were decorated with rows of eyelet embroidery or lace.

The size of the coffin depended on the body measurements of the dead but was three feet high and had a lid that could be closed with screws. Coffins came in different shapes, from rectangular to those shaped wide at the shoulders and narrow at the head and feet.

Those who could afford to would send a near relative to town to pick out a casket. In most cases, all the undertaker got out of a funeral was a chance to sell the casket. Only well-to-do people had the undertaker lay out the dead or furnish a hearse.

Still other neighbors gathered to dig the grave. Sometimes, if there was a church near the graveyard, the digging tools might be stored there, but usually "The neighbors would just gather their picks and shovels and just go to the graveyard," Elva Hough said. "We'd measure off our grave, what we had to have, and take turn about. One would get in there and dig him up a patch of dirt and another'd get in and throw it out. And we just kept that up until we got down where we wanted. We've done that until just the last five years or so around here."

The grave was at least six feet long, four feet wide, and six feet deep. The men would usually leave something to do for the day of the funeral, even if it meant just removing a few final shovelfuls.

The neighbors dug the grave even if it rained, snowed, or the ground was frozen. If the ground was frozen or there was lots of rock, the men sometimes dynamited. Since the soil in the Ozarks is so thin and the hardpan and rock layers are close to the surface, some graves were especially hard to dig. We heard cases of dynamiting being done while the funeral service was in progress. Sometimes a person had expressed the wish to be buried on his or her own farm, in which case the neighbors dug the grave right by the house, garden, or wherever it was requested.

In the meantime, other neighbors sat up with the dead. Charlie Mc explained, "This meant that someone stayed with the body all the time, usually a group of three to six people. It was done out of respect to the dead. The

Most coffins used in the Ozarks in the early twentieth century were homemade. In addition to the rectangular shape, many were pointed or shaped to the body.

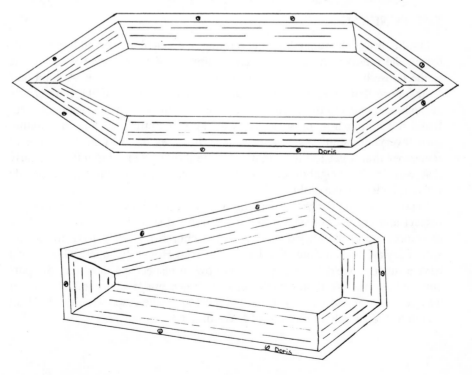

relatives were not expected to sit up. They were worn out. There had been sickness and death. They were supposed to go to bed to sleep."

Neighbors provided plenty of food and coffee for those who sat up. At least one person had to be awake all the time while the others might doze off in their chairs during the night. But the light was never blown out. Different neighbors would relieve them in the morning.

Pets, especially cats, were usually kept out of the house during this time, because of the fear that they might try to harm the body.

The home where there was a death was very busy, but though it was a sad occasion for the adults, it meant a chance to see one another once again to renew family bonds. "The atmosphere in the home after a death was not like at a funeral home now," Dorothy McMicken said. "I think there was a deeper feeling between the people then. Your neighbors were close to you, and they were the ones that came and stayed by you. That in my opinion created a deeper feeling than there is now in a funeral home where anybody can come. In my case we knew some of the neighbors were elderly, and they made a special effort to come for the love of being with us."

Myrtle Hough prefers the way we use funeral homes now. "I think it's much better," she said. "It's better for the family all the way around. You don't have the memories. They look so much nicer now. Just take you and me and somebody else, we wouldn't really know what to do except to dress and wash them. I think it's better for the family to have the dead person away so you can come home to relax. It's an awful trial on a family if you had to see that the meals were there and your house was crowded."

THE FUNERAL

On the day of the funeral, or the burying, the neighbors served a big dinner for all the relatives, a custom which continues today. Relatives would come to the house before noon, for most funerals were at two o'clock. A good half hour before that time, everyone would gather in the yard, if the funeral was at the home, or go to the church, enter, and sit quietly until the family arrived. It did not matter how busy anyone was, even if putting up hay or planting corn, everyone went. As Myrtle said, "Busy season or not. I can't ever remember that it got too busy that everyone didn't go to a funeral. It's nearly that way in this neighborhood now. And years ago, a number of people walked, including the children."

Lenora West remembers when she was in school how her teachers taught respect and correct behavior. "When we went to school they'd teach us how to respect the dead. They'd take us to the church and we'd have to sit real still. They'd let school out. We'd walk down to Hough [Chapel] when they'd have a funeral. We'd have a lecture on how to respect the dead and the parents and people. We didn't think about it. When our teachers talked to us, it was just natural and we had to have respect and take responsibility. We'd all march to the church and we minded. We didn't get out of line."

Lois Beard believes that children used to understand death better than they do now. "That's where I think a big mistake is made today," she explained, "because people don't let a child grow up knowing that there's life and death. If they knew that, when the parents died the children could be consoled. They could be talked to, but the way it is now, they've never been to a funeral and they don't know anything about it, and they don't realize life and death are some of the things we have to endure."

On the day of the funeral people wore their Sunday dresses and suits. The school children who sometimes served as a choir, especially where the church and school were close, just had their regular school clothes on. The members of the family wore dark, mostly black, clothes. If a husband or wife had died and the one left did not have black clothes, some neighbors would sew them or find suitable clothes for them. It used to be the custom for everyone attending to wear black. Each lady who could afford to had a black dress just to wear to funerals.

The women in the family wore black hats and veils to the funeral. The veils were square black pieces of material that went over the head so that you could not see the face.

A home funeral was usually simpler than one at the church. The atmosphere was also more informal. The yard was crowded with neighbors who had not found a place in the house. The choir or singers had to get along without music and used a tuning fork to get the pitch.

If the funeral was at a church, the coffin with the body in it would be shut and screwed down, loaded on a hack or wagon by six pallbearers, and pulled to the church by horses or mules. The wealthier people nearer the towns sometimes had funeral directors with hearses pulled by horses. The horses were black with black plumes or other decorations on them.

The opened coffin would be placed in the front of the church, usually just under the altar. The family would file in to sit on the first rows of benches and the services would begin.

If there was a preacher, the order would be quite similar to that used today. If there was no preacher, someone in the community would do his part. Helen Beard said, "There was always a man or woman in the community that could substitute with a prayer. If you couldn't get them in time, you'd always know there was a man or woman, usually a man, that could step up and do that."

Lois added, "I've never been any place where there wasn't somebody to carry on. If there wasn't anybody there, I'd do it myself. They took the place of the preacher and the undertaker and it was always carried out in a very dignified manner. I've never seen one that wasn't."

The order often went as follows: song, Scripture, song, obituary, sermon, prayer, viewing the body, last good-bys from the family, trip to the cemetery, prayer, interment, family visit.

The songs were sung by either the regular church choir, special groups, or individuals. Ashford Hough, who has sung in many funerals, told us he used to sing some duets but mostly quartets, and sang at many home funerals.

Occasionally the obituary was brief, as most are today, with just the dates when the person had been born and when he died, if he had been converted and when—just facts. But usually the obituary was much longer and more personal. It told about the parents, marriage, and children, when the person had joined the church, the survivors, and the age in years, months, and days with some interesting comments on his life—a complete life history.

Those writing the obituary always wanted to say something good about the dead person. Georgia Massey used to tell this story: "There was one man who was so mean and hateful, the preacher was hard put to it to think of anything good. He came to that part of the obituary and stopped. In a minute he brightened up and said, 'He's got the best set of teeth I ever saw.'"

The sermon was also usually longer than it is now, and it was very often addressed directly to the congregation. The preachers were not as well educated as today and some spoke quite bluntly of subjects now evaded. In the obituary it would be announced whether the person had been saved and in the sermon some preachers used the example of the dead as a warning to the people in the church that this end will come to all, so be ready, repent and be saved. Helen Beard said, "The country ministers weren't educated then. They just preached fire and brimstone. They would get wild at the funerals back at those times. It wasn't dignified like it is now and rather reserved. They preached! I've seen one preacher pound and run back and forth and then come up and pound on the casket. They just kind of whooped it up."

This kind of sermon would create reactions in the congregation, who probably then were not as reserved as they are today. Some people would kick and wail. Others would cry out loud to show sympathy.

The purpose of the service, of course, was and is to help the bereaved. Those who expressed themselves in this way were getting a sort of therapy. Of course, not all preachers behaved in this manner, but tried to help the living understand life and death, using other preaching methods.

The audience was very respectful toward whatever the minister preached. They all sat quietly, even the children, and listened attentively to the long sermon.

After the concluding prayer, which was also often long, the congregation viewed the body for the last time. As they passed the family they often paused to shake hands, to cry, or otherwise sympathize with them. Then they would go outside no matter how bad the weather was, leaving the family alone so that they could say their last good-bys to their dead.

THE BURIAL

The coffin was then closed for the final time; the lid was fastened with screws to the sides and loaded on the wagon again if the graveyard was any distance away. Many times it was beside the church, in which case the pall-bearers would carry it to the open grave.

The family followed right behind the coffin; behind them came the relatives and friends and neighbors, who would all stay for interment.

At the grave the people would gather around while someone spoke a prayer and the coffin was lowered.

Four men, two on each side, would slip ropes or harness lines underneath the coffin and slowly lower the coffin into a wooden box, which was already in the grave. The lines were of thin leather and could be pulled out from underneath the lowered coffin quite easily. Someone would jump inside the grave to nail the lid on the outside box, which acted as a vault. Then the preacher would say, "Ashes to ashes, dust to dust," and throw some dirt on top of the casket.

After this the men would fill the grave with dirt. Sometimes while the casket was lowered or the grave was being filled there would be more singing. While the grave was being filled, everyone visited and sympathized with the family.

If there were any flowers on the grave, they were wild, fresh picked and few in number. Later some people made homemade crepe paper flowers to put on the grave to keep it from looking so cold and gray, but flowers were never bought from a florist until recently.

On top of the grave came a marker of some kind. Sometimes it was noth-

A wreath of homemade flowers decorates this black casket, which was rather ornate for the time.

ing more than a wooden cross with the name and maybe birth date and date of death on it. Some families found a rock on which they crudely carved the information. Others put headstones on the grave, square or rectangular upright pieces of limestone which also had names and dates inscribed on them. Some fancy ones had a little poem or line from the Bible.

Everyone would visit with the family until the grave was finished. Then each went home or back to his business. Some neighbor women sometimes returned to the house to help straighten up, and the relatives who lived very far away would probably stay another night or two.

The cost of a funeral was very low compared to the cost today. The only expense was the coffin, which might have been around twenty-five dollars, including the satin lining, if made by a local handy man. The burial plots did not cost anything, for people used spaces available in the community graveyards.

AFTERMATH

After doing what he could, everyone continued his interrupted work, but for the widow or widower it was quite a different story. The widow often faced a very difficult situation: unless she had relatives to support her and her children, she had to run the farm alone, or look for work, which was very hard to find in the country where everybody else just barely made a living on his farm. Women rarely had any education or training for a regular job in town. With little children and a farm, she survived hard when she survived. A widower left with little children also had a hard time unless he had a female relative who could come into the home to help.

The widow was almost isolated from society. She was supposed to wear black clothes when in public for a year after the death, and she could not attend any "questionable" events, such as dances, social meetings, plays, or shows in town. About the only place she could go was to church. Her moral standards would be questioned if she remarried before the mourning year was over. But if she had several small children and was in desperate financial situation, it might be considered a blessing if she remarried before that year because it might mean survival for her.

One way or another, life goes on after a death. For the people in the Ozarks, their faith in God and their very religious attitude toward life often helped them more than anything else to find the way back to a normal life. This was God's will, and therefore it was nature's way—to give life and to take it away. People accepted death, for they could not change it and they believed God knew best.

Emblems of Life

Cemeteries, a very common sight in the Ozarks, often slip by with the landscape as we drive past without giving them a second glance. Many consider a cemetery only an emblem of death, something they want no part of, feeling that cemeteries are of no value to anyone but a corpse. But those who choose to accept them in a more realistic manner find them interesting and intriguing, as well as beautiful and overwhelmingly peaceful.

Cemeteries are not a place of the dead but rather an emblem of the fulfillment of life, since death is the perfectly natural end of life. The dead do not need the markers, for only the living care about dates of birth and death, inscriptions, and favorite objects. Because of this, cemeteries are a valuable link to the past, a place for living memories and philosophic thoughts.

Like most other things, cemeteries, too, are changing. Gravestones used to be wooden boards, then changed to cement slabs which stood upright out of the ground at the head of the grave with a smaller footstone placed at the foot. In some cemeteries the markers lie flat on the ground now, instead of standing upright, because it is easier to mow around them. Often graves had fences around them, and family plots were sometimes bordered with a cement curb. The foot markers were sometimes used as headstones on the graves of babies and small children. The size of the headstone often corresponded with the importance of the person buried under it.

Many gravestones were inscribed with sayings like "Gone but not forgotten" or "Traded a cross for a crown." Gravestones were sometimes decorated to reflect something about the person. One grave we observed was adorned with sea shells. The woman whose grave this stone marked was a collector and these shells were part of her collection. Another stone had musical notes inscribed on it. These were from a stanza of a song which had been a favorite of the musically talented girl who occupied the grave.

There are numerous graves that are not in marked cemeteries. They can be found right along the roadside. A few large rocks placed together could be the graves of early frontier pioneers who became infected with smallpox, a killer at that time, and were buried alongside the trail.

Today gravestones are not as personal as they used to be. There are no inscriptions or decorations which reflect upon the person under it—just names

and dates. It seems that mass production has even touched the cemeteries as the stones are becoming more and more alike.

To walk through an old cemetery and observe the markers and read the inscriptions imprinted on them is an intriguing experience in itself, but to research different graves and to listen to persons who have lived in the area for many years tell the stories behind some of the graves is fascinating.

In the Lebanon City Cemetery there is a grave marker which has the actual shoes and socks of a little boy preserved in the stone. The footstone on this grave is a preserved tree stump. On the stump is a little hammer. The young boy buried there was given the hammer as a birthday present by his father, who was a carpenter. The small child was following his father around a construction site when he stepped on a nail which penetrated his shoe and pierced his foot. The puncture became infected, and the child died of blood poisoning. In remembering the son the parents left him his prized hammer. The shoes and socks were left as a reminder to them of how fate had deprived them of their son.

On one side of an open field lies the grave of a Union soldier who was captured by the Confederate forces in the Civil War. His marker says that he was murdered by the Rebel troops. On the opposite side of the same field lies the grave of the soldier's wife, who died years later. According to local legend, she was buried so far away because she and her husband fought. Since then, they have been separated even further by Interstate 44, which now runs between them.

5. THE SWEET

A home, the means to make a living, and a sympathetic community provided only the essentials for a social life. For the Ozark people who wanted a fullfilling life there was more. There was freedom in self-sufficiency and pride in craftsmanship. There was satisfaction in creating and catharsis in fun. There was beauty in the forms, colors, and sounds in nature and in their homes. All these qualities combined to enrich their lives and balance out the bitter.

It is no accident that "sweet" follows "bitter" in "bittersweet," and it is not just because the words sound better in that order. Most people like to think positively—times will get better. Like the word "bittersweet," their lives were full of opposites. Working fifteen hours a day for weeks putting in a crop was "rewarded" with a few days' quiet fishing in a homemade johnboat. The drabbest, draftiest cabin could have colorful, warm quilts sewn with the tinest stitches in elaborate designs. The roughest gray floors could be made soft and bright by hand-woven rag carpets. The rockiest, poorest ridge land fit only to hold the world together would have the most dogwood blossoms and the best view of the valley.

It is not possible for people to live and work so closely with a land so beautiful without some loveliness entering their lives. But in bittersweet country the sweet comes last.

Crafts

The Ozark Johnboat

One of the most interesting indigenous products of the Ozarks is the john-boat, a combination produced by the ingenuity of the people and the natural features of the region. The johnboat is a long, narrow, flat-bottomed wooden boat designed for fishing the pools (called eddies) of the Ozark rivers and floating over the swift shallow riffles. It floats downstream with the current and is paddled by one person in the back using a lightweight paddle.

No one knows for sure when the first johnboat was built or where it got its name, though it is generally agreed that it was first designed by a man named John for float trips on the White River. The same general style of boat was used throughout the Ozarks on most streams. Each river had its own boat which was adapted to the characteristic features of that river.

Not many wooden johnboats are made today, for they have been largely replaced by inexpensive, easier-to-transport aluminum boats which are pro-

duced by several boat industries in the area. These aluminum johnboats are popular; yet many fishermen familiar with old-time johnboats prefer the wooden ones.

Desiring to record the art of making the wooden johnboat, several *Bittersweet* staff members helped Emmitt Massey, who has built many johnboats for floating, fishing, and trapping on the river farm where he grew up, construct one. He explained more about the boats.

"Originally they were built right on the riverbank. They were a heavy, durable boat made strictly for floating and fishing Ozark rivers. They were long. I've heard of some as long as twenty-seven feet to haul freight on Current River, but most around here were sixteen to twenty feet. The longer they are the more buoyancy they have. I wouldn't want one less than sixteen feet. They were designed to be stable enough to stand upright in while fishing and to float in four inches of water. They are narrow to go through brush and around log jams. Each boat I make, I do it a little different. Many people will disagree with me on building this boat, but this is my way now. Another time maybe I'd make it completely different."

MATERIALS FOR JOHNBOAT

50 feet of 1×8 cyprus for floors, ends, and keel
40 feet of 1×12 mahogany for sides
10 feet of 1×12 white pine for seats
⚹6 cement-coated nails
4 barn door handles
100 ⚹9 1¼-inch flathead screws, cadmium plated, no rust
marine paint
waterproof caulking
sandpaper
resin glue

PREPARING THE FLOORING

Emmitt spent the first day getting the flooring ready. The lumber he used for the floor was cyprus because it is fairly hard and will resist water. It takes about 50 feet of 1×8 boards to lay the floor. If the lumber has waves in it and won't lie flat, it should be split lengthwise. The boards are then cut into about 3-foot lengths. Select only good boards with no cracks to be tongue-and-grooved.

Use a ¼-inch tongue. The tongue-and-groove are used so the floor will fit tightly and securely. When the boat is put into the river, the boards will swell up, sealing the floor tightly, thus preventing leaks. Lay aside the flooring while you prepare the frame. Emmitt did his own tongue and grooving because he could not get good enough prepared flooring.

PREPARING THE FRAME

Mahogany or redwood are good woods to use for the sides. They are both tough woods that are not affected by water. Emmitt used mahogany, and prepared the two 16-foot sides by cutting a slope on each end so the front

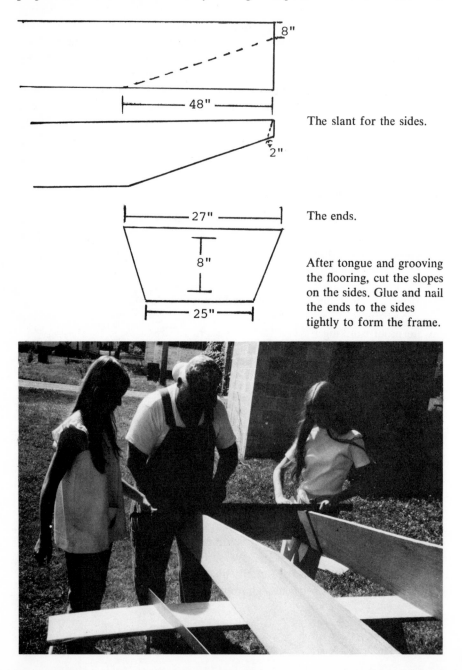

The slant for the sides.

The ends.

After tongue and grooving the flooring, cut the slopes on the sides. Glue and nail the ends to the sides tightly to form the frame.

and back of the boat will rise out of the water. This makes the boat much easier to steer. Use the same cut on each end of both boards.

Before cutting the ends, cut a board 35 inches at the top and 29 inches at the bottom to tack between the two sides in the center so the middle of the boat will be wider at the top than at the floor. This positions the sides of the boat to get the slant needed for the ends. When the floor is laid this board is removed.

Cut two ends 27×8×25 inches as shown in the diagram. Glue and nail the ends to the sides with ⚔6 cement-coated nails. It may be necessary to clamp the sides to make it tight.

LAYING THE FLOORING

Laying the flooring is probably the most time-consuming work on a johnboat, not because it is hard, but because there is a lot of it.

The bottom of the boat is sloped. After having laid the sloped edge facing upward, mix a small amount of waterproof glue and have ⚔6 cement-coated nails ready.

Put waterproof caulking into each groove of the flooring before inserting the board.

Use resin glue on the sides before laying down the floor boards.

Starting at one end of the boat, put glue on the ends and sides where the first tongue-and-grooved board will be placed. Then place the board so that the tongue faces inward and nail securely. On all the rest of the boards for the floor, a waterproof caulk must be put into each groove to help seal the boat. Use three nails on each board: two driven from the top and one driven slanted just above the tongue into the sides. Set all the nails on top and then fill each hole with wood putty. Many times it is necessary to use a clamp to get the flooring to fit tightly together.

After completing the floor, saw off any overhang and sand the entire boat smooth.

Nail each board securely with #6 cement-coated nails, two on top and one nail driven in slanted just above the tongue.

REINFORCING THE ENDS

After sanding the boat, attach the reinforcing ends. Emmitt made these of cyprus wood and cut them to cover the entire ends of the boat, including the ends of the side and flooring boards. These pieces will be about 29×8½×27. Glue and then tightly screw them onto the boat. One of the reasons for adding these second ends is to make a stronger end in case a motor is used.

Before placing the keel, check the floor for spaces between the boards. If

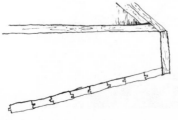

Reinforcing the ends.

there are any, fill them with waterproof caulking and remove excess caulk with a rag soaked in paint thinner.

LAYING THE KEEL

Laying the keel is one of the easier parts of making a johnboat. Take a sixteen-foot board four inches wide and lay it down the middle of the underside of the boat. Start at a reinforced end and place screws in a zigzag pattern in every flooring board the entire length of the boat. When you reach the middle, someone will have to stand on the keel so it will bend with the curve of the boat. Do not cut the keel into pieces because they might tear off in fast water. The screws must be set-screwed into the wood and the holes filled with wood putty. Sand the keel smooth.

Since the keel will not bend easily, use a weight to hold it securely to the boat. Attach with 1¼-inch flat-head screws.

INTERIOR

Before working on the interior, sand it thoroughly and fill any places of possible leaks with waterproof caulking.

The inside braces take a little time. They are 1×2s laid inside the hull of the boat for extra strength at the floor alongside the sides. Because both the front and back slope upward, it is necessary to cut the braces into three parts for each side. Cut the ends of each board so that they fit tightly against each other and the boat. It may be necessary to use a clamp to push the braces

The inside braces must fit flush with the floor. Secure the 1×2-inch braces with screws.

Screw in the seat braces (1×4×12). Set one pair at one end, one pair in the middle, and the third pair twelve inches from the other end to allow for leg room or a motor.

tightly alongside the hull. Use ⅛9 screws, 1¼ inches long, to screw the braces in tightly.

The seats come next. First install the seat braces or supports. Cut six 1×4s twelve inches long for braces, two for each seat. Place the first two at one end of the boat, one on each side about one and a half inches from the top. Using ⅛9 screws, screw the braces into the sides of the boat. Repeat this at the middle and front of the boat. Then cut the seats from 1×12 white pine so they fit tightly to the boat, and screw each seat to the brace. One end seat is positioned 12 inches from the end to leave room for a motor or to give leg room for facing forward.

SPRAY RAIL

The spray rails have to be nailed on. Set two sixteen-foot-long mahogany 1×2s along the edge of the sides and nail them down so that the overhang is on the outside. This strengthens the boat and makes a wider surface to draw the trotline over to keep hooks from catching.

Nail spray rails on top. Set the 1×2-inch boards so that the insides are flush with the inside of the boat. Bend them with the curve of the boat and nail tightly.

HANDLES

The handles are next. Get four barn door handles, two for each end, and screw in securely. These are to help carry the heavy boat.

Screw in four barn door handles—two on each end. Next paint with two coats of marine paint.

FINAL FINISHING

Plane and sand off square edges especially on the bottom, keel, and tip rail.

After a complete sanding, the boat is ready to paint. Use at least two coats of good-quality marine paint to help seal the outside of the wood to prevent leakage and protect the wood. Periodic painting will increase the life of the boat.

Before putting the boat into the river, fill the bottom with water for a few hours to allow the wood to swell together.

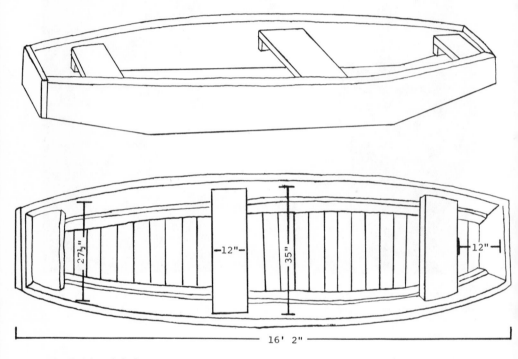

The finished johnboat.

A Talk with Emmitt

We spent several mornings working with Emmitt as we built our johnboat. Since most of us knew nothing about johnboats and carpentry, we were full of questions. Between the noise of the power tools and hammering, we did a lot of visiting. Turned upside down on saw horses near where we worked was his aluminum johnboat. We asked him what was the difference between the wooden and aluminum johnboats.

Well, the wooden johnboat is about a hundred pounds heavier than an aluminum boat. I'd rather have a wooden boat. It don't make near the noise that a metal one does on the river. It doesn't rattle like the metal one does scrap-

"Oh, I've caught fish that long from johnboats."

ing over riffles. It just kind of thuds when it hits something and that's all
there is to it. Also the wooden ones actually handle easier.

How many johnboats have you made?

Oh, I've made twenty-five or thirty. No two of them alike. You know, in
building a boat, you throw away your square and rules and just build them
with what you got to build them with. Actually there's no straight lines on the
boat; they're all curved lines, so when you go to square up your boat you
eyeball it. This boat will hold three, comfortable. We've had as many as ten
or twelve people in them playing around and we've carried a lot of supplies
when we went trapping. We trapped on the Osage Fork of the Gasconade
River for mink and muskrat.

How fast will one of those boats get up to?

You couldn't go very fast. They aren't made for speed. Even if you tried
you'd run into a log jam or a big rock, unless it was a big river.

Did you ever have your boat to tip over?

Yes. It wasn't the boat's fault. It was my fault. Here's the way you get into
trouble with a boat on the river. There'll be a limb or a tree overhanging and
a swift place, and you run underneath that and get the boat kind of turned.
The fast current then can fill the boat, swamp it, or flip it over. But usually
it's awful hard to turn over a johnboat. Just stay halfway awake and you
won't have any trouble.

Tell us about a log jam.

Well, it's just driftwood or logs and things that's gone down the river and
they'd just started building up. One would land, then another, until the jam
might get as high as this building. Of course the river would run under it and
all around it. It makes it kinda aggravating to get your boat around it. You

couldn't go under it, you had to go around or over the top of it. Hauling these boats over a big pile of logs isn't easy.

Back when you didn't have power tools to tongue-and-groove with, what did you do?

We made lots of boat floors by butting the edges together. They wouldn't leak much when they swell up. We didn't used to use cyprus. It was too hard to get. We very seldom got cyprus here then. We bought black gum. It doesn't have any grain to it. It looks like a sycamore. It gets real hard and you can't use ordinary nails. Sometimes we drilled holes to drive nails because it would be so hard we couldn't drive nails without bending too many. Lots of times we used them rough and didn't plane them.

Black gum will resist the water pretty good; now it's better than oak or anything we could buy on the market. We didn't have a lot of money to spend, so we just built them out of whatever we could get to build them out of because we very seldom ever took one off the river.

We'd cut our own trees, linn [linden] and butternut. You know what butternut is. It's really light. There was always a sawmill around close. We used maple, soft maple, 'cause we didn't have any hard maple. Once every couple of years, we'd get out and hunt us a tree, take it to the sawmill to have it sawed into lumber, and we'd stack it up in the barn loft or some other building to dry it. We'd usually get enough out of a tree to make a couple, sometimes three, boats. The problem was finding a tree tall enough to get an eighteen- to twenty-foot log.

How does water affect lumber?

Well, you take any other lumber besides cyprus and redwood and it'll absorb water. You can paint it and it helps, but it still absorbs the water. And it dries out, then absorbs water, then dries out, and after a bit that does something to the cells of the wood. It just comes to a certain place and stays there, usually leaving a big crack. When pine or other wood comes to that stage it loses its elasticity, becoming kind of crumbly. This'll never do. The only fault with cyprus is it's soft and wears a little faster, but it'll still outlast pine or most other lumber, because after a year or so it just—well, I don't know actually what happens, but something happens to the cells of the wood that it becomes soft and just crumbles off. Anything that hits it takes out a big chunk.

How long would it take you to wear one out?

Oh, we trapped a lot and in the winter gigged. Three or four years. Back home the river was shallow and we were always dragging over the riffles. Usually after we wore the bottom down and renailed it two or three times, they got to where they leaked constantly and there was no way to stop them. Then we'd take them to the house to make a feed trough and build a new boat.

What's the reason, besides the fact that it's awfully heavy, for leaving the boat in the river all the time?

The wood stays swollen up all the time. You just flip the water out of it if it rained. If they're out of the river, or course, they're going to dry some, and when it dries, the lumber shrinks and it's apt to leak. Now when we left boats on the river, we'd just pick out a place along the shore—the bank, we called it—a good place to get in and out, and just padlock it to the tree. The boat would just stay out in the river all the time. Never did lose but one; what I mean is plum lose one because usually, if somebody got your boat, when they got through with it they'd fasten it up to the bank. 'Course maybe they'd pick the lock or something, but usually they'd tie it up, because they'd want to use it again. They never take them up the river, that's too hard work. They take them down the river, so we'd just take down the river. Usually someplace around the bend we'd find it.

We never lost a boat due to high water. There was a place down in the field, well, you'd call it a little cove, and we usually tied our boat up there. We'd reach up as high as we could. There was a little sycamore tree there and we'd fasten the chain. Well, as the river comes up and the boat floats up and being in that little cove, very seldom did anything ruin our boat. If a log or tree comes down the river and get against it, you can imagine what that does to it. Just caves it in, tears them all to pieces.

How much did the boats you used to make cost you since you cut your own lumber?

Oh, five dollars, maybe, for sawing, nails, and screws.

How much will this boat we're making now cost?

Emmitt looked at us with a twinkle in his eye. We knew the cost of materials alone would be close to sixteen times what it cost when he was in high school.

Well, if you've got to ask, you can't afford it.

From Rags to Rugs

In the Ozarks, a piece of cloth endured much use until it reached the rag bag to be made into rugs. The cloth—perhaps hand-carded, spun, and woven of wool or cotton produced on the farm—might start as a small child's shirt. Then it was handed down through the younger children in the family, gathering holes and losing its original buttons along the way. After serving many years of wear as a shirt, it was added to a rag collection of Mother's worn-out dresses, Father's old pants cut down to fit his sons, and many other garments which could no longer be mended or remodeled. When the collection was big enough, all of these rags would be used in making rag rugs, prolonging the life of the material many more years. Since clothes were not worn just a few times in those days, it took years of saving to have enough rags to make a rug, especially enough to weave the four or five room-length strips needed for a carpet.

The many-colored and often faded rags didn't look like much, by themselves but when ripped, tacked together, and woven through a loom into a rug, they made attractive, useful, and durable floor coverings.

Ella Dunn has made many cotton rag rugs and said they would last for years if taken care of properly. Wool rags can last even longer than cotton, often outwearing the warp that held them together. The wool weft could then be cleaned and rewoven with a new warp to make a new rug.

Edith Fulford showed us some beautiful rich-colored wool rags she was saving to weave into a rug. The wool rags came from wool coats, jackets, and even old wool blankets. Wool takes dye better than cotton and, since the wool was not laundered like cotton when used as a garment, the color tones would still be very warm and rich.

Rugs woven for room-sized carpets usually didn't have any real patterns. The rags of various colors and designs, cut into strips, were all tacked together in random order, resulting in a varicolored design.

Though the term was not used then, the rugs were "wall-to-wall." The carpets were usually a yard wide and as long as the room. The weaver would continue weaving, rolling the carpet layer over layer on the cloth beam of the loom. Later she would unroll what she had woven and cut it in lengths to fit the room. She then tied the warp at the cut ends to keep them from raveling, and whipped the strips together side by side with a heavy thread. Some used a strong mending thread called boss ball.

Ella said the parlor or front room was the only room in which her family used rag rugs as carpeting. Carpeting wasn't for everyday use because of the difficulty of cleaning it. She did not use small throw rugs as we do now. "We didn't have rags enough for all the rooms. We scrubbed the other floors every Saturday with homemade soap and sand until they were so clean you would be willing to eat off of them if necessary. We carpeted the best room and saved it for when we entertained our young company."

To save the rug, her family rolled it up in the spring, beat the dust out of it, and stored it until the next fall. During the summer they had bare floors. Then in the fall they brought in freshly threshed straw and spread it over the floor about three or four inches deep. They unrolled the rug, stretched it, and tacked it down around the walls with carpet tacks, turning the edges under to hide the rough edge where the strips were cut apart. The result was a very smooth and soft carpet which blended with any color scheme. Ella remembers her son taking an old coal oil lamp and stretching out on the soft, warm rug carpet to work on his lessons.

THE LANGUAGE OF WEAVERS

Weavers have their own distinctive and interesting vocabulary. Before we see how a rug is woven, a short explanation of the most common terms is useful.

Beater—The reed is inserted in it, and it beats the filling (weft) into place.

Bundle—A group of warp threads, usually twenty-four, handled as a unit on the warping board and in threading through the loom.

Cloth Beam—The cloth beam is the roller at the front of the loom on which the cloth is wound.

Cross—The alternating of warp yarns around the pegs of the warping board describes a cross. The purpose of the cross is to keep the yarns in proper order for threading.

Dent—Slots in the reed through which a single warp thread is sleyed.

Parts of the loom: 1. Treadles 2. Cloth beam 3. Beater 4. Reed 5. Harnesses 6. Heddles 7. Warp beam.

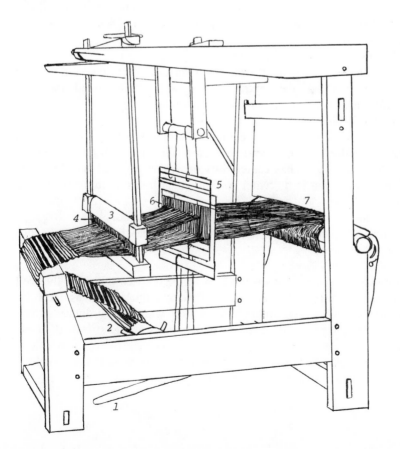

Harnesses—Two horizontal bars between which the heddles are strung.

Heddles—Lengths of metal, wire, or string suspended between the harnesses. They have a center loop, or eye, through which the warp yarn passes.

Leash Sticks or Rods—The narrow sticks or rods placed on each side of the leash or cross which are tied together to keep the warp in order when treading the loom.

Loom—A frame or machine used to hold one set of threads (the warp) in order while other threads (the weft, woof, or filler) are interlaced with the warp.

Pick—A single passage of filling thread (weft) through the shed, also called the shot.

Plain Weave—Weaving over and under one row, under and over the next row. Sometimes called tabby.

Ratchets—Wheels with teeth to maintain the proper tension. There is usually one at the back of the loom and one at the front.

Rattle—A toothed board for guiding the warp bundles when threading from the front.

Reed—A comblike device inserted in the beater. It spaces the warp in slots called dents. Reeds come in various sizes. The size indicates the number of dents per inch. For example, a reed with twelve slots is called a twelve-dent reed and means twelve threads per inch if single-dented.

Selvage—A woven edge of cloth.

Sett—The number of warp ends per inch.

Shed—The V-shaped opening formed by the raising or lowering of warp ends through which the shuttle carrying the filling thread (weft) is passed to make a row (pick or shot) of weaving.

Shot—Refer to Pick.

Shuttle—The stick or boatlike container which holds the thread when weaving. Shuttles come in various forms. The stick shuttle is long and flat. The boat shuttle has center rods on which to wind the weft. One kind has a steel pin in its center section which holds a removable bobbin or quill.

Sleying—Threading the warp through the dents in a reed.

Spool Rack—A wooden rack with holders for at least twenty-four spools of warp thread.

Tabby—See Plain Weave.

Take-up—The amount of warp used up through space taken by the weft. This is important when the weft is especially thick, such as large rug yarn or extra bulky rags—these take up more warp than ordinary weft.

Tension—The degree of tightness to which the warp is stretched on the loom.

Treadles—The pedals or foot levers to which the harnesses of a floor loom are attached to obtain the desired shed.

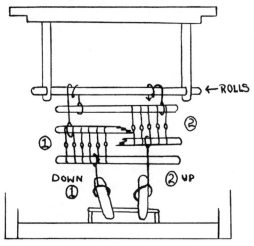

Treadles and harnesses. As pedal ⚹1 is pushed down, harness ⚹1 lowers, separating half of the warp. Simultaneously, harness ⚹2 raises since this harness is fastened on each end with a rope looped over a rolling wooden bar to harness ⚹2. Pressing pedal ⚹2 reverses the position of the harnesses and crosses the warp for weaving.

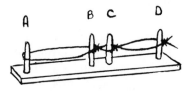

Making string heddles. Put pegs or nails on a 12-inch board as shown. The two center pegs should be no more than ½ inch apart. Begin with a warp string at least 24 inches long. Loop the center over peg A. Tie a square knot against peg B (on peg C side). Tie another square knot against peg C (on peg D side) and finish by tying a square knot at peg D as shown. The loop at pegs A and D will slip over the top and bottom harness boards. The hole created at pegs B and C is the eye through which you thread the warp. For a 28-inch-wide rug, you will need to tie 336 of these string heddles.

Warp—The threads which run lengthwise of the loom on which they are stretched to form the skeleton of the fabric.

Warp Beam—The roller at the back of the loom on which the warp is wound.

Warping Board—A wooden frame with spaced pegs around which the warp is measured and wound.

Warping a Loom—Stretching the threads for the warp to a desired length, beaming them, threading them, sleying them through the reed, tying them down. Sometimes called dressing the loom.

Weaving—Weaving is the crossing and interlacing of threads or fibers to form cloth.

Weft—The weft is put in at right angles to the warp and binds them together, thus completing the cloth. May be called woof or filler.

Woof—Refer to Weft.

Expressions:

Open the shed, close the shed, change the shed—refer to manipulating the treadles to form the V-shaped opening. When there is no shed or opening, the threads are said to be in a neutral position.

THE OLD LOOM

The old loom pictured in this story was built about 1857 or earlier by Silas Barr of the Russ Community of Laclede County, Missouri. According to Sherman Edwards, Silas' great-grandson, Mr. Barr made furniture for his family's use in his workshop and made this loom for weaving rag carpets.

Mr. Edwards remembers his grandmother, Mrs. Marion Barr, (Silas' daughter-in-law) weaving carpets on the loom. After being in the Barr family for three generations, the loom was sold to the neighboring Alfie Griffin family, where it was used for two more generations. In recent years no one used the loom any more and as space was needed in the house Alfie's son Harvie moved it to an unused chicken house where the *Bittersweet* staff located it and purchased it in 1972, just before Mr. Griffin's death.

There are no nails in the loom. All the permanent parts are fastened together with wooden pegs. The loom is readily disassembled for moving or storage as the warp and cloth beams lift out of their holders and the cross braces all fit into slots. It is made entirely of oak, with no metal parts. Even the cogs and ratchets are carved out of wood.

The original reed was gone, but a modern reed fits perfectly into the hand-grooved and adjustable reed holder. The reed is like those used years ago. The old wooden harnesses with string heddles were there, though the strings, of course, were rotten. Instead of string heddles, the loom now has metal heddles and a set of harnesses to hold them. With those two exceptions, the rest of the loom is as Silas Barr built it.

Rough oak lumber joined by wooden pegs and slots.

Hand-hewn ratchet on cloth beam.

Today a wall-to-wall rag carpet would be even more of a luxury than it was years ago, as the labor involved would make it very expensive. The greatest demand now is for small scatter rugs placed at doors and other spots to give accents, color, and charm to the room.

Using the old loom, we have learned how to weave just as women did long ago. Much more goes into making rag rugs than weaving the rags together. There is the warping of the loom to prepare the loom for actual weaving, the cutting and tacking of the rags, and finally the steps of feeding the tacked rags through the warp to weave them into rugs. These three processes are described as the first owner of this loom would have done them.

WARPING THE LOOM

Woven rag rugs are made of rags held together by a cotton string or cord called warp. Though the rags were readily available many years ago, the warp was not. It had to be purchased on four-inch spools very much like those weavers use today. Warp is sold by weight, with most spools holding half a pound or about eight hundred yards. Usually weavers purchase twenty-four spools, enough warp to weave many yards of carpet. Today warp can be obtained in many boilproof colors, but years ago most weavers used natural warp.

Preparing the warp is a harder job than weaving. It is tedious to thread the hundreds of threads through the reed and heddles correctly. Therefore, weavers would wind enough warp to weave many strips of carpeting onto the warp beam at one time.

There are several ways of warping a loom. We will describe a method which uses a warping board and threads the warp from the front. Ella Dunn remembers her mother doing it this way and our loom was designed for this method.

Warp beam wheel and lever for tension.

A warping board allows the weaver to handle several hundred individual warp threads and wind them onto the warping beam at one time. This process was used on looms which had no divided partitions on the warp beam. Most big looms today have divisions on the warp beam, allowing the weaver to wind a bundle of twenty-four warp threads at a time instead of the total number needed for the complete width of the rug.

WINDING ON THE WARPING BOARD

The first step in warping the loom is to put the warp onto the warping board (Plate 1). Place the spools on a spool rack so that the warp unwinds from the top of each spool. Pull about two feet of warp from each spool, getting all the ends even (Plate 2). You are ready to start winding the warp onto the warping board.

Place the warping board upright in a comfortable position to wind onto. Usually the boards are fastened on a wall, though some prefer to lay them on a flat surface. Be sure that the spool rack is placed so that winding will not be awkward and so that the threads will not get tangled.

Usually twenty-four spools are used. The ends of all twenty-four threads together are treated as a unit and are called a bundle. Tie a slip knot over peg A (Plate 3). As you wind the warp on the board, make a cross with pegs B and C. The cross is necessary to keep the bundles of warp separate and in the correct order while threading through the reed and heddles. Begin winding by going over peg B and under peg C. Hold the warp in both hands, one to guide the warp and the other to keep the tension. Pull the warp

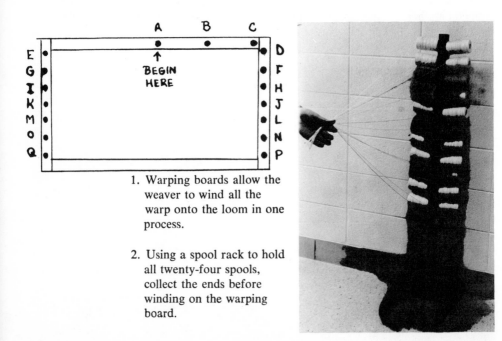

1. Warping boards allow the weaver to wind all the warp onto the loom in one process.

2. Using a spool rack to hold all twenty-four spools, collect the ends before winding on the warping board.

around peg D and go to peg E (Plate 4). Now proceed to peg F, back and forth until you reach peg Q, or the last peg on your board. Go around peg Q as you have the other pegs, except go back to peg P and retrace the first pattern of warp. Continue up the board to peg D and go around it. But this time, instead of retracing the pattern, go over peg C and under peg B—the reverse of the first time. By doing this you have formed a cross.

Continue around peg A, and you have completed one round on the warping board. Now go over B and under C as you did the first time. The rest of the work of putting the warp on the board is simply following the pattern you have made on the first complete round. Be careful not to overlap the bundles on the pegs or let them slip off. Only one person should wind the warp onto the board, so that the tension will be equal throughout the entire length of warp. This will prevent the warp from tangling while rolling onto the warp beam.

Continue putting rounds on the warping board until you reach the desired width of your rug. Cut the warp and fasten with a slip knot around peg A as you did when beginning.

To determine the width of the rug, you must know two things—the sett of your loom and the number of spools you are using. If you have a common twelve-sett loom (twelve warp threads per inch), and you are using twenty-four spools of warp, a half round will be two inches, and a complete round will be four inches of warp when threaded on the loom. To weave a rug twenty-eight inches wide, you will need to put seven complete rounds on the warping board.

The length of your warp is determined by the size of your warping board. The one pictured is small and will weave only about fifteen yards of warp.

Since warping the loom is such a tedious job, in the old days women warped using much larger warping boards, nine or ten feet wide and three or

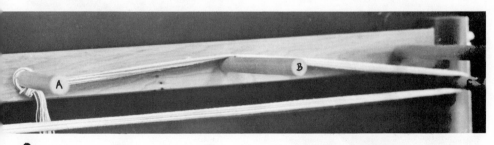

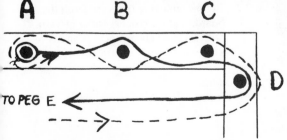

3. Fasten the ends on peg A, go over B and under C the first time.

4. When returning, go over C and under B to form a cross.

four feet high. Fastened to the side of the smokehouse or other building, these boards could allow many yards of warp to be put on the loom at one time. Warping like this would permit the women to weave for months without having to rewarp the loom after weaving only a few rugs.

REMOVING THE WARP FROM THE WARPING BOARD

When enough warp is wound on the board to reach the desired width of rug, one must transfer the warp from the warping board onto the loom. This is done by making a large chain of the warp on the board. But first a few preparations are necessary.

Make a small chain with a piece of wool yarn about four feet long at the cross between pegs B and C. This keeps the bundles in the correct order to place on the rattle when threading the loom. The chain resembles that made with a crochet hook. Double the yarn, making a loop at one end (Plate 5). Place the loop beneath the first bundle wound onto the board. Pull the dou-

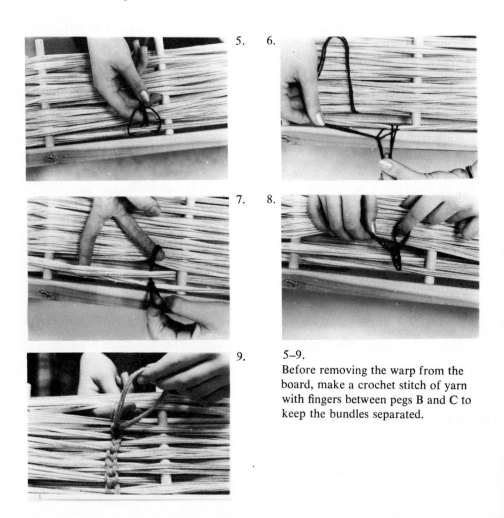

5.   6.

7.   8.

9.

5–9.
Before removing the warp from the board, make a crochet stitch of yarn with fingers between pegs B and C to keep the bundles separated.

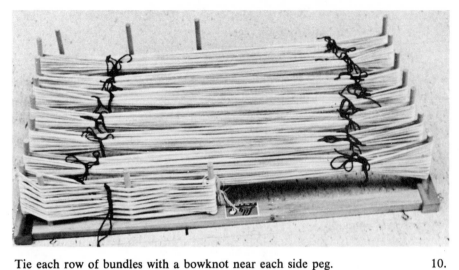

Tie each row of bundles with a bowknot near each side peg. 10.

11.

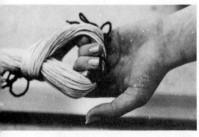

12.

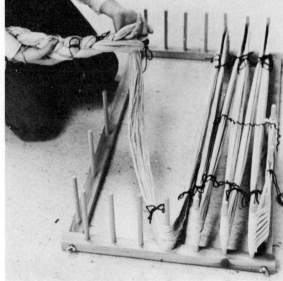

14.

Remove the warp from the
board by making a large
chain with your hands.

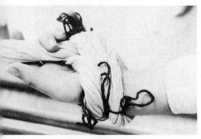

13.

ble threads partially through the first loop to form a second loop (Plate 6). Do not pull the ends through. Tighten, and repeat this chain, making a link around every bundle (Plate 7). When you reach the last bundle, pull the ends through the loop (Plates 8–9).

Use more wool yarn to keep groups of bundles in their correct order while removing the warp from the warping board. Tie the yarn in bowknots around all the bundles, about two inches from every peg. A bowknot is best because it can be easily removed (Plate 10).

You are now ready to remove the warp from the warping board by making one large chain of all the warp threads. Tie a piece of yarn at peg Q to mark the center. Begin the chain at peg Q by slipping all the bundles of the warp off the peg together as one unit. Slipping your hand through the loop that was around peg Q, get hold of all the warp bundles and pull them through, forming a second loop (Plates 11–14). Gently slip the hand through the loop that was drawn through the first loop. Continue the chain, removing the warp

After chaining off the entire warp to peg D, tie the chain in an easily removed bowknot to hold in place while threading through the loom.

15.

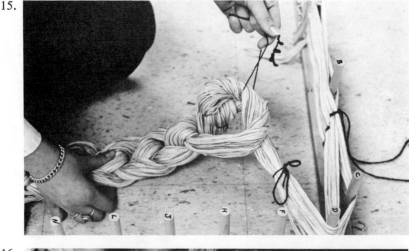

16.

17.
Insert leash sticks on either side of small yarn chain before removing it from the warping board.

from the board as you progress up to peg D. At that point secure the chain with a piece of wool yarn so it won't come undone (Plate 15). Now tie a piece of wool yarn at peg A as you did at peg Q to mark the center (Plate 16).

It is time to insert the leash sticks, one on each side of the yarn chain you fixed earlier. Leash sticks can be made from one-half- to one-inch dowel pins. Tie a piece of yarn at each end of the leash sticks to hold them together and keep the bundles from slipping off (Plate 17). Remove the remaining warp from the board (including the yarn chain, leash sticks, and cross) by simply pulling it off the pegs. The warp has been chained off the warping board, looped into a manageable chain which keeps all the threads in place and prevents them from becoming tangled. You are now ready to put the warp onto the loom.

TRANSFERRING THE WARP TO THE LOOM

The chain from our warp board consists of 336 individual warp threads fifteen yards long. This method of transferring the chain onto the warp beam of the loom feeds the warp from the front, through the rattle, the reed, and the heddles, before being wound onto the warp beam. When the warp is all threaded and fastened to the warp beam, the warp beam wheel is turned. The wheel pulls the warp out of the chain and draws it through the loom. Enough warp is reserved to fasten to the cloth beam. We are describing warping for a two-harness loom using plain (or tabby) weave with no pattern in the warp.

Cut the warp through the center which was marked by the wool yarn. (This was the loop around peg A on the warping board.) In order to keep each unit separated, tie a slip knot at the end of each bundle before taking

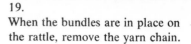

18.
The rattle helps hold and separate
the bundles of warp while still
chained together.

19.
When the bundles are in place on
the rattle, remove the yarn chain.

the chain to the loom. You should now divide the warp bundles, separated
and held in place by the yarn chain, between the pegs of the rattle (Plates
18–19). The rattle fastened in front of the reed helps hold the many bundles of warp in place while threading them through the loom. One can be
made easily with nails or pegs spaced about two inches apart on a board as
long as the reed.

   Place the center bundle between the center pegs of the rattle, spreading out
the bundles on the pegs in each direction. To keep them from falling off the
rattle, tie two bundles together. Remove the yarn chain (Plate 20).

20.
The rattle continues to hold the yarn bundles even while threading through the
reed.

21.
Thread warp threads one at a time through the reed without skipping any dents.

The warp is ready to be threaded (or sleyed) through the dents in the reed. Begin with the center bundle at the center sett of the reed, and individually draw a single warp thread through the reed with the threading hook (Plate 21). This job goes much faster with two people—one in front holding the correct thread and the other behind the reed pulling it through the hook. Always begin in the center of the reed and work one way and then the other so the warp will be centered on the loom.

Continue drawing the individual warp threads through the reed until you finish the first bundle. Secure each bundle behind the reed with a slip knot to keep the warp threads from slipping back through the reed. Repeat this process with each bundle until you reach one end. Some people prefer to draw two warp threads through the last dent of the reed to make a stiffer selvage.

You are now half finished drawing the warp through the reed. Return to the center and draw through the remaining half of warp threads. When sleying, be very careful not to skip a dent, which will cause gaps in the finished rug.

Next thread the warp through the heddles. Standing behind the harnesses, pull each thread through with the hook. Begin with the same bundle that you began with when sleying the reed. Have both harnesses at the same level. Untying one bundle at a time, draw the first individual warp thread through the

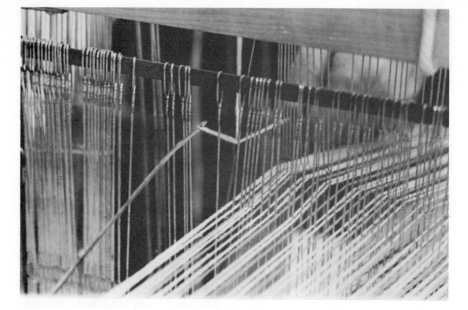

22–23.

The warp goes through the eye of the center heddles of the first harness and between the center heddles of the second harness. The second warp goes between the heddles of the first harness and through the eye of the center heddle on the second harness.

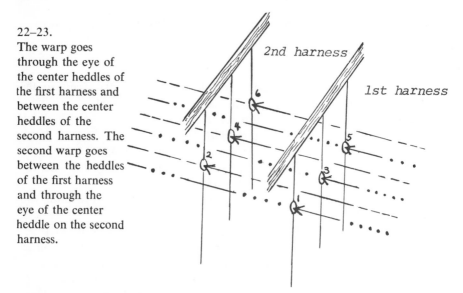

2nd harness

1st harness

eye of the center heddle on the first harness and between the two center heddles of the second harness. Draw the second warp thread between the heddle you just threaded and the next heddle of the first harness and through the eye of the heddle on the second harness (Plates 22–23). It is very important that you do not skip heddles or fail to alternate harnesses, as every mistake in threading will give an imperfect weave. To correct the mistake you must take everything out to the mistake and rethread.

24.
Turn the warp beam lever (at
rear) to wind the warp through
the reed and heddles onto the warp
beam.

Tie the bundles together after threading through the heddles as you did after threading through the reed to keep them safe until ready to fasten them to the warp beam.

You are now ready to tie the bundles onto the rod attached to the warp beam. The tension must be the same all the way across the beam, which can be achieved by tying the two end bundles onto the rod with the same tension. Then tie on the center bundles, keeping the tension equal.

The next step is to wind the warp through the loom onto the warp beam (Plate 24). At least three and possibly four other people are needed to do this: one person is needed to turn the warp beam wheel, one to hold the leash sticks together to put tension on the warp as it goes through the reeds and heddles to wrap firmly on the beam, and the others to hold the warp chain, remove the bowknots of yarn in the chain, and keep the warp smoothed out as it is drawn through the reed. The warp will sometimes become tangled at the reed, but simply comb out the tangles with your fingers and continue turning the warp beam wheel.

You should wind all but about one foot of the warp through the reed. Before you get that far, cut through the looped end of the warp chain and tie each bundle together as you did at the other end of the chain. Tying prevents the warp from accidentally slipping through the reed. Next, tie the warp that has not gone through the reed to the rod which is attached to the cloth beam. Do this in the same fashion as you tied the warp onto the warp beam by first tying both end bundles to get the correct tension, then tying those in the middle. These ends must be tied carefully with equal tension across the width of the beam. As the rug is woven and wound onto the cloth beam, it should wrap evenly.

You are finished warping the loom and are ready to prepare the rags for the weft.

TACKING THE RAGS

The first consideration in preparing the weft for a rag rug is the kind of rags you will use. In older days the only types of fabric people had were cotton and wool. Even though it is not as plentiful as it once was, cotton has continued to be the most popular fabric for rugs for several reasons. Rugs made from cotton rags are easy to clean; they can be washed in very hot water with no fear of shrinking or fading; and cotton is easy to work with since it is not bulky and tears easily, yet is strong enough to withstand the pulling and pounding of the loom.

Wool also makes lovely rugs. Its colors are brighter than cotton as wool takes the dye better and wool weft lasts longer than cotton. However, wool has some disadvantages. Since wool does not tear like cotton, it takes longer to prepare the strips, as each strip must be cut with scissors. Wool cannot be washed as easily as cotton; rugs made of wool rags should be washed in lukewarm water because wool is likely to shrink. Most people do not wash wool rugs, but shake and beat them clean.

After tacking the rags together, wind them into balls. Edith Fulford is winding for a varicolored rug.

Today many weavers like to use knits. They make pretty, colorful rugs since knits come in such a variety of bright colors which never fade and hardly ever wear out. They also wash easily, but, like wool, knit fabrics are bulky and have to be cut into strips instead of torn.

Whatever kind of rags you use, never change types of fabric in the middle of a rug because different fabrics wash differently than others, and they often don't wear the same, or produce a consistent finished product.

When you have collected and sorted all your rags and put them into piles according to the kind of fabric, you next need to sort according to weight. Cottons vary from heavy duck and denims to very sheer organdies. Most can be used in weaving rugs, but for best appearance and even wear do not use them together. However, it is possible to use different weights of fabric in the same rug by adjusting the width of the strip. Thinner materials would be cut wider than heavier ones. In that way, when woven through the loom and beat down, each row of weft would be the same width.

Remove all snaps, buttons, and zippers, and take out the seams. Seams in the strips make it harder to pull the weft through the warp and cause hard or bulky spots in the finished rug.

Next, tear the rags into strips. To do this, cut a little strip about two inches long with the grain of the fabric and tear (or cut) it the rest of the way. The ravelings don't matter as they will be folded into the weft; those that do stick up through the warp will soon wear off.

The length of the strip is determined by the length of the scraps. There is no one width for tearing the fabric as that depends on how thick you want the finished rug. Most people cut cotton rags about one inch wide and the wool or knits narrower. The wider the strips, the heavier the rug and thicker the width of each row of weft. Edith Fulford said, "You just take your garment and work with it and whatever it says to do, why, you do it."

Cut the strips depending on the fabric. If it is heavy, it should be torn narrower than a thinner piece. For knits and wools the width of the strip should probably not be more than three fourths of an inch.

There is an easy way to make the rags go much further when you have a few little scraps. Begin at one side of the scrap (Plate 25). When tearing the first strip, do not tear completely to the end of the piece. Leave about half an inch. For your next tear, begin at the other side, and tear up, again leaving

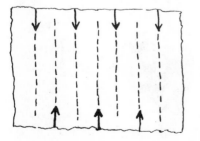

25.
Use even small scraps of fabric by tearing as indicated by arrows. Leave about ½ inch at end of each tear for one continuous strip.

about half an inch untorn. Continue in this manner until the scrap is torn. This will produce one long piece which does not need to be tacked.

As you tear the strips, put like colors together into piles. Before you tack the strips together, you need to decide on the design. No two rugs will be alike, unless, of course, you use a solid color. Since there are an infinite number of designs you can use, just use your imagination. The design could be very simple or more complicated—twelve inches of white followed by an inch of color, then an inch of white, repeat and finish off with one last inch of color and twelve more inches of white. You could also just mix the colors together with no specific pattern.

After you've torn your rags and have decided on your design, you are ready to start tacking the strips together. If you plan to use sections of one color, followed by another, tack each color together and wind in separate balls. If you want a staggered effect, tack a different color on each time in the design you wish.

Rags can be tacked by machine or by hand. Lay one strip on top of another and sew flat, not in a seam. This makes a smoother, less bulky joining. Edith sews her strips together by overlapping about one inch of the end of one strip over the end of another with the right sides down. Then she folds them over together lengthwise once and then a second time.

Next, she sews diagonally across the folds. Sewing diagonally allows you to work faster and prevents loose ends which get caught or stick up in the rug, leaving a rough finish. Sewing on the bias also allows some give to the strips so the stitches don't break as easily when they are stretched in the loom.

An economical way of saving thread and time when sewing these strips together on the machine is to sew many strips together before cutting the thread. Edith laps them over as shown in Plate 26.

While lapping them over, she loops one string in one direction and the next

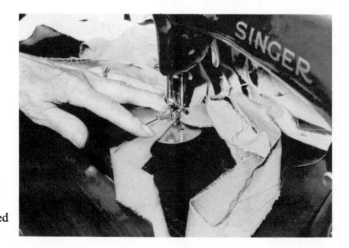

26.
Tacking with the machine makes the job easier. Sew diagonally on folded strips.

string in the other with no space between until she has sewn together as many as she wants. She then clips them apart and rolls them into a ball.

Even if you sew the strips together on a machine you will need to do some hand tacking. If your strip breaks on the loom, or if you need to cut it to fix a mistake or when changing shuttles, you can sew the strip back together by hand.

Though machine tacking is faster, some people prefer to tack the strips together by hand. The method is the same, except that you will probably not want to fold the strips before tacking if the material is heavy. When hand sewing, use double thread and take small stitches diagonally across the strips. Fasten your thread well after each strip. Some prefer weaving with hand-tacked strips since the looser hand stitches do not make such a stiff place in the weft.

Preparing the rags is the most time-consuming part of weaving rag rugs, but when they are all tacked, the real fun of weaving begins.

WEAVING THE RAG RUG

Weaving is defined as crossing the warp and the weft, or interlacing threads. The two-harness loom helps the weaver do this process quickly. Every even warp thread goes through the heddles of one harness and the odd numbers are threaded through the heddles of the second harness. Each harness is controlled by a foot treadle. As one treadle goes down, it lowers one harness and raises the other, separating the warp threads. The weft is put through the shed that is created. When the other treadle is pushed, the position of the harnesses reverses. The warp that was on top is now on the bottom. This makes a cross which produces the weave.

As each row (called a shot or pick) of weft is put through, the beater is pulled forward against the strip, mashing it into a tight string. When the warp is crossed and the beater applied again, the weaving is tight.

By now you have the rags already tacked and the design decided for the rug. But before you start the actual weaving, there are a few things to get ready at the loom. First you need to wind the rag strips from the ball onto a shuttle. Shuttles designed to carry the weft through the shed of the warp come in several sizes and styles. Rack or boat shuttles slide easily through the

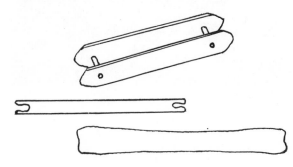

Some shuttles used in weaving rag rugs.

Note the changes in a modern loom. Edith Fulford (standing left) teaches *Bittersweet* members to weave.

warp on wooden runners and are preferred by most rug weavers. If you have several shuttles and are using more than one color, fill a shuttle for each color.

Next you need to tighten the warp. The tension of the warp should always be released when not weaving to prevent stretching the warp. On our old loom this meant tying the lever on the wheel of the warp beam.

You also need to be comfortable and have all your equipment handy. Sit on a stool, bench, or chair which will enable you to work the pedals easily and to avoid any unnecessary bending and stretching while weaving. The weaving rhythm should be steady and not tiring.

Provide a place for scissors, needle, and thread so that you do not have to get up or hunt for them. We fixed a place by taking a scrap of fabric and wrapping it around the front bar of the loom. We made a pocket for the scissors and thread.

The basic steps in making a rag rug are simple. Begin with a narrow tight border of warp, then weave the rags in the pattern desired for the length of the rug, and finish off with the same number of rows of warp for the other border. Then leave a space of several inches of warp before beginning a new rug.

When everything is ready to weave, begin the first rug about six inches from the rod where the warp threads are tied (Plate 27). If this is the sec-

27.
Beginning the first rug.

ond rug, leave at least six to eight inches from the rug you just finished (Plate 28). Edith likes to run an old rag strip through as a marker. Tamp it in straight with the beater, cross the warp, and run it back through. This enables you to start the rug on a straight line. You will pull this strip out once the rug has enough rows to keep it going without the marker.

After you have the marker in place, you are ready for the border. This gives a tight finish to the ends of the rugs. Many weavers use a few rows of warp thread, though it is not necessary to do so.

When the border is done, you are ready to run the weft (or rags) through. Push down on one of the pedals, making a shed. Run the filled shuttle

28.
Leave about eight inches between rugs.

29.
Leave a few inches of rag in the first row. Turn it back in when weaving the second row.

through, leaving about four inches of the end sticking out the edge (Plate 29). Now tamp the rag strip tight against the border with the beater, making a hard line which will eventually contribute to the design of the rug. With your feet on the two pedals underneath you, press down the one that is up. This crosses the two rows of warp and holds the rags tightly in place. Once again tamp two or three times with the beater to make a nice straight line in the rug.

Leave a few inches sticking out when beginning and ending the borders and rag strips. Then cut the excess part of the rag strips thinner and turn it back in the rug with the next row. The crossing of the warp will hold it tightly in place and turning it back will avoid ragged ends sticking out.

Now run the shuttle back through the other direction and repeat the process to make a second row. Repeat this until you are finished or until you want to change the color. Then cut the line of rags, tack on the other color, and continue weaving. Try to keep a big enough shed so the shuttle slides through, and do not wind too much weft on the shuttles or it will be difficult to slip the shuttle through the shed.

An important thing in weaving is to keep a straight selvage, for uneven sides will ruin the looks. When running a single shot through the shed, do not pull it through too tightly. Leave a little loop at the edge. When you bring down the beater that looseness will be taken up, leaving a straight selvage.

A piece of equipment called a template helps keep the selvage even. It is a long jointed board, adjustable to any width, with sharp clasps on each end to grip into the rug. You can fasten this on the rug when you have woven about three or four inches. The nails clasp into each edge, holding the rug taut and straight. The template serves as a guide as to how tight or loose to weave the selvage and helps keep them straight. When you weave another few inches, move it up. The template follows you through the rug, assuring that the rug is the same width throughout.

When you make a mistake in the rug, simply unweave. If your right pedal is down, push the left one down in order to uncross your cross and run the shuttle backward, pulling the line of rags back out. Repeat this uncrossing,

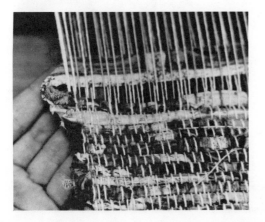

Getting a straight edge is difficult for a beginner.

and pull out all the way back to your mistake. We had to unweave almost half a rug just for a mistake, but it is worth it when your efforts produce a beautiful rug.

Actually it is personal preference as to how much warp you leave between rugs. Edith leaves six inches to allow for three inches fringe for each rug when you take the rugs off. Other people may want more fringe than that. In deciding on the amount of fringe you want, remember that the knots you tie to fasten the fringe will take up some of that length. Mark off the desired length and start a new rug.

It is better not to cut the rugs apart as you make them, because you waste warp and time: each time you cut off a rug you have to retie the ends back into the cloth beam. Leave the rugs on the loom until you use up the warp and then take them all off together. As you weave the rugs, just wind them onto the cloth beam. Leave the rugs on the loom until you use up the warp.

While weaving the rugs, keep working until you have no more room to run the shuttle through the shed or until it gets to be uncomfortable. Then roll the finished portion onto the cloth beam. Release the tension on the warp beam, roll the warp off the warp beam, and roll the woven rug onto the cloth beam. When you have rolled it as far as you need to, secure the ratchet on the cloth beam, tighten the tension on the warp beam, and resume weaving.

When you take the finished rugs off the loom, release the cloth beam ratchet, cut the warp threads, and unwind all of the rugs onto the floor. Cut the warp with the scissors halfway between each two rugs to separate them.

Using the template.

Roll finished rug on the cloth beam.

When all warp is rolled off the warp beam, cut the rug from the loom, leaving enough warp for a fringe.

Secure the weaving by tying small knots in the fringe.

Use the table edge to cut fringe the length desired.

To keep the rugs from gradually unweaving, the fringe needs to be tied. Lay each rug on a flat surface, then, beginning at one selvage, tie three to five warp strings into an overhand knot. Push the knot securely against the border to hold the weft tightly.

The rug is now finished except for trimming off the ragged ends of the fringe. Lay the straight line of the rug's border back from the edge of a table, then cut the ends sticking over the length you want the fringe to be.

We found the weaving relaxing, and it was exciting to see the rugs form. The most gratifying part, though, was to sit back and look at the rugs you had woven out of rags most people would throw away.

Pieces of the Past

The basic patchwork technique came to America in the seventeenth century with the early colonists, but it was far from being the art it later became. The frugal nature of American women combined with their love of beautiful things and caused them to develop quilt making to a sophisticated art practiced by most women as early as the eighteenth century. In the early American homes quilts were a necessity of vital importance to all, especially in the Northern settlements where the winters were cold. The pioneers' poorly heated log houses made it necessary for an adequate supply of bedding.

To make the great amount of bedding needed, every scrap and remnant of leftover fabric from rare manufactured material was saved. The best parts of worn-out garments were carefully saved and cut into quilt pieces. Women eagerly exchanged different-colored pieces with one another, storing every scrap in boxes or special bags to sew later into colorful quilts. The main idea, though, was to produce a quilt that was warm and would withstand the greatest amount of wear possible. Patched and repatched, the older ragged

The ladies of White Oak Pond Cumberland Presbyterian Church quilt every Thursday. Here they begin work on an Improved Nine Patch.

quilts were even used to fill newer ones, tacking a new cover and lining together. Nothing was wasted.

The piecing and quilting was a favorite pastime of both old and young. In
both rich and poor homes the women and young daughters would sit in their
rocking chairs close to the fire, piecing, tacking, and quilting after the housework and chores were finished for the day. This was a period of relaxation
and a time for visiting.

Piecing was one of the first things a young girl learned. A girl would usually start piecing her first quilt around the age of eight. Usually the quilt was
a simple Four or Nine Patch. This block-style quilt was easy for the beginner
because the straight seams of the square blocks repeat to create a geometric
design.

There is a difference between "patching" and "piecing." The patched quilts
were commonly associated with unfortunate circumstances: people only had
old patches with which to make quilts. Patches were cut out of old garments
and sewn together in no particular pattern though many of the "scrap quilts,"
as they were called, were very pretty when made from gay pieces carefully
blended of various shades of a color.

The pieced quilts were of special appeal to women who delighted in precise

At a favorite spot Ray
O'Dell spends many
pleasant hours piecing
tops she will later quilt.

and accurate work. The pieces were usually of uniform shape and size and of contrasting colors which made a pattern.

Whether it was a patched or a pieced quilt, each woman prided herself on creating a quilt that was artistic. For those who enjoyed making pieced quilts, there was practically no limit to the variety of designs available. Women often made up their own patterns from the basic Nine Patch to rather complicated patterns like My Mother's Dream.

The quilt maker was not an artist and did not think of herself as an artist. While making bedding for her family, she experimented with design possibilities, creating patterns to suit her taste and moods. She used color and geometric forms to represent objects (Fish Block quilt), movements (Fifty-four Forty or Fight), ideas (Improved Nine Patch), and emotions (My Mother's Dream). Her patterns looked modern because of the bold striking colors and the almost three-dimensional design effect which looked like abstract art.

The beginning of a utility quilt or pieced quilt was the basic square, which could easily be segmented into many different straight-line forms to create many different patterns by rearranging, adding, and subtracting pieces. These pieces were also easy to stitch together because of the straight lines. (Quilts

The Carpenter's Square
quilt pieced in 1860s looks
like modern abstract art.

with curved lines were appliquéd—pieces sewn on the surface of another block.)

A great number and variety of names were given to quilt designs. The many days spent in creating even a simple quilt gave the maker time to ponder over a name for the new design. Quilt names often reflected the moods and personalities of the people who named them. Some names were quite humorous, some show sadness. Some quilt patterns got their names from historical or political events. Fifty-four Forty or Fight, Democrat Rose, Lincoln's Platform, Confederate Rose, and Pilgrim's Pride are examples of this. They were given also biblical and religious names such as Crown of Thorns, David and Goliath, Joseph's Coat, Crosses and Losses, Solomon's Temple, Job's Tears, and Star of Bethlehem. Quilts were named from outdoor life, recreation, and occupations: Flower Garden, Sunshine, Snowball, Four Frogs, Cats and Mice, Eight Hands Around, Hands All Around, Baseball, and Carpenter's Wheel. The subject of love was not left out—Hobson's Kiss, Lover's Link, Wedding Ring, and Wedding Knot.

Women who were artistic delighted in changing and improving designs, using old patterns as a foundation as they worked out new ones. From the

Crazy quilt of dress
scraps and old ties.

Nine Patch pattern new patterns and names were derived such as Improved Nine Patch, Split Nine Patch, Double Nine Patch, and the Nine Patch Star. Therefore, it is not unusual to find patterns of the same design having many different names. The pattern Crown of Thorns is also called Georgetown Circle, Rocky Mountain Road, and Memory Wreath. When called Memory Wreath, it was made from pieces of clothing worn by the departed with their names embroidered in the center. Crosses and Losses is sometimes called Fox and Geese, Triple X, and Hovering Hawks. Missouri Rose is called Rose Tree and Prairie Flower. Jacob's Ladder is called Stepping Stone, Wagon Track, and Underground Railroad.

Even the everyday quilts were considered worthy of names. Children named them, too, and the results were quaint names such as Pig Pen and Pin Wheel. They were delighted when they were able to name a quilt and pick out the blocks of material that were once parts of their own dresses or shirts.

When a woman made up a new pattern she was anxious to give it or trade it for another one with her friends or relatives. They would meet at one another's homes and discuss new patterns and names, sometimes accumulating a hundred or more different patterns until even the most ambitious quilt maker could not hope to make a quilt for every design she admired.

Even though pieced quilt patterns were loaned and shared readily, none of the quilts of the same basic pattern would be alike because the makers might vary the size of the pattern by making it smaller or adding more pieces. They would all have different color combinations and use different materials. They

Friendship quilt.

would also add a variety of borders that would give each quilt a different effect.

Women and girls cut out quilt blocks and pieced them together throughout the year in their spare time. When the quilt top was pieced together it was ready for quilting or tacking. The lining is usually a whole cloth stretched over a quilting frame, on which the filler of wool or cotton is laid. The finished top is stretched on last. The three layers are then stitched through, following lines marked on the top. Quilting or tacking keeps the filler from shifting and bunching up. Both are methods of keeping the top, filling, and lining in place, making a sort of cloth sandwich. You tack a comforter and quilt a quilt. Tacking ties the layers together and is always done by hand. Quilting is sewing together material with very fine stitches, but in a definite, usually very artistic, pattern. Quilting takes more skill and is more time-consuming than tacking. The result is also much more artistic and valued.

The quilting bee was a special occasion not only for women but also for the whole family. On a warm summer day the women would set up the quilting frames under a big shade tree in the yard, stretch the lining, filling, and pieced top in the frames and start marking the design on the top of the quilt.

Women and girls of every age would gather around the quilt, happily visiting and exchanging news of the community. Often friends and women of the church would have a quilting bee to make a quilt for a special occasion.

At noon the women stopped to spread their basket dinner on tables, calling the children from their games. After the meal, they would again gather around the quilting frames. The quilt was to be finished by suppertime because often the men came from the fields to supper and later played games, danced, or sang songs. The quilting bee was a day of work and fun for all, a social pleasure second only to a religious gathering. Quilting bees were also occasionally used to raise money for neighborhood or church projects.

Quilts for family use were usually quilted at home. Many women had frames set up in a room of the house and some had smaller lap frames on which to quilt. When it was time to put a new quilt into the frame, a neighbor would come to help and sometimes stay to help quilt. Helping each other quilt made the work go faster and more pleasantly.

Skill and speed could only be acquired through much practice. Quilting was a slow process especially if the quilt was to have lots of fancy designs. Patterns of quilting are not as plentiful as designs for the pieced tops of quilts; only about eight or ten standard patterns are in general use. These designs are arranged in wavy lines and circles. One of the most popular was the feather design.

Mothers and grandmothers made special quilts for each child in the family for the time when they would set up housekeeping, boys as well as girls. Cherished heirloom quilts were sometimes passed down to granddaughters as wedding gifts. Most quilts were used every day. However, the best quilts were often saved for occasions when special guests stayed overnight. Sometimes, to protect the quilt, an extra binding like a slipcover would be placed over the top of the quilt near the face. This cover would reduce the number of times the quilt needed to be washed. Though quilts are washable, washing is hard on them and they rarely look as nice afterward.

The American woman has continually turned the production of basic necessities into creating works of art, using a skill that has been traditionally hers—needlework. In addition to making rugs, crocheting, knitting, embroidering, tatting, and needlepoint, perhaps the finest, most accomplished, and sophisticated as well as most widespread endeavor was the making of quilts.

Her works of artistic beauty and fine craftsmanship at the same time afforded her a means of expression, an enjoyable individual pastime, and a reason for neighborliness and social gatherings. She accomplished all this from tiny scraps of waste material.

Quilt making epitomizes the best of the American woman's pioneer spirit of conservation, ingenuity, and appreciation for fine things. And the quilts these women made give us pieces of the past.

PIECING THE TOP

The Nine Patch quilt is one of the oldest and probably the most popular of the quilt patterns. Though there are many variations, they are all based on the basic simple Nine Patch pattern which we will describe.

Some patterns vary in the size and shape of the squares, changing from squares to rectangles to the more difficult curved sides, but most of the variety in the quilt is in the color arrangements of the blocks. There are endless possibilities for originality even within the simple square Nine Patch, ranging from a hodgepodge of colors with no pattern at all to the stylized arrangement of our quilt. Each person piecing a Nine Patch will create her own design.

Since the Nine Patch is perhaps the simplest quilt to piece, it is a very good one for beginners. Based on the square, all the seams are straight and there are only two basic sizes of blocks to cut out.

EQUIPMENT

You will need a hem gauge, scissors, tailor's chalk, needles, thimble, and thread.

The hem gauge is used to measure each seam to be sure it is exactly one fourth inch. If the seams are not all the same the block will not be square, and if the blocks are not all square, the finished quilt will not be square either.

The scissors and tailor's chalk are used to cut out the quilt pieces.

The needles and thimble are very important parts of your equipment. You need size 7 or 8 quilting needles and a thimble that is comfortable, but not tight, on your middle finger.

The thread used to piece and quilt is a special kind called quilting thread 70. It is stronger than regular sewing thread and will not fray as badly. You will need two or three spools of thread to piece this quilt.

FABRIC

The fabric for your quilt should all be the same texture so that the quilt will be uniform and will piece smoothly. The best fabric available to use today is a cotton blend of 65 per cent polyester and 35 per cent cotton; 100 per cent cotton will shrink, which means you will have to wash it before making your quilt, necessitating ironing to prevent it from being wrinkled and old-looking. The polyester and cotton blend will not wrinkle. Years ago women used what material they had from leftover scraps. As manufactured material became available, they began to purchase white and solid colors to set the blocks together, but they rarely thought of purchasing all the fabric needed. The real reason for piecing the top in the first place was to use up scraps on hand. Today, however, quilt makers often purchase all their fabric to make the quilt.

To piece a 72×96-inch quilt following the Nine Patch pattern described here you will need the following solid colors:

½ yard each of three colors for piecing the blocks (we used olive green, maroon, and orange)
¾ yard of a fourth color for piecing blocks and for setting them together (we used gold)
1⅓ yards of a fifth color to set the blocks together (we used brown)

It is advisable to purchase all the solid-colored fabric at the same time to ensure that the colors will be the same. In addition to the above, you will need print or figured fabric to co-ordinate with the solid colors. The print may come from scraps of new fabric left over from garments that you have made, or perhaps from a friend or relative. This will give an interesting variety to the quilt. If you wish to purchase this material and use only four prints, you will need ½ yard of each.

THE PATTERNS

Only two sizes of blocks are needed for this Nine Patch pattern—a 3½-inch square and a 9½×3½-inch strip (used for setting the blocks together). The two patterns should be cut out of a thin stiff cardboard. Some women use a piece of sandpaper for the pattern as it will stick to the material and keep it from slipping. Make several copies of each pattern piece because the pattern edges become frayed from marking and thus incorrect in size.

CUTTING

Press all fabric smooth. Pull a thread on the edge of the fabric to get it straight, and trim away the uneven edges and the selvage. The selvage will not stretch the same as the rest of the fabric and will make your quilt top pucker if it isn't removed. Place the square pattern on the wrong side of the fabric, aligning it with the straight grain of the fabric. Trace around the pattern with the tailor's chalk. Trace 10 or 15 squares before cutting them out. If you have them, use pinking shears to keep the edges from fraying.

Cut forty squares of each of the four solid colors and forty squares of each of the four co-ordinated printed colors. This will give you a total of 320 squares—160 print and 160 solid. When these are sewn into strips—nine squares to the strip—they will form thirty-five large blocks.

After cutting the squares, place them in a safe dry place. One good way to store the pieces is to place them in a flat rectangular suit box with each color and design in an individual stack. With this plan you can readily find any color and its co-ordinate.

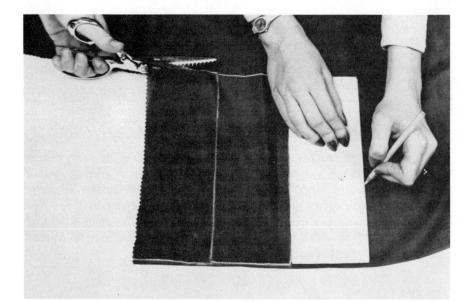

Mark the pattern on fabric with chalk and cut out with pinking shears.

PIECING

To begin piecing, place the right sides of a solid and a co-ordinated colored print square together. Hold them firmly and with a needle threaded

It takes hundreds of thousands of tiny stitches like these to piece a quilt.

with a single thread make tiny running stitches one fourth inch from the edge of the fabric. Begin with a small knot in the end of the thread and end with a few back stitches. Be sure the seam is straight and the edges are even. Press the seam open.

To complete one strip of the block, sew another solid square to the other side of the print square with right sides together as before. Repeat the same pattern, making two identical strips. Now make another strip by reversing the pattern, putting a solid square in the middle.

Next sew the three strips together to make a square. Sew one of the first strips to the last one. Notice that this makes a checkerboard effect. Place the right sides together, get the seams even, and slip a pin through the seams to be sure to hold them in place while sewing. Stitch as before. Then sew on the remaining strip to complete one block. Press all seams open. Make seventeen more blocks with the solid block in the middle like this and then make seventeen blocks with the solid and print reversed, the print in the middle.

It is very important that the seams match exactly when setting the blocks together. If the blocks are cut true and are sewn with exactly quarter-inch seams, the seams will match. But when putting the blocks together, always match the seams first and, if there is any irregularity, let it be on the end where the extra material can be trimmed even. Seams matching exactly give straight lines to the quilt patterns. Every block that is not true will show.

After completing all thirty-five blocks, you are now ready to begin setting the blocks into quilt-length strips. The pieced blocks are first set together with the rectangular blocks ($9\frac{1}{2} \times 3\frac{1}{2}$ inches) of a basic co-ordinating color (we used brown), not used in the blocks, and the $3\frac{1}{2}$-inch squares of one of the solid colors used (we used gold).

Cut out 58 strips $9\frac{1}{2} \times 3\frac{1}{2}$ inches and 24 of the $3\frac{1}{2}$-inch squares just as you did the first blocks.

To set the blocks together, sew one brown rectangular strip on the left side

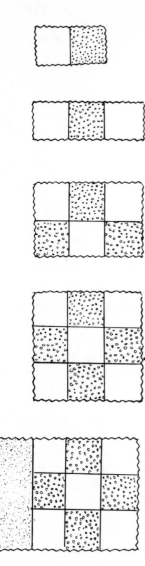

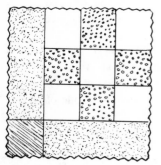

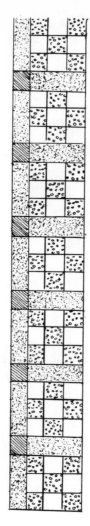

The step-by-step process of piecing a Nine Patch, from the first two squares (top left) to the finished quilt (top right).

Piece the long strip to the block. Note the tiny running stitches.

of the first block. Next sew a gold square to the left of another rectangular strip, then sew this strip to the bottom of the pieced block. This is one complete block. You will need seven of these to make one strip the length of the quilt.

Continue sewing the strips and squares to each block and then sew these blocks together until the first strip of seven blocks is complete. Alternate blocks with solid and print patterns in the center. A rectangular strip is not sewn to the top or bottom of the first or last blocks in the strip because the border, added later when the top is all pieced, makes the pattern symmetrical.

After you have finished one strip, begin the second in exactly the same way but alternate solid and print centers. Then sew the second strip to the left side of the first strip, continuing until all five strips are together. Do not sew a brown strip or gold square to the left side of the last quilt-length strip because the border will be added later.

To stagger the colors and achieve a pleasing effect, before you sew the blocks together, lay all of the individual blocks down on the floor or on a large surface to determine which pieces to sew together. Be careful not to put two of the same color together. When the pieced blocks are arranged in the design that is pleasing to you, pick them up in order and stack in piles so that you can sew them together in that order.

When you have sewn all 35 blocks together, sew the border to all four outer edges of the quilt, mitering the corners. The quilt we describe could be finished with a 3-inch border of brown, but there are a great variety of borders you can use. Any one will make your quilt unique. You now have your quilt top pieced. The next step is quilting.

THE QUILTING

Quilting has been practiced for hundreds of years. During the summer women and girls would quilt their petticoats for protection against the drafts of cold air in the winter. They quilted backs of chairs, fireside benches, and coats as well as coverlets for the bed. The quilting is necessary to hold together the three layers of cloth used to insulate against the cold. But just as the tops were beautiful as well as functional, so the quilting was decorative no matter what pattern was used. Many quilts were quilted with rows of stitches in horizontal and vertical lines (or diagonal lines) without regard to the pattern of the top, or the quilter could follow the pattern of the top, quilting inside each block. More ambitious quilters created fancy quilting patterns to fill the larger solid blocks set between the pieced blocks. Usually the same basic pattern was repeated in every block, but sometimes quilters would put a different design in each block.

The finest quilts are prized not only for their beautiful pieced tops, but for the undersides which have a less obvious but just as ornate design created by thousands of tiny running stitches. The appeal of the quilting is enhanced by the three-dimensional effect the soft filling creates as it fluffs up in the spaces between the tight stitching.

To save time, women today are quilting by machine, but there still remain a few who share the pride that their mothers and grandmothers had in being able to create something by hand that was of use to their family. The following directions are for the growing number of people who still wish to learn to quilt by hand.

MATERIALS

lining slightly larger than the top	pins
quilting frame	quilting thread 70
one roll of cotton or polyester batting	quilting needles size 7 or 8 thimble
C clamps	scissors

Years ago the lining or back of the quilt was often unbleached muslin or domestic homespun. For a warmer cover wool was sometimes used. When they became available, some women purchased broadcloth or finer muslins for the lining. During the thirties, forties, and fifties, the days of cotton feed sacks, many women sewed four of them together to use for the lining of their everyday quilts. Preferably the lining should be in one piece and should be slightly larger all around than the batting and the top. Most people prefer a solid color, usually white, though beautiful effects are created with colored backs which emphasize the quilting.

The batting or filler was used originally to add a third thickness to the quilt—an insulation for more warmth and comfort. The batting itself was often wool which was home-produced and hand-carded into a fine thin layer which was then spread over the lining of the quilt. Some people grew cotton and made carded cotton batts for the filler. Later most quilters bought the prepared cotton batting stocked in country stores and available from mail order houses. Today polyester filling available at most fabric stores is used more often than cotton, mainly because it can be quilted more easily.

THE FRAME

The frame stretches the three layers together tightly while the quilting is being done. Frames are usually nothing more than four narrow boards, usu-

Esther Griffin quilts her Flower Garden quilt on a lap frame. The three layers have to first be basted together to hold them in place for quilting.

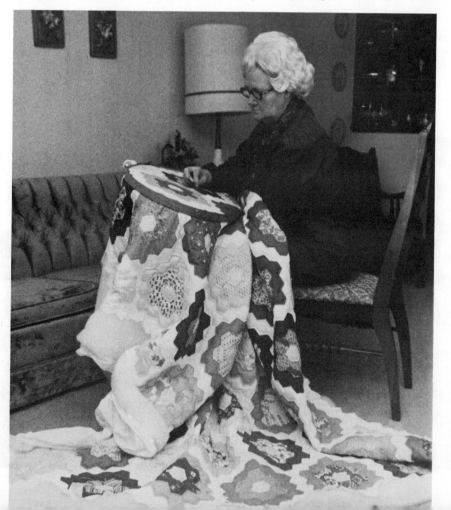

ally walnut 1×2s or 1×4s, which sometimes have holes drilled every three or four inches. Frames are most commonly 103 inches long and 72 inches wide. The four sides are placed at right angles in a rectangle clamped together with C clamps, spikes, or some other means. When the frame is put together, it can be placed on handmade stands or even on the backs of four straight chairs. Another way of positioning the frame is to screw four hooks in the ceiling of a room and run ropes down to each corner of the frame. This way the frame can be lowered to working position or raised to the ceiling out of the way.

The lap frame is also used and can be purchased from hardware stores or mail order houses. The lap frame works in the same way as an embroidery hoop does. You can move the frame to the area of the quilt you want to work on and clamp on the outer rim to make the tension for quilting. The frame comes on a stand and adjusts to a comfortable angle. Unlike the other type of frame, it can be moved and stored easily. Before using the lap frame you must baste together the three layers.

STRETCHING THE LINING IN THE FRAME

When putting the lining in the frame, it is important to get it stretched evenly and squarely, for it is the basis of the quilt: the filler and top are fastened to it. If there is a right and wrong side to the lining, put the right side down.

To put a quilt in the frame, first pin each side onto the longer quilt frame.

Next place the side frames on the ends.

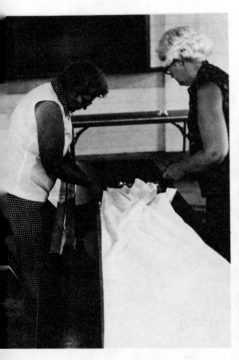
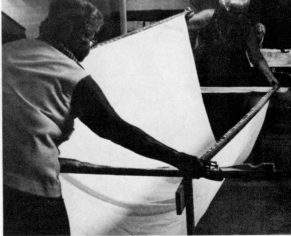

There are two methods of fastening the lining to the frame—sewing it in and pinning it in.

To sew the lining in you will need some kind of heavy thread or thin cord and a big needle. With these you whip the thread through the lining and through the holes drilled in the frame. First, secure the long length of the lining to one of the side frame pieces, stretching it as tightly as possible. Then secure the lining on the other side. This can be done on a table. Now attach the end pieces with C clamps forming the rectangle, and stretch and fasten the ends of the lining to the frame.

If you wish to pin the lining to the frame, you will first need to tack a long narrow strip of sturdy fabric along the four pieces of the frame. Then, spreading the lining inside the frame, pin the edges of the lining to the fabric on the frame.

After the lining has been sewn or pinned to the frame, roll out the batting on top of it. The batting is stretched carefully and pinned onto the lining all around the edges. Pin the batting onto the lining even if you sewed the lining onto the frame. Extra heavy pins with big heads hold well and are easy to

Fasten the corners with C clamps.

Stretch the lining and pin, or, as is shown, lace it in.

The filling comes next.
Get it smooth and trim
off the excess.

The lining, filling, and
pieced top pinned tightly
in the frame are ready for
quilting.

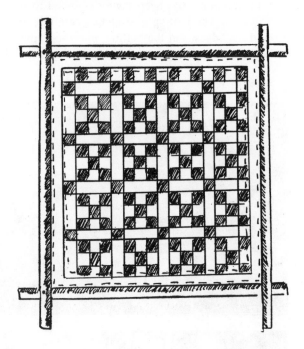

remove later when the quilting is done; they are, however, harder to pin
through the thick layers.

Next spread the pieced top right side up over the lower two layers. Stretch
the top carefully and tightly across the whole, pinning the edges onto the batting and through the lining. The hundreds of seams on the top make it essential to stretch the top very carefully to have a smooth, unpuckered top to
quilt. After pinning the top all the way around, you are ready to begin the actual quilting or tacking process.

TACKING

Large needles and yarn are generally used to tack the quilt. The thread can be doubled to make it stronger. To begin tacking, you must decide on the pattern you want to follow. Leaning over the comforter with your sewing hand on top and other hand underneath the quilt to guide the needle, take a

Tacking is easy. Even Robert McKenzie, our photographer, got in the act.

Essie Hamilton unlaces the tacked comforter from the frame.

stitch through all three layers in the place you want it tied. Leave about one inch of thread and cut. Now tie the strands of yarn together with a hard knot. Thus lining, padding, and the top piece are "tied" together. Repeat this process throughout, following the pattern of your choice.

It is important to note that even though you are following a pattern when tying, the mislocation of a tie is never important enough to take out. As Myrtle Hough says, "You can't make it wrong. You can't hurt it when you're tacking it. Now if you were quilting I wouldn't tell you that. With a comforter it doesn't make much difference, 'cause you'll never notice it after it's all tacked."

THE QUILTING

The quilting can be done by sewing machine or by hand. The quilt that is quilted by hand tends to be more creative than the one quilted by machine, because the designs can be more ornate and varied. Quilting on the machine is a skill all its own, requiring a special head to accommodate the huge quilt and frame. Obviously the quilts of long ago were all hand-quilted.

The length of time it takes to quilt a quilt depends on many factors—the size of the quilt, the closeness of the rows of quilting, the number of people who are quilting, and the skill of the quilters. The women at White Oak Pond Church, who quilt every Thursday to raise money for the church, can quilt one in about twenty-five hours when eight or nine work together. Ray O'Dell and her sister, working together, would quilt one in a week to ten days, working each day until they tired. Bending over and reaching to quilt makes the shoulders ache; fingers tire and the women would prick their thumbs on the point of the needle as they use their thumbs to guide the point of the needle to make the tiny stitches. They would sometimes put tape over their thumbs to protect them, then rub them with Vaseline afterward. The ladies at White Oak Pond Church toughen their fingers with rubbing alcohol, which also acts as an antiseptic for the needle pricks. All these women are accomplished

Skillful hands quilt an Improved Nine Patch quilt.

Fancy quilting patterns decorate large white blocks. Though harder to quilt, they give a beautiful effect.

quilters. An inexperienced quilter will find herself spending three or four times that many hours to quilt an average-size quilt.

The choice of needles and thread is important. Short strong needles make taking tiny stitches possible and the special thread is stronger and does not tangle as much as regular sewing thread. Use special quilting thread 70. Depending on the size of the quilt and the closeness of the quilting, it takes from 250 to 500 yards of thread. Women who quilt for others charge by the yard of thread used.

When the quilt is stretched and tied and all supplies are ready, it is time to mark the quilting lines or patterns. Some prefer to mark the pattern before it is stretched.

Many geometric quilt patterns like the Nine Patch and Flower Garden need no quilting pattern as the quilter usually stitches just inside each piece. Sometimes quilters draw lines making squares or diamonds, circles, ovals, or fans across the whole quilt. Sometimes they use a fancy pattern to get a more artistic design on the quilt.

To mark the overall quilting lines on the quilt, use a hard-leaded pencil

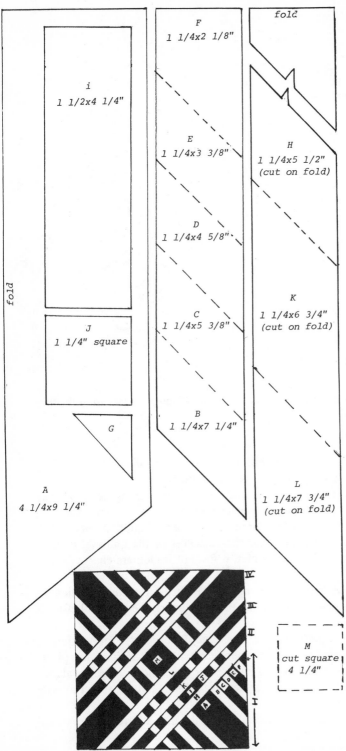

F
1 1/4x2 1/8"

fold

i
1 1/2x4 1/4"

E
1 1/4x3 3/8"

H
1 1/4x5 1/2"
(cut on fold)

fold

D
1 1/4x4 5/8"

J
1 1/4" square

K
1 1/4x6 3/4"
(cut on fold)

C
1 1/4x5 3/8"

G

B
1 1/4x7 1/4"

L
1 1/4x7 3/4"
(cut on fold)

A
4 1/4x9 1/4"

M
cut square
4 1/4"

Carpenter's Square

1. Piece together pieces for triangle I. Begin with piece A, add B,C,D,E,F and G keeping straight edge even.
2. Sew strip H on to triangle I.
3. Piece together strip II using 1 piece i, 4 red J, 6 white J's and 2 E's.
4. Sew on to strip H. Match red lines from triangle
5. Sew on strip K.
6. Piece strip III as strip II only use C's instead of E's for end.
7. Sew on strip L.
8. Piece strip IV using 1 M, 6 white i's and 4 red i's and 2 A's.
9. Sew strip IV to strip L, matching red blocks as before.
10. Repeat steps 1-7 for other half of block and sew halves together.
11. This is one block. The completed quilt will use 9 blocks, 3 each way.
12. Put on border as desired

For one 25" block cut:	For complete quilt cut:
A-4 red	A-36 red
B-8 white	B-72 white
C-8 red	C-72 red
D-8 white	D-72 white
E-8 red	E-72 red
F-4 white	F-36 white
G-4 red	G-36 red
H-2 white	H-18 white
i-8 red	i-72 red
6 white	54 white
J-16 red	J-144 red
24 white	216 white
K-2 white	K-18 white
L-2 white	L-18 white
M-1 red	M-9 red

Complete quilt takes approximately 3 yards of 36" material for each color.

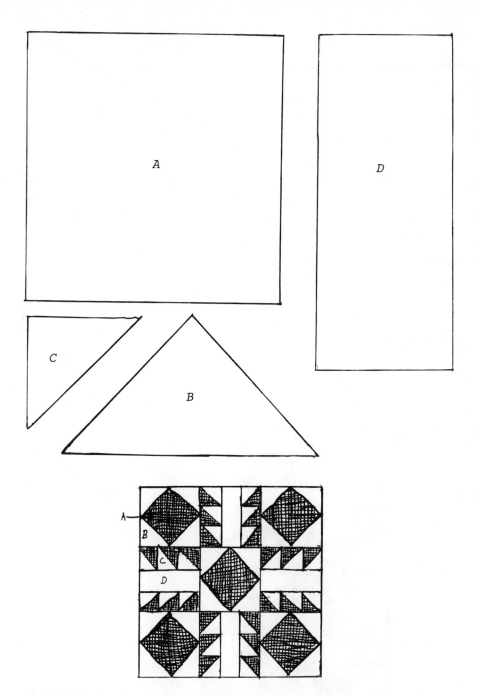

My Mother's Dream—Each block of this complicated quilt composed of sixty-eight triangles in a design featuring five squares is a study in patience and skill. For complete quilt cut: A—210 print, B—840 solid, C—1,008 print and 1,008 solid, D—168 solid.

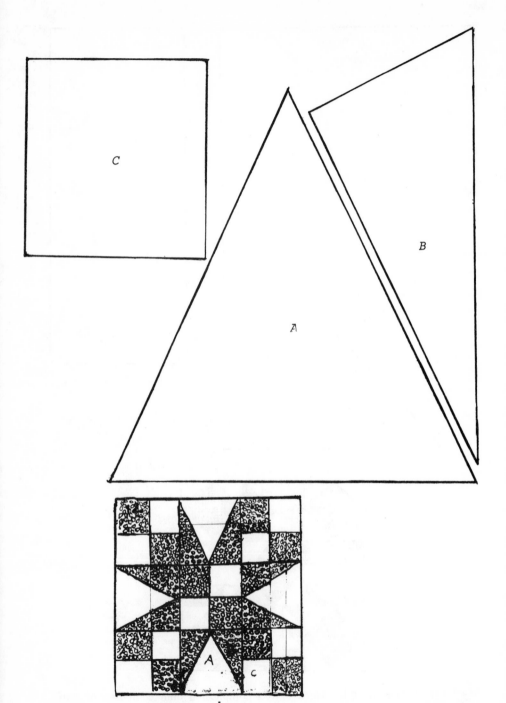

54–40 or Fight—The campaign slogan of James K. Polk in 1844 regarding the dispute over the boundary of the Oregon Territory was the inspiration for this complicated block of many pieces. For complete quilt cut: A—112 white, B—224 print, C—280 white and 280 print.

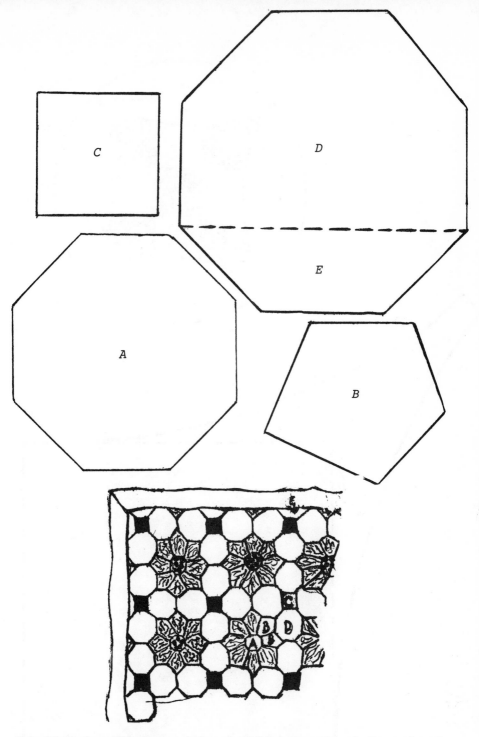

Colonial Garden—This flowery design of small hexagons gives the impression of a flower garden when pieced in colorful prints. For complete quilt cut: A—130 yellow suggested, B—1,040 print, C—green suggested, D—566 white or light solid, E—50 white (to fill in next to border).

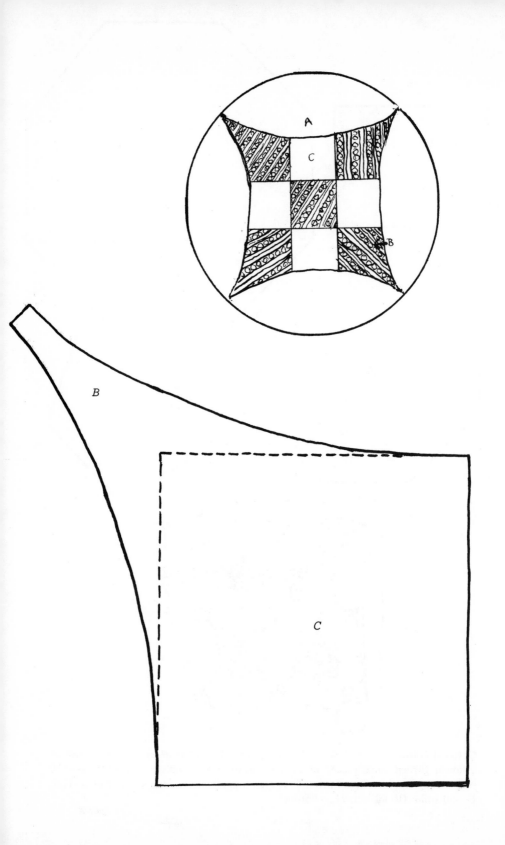

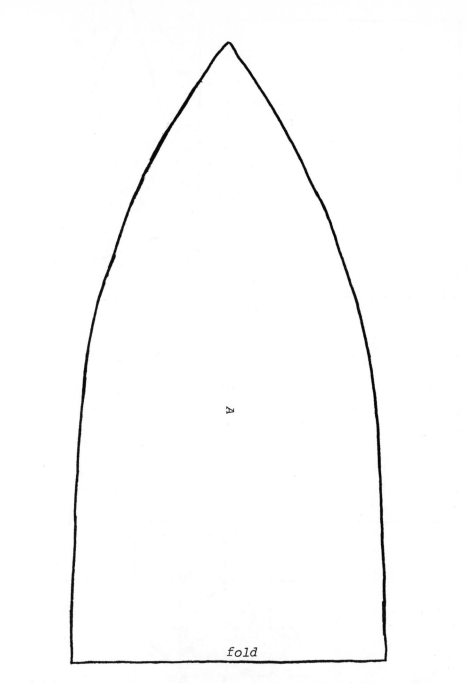

A

fold

This newer version of the old faithful Nine Patch turns squares into an allover circle design. Because of the curved edges, this is more difficult to piece. Requires forty-two blocks. For one block cut: A—4 white, B—4 print, C—4 white and 1 print. For complete quilt cut: A—97 white, B—168 print, C—168 white and 42 print.

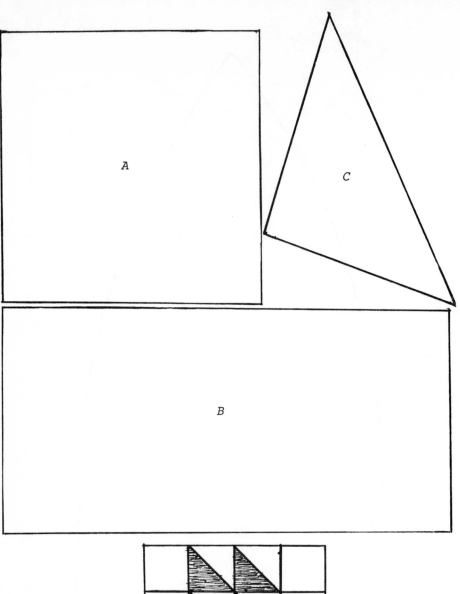

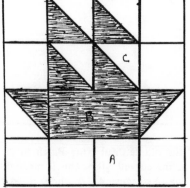

Mayflower—This design commemorates the Pilgrims crossing the Atlantic. Any little boy would enjoy the many boats sailing on his bed. Fifty-six blocks make a quilt. For complete quilt cut: A—448 solid, B—56 print, C—336 solid and 336 print.

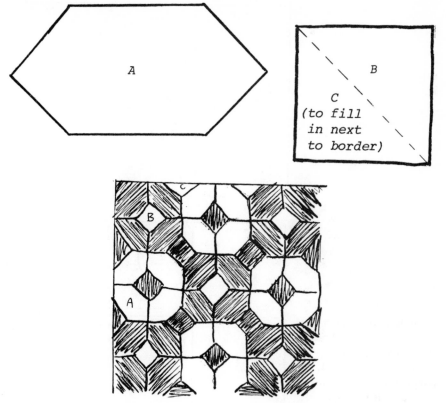

Kansas Dugout—A hexagon and a square complete the patterns for this abstract
design which would brighten even a Kansas dugout. For complete quilt cut:
A—840 print and 210 white, B—586 print and 672 white.

and a yardstick and mark the entire quilt before beginning. Pencil is used instead of chalk which would soon disappear, but be careful not to mark too
dark or the lines will show after the quilting is done.

Quilting patterns can be purchased at fabric stores and transferred to the
quilt. To transfer the pattern, cut it out first in cardboard, lay it on the block,
and mark every line you intend to quilt.

To quilt the Nine Patch or other simple geometric designs that you do not
need to mark, begin in one block about arm's length from the edge of the
quilt one fourth inch from the seam. Make a small knot in the end of the
thread, put your needle in the top right corner of the right-hand square (if
you are right-handed), and pull the knot through one layer of cloth to hide it.
Then quilt parallel to the quilt's edge, taking as many tiny running stitches as
you can get on the needle. A good quilter can get about seven or eight
stitches on the needle. Be sure each stitch goes clear through all three layers.

Continue quilting, always staying one fourth inch from the seam across the

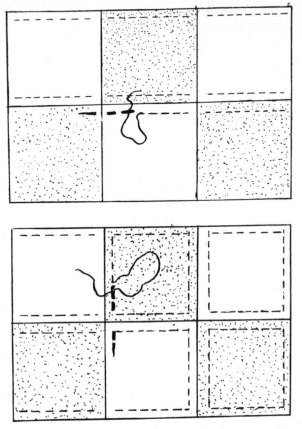

To quilt a Nine Patch first quilt the horizontal lines (top), and then the vertical lines (bottom), skipping the seams. This looks as if it were quilted in a square.

block until you reach one fourth inch from the first vertical seam of the next block. The best quilters do not quilt across the seams but slip their needles under the top between the layers to come out one fourth inch on the other side of the vertical seam on the next block. Continue quilting this same line until your thread runs out or you have gone as far as you can comfortably reach. Then fasten the thread with two back stitches on the last stitch and draw the remaining thread on the needle under the top layer so that no thread ends hang out.

Rethread the needle and quilt the next horizontal row nearer you. When you have quilted all the horizontal rows you can reach, quilt the vertical rows in the same manner, reaching in as far as you can comfortably quilt and working toward you. When you have quilted this entire area, move your chair to another spot and continue.

ROLLING THE QUILT

When you have quilted all around the frame as far as you can comfortably reach, you need to roll the quilt. Take the pins out of the batting and lining

The ladies at the White Oak Pond Church are about to finish another quilt.

Eppah Humphreys and Ida Fike unpin a finished quilt while ladies in the background begin a new one.

on the side you are rolling (they are no longer needed as the quilting holds it securely), and remove the string or pins holding the quilt to the cross frames as far as you have quilted. With one person on each end of the long frame piece, remove the two clamps and roll the quilt inward, turning under the part already quilted. Refasten the frame onto the cross frames and continue quilting. Most quilters quilt on both sides of the frame until they have enough to roll under. Continue quilting and rolling until the whole quilt has been completely quilted and is ready to take from the frame.

To remove the quilt from the frame, unroll the quilt to its original size, unpin all the pins, and remove all cords holding the lining, batting, and top to the frame.

The quilting is now done, but the quilt is not completely finished, for the edges are still raw. There are several ways of completing the edges. Many prefer to put a decorative bias binding of a co-ordinating color all the way around. First trim so that all layers are even. Usually the binding is sewn through all three layers from the top by hand (or with the sewing machine), and then turned and whipped by hand onto the lining. If the lining is larger than the top, the extra lining edges can be turned over the top and hemmed in place, mitering the corners.

The quilt or comforter is now completely finished, a useful and beautiful creation made from otherwise worthless scraps of material.

Making Music

Singing with So-Fa Syllables

sings the teacher of the singing school. All the pupils take their pitch, sopranos high Do, altos Mi, tenors So, and basses the low Do. The voices unify, making a chord. The teacher holds his hand upraised until everyone finds his beginning pitch. The pupils, also with hands raised, await the signal to begin. When the teacher's arm lowers for the first count, everyone sings through the song first with So-Fa syllables, following the spirited tempo of the leader, keeping time with the down, in, up arm movement pattern of ¾ time.

"Good," compliments the teacher. "Now you know the notes, let's sing the words." Once more he sets the pitch, beginning with high Do. By the last session of the singing school, everyone can sing through the new gospel song correctly in four-part harmony.

Once singing schools were common in most every Ozark community, where everyone from babies to grandfathers attended daily for two to three weeks for music instruction. Most of the instruction in teaching music was learning to read the notes by their shapes, rather than their position on the staff. When the singer saw a ▽ , or Ti, he would know immediately what pitch to sing. This type of singing was called shape note singing to distinguish it from round note singing, which later supplanted it.

Today singing schools and the use of shape notes are departing the scene, but in our community two schools have been held in the past few years in local Churches of Christ. Accepting the warm hospitality of the two groups and the singing school teacher, Richard Nichols, *Bittersweet* staff members were privileged to attend both schools and share another Ozark tradition.

Everyone learns to beat time so he can
lead a song.

Richard Nichols has witnessed a rapid decline in singing schools. "I hate that," he said. "It's sad because it's such a good thing for the people. Not just certain talented individuals, but everyone can enjoy it."

Why the decline? "I really couldn't tell you unless it's just a lack of interest." But he has seen people who couldn't read music learn the shape notes. "The beauty of learning shape notes," he told us, "is you can pick up a song you have never seen before and you are able to sing it. Because of the aid of the notes, it's easier to learn the song quickly.

"It's a feeling of accomplishment when you can pick up a new songbook and sing the songs through. I'm talking about brand-new songs, and I mean four parts, all the people, the whole congregation."

He then told us how he felt about using shape notes. "I'd like to see people impressed with the idea that it's a tool or an art a person can learn in their youth and use all the rest of their lives. I feel it's an aid for us to worship God, so I feel it's very important."

Singing schools were started to fulfill a definite need. The tight schedules of the crowded one-room schools allowed for no music instruction. But the Ozarkians have always been a musical people; they enjoy music, and many play quite well by ear. Even so, they wanted more formal teaching. They also wanted to learn music that they could use in their church services. Most churches emphasized good gospel singing as an important part of worship. Being very religious, Ozarkians wanted to "sing a joyful noise unto the Lord."

Sonny Gay leads the singing.

Singing schools were once an integral part of life in the rural community. Held as often as once a year, or as infrequently as three years or more apart, they were always anticipated, for they were a time of fun and fellowship, as well as a time to learn.

Several factors have contributed to the decline of singing schools, but the most devastating has been the move away from shape notes. Shape notes were used mostly in gospel and folk songs, which were not taught in public schools: the teachers in public schools received their background for teaching in colleges, and colleges did not teach shape notes. Therefore, when school attendance became widespread, many children did not learn shape notes.

Shape notes began to lose their importance when musical instruments for accompaniment became widespread. The advantage of shape notes, and one reason singing schools used them, was that the notes allowed the songs to be pitched comfortably for all the singers. An instrument is pre-pitched, that is, the pitch may be raised or lowered only within a very narrow range, as compared to the voice, so it is extremely difficult to alter the pitch for each song. On a piano or organ it is impossible to do this without extensive and time-consuming retuning. As instruments have become more prevalent, the leader has taken the predetermined pitch from the instrument, and the printed shape notes have begun to function like regular round notes.

Thus singing schools have, over the years, evolved from community affairs which everyone attended into specialized affairs which teach shape notes and music rudiments to congregations of certain denominations that continue using songbooks written in shape notes.

AN EARLY SINGING SCHOOL EXPERIENCE

We visited with Lois Beard who told us about the role singing schools played in people's lives in the early 1900s.

You don't know what it is to try to receive an education in three weeks until you have attended an old-time singing school. The music teacher that we had most often in this county was Professor J. W. Dennis, who was raised in Laclede County. He went to Oklahoma and lived many, many years, but he always came back to teach our singing schools and he would stay several months in the communities, teaching at one place and then the other. Singing schools usually lasted three weeks. But he really taught you the music in three weeks. I have never had the opportunity to attend too many, for you can see by this picture I wasn't very big in this one, but it was a wonderful thing.

We did have others that turned out to be very successful teachers here in our own county that went to school to him, but he stayed with it the longest, through the most number of years, and taught the most number of pupils, I would say.

As you can see from the picture, there was all age groups. They went from my grandmother to me. Grandmother was real old and I was only a child in

After the big dinner on the last day of the Morgan Singing School, January 22, 1907. The arrow points to Lois.

this picture. But they all learned. They learned to read the shape notes or the lines and spaces. I prefer the lines and spaces because I can't just say Do, Re, Mi every time I look at a note and tell what it is, so I read the lines and spaces because I didn't go as far in his music teaching as others. Mr. Dennis always carried a baton, a Do-stick. He kept time and he was very, very strict on time. That was one of the greatest things he taught because, if you lost time in music, you'd lost it all. But we did learn to sing and he didn't sing just this old-time "Nearer, My God, to Thee." He sang the fastest, liveliest songs of anyone in the world and he wanted all four parts when he started one, too.

In the old-time singing schools, they'd have it three weeks and they'd teach it usually in the daytime if it were through the winter after our grade schools were out. At this stage of the game, this was in nineteen and seven, we would usually have a fall term and then a spring term, and we'd have a dull spell in the wintertime with no school. And that's when he usually came to teach. That was a lot of time, spending a whole day singing. We'd take our lunch each day, and on the last day we'd have a big dinner when everybody came and we sang all day long. Now sometimes they'd teach a night school if there was school going on in the community.

The whole family would go?

Yes, yes, it was great fun. It was not only a good time socially and a fellowship that was enjoyed, but it was a something of learning. And after we had one of these singing schools, you'd be surprised how many nights groups would gather in the homes and sing until the wee hours. Our home was always an open house for it because we had an organ. It was very enjoyable. And we knew when we made a mistake that way. If we hadn't had the learning, we wouldn't have.

Did you have to pay any kind of tuition?

They usually gave him a free-will offering, a donation. I can remember a few teachers other than he that you would take a subscription and a family

Keeping time while singing in a folk festival in a bluff shelter near St. Joe, Arkansas, in 1939. (Photo courtesy of Townsend Godsey)

could all go for a certain fee. If there was a half dozen they all went, the father and mother and all the children went on the same price, but usually they just gave what they wanted to give.

What would it amount to?

I'd almost have to guess that, but it wouldn't be very much. Now he'd get his board free because he would stay with the people in the community, and it wouldn't cost him anything. But I would say that ten dollars a week would be a fair guess—thirty dollars for three weeks.

What were the subscriptions for families?

I would say a dollar and half for the whole family for three weeks.

Did they just have it during the weekdays?

Yes, not on Sundays. On Saturdays we'd go, yes, but not on Sunday. They all went to church on Sunday.

About what time would it start?

Just like your regular school, about nine o'clock, and run till about four in the afternoon.

Men could go because there wasn't any farm work?

Not a lot in the winter. That's the reason it was a good time in the daytime. You know people didn't used to stay up as late as we do now.

Did you have any accompaniment?

Oh yes. We had an organ. In a school like this we'd take our organ from our home or someone else would bring it and leave it there the whole three weeks. We'd carry the organ in the back of the hack. The back seat of the hack would come off and you just set that seat off and put the organ in it and hauled it over there. It wasn't hard to do and everybody was willing to do their part.

Did the teacher use a tuning fork?

Well, he could. And I've seen him do it many times, yes. They had to go lots of places where they didn't have an organ.

Would they usually hold them in churches if they had one?

They didn't always in all the places. It would depend on—if the leaders of the church were interested, they were at the church, but if they weren't, they held them at the schoolhouse.

What kind of songs would they sing? Mostly hymns?

It would be hymns but not the old, old hymns. He taught a lot of songs—a lot of his teaching was from company books like Vaughn Music Company and they were fast. I mean they put the pep in them. They weren't draggy songs. We could sing the old-time slow-moving songs but we didn't like them.

Each person learned to lead a song. Did girls do it as well as the boys?

Yes.

Did he deal mostly with the men? Was there any difference?

No. I really don't think there was. I know what you're driving at, because in early days there was a difference made. A woman stood back more. The women didn't step forward and do the things they do now, but when we had an organ it was always women that played.

The women were equal in the singing then?

Yes. They have to be taught and you have to have it equal or you couldn
have a good quartet. And that was one thing this teacher stressed was to hav
all four parts and make a good quartet showing, or double quartet, and hav
the whole congregation balanced.

Everyone had to lead a song. I can remember one that I wasn't old enoug
to go to school. I'd say it was about nineteen and nine or ten that he cam
here and I went to the singing school that was held in the daytime. Whe
they went to have the last day, of course, everybody was going to direct
song, I mean with a Do-stick. But oh, they'd practiced me at home on m
song. They just drilled and drilled me on that. I couldn't read, see, I couldn
read the words, and they had taught the words to me. I had the one song a
memorized, for I'd been singing all the way through that three weeks. An
when I got up and called my number, my mother held her breath. They a
just took a long breath and like to fell over, for I just directed another son
completely. Didn't call that number, sang another song and didn't miss
note!

Were there about fifty people at every singing school?

About that number.

How did people dress when they went to these schools?

Now they usually went about like they are there in the picture, for they wer
going someplace. It was an occasion to dress up. That's another thing tha
we've gotten away from a little bit, is the pride. It didn't make any differenc
where you were going, you were supposed to be proud enough to dress u
and be in nicest clothes.

What other kinds of music did you used to have?

We had all kinds of music, but we didn't have it in school like they d
now. When times began to change and we began to have cars and could g
places, this way of teaching sort of died down and we began to have ou
teaching more in the schools. But we kids there in that picture, there wa
never any of us that was privileged to go to high school.

How often would you have a singing school in the same community?

I'd say sometimes we'd have one every year, because there was a deman
for that type of learning in that day and time. It was one of the things of yes
teryears that has been appreciated, I think, the most of any one thing we eve
had in the community. We appreciated the church services, but it wouldn
have been church services without good music, and that was the only thin
that really we needed music for, only in the homes, for we didn't have an
occasion to have it anywhere else. People were more—in a way—mor
musically inclined. I don't mean to criticize, but there was more music in tha
music than the rock you hear now, and it had more depth to it and it staye
with you, I think. I don't mean to be partial or critical, but to me there's s
much music today that doesn't have any meaning and music should hav
meaning to it. It should leave you with a better feeling.

I think that now television has taken the effort away from us. We sit dow

SINGING WITH SO-FA SYLLABLES

and lazily relax in front of a television program instead of the outlet we have of our own. That isn't an outlet to sit and listen or watch. Music, if we participate in it, takes care of that problem. We all have our blue days. We all have our moods, I don't care who they are. We all have those things in our life that we have to cope with and we better learn as we're younger how to cope. Music is a great way. It's one of the best, I think. Now I think all sports are wonderful, but as you get older sports are gone. You can't participate in them. I couldn't go down here and do very much ball playing even though I played ball as a kid like nobody's business and enjoyed it, but I couldn't do that now. We can participate in music as long as we live if we get to be a hundred. It is an outlet.

HISTORY OF SHAPE NOTES

The primary step in learning to sing by the use of shape notes is learning the So-Fa syllables. These syllables are Do-Re-Mi-Fa-So-La-Ti-Do. The syllables Fa and So were often joined together in their description.

The present system of singing names for the tones of the scale developed from what is known as the Guido System of Syllables. An Italian named Guido (990–1050) took the first syllables of the first word of each line of a poem and came up with Ut-Re-Mi-Fa-Sol-La. He applied these syllables to the tones of the scale that was known then. Later Ut was changed to Do and another syllable called Se was added, giving the scale seven syllables called Do-Re-Me-Fa-Sol-La-Se. Do was repeated after Se to complete a full octave. This is the scale many early American composers and publishers used. The syllable Se was later changed to Ti to give a smoother sound pattern.

An early variation of the syllables was sacred harp singing, used in the South. It had only three syllables—Do, So, and La.

There have been other changes in the syllables and the shape notes which accompany them. The syllable Sol as been shortened to So, so that all syllables end with a vowel.

The early shape notes had stems which came out of the center of the note. Present-day shape notes have the stems on the edge as do regular round notes.

There have also been some changes in teaching the music. Many teachers now say sextuple time instead of sixtuple for $\frac{6}{4}$ time. Most people accept that the staff has five lines and four spaces, but it used to be taught five lines and six spaces, counting the spaces above and below the staff.

Regardless of how much or how little change is involved, many people, es-

DO RE MI FA SOL LA TI DO

Early shape notes with stems in center of the note.

Singing school teacher Richard Nichols leads.

pecially singing school instructors like Richard Nichols, are quick to recom-
mend the shape notes. "I don't see any point to avoid using shape notes," he
said. "I would advise any congregation or group to learn the shapes."

SCALE

The scale is the basis for all music. It consists of a family of seven tones,
with the first tone or key tone being repeated an octave higher. There are
different scales for different keys. To find a new scale in a new key, go up a
fifth for sharps. The old So becomes the new Do. For flats, go down a fifth—
the old Fa becomes the new Do.

There are five full steps and two half steps in the scale. The full steps are
between tones 1–2, 2–3, 4–5, 5–6, and 6–7; there is another tone, midway or
a half step, between the two. However, between tones 3–4 and 7–8 there is
only a half step. The syllables show this. The tone between 3–4 is Mi, and
between 7–8 is Ti. Both end with an "i," which indicates that the next pitch
will only be a half step higher, while another vowel indicates a full step.

The chromatic scale is composed of all half steps between the key tone and
its octave-higher interval. The notes are called different names ascending and

Simple scale in shape notes.

To find a new scale in a new key go up a fifth for sharps and down a fifth for flats.

Major chromatic scale in shape notes.

descending. A sharped La is called Li, while a flatted La is called Le. You can also see that Le is the same interval from Do and Si. They sound the same pitch, however, as do Ab and G♯, the pitches they represent in the key of C, or the natural key (no sharps or flats in the key signature).

PITCHING

One advantage of using shape notes (without an instrument) is that they allow the range of the voice parts to be placed where it is neither too high for the sopranos nor too low for the basses. Placing the range in this manner is called pitching.

To pitch a song, use the notes of the tonic chord, or the arpeggio of the key. The tonic chord consists of the first, third, fifth, and eighth tones of the scale. However, since the first and eighth tones are called by the same name, we can say that the chord is made up of Do, Mi, and So. Disregard any note not in the chord. If the high note in the soprano is a Fa, the note used for pitching is Me, unless there are many Fas. In that case, it would probably be best to use So.

There are five rules for pitching.

1. Look for the high soprano tone of the tonic chord.
2. Pick the correct Pattern (see below). The pattern is determined by the high soprano note. Pick pattern number 1 if the high note is Do, number 2 for Mi, and number 3 for So.
3. Look for the low tone in the bass. The two bottom notes of each pattern are in parentheses because they do not have to be used.
4. Begin sounding the pitches in the pattern in order from the highest to the lowest, making adjustments so all voice parts will be comfortable.
5. Come up to the beginning pitch of the soprano. If the soprano does not begin on a pitch in the tonic chord, come up to the pitch which is closest. For example, if the starting pitch is Ri, you would come up to Mi.

Many song leaders use a tuning fork as a basis for absolute pitch. A tuning fork is simply a prong-shaped device which, when struck, sounds a certain pitch. It is an indicator to determine if the group is near the correct pitch. If they are too far off, they should repitch the song. Also, many song leaders who have low voices check to make sure their pitch has not dropped too much.

Patterns for pitching.

#1	#2	#3
△ - Do	◇ - Mi	O - So
O - So	△ - Do	◇ - Mi
◇ - Mi	O - So	△ - Do
△ - Do	◇ - Mi	O - So
O - So	△ - Do	◇ - Mi
(◇) - Mi	(O) - So	(△) - Do
(△) - Do	(◇) - Mi	(O) - So

VOICE PARTS

There are four voice parts to songs written in shape notes. Most songs written in regular round notes also have four parts but can have many more. The four most commonly used parts are soprano, alto, tenor, and bass.

The soprano and alto are higher parts written on the treble staff and usually sung by women, though men sometimes sing the soprano part an octave lower. The soprano part is always the lead part carrying the melody, except where a special effect is desired. A song leader always sings soprano while leading. The tenor and bass parts are lower parts written on the bass staff and are usually sung by men.

The four parts are shown (below, top), arranged in the proper position on their respective staffs, formerly named staves.

The parts used in a male (barbershop) quartet are two tenor parts, a baritone part, and bass (below, middle). The tenor parts are written on the tenor staff, the same as the treble staff, but an octave lower. The tenor staff is shown in relation to the others (below, bottom).

Voice parts.

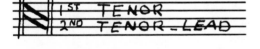

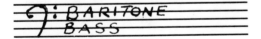

KEY SIGNATURE

The name of the staff is determined by the clef sign. There are three clefs (formerly claves) used in singing. The treble clef centers around the second-line G, the tenor clef around the third-space C, and the bass clef around the fourth-line F.

Immediately following the clef sign is the key signature. This tells you the key tone of the scale. If the key signature is in sharps, find the last sharp, and go up one half step to determine the key tone. For flats, the next-to-last flat names the key tone. Another way to determine the key is to find the last flat and go down a fourth (use the flat as the first step, and count down four steps).

RHYTHM

The time or measure signature is written after the key signature. It consists of two numbers, written like a fraction, for example ¼. The first number indicates how many beats there are per measure. The second number indicates which note gets a full beat. The number four indicates that a quarter note receives one beat, an eight indicates that an eighth note gets one beat.

Beating time helps you feel the tempo, thus enabling you to follow rhythms better. It also helps keep everyone together, and keeps them from rushing or dragging the tempo. If you do happen to get off, you can look at the song leader, who is beating time, too, and get back on.

There are different patterns of arm movement for different time signatures. The simplest pattern is down, up. The time signature will be either ²⁄₄ or ⁶⁄₈ (two or six beats per measure, with a quarter or eighth note receiving a full beat). The pattern for ¾ time is down, in, up. This pattern is also used for ⁹⁄₈ time. The most common pattern is used for ¼ and ¹²⁄₈ time—down, in, out, up. The most complex and least used pattern is that for ⁶⁄₄ time: down, in, up, down, out, up.

BREATHING

Breathing is very important to good singing. You must have good projection and proper breath support, or a song will drag and die. Richard Nichols used the following exercise in singing schools to increase lung capacity and breath support. While standing, inhale, exhale, inhale, exhale, inhale, and count aloud fairly slowly to about 25. Repeat—inhale, exhale, inhale, exhale,

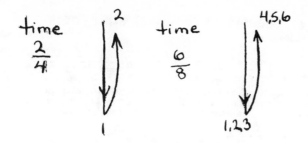

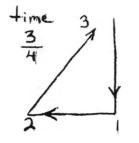

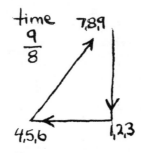

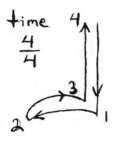

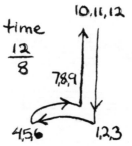

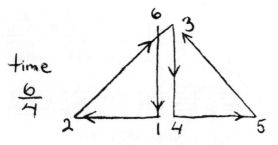

Patterns for beating time.

No. 14 Leaning On the Everlasting Arms

Rev. E. A. Hoffman

A. J. Showalter

1. What a fel-low-ship, what a joy di-vine, Leaning on the ev-er-
2. Oh, how sweet to walk in the pil-grim way, Lean-ing on the ev-er-
3. What have I to dread, what have I to fear, Lean-ing on the ev-er-

last-ing arms; What a bless-ed-ness, what a peace is mine,
last-ing arms; Oh, how bright the path grows from day to day,
last-ing arms? I have bless-ed peace with my Lord so near,

Chorus

Lean-ing on the ev-er-last-ing arms. Lean - ing,
Lean-ing on the ev-er-last-ing arms.
Lean-ing on the ev-er-last-ing arms. Lean-ing on Je-sus,

lean - - ing, Safe and se-cure from all a-larms;
lean-ing on Je-sus,

Lean - ing, lean - ing, Lean-ing on the ev-er-last-ing arms.
Lean-ing on Je-sus, lean-ing on Je-sus,

A hymn familiar to most is written here in shape notes.

inhale, and this time count to 35. Now that you are warmed up, repeat again —inhale, exhale, inhale, exhale, inhale, and count as far as you can without sneaking another breath.

After attending a singing school, no one could sit silently during congregational singing at church or funeral services. They participated in the singing, which helped them to share in the experience to the fullest measure.

"I've Sung at 5,000 Funerals"

A VISIT WITH ASHFORD HOUGH

I've been singing for over sixty-five years, ever since I was a boy possibly around seventeen or eighteen years old. I had my eighty-eighth birthday last March. That's a long time to sing. I've kept track up to nine years ago when I had a stroke and couldn't sing for a while. I've sung at five thousand funerals.

I started singing where we lived out in the country about eighteen miles. We had a cemetery there—Hough Chapel—a church and a cemetery. For miles around they buried there at the cemetery. When I started to singing, there was eight of us youngsters in the family and we all sang—the whole family. When we were just kids, we sang at that cemetery at funerals. They'd have the funeral in the church, then we'd go to the cemetery and sing while they were taking care of the grave—filling in. We'd sing three or four songs while they were doing that. The crowd was all standing around there listening to the singers until it was all completed.

We done that almost every time when we were out in the country. They ex-

pected us to sing. It was the custom then. Now, everybody is too busy for all that. They just want you to sing just a couple of stanzas at the service inside. Funeral homes now prefer for you not to sing all of a song, just a stanza or two—everything's over in half an hour.

But all my life, you might say since I was large enough to sing, I've sung at funerals—at first just in that neighborhood, but after I got up in the twenties, we'd go to different places in the community where they had a church and cemetery. That was more a community thing—not just one group. By that time, most of my funeral singing was quartet singing. During the years from the time I was thirty to fifty, I expect I might have sung possibly fifty duets in that period, but not much duet singing. It was mostly quartet singing.

I haven't sung much since I had my stroke. Of course people knew I was knocked out and they wouldn't ask me to sing. There's a quartet that I did sing with some after that when they'd ask me to sing. I wasn't a steady member in it, but if one of them couldn't go, why, they'd get me to take their place.

Did you ever have any singing lessons or training in music?

Oh yes, but I never did take voice. I'm singing in my natural voice. When I was a lad between fifteen and twenty I went to half a dozen singing schools to learn music, but not voice.

Just community singing schools, not in school?

No. I never got much of that in my other education. I'm just kind of what you call an ignorant boy!

Did you ever sing at a home funeral?

Back several years ago we sang at lots of funerals at the home. It was people we knew like that. It wasn't like we had to go out and do things perfect. They understood we didn't have any music and we were out in the open. In most cases if the weather was fit, they'd have the service out in the yard. Of course, it wasn't that way all the time. Sometimes there were funerals in the house. Usually several hundred people would attend these country funerals— the whole neighborhood would come. Back in those days we sang without accompaniment. Just take a tuning fork and tu-u-n-n-n-g. Get the pitch and away we would go.

Would there be more funerals at the weekend?

Not necessarily. They couldn't pick the day. In older days they didn't embalm the body and they couldn't keep them. There was a few years here that the funeral homes wouldn't have a funeral on Sunday. They'd have it the day before or the day after. The ministers were busy. It interfered with church work in every way. It just wasn't satisfactory. It would just spoil the Sabbath day for a lot of people.

Have you been asked to more than one funeral in a day?

We had three one evening at the same hour. I'd promised my organist who had a relative pass away. The evening before a group come up to my store and wanted my quartet to sing at their funeral at two o'clock the next day. That was the same time as the one we had. Well, I couldn't go back on my

organist—I had to go through with that—so I said, "I'll find you a quartet."
And I went out and got another quartet for them. Then it wasn't an hour
until there was another group come in. These folks brought somebody back
to bury, so they come and wanted me—I guess the funeral home sent them.
The one we had was a different funeral home—it wasn't from here—so they
come and told me their story, and I said, "We'll have to find you a quartet.
We've already got a funeral for tomorrow evening at two o'clock." They
wanted theirs the same time, so I said, "Come go with me. I'll get you a
quartet." And that evening after they got back to town, both of those groups
come in and thanked me for helping them out. We had the three that evening
at the same hour.

Have you actually sung at more than one in any one day?

It's been several years ago—we had a singing convention over in Dallas
County on Sunday and they was having a funeral there the next morning and
they asked me to do that funeral. So I agreed to do it. They were having one
at Hough Chapel at eleven o'clock the same morning. So they had the first
one over there a little early on account of me having to go to Hough. So we
done our singing before the service at the one in the other county, then got to
Hough just in time to sing there. Then we had to drive back to town for one
at two o'clock that afternoon. It just kept us on the move. You can have two
funerals in a day and get along with it, but it is hard to have three of them
twenty-five or thirty miles to go over to do that.

*If people asked you again and again, you must have been a good singer.
Did you ever need to practice?*

My policy was to never go and try to sing a quartet at a funeral until I
knew how it was going to sound. I wouldn't go and just sing any way. I
wanted to know just what we were going to do, because that could be em-
barrassing. And that was not my way of doing. I wanted to do the best that I
could do with what I had. We always tried to get together the night before or
just before the funeral and run over the songs we were going to sing. We
knew which part each was going to do so that we didn't have to organize
after we got there. That was my policy when I was running the quartet and I
run it for several years—possibly twenty-five or more years.

I was the leader in the quartet. If one of our men would get a job
someplace and couldn't be in, why, it was up to me to find someone to do it
and get it balanced so it would be all right. We were noted as a good quartet.
Everyone in the county and out of the county would call on us to sing at funerals. I'd say for twenty years after I began singing for the funeral homes,
each funeral home would call me and tell me when they wanted me to do it.

I sang all parts. In early days I sang tenor a hundred per cent. Then it got
to where I had to take some other parts in order to have the quartet balanced, see. Then I sang the lead. But I've sung bass and alto. And I sing
some just mud!

What are the four parts in a quartet?

Bass, tenor, alto, and soprano. Sometimes we had women singing, but most

"I've been singing for
sixty-five years, ever since
I was a boy possibly
around seventeen or
eighteen years old."

of the time it was men. The men sang the soprano and alto parts an octave lower.

My daughter sang in the quartet when it was so she could go with us. Sometimes she was in school and couldn't go, but I took her out of school a few times. I used several of the schoolgirls here. Some of them were good players. All the time you don't have someone to play, you know, and I had two or three different girls that would play—get out of school and do it. They were all happy to go when I needed them.

I've just sung any way. I've had to. I used to—in my younger days I could sing the alto high, like a lady. I can't now. I can sing it, but I sing it low. I don't try to sing it up the octave high. But once in a while there is a song I can still go that high on, but I don't try to any more. I know when I can and when I can't and I try to not do something I know I can't. I've always figured that way. Sometimes they'd select something that I'd never heard even. But if I could run over it before I got there, it was always good. I'd say, "Oh, we'll do it anyway."

Did it ever hurt your business to be gone so much?

I think it brought me business. I'd sometimes just have to walk off with folks in there. When the time comes, you just have to be there. My wife part of the time had her office in my store and she could keep them pacified, see. We had one man—an agent, showing me stuff—he was there different times when I'd just have to go. Well, he'd just sit there and visit with her till I got back. He didn't think anything about it. In fact he appreciated it.

THE SWEET

Didn't it cost you? Did you feel you lost a lot of money to drive to funerals and take off from work?

I didn't feel I was losing anything. I gained.

Did you ever get paid?

Not very often. In later years sometimes the undertaker would leave some money, but that first was all free.

You never asked to be paid?

No. They got to where they'd give us a ten-dollar bill. That'd be two dollars apiece for the player and four singers. We'd take that and be tickled to death, or we'd go and do it and be just as well tickled as we was that way. We never asked for money. Then other places it'd be out of the county and we'd go and we'd sing and they'd give us twenty dollars, see. And that just made us almost rich! But it was nice to be able to do it and people appreciated it. We give them our best. All seemed to think it was good enough.

When we started out we never thought about getting pay when we was in the country before we come to town. We didn't just have an organized quartet until we come to town. We all sang. At that particular time sometimes we'd have to change parts with the condition like it was to balance up and go. But after we come to town, we had quartet singing. I was convenient to the funeral homes here where they could get in touch with me on the phone more than the rest of them. They would just call me and tell me who it was and where it'd be and if they had any special songs they'd tell me what they wanted. It was practically all done in that way for twenty years. It got to be known as the Ashford Hough Quartet because they used me to organize the singers.

Of course you can't always get the same quartet. That changes with maybe a year or two's time and you have to get someone else to take a place. That's the reason for me singing different parts. Maybe if we'd get someone who could sing the tenor, I'd have to give that up and take another part. It wasn't that I was a good singer that I would do that, it was a necessity. In fact, it wasn't that I was such a good singer that I sang at so many funerals. It was convenient for them to get me.

If the family wanted you to pick a song, would you, or would you talk to the minister?

No, I didn't fool with the minister. If the family had give the minister something for us to sing, why, I'd sing it. I never asked a minister what I ought to sing. I figured his business was to do the other and it was my business to take care of that. You can't let everybody take a hand in it if you are trying to do something. And I tried to do it so the family would be happy with what we done.

Most of the deals in those days, the relatives would pick the songs they wanted sung. Then it got to be where they'd call me and say, "You just sing what you think would be right." A large majority of songs, when we'd sing in quartets, they wouldn't even suggest a song. They'd say, "You know what's good to sing and you just go ahead and do it."

Did you have certain songs you used a lot?

"Going Down the Valley One by One," we sang that so often. They'd ask for that. I haven't heard it for a while. The songs would be from the church songbook. "In the Garden," "We'll Never Grow Old," "Heaven Holds on to Me." We sang that quite frequently. "The Circle Be Unbroken," "Each Step I Take."

"When They Ring the Golden Bells," we sang that. It's really not a funeral song, but we've had folks ask for it and we tried to sing it, not in a jingle fashion, but like it meant something.

WHEN THEY RING THE GOLDEN BELLS

There's a land beyond the river,
That we call the sweet forever,
And we only reach that shore by faith decree;
One by one we'll gain the portals,
There to dwell with the immortals,
When they ring the golden bells for you and me.

Don't you hear the bells now ringing?
Don't you hear the angels singing?
'Tis the glory hallelujah jubilee.
In that far-off sweet forever,
Just beyond the shining river,
When they ring the golden bells for you and me.

It was mostly on request we sang that. We had the Baptist preacher here— it's been several years ago—and a lady passed away. The family asked for that song. Now he came to see me and he said, "Now you don't need to sing that. You can change it and sing something else." To him it didn't make sense. But I said, "Oh yeah. We'll sing it and it'll be all right."

They all liked it. He did when we sang it, but we didn't sing it like he thought it would be. But it's a nice song.

Do you have any favorite songs?

Oh, I don't know. I've sang them so long and so much. I love "Precious Memories."

> Precious memories, unseen angels,
> Sent from somewhere to my soul;
> How they linger, ever near me,
> And the sacred past unfold.
>
> Precious memories, how they linger,
> How they ever flood my soul,
> In the stillness of the midnight,
> Precious, sacred scenes unfold.

I sang that at the funeral of three boys that were drowned. I counted the people at that funeral. I was setting up on the front seat and the caskets were just over at the side and, as they come in, I counted them and they was close to nine hundred people that passed through there.

I'll bet it's been hard for you at times to sing, hasn't it, especially for close friends?

I called on one man I'd sung with to sing with us at a funeral, but he was sick and couldn't go. I went down to see him that morning at the hospital before I went to the funeral. But he got worse. When I got back from the funeral after supper, I went back to the hospital and he died while I was there. And the next morning they called—wanted me to do the funeral. That was a pretty hard one. I'd sung with him no telling—I expect a thousand funerals that he had sung with me and then have to sing on his.

Then Rob Dennis. I'd sung with him from the start, but he was out several intervals as he wasn't around, but I sang at his funeral. And I had a buddy that was in with me in real estate—I done that some—and he passed away. They called me to come sing at his funeral. And I had another buddy that was as close to me as anyone gets. He passed away and they called on me to do that funeral. I've done funerals that was so close it was hard to even think about.

My brother-in-law, Wright. He got in bad shape and we just couldn't do anything for him. We were there. We lived just about a quarter of a mile from them. Ella and I hadn't been married too long and we visited back and forth—lived together almost—and we were over there when he passed away. He—oh, an hour before he went—he asked us to sing. We did and he even sang with us. He didn't have all the words, he just didn't have the breath to say all the words, but he was right along with us in the songs. And he passed away while we were singing. And I sang at his funeral.

Mom, play one. Let me just run over one for the girls. It won't take but a minute. Just a verse. I've been out a-sprouting all this morning. I'm not in very good shape. I'll sing the first verse soprano and I'll sing the second verse tenor. How's that?

Face to face with Christ my Saviour,
Face to face—what will it be
When with rapture I behold him,
Jesus Christ who died for me?

Face to face shall I behold him,
Far beyond the starry sky?
Face to face in all his glory,
I shall see him by and by!

The Mountain Dulcimer

There's a sound that comes from these hills, a sweet, haunting sound, a sound that few people know about and fewer still have heard. It's the song of the mountain dulcimer, also known as the Indian walking cane or Jacob's coffin.

The dulcimer is a long, narrow, stringed instrument, sometimes rather resembling an elongated guitar without the neck. The actual body shape of a dulcimer is not standardized but subject to the creativity of its maker. Most dulcimers have three strings, but the four-stringed instruments are gaining in popularity. Because there is no neck and the frets are over the body of the instrument, the dulcimer is classified as a fretted zither rather than a lute.

No one knows exactly where or when the first dulcimer was made, but it is truly an American folk instrument, having no European counterpart. Most information points to the middle of the 1800s as its time of genesis. Most people feel that the first dulcimers were made in Appalachia and brought to the Ozarks; others think that the dulcimer was made in the Ozarks and spread to the Appalachians. All agree that it is truly the instrument of the hill people.

Bill Graves has one theory about the origin of the dulcimer. He claims that his grandfather, John Mowhee, a full-blooded Cherokee, first thought of and made the Indian walking cane—Indian because he was a Cherokee and walking cane because of its long, narrow shape. John Mowhee was a scout for the Northern army in the Civil War and traveled all through the South. It was during this time in the army that he first created the pattern. Already an accomplished fiddle maker and player, he spent his long evenings in camp making walking canes and entertaining his buddies, singing the old songs of home and family. This is what Bill told us about his grandfather.

"He studied up the pattern during the Civil War. He drew his own pattern, the best I can tell. I've seen his pattern; it's a little stick notched down. Each notch told him something. [This is similar to the pattern stick used by old-timers to determine the dimensions to use in building a new barn.] Some company wanted the pattern. He was offered several thousand dollars, but he wanted to keep it. He didn't need the money. He was on two pensions and that was a lot of money back then. He didn't make them to sell. He just made

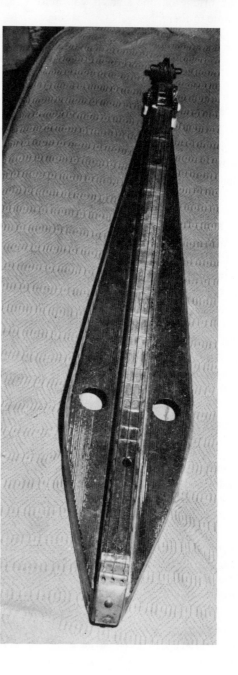

Mountain dulcimer made in 1912
known as Indian walking cane.

them for a hobby. He traveled around and stayed with people and if he liked them, he'd make them a dulcimer.

"He put his name in every one he made. He's got his name inside here on the bridge on one side. If you hold it in the light just right you can see his name in there."

John Mowhee built the dulcimer illustrated here about 1912 in Conway, Missouri. Most of his dulcimers were built of cherry or apple wood. The dulcimer makers would use whatever native wood was available.

PLAYING THE MOUNTAIN DULCIMER

The mountain dulcimer is played by ear. What little music there is available for it has only recently been prepared for the beginner. When he learns how to tune for different modes or keys, the position of the notes on the fret board for each mode, the basic strum and thumbing techniques, and, if desired, the more modern picking and chording methods, he will then throw away books and music and play the music as he feels it.

Most native traditional players play by ear and, like Bill Graves, say, "You're out of my category when you ask me about notes." They played other stringed instruments and picked up the dulcimer, or they learned from someone who gave a few instructions and encouragements. Many musicians grew up in musical families as Bill did. He said he learned to play from his mother. "They only had one violin when I was a kid. My mother was a violin player and Dad was, too; my brother played the fiddle and he played and called at dances. They were so afraid for me to touch that fiddle or I'd knock it out of tune. I didn't get to learn to play the fiddle for years. So Mom said, 'Well, if they ain't gonna let you play the fiddle, you can learn to play the walking cane.' So I learned to play it."

HOLDING THE DULCIMER

The common way to hold a dulcimer is on your lap. This is a more personal way of playing for your own enjoyment. If this appeals to you, you will need a low seat, so your legs will provide a level resting place for the instrument. Lay the dulcimer on your lap with the scroll end on the left. The instrument should be at an angle, with the scroll end farther away from your body. This allows more room for your left hand to move while noting, and your right hand will be at a more comfortable angle. Your knees should be slightly apart to provide more support for your dulcimer.

Another method is to place the dulcimer on a low table. Bill much prefers to play this way. He puts small legs on the bottom of his dulcimer.

"Take a spool," he explained, "and cut it in two, glue it on there [underside] and put you a plug in that hole and put a little tack in the plug to set it on a table. You put two little legs up here [bridge end], and one over there [scroll end]. This clears your music up. It gets rid of all that ring sitting up on a table."

THE NOTER AND PICKS

The tools needed to play your dulcimer are the pick and the noter, though you can use your fingers. The pick, held in the right hand, can be a guitar pick, a thumb pick (for modern playing styles), or, if available, a turkey quill. The turkey quill is often used in traditional styles of playing. To prepare a quill for use, first pull off the feathers, then clip the small end at the desired length and thickness. Use this end for strumming, as it gives the needed flexibility.

The purpose of the noter is to hold down the melody string. On a four-string dulcimer, there are two melody strings which are played as one. Holding down or fretting the melody string results in a change in pitch, producing the tune. The noter may be any of several materials, but most players use a piece of wood that is tapered on the end to move smoothly up and down the fretboard, and carved to fit the hand. Wood produces a mellower tone than either plastic or metal.

The noter is held in the left hand with the fingers underneath and the thumb on top. The thumb exerts pressure to hold down the melody string. The index finger held lightly against the fret board keeps the noter from slipping. In playing the notes, the noter slides along the fret board so that one note flows into the next—the characteristic sound of the dulcimer. However,

A turkey quill pick is simply made by removing the feathers from the quill.

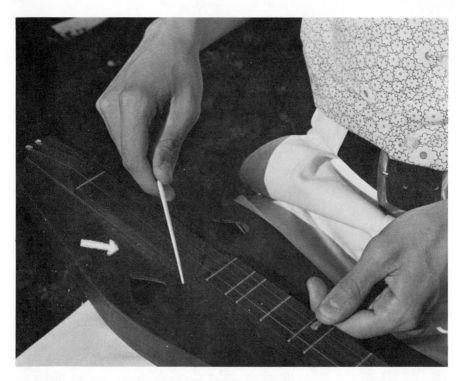

How to hold the quill pick and homemade noter of dogwood. Arrows show the direction of strumming.

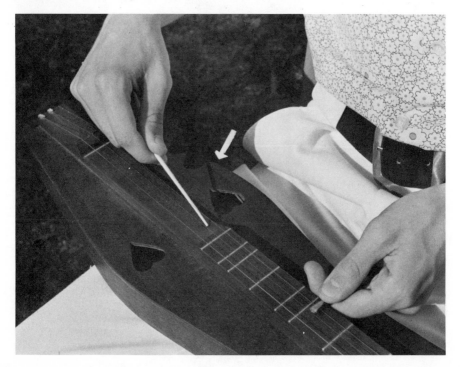

the noter may be lifted occasionally to give a break in sound. Coming down again with the noter gives an emphasis to the note and a slight twang, an almost oriental sound.

TUNING

A dulcimer should be tuned frequently as changes in heat and humidity can throw the wooden instrument out of tune, and if the strings are tightly adjusted for long periods of time, they are apt to slip.

There are many ways to tune a dulcimer. Though we won't list them all, the three most common tunings needed by the beginner are:

1. Major or Ionian tuning. Tune the bass string to the pitch most pleasing to you. Then fret the bass string at the fourth fret. The remaining strings are tuned to this pitch. To tune to a piano, the bass string is tuned to C one octave below middle C, the other strings to G below middle C. The key is C, and the scale starts on the third fret. Major tuning is the most useful for beginners.
2. Minor or Aeolian tuning. Tune all strings to a low major tuning. Fret the bass string at the sixth fret, and tune the melody string to this pitch. The middle string is not changed. The key is C minor, and the scale begins on the first fret.
3. Mixolydia tuning. Tune all strings to a low major tuning. Fret the bass string at the seventh fret, and tune the melody string to this pitch. Again, the middle string is not changed. The scale begins at the seventh or open fret.

STRUMMING

Strumming is the simplest and most traditional style of playing the dulcimer, the way that is as old as the dulcimer itself. The strum is used principally on fast tunes.

In strumming, all strings are played but only the melody string is noted with the noter. (The other strings may be noted in chording, which is discussed later.) The other strings, therefore, sound constant pitches, a fifth apart.

Songs that employ the strum are written in $\frac{1}{4}$ or $\frac{2}{4}$ time, using similar strums, or in $\frac{3}{4}$ or $\frac{6}{8}$ time.

In $\frac{1}{4}$ and $\frac{2}{4}$ time each beat is subdivided. As each measure is broken into beats, each beat is broken into strum movements.

A. Strum toward you across all strings, stressing the melody string. This beat receives the heaviest accent.
B. Strum away from you across all strings. This beat can be silent to add variety to the tune.
C. Strum toward you across all strings.
D. Strum away from you across all strings.

In ¾ and ⁶⁄₈ time, each beat is also subdivided, but into two parts instead of four as in ¼ time.

¾ time

BEAT 1

A. Strum toward you across all strings. This beat will receive the accent.

B. Silence.

BEAT 2

A. Strum toward you across all strings.

B. Strum away from you across all strings.

BEAT 3

Repeat beat 2.

The ¾ pattern doubled is used for ⁶⁄₈ time.

THUMBING

Thumbing is another old and traditional way of playing the dulcimer. The melody string is plucked with the thumb, sounding the melody note. If a note is sustained, the thumb should continue softly over the remaining strings. Thumbing is very good on slow tunes and ones in ¾ and ⁶⁄₈ time.

Thumbing.

Bill Graves using a turkey quill pick on his Indian walking cane made by his grandfather in 1912.

A variation of thumbing, used by Bill, who calls it "thumping," is to sound all strings instead of just the melody string. He cautioned us, "If you don't watch it you're going to wear a blister. I tell you, when I learned that I had all the hide torn off that right there. You might not think there's quite a trick to that, hitting those strings, but, brother, I had that off clear to the quick more than once. But I was anxious to learn to play and that's a lot of it, I guess."

With the recent revival of interest in the dulcimer, and the influence of the guitar and banjo, other styles of playing have developed from the traditional thumb and strum.

DOUBLE-THUMBING

One of the modern styles is double-thumbing. A thumb pick may be used, but the thumb is all that is really required. In double-thumbing, as in strumming, each beat in $\frac{4}{4}$ and $\frac{2}{4}$ time is subdivided into four parts.

A. The thumb picks the melody string away from you.

B. The index finger plucks the bass string toward you. This beat can be silent to add variety.

C. The thumb picks the middle string away from you.

D. The index finger plucks the bass string toward you.

Double-thumbing may also be used in $\frac{3}{4}$ and $\frac{6}{8}$ time. As in strumming, each beat is divided into two parts.

BEAT 1

A. The thumb picks the melody string away from you.

B. The index finger plucks the bass string toward you. This beat may also be left silent.

The pattern for double-thumbing. A—Strike melody string with pick away from you. B—Pluck base string with index finger toward you. C—Strike middle string with thumb away from you. D—repeat B.

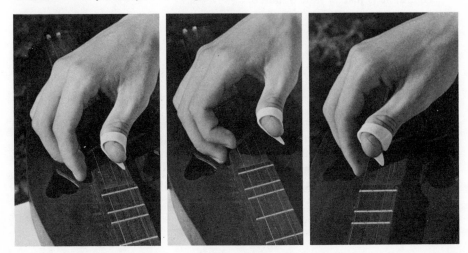

BEAT 2
A. The thumb picks the middle string away from you.
B. The index finger plucks the bass string toward you.
BEAT 3
A. The thumb picks either the middle or melody string away from you.
B. The index finger plucks the bass string toward you.

THREE-FINGER PICKING

Another of the modern styles is three-finger picking. It is borrowed from guitar-playing styles, as is double-thumbing. The sound is only slightly different but contains less bass.

The following is the pattern for three-finger picking in ¼ time.
A. The thumb picks the melody string away from you.
B. The index finger plucks the middle string toward you. This beat may be left silent.
C. The middle finger plucks the bass string toward you.
D. The index finger again plucks the middle string.

The pattern for three-finger picking in ¾ time is arranged as follows.
BEAT 1
A. The thumb picks the melody string away from you.
B. Silence.
BEAT 2
A. The index finger plucks the middle string toward you.
B. The middle finger plucks the bass string toward you.
BEAT 3
A. The index finger plucks the middle string toward you.
B. The middle finger plucks the bass string toward you.

Again, 6/8 is just ¾ time doubled.

CHORDING

The last modern style is chording, which may be used with the strum, thumbing and double-thumbing, and three-finger picking. All strings may be fretted with the thumb and fingers to change their pitches. Page 391 illustrates the chords for major usage. By using them you will be able to accompany many songs, such as the two shown on page 392.

Chords for the mountain dulcimer.

Chording one of the C chords with the left hand.

Elliott Hancock demonstrates chording in the lap position.

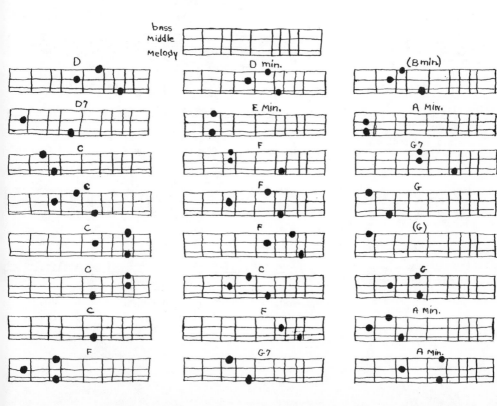

bass
middle
melody

D   D min.   (B min.)

D7   E. Min.   A Min.

C   F   G7

C   F   G

C   F   (G)

C   C   G

C   F   A Min.

F   G-7   A Min.

SKIP TO MY LOU

Two simple songs for the mountain dulcimer.

Old-time Ozark Square Dancing

"Are you ready?"

The fiddle led off with "Chicken Reel." The four couples began to sway with the rhythm, anticipating the caller's first directions. Assured all were ready, the caller chanted with the music:

> All to your places
> And straighten up your faces.
> All join hands and circle eight.
> Ladies face out and gents face in
> And hold your holts and gone again.

The dancers followed his directions, their feet beating out the rhythm of the music.

> Break that swing and balance eight
> As you would eight till you get straight.

Warming up to the music, the head man let out a whoop. The contagious rhythm infected the ring of people tucked out of the way around the living room. Most clapped in time to the music, while a couple of men stood up in

the double door to the kitchen as the dancers got into the dance and clapped and stomped their feet loudly.

The fiddle and guitar played the melody over and over as the dancers jigged and whirled through the dance.

> Wave the ocean, wave the sea,
> Wave that pretty girl back to me.

All four couples in turn led the others through the dance. Ten to fifteen minutes later the caller finished.

> Promenade and put her on a shelf.
> If you want any more you can call it yourself.

While most dancers sat down, one couple executed a few more extra-fast steps before the fiddle finished off the song.

Square dancing and round dancing were the two kinds of dancing in the rural areas of the Ozarks. In the local language, anything not danced in a square was round dancing. Round dancing did not mean folk dancing, but social dancing where a couple dances alone, doing the popular dances of the time, the waltz, two-step, and the even more modern jitterbug and twist.

Square dancing is a folk dance developed in America from adaptations of the English running sets and the stately French cotillion which later developed into the less formal quadrilles and, in America, the Virginia reel. In square dancing four couples are in square formation, dancing always as a group. Under the direction of a caller, or, as he was formerly known, a prompter, they perform intricate figures and patterns, often changing partners, to the rhythm of stringed instruments playing lively tunes.

The old-time square dancing brought to the Ozarks by early settlers from the mountains of eastern Tennessee and Kentucky followed the basic folk pattern. Each of the four couples in turn led the others in the same dance. Couple number one would go as directed by the caller to other couples in turn to "Take a Little Peek" or lead the others in the "Wild Goose Chase." Then couple number two would lead in the same call, going to the other three couples in turn. Depending on the dance, couples would sometimes stand for periods of time doing nothing, waiting their turn while the other couples were dancing. The jig step which is characteristic of some dancing in this area probably developed as a way of participating or filling the time so that everyone was dancing all the time.

Square dancing in more recent years, especially Western style, involves all dancers most of the time and has developed some more involved patterns and movements. However, the dances usually do not last as long or allow dancers as much individuality. The old way, with each couple taking turns leading and going through several variations, could last twenty minutes if the caller had an energetic group. Also, to vary the dance a caller with experienced dancers might call a different dance for each couple. Couple one might do "Cowboy Loop," couple two "Sally Good'in," couple three "Roll the Ball," and couple four "Form a Star" with a variety of figures among the couples.

A letter from Charlie McMicken gave the *Bittersweet* staff the needed push to learn the old way of square dancing. "You wish to write articles about some of the dying arts," he wrote, "and a suggestion of mine would be an article about square dancing. I am referring to the old-time jig-style, foot-stomping, hillbilly type which is possibly unique to the Ozarks. The calls, the dances, the fiddle music have surely come from rural regions."

This letter began a chain of events with Charlie and Dorothy telling us about square dancing and Charlie teaching us how to do it with the help of the Ridgerunners, four couples who still carry on the older tradition of dancing.

Years ago the square dance was held in the dancers' homes. Charlie and Dorothy frequently converted their living room into a dance floor by taking down the stovepipe and pushing the stove out of the way, making a larger floor space. Local musicians and neighbors would gather at the house for a night's entertainment. Usually there would be just one set going, but sometimes there would be a set in the living room and another in the adjoining dining room with the caller standing in the doorway directing both sets.

During the Depression, the McMickens and their friends helped relieve the boredom of many teen-agers who had no cars or money by inviting them to the house and teaching them how to square dance. Although this did help to entertain the teen-agers, many of the adult dancers met with some interference from local churches, who at that time frowned on dancing. Any dancing was suspect, but square dancing was considered especially bad. The bad reputation was probably associated in the beginning with drinking. The preachers and many people in the community seemed to think that where there was dancing there was liquor, and that the square dancers were "leading the children astray." But Dorothy explained the views of the group she danced with. "We didn't have much else for entertainment and we'd get together as people will do, you know. There were no strangers and there was no liquor allowed. That was understood." Charlie added, "With us at least. There were some places that weren't so particular, but with us there was no liquor." The places that weren't so particular were usually the dances held outside on a platform, frequently seen at picnics or other public places.

Nor is the objection to square dancing all in the past. Some churches and preachers today still share the feelings of the churches fifty years ago, teaching the evils and future consequences of dancing. "For all I know they may be right, but we've enjoyed it," Charlie said.

The enjoyment square dancing gave everyone was obvious in the attire of the people years ago. The women dressed up in their good Sunday dresses and the men wore their nicest overalls.

A special feature to the square dance was the person known as the clapper and stomper, who would clap and stomp loudly with the music, helping the

Bill Fenton helps dancers keep in time by clapping and stomping on the side lines.

dancers keep time. Sometimes several persons would clap and stomp. Each person in the room adds to the total effect of the dance—the chant of the caller over the musical lead of two or three instruments with the clappers' and dancers' feet supplying rhythmical background, all punctuated frequently by whoops from the men and laughing exclamations from the women. The onlookers are pulled into the rhythm by clapping, swaying, tapping feet or even jigging on the side lines. The dancing was so entertaining and enjoyable that several times Charlie and Dorothy literally danced all night. "We've got home in time to do morning chores a time or two. Isn't that awful?" he laughed.

A great part of the enjoyment of square dancing is the lively tunes of the musicians in the room playing tunes like "Up Jump Trouble" and "Chicken Reel." Charlie Mc and dancers in general much prefer live music to records. "A record some way or another is not right," Charlie said. "I've tried calling from records with the best fiddler in the United States but I can't quite get with it. I get close."

In Ozark square dancing the fiddle is the lead instrument. Its high-pitched tone adds a special flavor to the music. Sometimes it seems that the fiddle is telling its own story about what happened at "Cripple Creek" or what "Dusty Miller" did. A good fiddler can make the old fiddle tunes come alive, transferring his enthusiasm to the dancers.

The fiddle is played by ear and often held on the shoulder instead of under the chin like a violin. For best results a fiddle needs a second instrument for background and fullness. A guitar, mandolin, or banjo is used as a second, following the rhythmic lead of the fiddle, to make a foundation of chords for the fiddle to carry the melody. The piano was sometimes used as a lead instrument when there was no fiddle player available. But Charlie said, "A fiddler is always best. We've danced to others, but a fiddle is the instrument for square dancing."

The musicians also enjoy square dances. They can meet their friends, play their favorite tunes, and show off their expertise on their instruments. They play different tunes all evening, seemingly without tiring, even playing or practicing between the dances, staying as long as anyone still wants to dance.

There are hundreds of old fiddle tunes used for square dancing which have been handed down and played by ear. Certain favorites like "The Eighth of January," "Turkey in the Straw," and "Lil' Liza Jane" have been written down in music books, but some lesser-known ones have been forgotten because today very few young musicians play the old tunes.

The most noticeable regional difference in square dancing is the jigging, in which each one dances as he or she wants to. Some shuffle to the music, some step around in time to the music, and some do a more difficult step often called a jig. Especially good dancers do a still more difficult back step, dancing backward with a shuffle.

The jig is similar to clogging, which goes back to the pre-classical folk dancing of Ireland and other places. It is a fast step—first on one foot, then

Charles Holloway
and his daughter
Cindy jig to the last
strum of music.

the other. The weight is transferred in the air as in running. The step itself varies from region to region and dancer to dancer. The movement is done in the legs with the bent knees absorbing most of the movement. The best dancers are described as smooth. The hips do not move a great deal and there is not much up and down movement of the body. The dancers are loose and relaxed in the knees and feet as well as the upper body. They like to wear taps on toes and heels to emphasize the step.

When we asked Charles Holloway of the Ridgerunners how he did it, he replied, "I don't know. I just do it." His daughter Cindy was more explicit. She said she alternates feet in a sort of hop-step on one foot, sliding backward almost in one motion, hop-step on the other, sliding backward, rapidly shifting weight in time to the beat of the fast music. Another dancer might give different directions, for there are many styles of doing this. None of the Ridgerunners does it exactly alike.

The dancers jig most of the time. Their own individual step is especially noticeable when a single dancer is being circled by the others as in "Rattlesnake Shake" or "Bird in a Cage." This is a chance for him to dance alone and show what he can do, rather than stand still while everyone else is dancing.

Completing the normal figures of the square dance itself requires a lot of exertion. The almost constant jigging added to this makes all but the most hearty want to sit out some of the dances. Dorothy said, "It keeps you limber and is good exercise."

Charlie grinned. "And lots of fun."

The caller in the square dance is the most important person on the dance floor. He is responsible for the dancers dancing correctly and keeping in time with the music. He should call in a musical voice, speaking loudly and distinctly so that the dancers understand exactly what figure they are to do. The caller should be a leader forceful enough to direct the dancers, because he is the one who determines the dance he calls, whether or not there are variations in the dance, and the length of the dance.

"The old way of dancing was for the caller to be in the dance," Charlie explained. "He wasn't off to one side, but he was right in the set and he called and danced at the same time. I don't pretend to do that any more. I stay to one side now. At that time, of course, instruments weren't amplified. No one had electricity and a fellow didn't have to holler loud anyway to get above the music. Of course, now I stay on the side lines and use the mike. I have to get above the amplified instruments. Oh, I'm not near as good on the mike as I would be without the mike and I'm nowhere near as good as I was years ago."

The caller has to be in time and in tune with the music so that, when a phrase of music begins, a phrase of calling begins also. A good caller uses extra words, or patter, to make his calls more complete and to help keep the rhythm for the dancers.

Charlie explained, "The caller is supposed to have a lot of patter in through there—a lot of other things to say. The caller is directing. He's telling the dancers what to do, and when and how to a certain extent at least. Take a call now, for instance, 'Once and a half.' Now, no telling how many different calls there are to go along with that, I mean patter to go along with that, like,

> Once and a half and a cow and a calf
> And twice six bits make a dollar and a half
> And hoorah, boys, we're a having us a time.

"Now the only thing I ever said in through there to do any good was just 'Once and a half.' The rest of it was just throw-in stuff, see? And there's a dozen different ways of calling 'Once and a half,' and they all are adding the patter in there.

Once and a half and pat her on the head.
If she don't like biscuits, feed her corn bread.

Once and a half and a half all around.
Rabbit on a hillside a-jumping up and down.
Swing that pretty girl round and round,
Make that big foot jar the ground.

"See what I mean? There's just dozens of different ways of saying that same thing. It all means the one thing, 'Once and a half.' That's all you ever did tell them, too. A lot of patter adds to the rhythm of the dance. It just helps the thing along some way or other."

Charlie went on to tell why he started calling. "I started calling probably when I was about twenty years old. We needed someone to call. A bunch of us got together and there was no one to call. 'Now you can,' 'No, I can't either,' 'Well, you can,' 'No, I can't either.' And it just went the rounds and finally I said, 'Well, I'll try it.' And that's where it started with me. I've enjoyed the calling. I started calling a long time back, over fifty years ago. Oh, I don't know if I get better as I go along. I should learn from other callers. I'd go to a dance where someone else is calling and I'd pick up some calls I didn't know previously. I don't know, to get good you're going to spend ten, fifteen, twenty years on the whole thing. But all I'm doing is repeating what the other feller taught me. But there are dozens of different dances. Ask a fiddler how many different tunes he knows and he says, 'I can play all night,' which means he could play all night and never play the same tune twice. The caller can call a different dance for each different group or just call all night and not repeat himself. At one time I could have done that. I've lost a lot of calls—a lot of the dances we just didn't use."

Charlie learned his calls from callers who learned them fifty years before him. We have written down his calls as he called them for our dance. Here is a glossary of terms, directions for the common figures, and several dances enjoy by the Ridgerunners and the *Bittersweet* dancers.

GLOSSARY

G—Gent
L—Lady
C—Couple
Across the hall—name for C 3.
Bird and crow—bird is the L, crow the G.
Corner—L to the left of G.
Couple up 4, 6, 8—Lead C holding hands go to C 2; join hands and circle to the left.
    With 6, add C 3.
    With 8, add C 4.
Form a star—Gs 1 and 3 (or Ls) hold right hands across clasped right

hands of Gs 2 and 4 and dance to the left. This is right-hand star. For lefthand, reverse, clasping left hands, thus moving to right.

Grandmaw—term for another L, often meaning L to the left.

Home position—position G starts the dance—first, second, third, or fourth. During the dance L often changes her position when she changes partners. She always starts and ends in home position.

Lady go gee and gent go haw—L goes to the right and G to the left.

Lead in 6, 8—While circling with 4, lead G drops hand of L 2; C 3 joins the ring. C 4 joins ring by breaking in between Cs 1 and 3.

Left-hand lady—another term for corner.

Left wing—another term for corner.

On the left by your left wing—give left hand to corner, move around, and give right hand to partner.

Opposite—name for C 3.

Partner—the L or G you're dancing with. Partners often change throughout the dance.

Promenade left—G takes corner L and promenades.

Rights and lefts all around the ring—alternate hands with other dancers, Ls going left, Gs to right until partners meet.

Sally Good'in—one of the other Ls, usually the corner.

Sashaway—G and L meet each other going around back to back to original position.

Sashay—used in "Scale the Wall"—two lines of three dancers facing each other rotate clockwise, changing places.

Square—eight dancers standing in position of a square.

Four couples in the square position.   The swing.

Swing—hold partner in dance position and circle in place.
Taw—another term for Gs partner.
Two hands across—in star formation, dancers join hands and circle.
Two-way swing—same as swing.
Whirl—another term for swing.
Your partner wrong—left hand to partner.

FIGURES

CIRCLE EIGHT

> All join hands and circle eight.
> Eight hands around the ring.

The 4 Cs join hands in set formation and circle to the left.
Variation:

> Places all and to your places
> And straighten up your faces.
> Ladies facing out and gents facing in,
> And hold your holts and gone again.

The Ls turn around and face the outside of the circle, still holding hands.

BALANCE EIGHT

> Break that swing and balance eight
> As you would eight till you get straight.
> Swing like swinging on a rusty old gate
> If you ain't too late.
> Hand over hand and wrist over wrist
> And meet your honey with a shoo fly twist.

Balance eight. The solid lines show
direction of the girls.

1. *Cs face their partners; clasping right hands, they move around one full
   time, then halfway around again, extending left hands to corner. Drop
   partner's hand.*
2. *Clasping left hands with corner, they move all the way around, then
   give right hand again to partner. Drop corner's hand.*
3. *Gs continue to right and Ls to left all around the circle, extending alternately left and right hands to the other dancers until they meet their
   partners.*

Variation:

> You swing Sal and I'll swing Kate.
> Hurry up, boys, don't be so late.

ONCE AND A HALF

> Once and a half and a half all around,
> Swing that pretty girl around and around
> And a post in the hole and a hole in the ground.

1. *Meet your partner and swing.*
2. *Gs then swing all Ls in the set in turn, moving to the left until they meet
   their own partners.*
3. *Promenade their partners.*

Variations:

> Swing that gal from Arkansaw,
> Swing that gal with the lantern jaw.
> Hurry up, boys, and swing grandmaw.
> Swing Sally Good'in, promenade your taw.

> Swing them east and swing them west,
> And swing that gal that you love best.
> Swing them west and swing them east,
> And swing the gal that you love least.

> Once and a half and don't fall down.
> Swing that pretty girl around and around.
> Swing them high and swing them low
> And swing that gal in calico

> Swing that gal that is so sweet
> And swing the gal that can't be beat
> And swing the gal that is so neat.
> Swing the gal that's got big feet.
> Promenade the next you meet.

> Once and a half and keep on raggin'.
> A four-horse team and a heavy wagon,
> Tongue a-hanging out and feet a-draggin'.

Once and a half you all jump up
And you never come down.
Swing that pretty girl around and around
And make that big foot jar the ground.

Once and a half as you go by,
Once and a half and on the fly,
And swing them low and swing them high
And meet the next one, say good-bye.

PROMENADE

Ice cream, lemonade,
And meet your partner and promenade.

1. Meet your partner skating fashion, right hands together, left hands under.
2. Dance to the right back to Gs home position.
Variations for the end of the dance:

Promenade that pretty little girl.
Promenade all around the world.
Promenade all around the floor.
Promenade home, for there ain't no more.

Promenade that pretty little thing.
Promenade all around the ring.
Promenade all around the floor.
Promenade home 'cause there ain't no more.

Meet your partner and promenade.
Promenade all around the hall.
Promenade home 'cause that'll be all.

Meet your partner and promenade.
Promenade that pretty little girl.
Promenade all around the world.
Promenade and put her on a shelf.
If you want any more, you can call it yourself.

DANCE TO THE RIGHT AND LEFT HAND TOO

First couple out and dance by the right
And left hand too.
Lady all around and gent cut through
On the inside circle and the outside, too,
And give them room and see them go through.
Dance again as pretty as you can.

1. C clasp right hands facing each other and move around each other half-way to the left, changing places.
2. They drop hands and face each other again.

3. Then clasp left hands and move to right, past each other, to original places.
4. G holds Ls right hand in his left and leads her around outside the circle to right.
5. When they reach the opposite C, they drop hands. G goes between C 3 while L continues around the outside.
6. They meet at the home spot.
7. Repeat steps 1–3.

"Lady all around and the gent cut through,
On the inside circle and the outside, too."

"Doe-si-doe and the little boy doe,
And the boy in the bread pan playing in the dough . . ."

DOE-SI-DOE

Doe-si-doe and the little boy doe,
And boy in the bread pan playing in the dough,
And the little boy doe by doe by doe,
And little boy doe and oh, by golly, and oh, by Joe.
Right hand across as you go through
And left hand back and how are you?
Don't forget that opposite lady.
Opposite right, your partner wrong
And hurry up, boys, don't be so long.

1. *Couple up 4.*
2. *Both Cs face their partners. They clasp left hands and move around each other until they meet their corner.*
3. *They clasp right hands of corner, dropping partner's hand, and move around corner.*
4. *They give the left hand back to their partners and move around partners halfway until Gs meet each other.*
5. *Gs clasp right hands as do Ls clasp their hands across Gs in star formation.*
6. *Circle to the right in star formation.*
7. *Dancers switch to the left hand and move to the left in star formation.*
8. *Break the star, give right hand to the corner, move around.*
9. *Left hand to partner, move around.*
10. *Circle up 4.*

Variations:

Doe-si-6 as you would 4.
Doe-si-8 as you would 4.

This can be done with 6 or 8, doing the star formation with all Cs.

One more doe and on you go.

Repeat doe-si-doe:

BASIC ORDER FOR OLD-TIME SQUARE DANCING

Directions are directed to men unless specifically stated.
1. *Circle eight*
2. *Balance eight*
   Once and a half
   Promenade

3. *First couple*
    Dance by the right and the left hand too
    Lady all around and gent cut through
        Do the dance
    Go to second, third, and fourth couples in turn
            Return home
4. *Balance eight*
5. *Second couple out*
    (*repeats what first couple did*)
6. *Balance eight*
    (*repeat with third, then fourth couple leading—end*
    with Balance eight)
Variations:
    Introduction
        Break and swing
        To the center and back
        Sashaway
    Between couples
        Any variation to add interest and keep dancers listening
    At end
        Waterbury Watch
        Extra swinging
        Doe-si-doe
        Sashaway

DANCES

ARKANSAW OR WILD GOOSE CHASE

First couple out and couple up four
In the middle of the floor.
Arkansaw and away back down in Arkansaw,
Follow the leader in a wild goose chase.

G 1 leads the other three holding hands in a snakelike dance in the middle of the floor as he cuts a figure eight.

Couple up four in the middle of the floor,
And Arkansaw and away back down in Arkansaw,
Follow the leader in a wild goose chase.

This time G 2 leads the others in a figure eight.

Couple up four in the middle of the floor,
And lead in six and don't you mix.
First old boy, follow the leader in a wild goose chase.

With three couples in a ring, G 1 leads in a figure eight.

> Arkansaw and away back down in Arkansaw,
> And follow the leader in a wild goose chase.

G 2 leads.

> Couple up six and don't you mix,
> And the next old boy follow the leader in a wild goose chase.

G 3 leads.

> Couple up six and don't you mix.
> And on to the next and open up a gate,
> And lead in eight when you get straight.
> Follow the leader in a wild goose chase,

etc.
Continue dance with four couples, each G leading.

BIRD IN A CAGE

> To the right and couple up four
> In the middle of the floor.
> Bird in the cage and three hands round.

L 1 goes inside the circle while the other 3 circle around to left while holding hands.

> Bird hop out and crow hop in.

L 1 rejoins the circle while G 1 goes inside the circle.

> Couple up four in the middle of the floor,
> On to the next and lead in six and don't you mix.

G rejoins circle and the two couples go to C 3 and couple up 6. L 1 and G 1 repeat all steps with six, then eight, circling. Repeat dance with each C leading.
Variation:
Lead C goes to each C in turn, circling four hands each time.

CHEAT OR SWING

> Opposite gents go across the hall,
> And cheat or swing and swing or cheat.
> Don't forget that cheating in the game,
> And back to your partners and everybody swing.

1. *G 1 goes across the hall, sashaways and then swings L 3 and G 3 goes across the hall and does the same with L 1.*
2. *Gs go back to their partners and everyone swings.*

To the right and all four gents go to the right.
And cheat or swing and swing or cheat.
Don't forget that cheating in the game,
And back to your partner and everybody swing.
Opposite gents go across the hall,
And cheat or swing and swing or cheat,
And don't forget that cheating in the game,
And back to your partner and everybody swing.
To the left and all four gents go to the left.
And cheat or swing and swing or cheat.
Don't forget that cheating in the game.
Couple up four over here and four over there,
And you know where and I don't care.
And doe-si-doe and little boy doe, *etc.*
Couple up four over here and four over there,
You know where and I don't care.
You open up a gate and lead in eight
When you get straight.

Repeat dance with Gs leading.

CORNER GIRL

Lead her up and through the hall,
Lady go gee and gent go haw.
Next time you meet her you meet her in the hall
And everybody whirl.

1. *G 1 leads his partner up the set and through C 3.*
2. *L goes all the way around outside the circle to the right, the G goes to the left*
3. *When they get back home, everyone swings.*

Opposite gents go across the hall and sashaway the opposite
girl.
Back to your partner and everybody whirl.
Lead her up and through the hall,
Lady go gee and gent go haw.
Next time you meet her you meet her in the hall,
And everybody whirl.

G 1 leads.

All four gents go to the right,
And sashaway the right-hand girl.
And back to your partner and everybody whirl.
Lead her up into the hall,
Lady go gee and gent go haw.
Next time you meet her you meet her in the hall,
And everybody whirl.

G 1 leads.

> To the left and all four gents
> Sashaway the corner girl.
> Back to your partner and everybody whirl.
> Doe-si-doe and little boy doe, *etc.*

Repeat dance with Gs 2, 3, and 4 leading.

COWBOY LOOP

> To the right and couple up four
> In the middle of the floor.
> First old boy in a cowboy loop.

1. *C 1 goes under the clasped hands of C 2, holding hands until they get under.*
2. *C 1 separates, L going around G and G around L. L 1 still holds hands with G 2 and G 1 holds hands with L 2.*
3. *C 2 ducks under their clasped hands.*
4. *The two couples form a circle again.*

> Second old boy will follow suit.

1. *C 2 leads in a cowboy loop, going under the arms of C 1. Circle four.*

> Couple up four and on to the next
> And lead in six and don't you mix.
> First old boy in a cowboy loop.
> Second old boy will follow suit.
> Third old boy fell in the coop.

1. *With six circling, each couple in turn does the cowboy loop.*
2. *C 1 goes between Cs 2 and 3.*
3. *C 2 goes between Cs 3 and 1.*
4. *C 3 goes between Cs 1 and 2.*

> Couple up six and don't you mix,
> And lead in eight when you get straight.
> First old boy in a cowboy loop.
> Second old boy fell in the soup,
> Third old boy has got the croup,
> Fourth old boy has got the roup.

1. *Repeat cowboy loop, each couple in turn dividing the ring.*
2. *C 1 goes between C 3.*
3. *C 2 between C 4.*
4. *C 3 between C 1.*
5. *C 4 between C 2.*

> Couple up eight when you get straight.

Repeat dance with each G leading.

FORM A STAR

Swing those ladies to the center and back.

Gs hold their partners' hands and parade them to the center of the circle, then back, walking backward.

Gents to the center with right hands across,

Gs form right-hand star.

And left hand back.
And skip that partner and take the next.

1. *Still holding star formation, circle right.*
2. *Gs pass their partners and take the next L. G 1 takes L 2, etc. G hold L's waist. L holds G's waist.*

Gents swing out and ladies swing in,
And hold your holts and gone again.

1. *Gs let go of left hands and swing partners with arms still around waists. Gs circle in place, L backward around him. They turn once and a half.*
2. *Ls form right-hand star.*
3. *Circle to left in form of a star.*

Ladies swing out and gents swing in,
You hold your holts and gone again.

1. *Ls let go their right hands. Gs swing the ladies backward once and a half.*
2. *Gs form a left-hand star.*

Break that swing and everybody swing,
And on the left by your left wing.
And rights and lefts all around the ring.

Repeat dance three more times until Gs have their own partners.

The Texas star.

LADIES MAKE A BOW

Couple up four in the middle of the floor.
Right hand across as you go through.
Left hand back and how are you?
Two hands across and form a basket
That won't hold shucks.

1. *C 1 and C 2 form right hand star.*
2. *Star to left.*
3. *Continuing circling to right, Gs hold both hands, Ls hold both hands under the Gs' hands.*

Ladies make a bow.

Still holding hands, duck under the arms of the Gs.

And gents know how.

Gs go under the arms of the Ls, still circling to right.

Don't forget your opposite lady,
Your opposite right, your partner wrong,
Hurry up, boys, don't be so long.

"Ladies make a bow,
Gents know how."

Break the circle. G takes L to left by his right, then his partner by his left.

> Couple up four in the middle of the floor,
> And lead in six and don't you mix.

Repeat all steps with six, then eight. Continue dance with other Gs leading.

RATTLESNAKE SHAKE

> To the right and couple up four
> In the middle of the floor.
> And doe-si-doe and little boy doe, *etc.*
> On to the next and round that lady with a rattlesnake shake,
> And it's out in the center and you cut a figure eight.

1. C 1 leads C 2, all holding hands, in between C 3 around L.
2. Back to the middle of the floor G 1 leads all in a figure eight.

> Round that gent with a rattlesnake shake,
> And out to the center and you cut a figure eight.

Repeat the figure, this time going around G.

> Couple up six and don't you mix.
> Balance six as you would eight.

Variation: six couples do the doe-si-doe.

> And on to the next and round the lady with a rattlesnake shake.

Continue the figure leading six.

> Couple up eight when you get straight.

Variation: Doe-si-doe with eight. Repeat dance with other Cs leading.

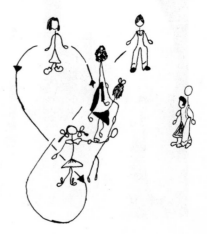

> "And round the lady with a rattlesnake
>   shake,
> And it's out in the center and you cut a
>   figure eight."

ROLL THE BALL

Lead her up into the hall,
Lady go gee and gent go haw.
Next time you meet her you meet her in the hall.

C 1 goes through C 3, L going right, G going left.
They go all around the circle back home.

Everybody whirl.
And promenade left all around the world.
Same old boy and brand-new lady,
Lead her up into the hall,
Lady go gee and gent go haw.
Next time you meet her you meet her in the hall.
Everybody whirl.
And promenade left all around the world.

Repeat until get own partner.
Repeat dance with each C leading.

SALLY GOOD'IN

(*For those who like to swing*)

Swing your partner
To the right and swing with a two-way swing.
Back to partner, everybody swing.
Across the hall and swing that gal from Arkansaw.
Back to your partner and swing your taw.
Everybody swing.
To the left and don't forget to swing grandmaw.
Back to your taw and everybody swing.
First two gents go to the right and swing, *etc.*

Repeat going to all Ls.
Repeat with 3 Gs, then 4 Gs. Repeat with each G leading.

SCALE THE WALL

First couple to the right and couple up four
In the middle of the floor.
You leave those girls and on to the next
With three hands round.

G 1 leaves his partner standing to left of G 2 and goes on to C 3 and the
three circle.

Take your partner, go on to the next,
And couple up four in the middle of the floor.

He takes L 3 by the hand and goes to C 4. Four circle.

"Forward up and sashay around
And the two little boys scale the wall."

And leave those girls and go on home.

Leave L 3 on left of G 4 and go home alone.

And forward up and back.

The side Gs, holding hands with a L on each side, go forward until they meet and back.

Forward up and sashay round.

Go forward again and all six, still holding hands, rotate to the left, then move back, changing sides.

Watch the two little boys scale the wall.

Gs 1 and 3 change places.

Forward up and back.
Forward up and sashay around.
Watch the two little boys scale the wall.

Repeat so Gs are in home positions again.

And promenade left all around the hall.

Repeat until Gs have their own partners.
Repeat with each C leading.

SWING THE OPPOSITE

Couple up four in the middle of the floor,
And ho, swing the opposite.
Couple up four in the middle of the floor,
And ho, swing your own.

The call is to Gs 1 and 2.

Couple up four in the middle of the floor,
And lead in six and don't you mix.
And ho, swing the opposite.
Couple up six and don't you mix,
And ho, swing the opposite.

Couple up six, and don't you mix,
And ho, swing your own.
Couple up six and don't you mix,
And on to the next and you open up a gate,
And lead in eight when you get straight.
Ho, swing the opposite.
Couple up eight when you get straight.
And ho, swing the opposite.
Couple up eight when you get straight,
And ho, swing the opposite.
Couple up eight when you get straight,
And ho, swing your own.
Couple up eight when you get straight.
Doe-si eight as you would four
And little boy doe by doe, *etc.*
Couple up eight and
Sashaway the left-hand girl.
Sashaway the corner girl.
Sashaway your partner all,
And sashaway all round the hall.
Meet your partner with a
Once and a half and a half all around, *etc.*

*Sashaway as directed, end by going to the right, sashawaying each L in
turn until you meet partner.*
Repeat dance with each G leading.

TAKE A LITTLE PEEK

To the right and around that couple,
And take a little peek.

*C 1 goes to C 2. L 1 goes halfway around G 2 while G 1 goes halfway
around L 2, still holding hands. C 1 pauses in this position and they
"peek" at each other behind C 1's backs.*

And back to the center and shake your little feet.

C 1 returns to center and each looks at partner.

Around that couple and peek once more.
Back to the center and circle four.
Leave that couple and on to the next.
Around that couple and take a little peek, *etc.*

Break the circle and repeat with Cs 3 and 4.
Repeat dance with all Cs leading.

TWO LITTLE SISTERS

Lady to the right and
Two little sisters form a ring.

L 1 and L 2 join two hands and circle.

> Back to your partner and everybody swing.
> On to the left by your left wing,
> Rights and left all around the ring.
> And meet your honey with a two-way swing.
> Once and a half all around, *etc.*
> Meet your partner and promenade.
> Two ladies to the right and
> Three little sisters form a ring.

Ls 1 and 2 circle with L 3.
Repeat with Ls 1, 2, and 3 circling with L 4.
Repeat dance with each L leading.

UP TO THE CENTER AND BACK

> First couple up to the center and back.
> Up to the center and cast off six. (*1*)
> Lady go gee and gent go haw.

Dance between the opposite couple, L to right, G to the left outside the circle back home.

> Everybody whirl.
> Up to the center and back.
> Up to the center and cast off four. (*2*)
> Lady go gee and gent go haw.

L goes between Gs 2 and 3 and the G goes between Cs 3 and 4.

> Everybody whirl.
> Up to the center and back.
> Up to the center and cast off two. (*3*)
> Lady go gee and gent go haw.

L goes between C 2 while G goes between C 4.

"Up to the center and back
Up to the center and cast off six."

Everybody whirl.
And promenade left all around the world.
Same old boy and brand-new lady,
Up to the center and back.

Repeat until regain own partners.
Repeat dance with each couple leading.

WAVE THE OCEAN

First couple to the right and couple up four
In the middle of the floor,
And on to the next and
Wave the ocean, wave the sea.
Wave that pretty girl back to me.

C 1, holding hands, followed by C 2, G behind G, L behind L, go between C 3, G to the left, L to the right in single file. Partners rejoin in center and swing when they meet.

Everybody whirl.
And wave the ocean, wave the sea,
Wave that pretty girl back to me.

Repeat above directions.

Everybody whirl.
Wave the ocean, wave the shore,
Wave that pretty girl back once more.
And everybody whirl.
Couple up six and don't you mix.
And on to the next and
Wave the ocean, wave the sea,
And wave that pretty girl back to me.

C 1 leads as before followed by Cs 2 and 3.

Everybody whirl.
Wave the ocean, wave the sea,
Wave that pretty girl back to me.
Everybody whirl.
Wave the ocean, wave the shore,
Wave that pretty girl back once more.
Everybody whirl and couple up eight, etc.

Repeat dance with each couple leading.

WIND THAT WATERBURY WATCH

(This figure is usually done at the end of a night of dancing.)

Wind that Waterbury watch and wind it tight,
Or we'll be here till broad daylight.
Wildcats squall and a house cat jumps through a hole in the wall.

1. *Circle eight.*
2. *Lead G breaks the circle, the rest holding hands in line. He leads all other dancers under the clasped arms of C 4.*
3. *After all the dancers have gone under, G 4 turns so his right arm is over his left shoulder, still holding on to the left hand of his partner behind.*
4. *Lead G circles around in position and goes under the arms of the next two dancers (Cs 3 and 4).*
5. *G repeats, cutting off one dancer at a time until all dancers have the right arm over the left shoulder, holding the left hand of dancer behind.*
6. *G joins hands back across his shoulder with L 4, thus winding up all the dancers.*
7. *In this formation, continue circling to left, then backward to right.*
8. *Break and swing.*

Variations while dancers are winding up:

>Walk that squirrel right off that limb to a hole in the wall.
>Hold tight if it's all right.
>Hold tight, circle right,
>Break that swing and balance eight.

MIXER FOR THE END

(Everyone can get in this. This dance is meant to involve
any number of couples.)

>Join hands and circle to the left.
>Ladies to the center back to back.

Ls go to the center and stand facing out with backs together.

>And gents run around the outside track.

Gs continue circling to the left single file.

> Don't get hurried, don't get vexed,
> Skip that partner, take the next.

Each G passes his partner and takes next for new partner.

> Now you're home, you balance all.
> Swing your partner with a right-hand swing
> And on to the left by your left wing.
> And right and left all around the ring.
> Meet your partner, promenade.

Repeat with each new partner until meet original partner.

In the Key of B for Bluegrass

The music had already started as we left the riverside parking lot and walked through the walnut and oak trees to the rustic platform where Bill Jones and the Bluegrass Travelers were picking a lively old-time fiddle tune bluegrass fashion. The men's yellow shirts matched the women's dresses and made a colorful splash against the rough-sawed oak platform.

We picked our way through the audience reclining in lawn chairs, leaning against trees, and even, in the case of some children, sitting up in the trees. We walked around quilts spread on the grass where small children played and a father stretched out with eyes closed, tired from his week's work, letting the music fill and relax him as old favorites and newer, unfamiliar songs came one after another all evening.

We found our way to some empty places in the impromptu seats of long boards nailed to whole logs. Our late arrival was not noticed in the casual, informal gathering. Several people smiled at us, and one even commented, "Oh, I see you're going to listen to bluegrass all during the week, too," as we set up our recording equipment. But most were oblivious to their surroundings as they felt and experienced the music all around them in the natural wooded amphitheater.

The clear unmistakable music of the fiddle was leading the other instru-

Charles Calton on the fiddle.

ments in "Sally Good'in" as the guitar, banjo, and mandolin pickers played rhythm. The steady beat of the bass fiddle was more felt than heard, causing the people all around us to move in time to the music, tapping toes or heels, swinging legs, strumming fingers, or swaying their whole bodies to the dominating rhythm.

On the next song the mood changed from the spirited hoedown to the slower gospel "Glory Road." This time the instruments played background to the Jones family trio singing three-part harmony, Carol leading with her mother and father harmonizing in alto and baritone. Between the verses the instruments again took the lead with the mandolin and banjo alternating in some rapid skillful picking.

At an especially intricate part of the picking, the audience spontaneously clapped and cheered. Their interest and enthusiasm were contagious, spurring the musicians to pick and sing even better. Everyone was thoroughly enjoying it, the musicians as much as any.

A slight cool breeze found its way through the trees, as the hot July sun began to disappear behind the hill across the river which made a bend around the level wooded area. The horizontal lines of sunlight for the first

Ralph Withers, Harold Rowden and the Bluegrass Five play for *Bittersweet*.

time this day found their way under the trees, momentarily giving a golden light to the performers. Captured by the strong rhythmic beat of the music, we were unaware when the sun sank below the hill and lights replaced it.

The Suns of Bluegrass were next, high school boys chauffeured all over Missouri and Illinois to bluegrass festivals by their father, Bill Klug, who is also their greatest fan. "Bluegrass is clean, wholesome music played in family-oriented surroundings," he said. "I'm pleased the boys love it so." Their own individual fast style showed the diversity of the music and the wide range of ages and backgrounds of bluegrass performers.

Group followed group, singing and picking music for people who enjoy living. They sang the songs their grandparents used to sing on Sunday afternoon or played at a square dance on Saturday night. They sang gospel music and more recent songs adapted to bluegrass styles. The songs were about real-live happenings, based on religion, love, joy, sadness, special events and occasions, with most of them telling a story or legend. "It's a simple down-to-earth music," said seventeen-year-old performer Randi Calton.

Bluegrass music is played with a strong driving beat and is sung in three- or four-part harmony. There is usually a lead singer with a high tenor and a baritone or alto with a bass added when a quartet sings. The songs are often sung and played in the higher keys of B flat, G, and C flat, which raises the voices up, giving the characteristic high tenor which is slightly nasal. Each group and each song is done differently, with singers switching different parts to suit the song. Even the same group does not always sing the song the same way each time.

Five string instruments are basic to bluegrass. They consist of the flat-top guitar, bass, banjo, mandolin, fiddle. Sometimes the Dobro guitar is used in bluegrass bands. Even though some say it does not belong with the five basic instruments, the Dobro is appearing more and more often in festivals throughout the Ozarks.

The Dobro guitar is both a unique and an original instrument. Created in 1928, it was put on the market in 1929 by three brothers named Dopera. They arrived at the name by taking the *d-o* from Dopera, and the *b-r-o* from "brothers." The guitar itself, made from rosewood, hardwood, or maple that mellows the tone as it ages, is much the same size as a regular guitar. But built inside the body is the thing that sets it apart from other musical instruments—the metal resonator that sends its tone one and a half times louder than other acoustical guitars. Because of this resonator, some say the Dobro was the forerunner of the electric guitar.

Though the size and shape of the guitar is the same as other guitars, the playing methods are completely different. Held flat like a table top by a strap around the player's neck, the guitar is picked with steel finger picks instead of being strummed. A slide bar is moved up and down the neck in place of chording.

The lonesome and homeless tones of the Dobro range from tenor to low

Farrell Stowe at the Do-bro guitar.

bass and add a special effect to bluegrass music. The sound itself, a mixture of Hawaiian and flat-topped guitars, can display the moods of the songs whether happy or sad, slow or fast.

The common guitar is the basic instrument, and one guitar player of the two or three is often the leader of the group. There are always some guitars for rhythm. Though the fiddle is not standard everywhere, audiences in the Ozarks expect the fiddle and miss its sweet melody when a group plays without one.

In addition to the guitar, another instrumental necessity is the bass fiddle, which is strummed. The bass supplies the steady background beat, the instrument's low rhythmic tones mingling with the higher ones of the mandolin or fiddle for the rounded musical effect.

About one third of the selections are instrumental, featuring the banjo, mandolin, and fiddle in turn. But since instrumentation is such an important part of bluegrass music, all instruments, including the bass, take turns doing solo parts as well as playing together in harmony and as accompaniment to

the singers. Even in the vocal pieces, it is not unusual for two or three different instruments to be featured between the verses. The instruments are more than a chording accompaniment for the singers. This variety of sounds and effects all united in one piece keeps musicians and audiences alike alert and interested. It is never dull or routine. Variety and spontaneity gives bluegrass so much appeal that viewers can listen to the same groups singing or playing the same songs over and over and know each time is special.

Ozark bluegrass musicians are resisting electric instruments, for they want to retain the natural sound rather than attain volume. Outdoors or before large groups they use microphones and sound systems to bring out the solo instruments.

It was midnight when the last group came to the stage. Just as intense and vivacious as the first group, the Battlefield Bluegrass Express began. "It's a pleasure for us to be out here picking for you," said Charles Lee, the leader, as he began singing in harmony with his wife and daughter. Though they, as do all the musicians, work all week at other jobs, they load up the whole family with tents or campers and supplies and travel all over the Ozarks to

Picking and singing go on
late into the night.

spend their weekends singing, playing, and enjoying the companionship and music of others. When the master of ceremonies indicated their thirty minutes were up, even at this late hour, the group wanted to continue. "Oh shucks," Lee said, "I was just getting started."

Even though the organized program was over, that didn't mean the audience or musicians had had enough. The children were put to bed, but jam sessions were going on in several places back at the trailers. "Hard-core grass musicians can stay up until dawn playing music, then get up in the morning and play more. They have an amazing resistance to sleep," said one enthusiast. As we walked back to our car, the lonesome Dobro of one group faded into the banjo picking of the next, which in turn was replaced by three fiddlers from different bands each seemingly trying to outrace the others as they sawed their way through an impromptu piece.

Saturday and Sunday were filled with repeat performances by the ten to twelve groups invited to the festival, with special performances by visiting musicians. Workshops, old fiddlers, and flat-picking contests offered a change in Saturday's program.

A very special part of a bluegrass festival is the Sunday morning service and gospel singing. In the open air of the Ozark hills, under the trees beside the gravel bar of the river, the presence of God is clearly felt as a few select groups sing bluegrass gospel, old-time songs like "I'll Fly Away," "Lift Your Eyes to Jesus," "Washed in the Blood of the Lamb," and "Leaning on the Everlasting Arms." The skill of the pickers, the beautiful harmony, and the intense poise of the singers leaves the audience with the feeling of actually being "Washed in the Blood of the Lamb."

Charles Calton, father of the Calton Family, has expressed this feeling in his song, "Bluegrass Music on Sunday Morning."

> Bluegrass music on a Sunday morning.
> We preach, we pray this day.
> We pray of our neighbor,
> We sing of our savior,
> We sing in the old gospel way.
>
> It matters not your religion,
> Nor the clothes you choose to wear,
> But the festivals Sunday mornings
> Are about our Lord up there.
> We feel each song in our hearts,
> Each group gets up to play,
> The fast, the slow, it matters not,
> It's the old gospel way.

In between events we wandered through the grounds, listened to jam sessions, met new friends, and talked with the band members who had donated their time to give *Bittersweet* its official start by playing for us at a benefit performance.

We visited with Jan Lee of the Battlefield Bluegrass Express, who helped us understand more clearly what bluegrass music is by comparing it with rock and country.

"Bluegrass is easier on your ears than rock and country both, because it emphasizes the instrument picking and playing in the band. It is important to really pick the instruments good and have good harmony. It's a more mellow sound and you can set back and listen without grabbing your ears. Country western usually has only one singer. Bluegrass involves quite a bit of harmony. Bluegrass is not a tear-jerking barroom-type song like country, chasing around with other people. It's not as draggy. It's faster, has more feeling. It's a challenge as it's harder to play."

Gerald Stowe added, "It's country soul."

Jan also described the different kinds of bluegrass music. She said there are three different types—basic, contemporary, and modern. "The basic or old-time bluegrass is driving. They hit it real hard. It's more nasal and sung higher and lonesome and through the nose, lots of it. The contemporary is done in minor chords and with different chord changes and

The Calton family sings at festivals all over the Ozarks.

sequences that are unusual. The tune is not real basic. It switches around. It's got prettier tunes, I think. Modern bluegrass is a little too modern for me when they go to electrifying their instruments. We don't go for that here in the Ozarks."

We asked Inez Calton how the groups kept together since they used no music and had no visible leader. "We all play by ear. I guess it just comes natural or we're born with it. I used to play with my brothers and sisters. I met Charles through music and we've always played as a hobby. Charles can play anything. We just sort of know what each is going to do. One is the leader, but we mainly play our own rhythm and play and sing to the lead instruments."

Bluegrass music is a true modern folk music. Though the origin of any folk art is obscure, Bill Monroe of Rosine, Kentucky, is credited with starting to promote bluegrass music in the 1940s and giving it its name. But folk, country, gospel, and family singers in the Ozarks as elsewhere had been singing and picking stringed instruments in similar styles for many decades. This type of music was natural for them and they gave it a distinctive rhythm, pepping it up.

Most of the Ozark musicians grew up in musical families, learning to sing and play as they learned other things from their parents. Their natural skill and liking developed as they grew. Perhaps the most characteristic aspect of Ozark bluegrass is its family-oriented groups. Not only does the whole family attend the festivals, but they all participate. The women in the Ozarks have always been included in music; therefore the bands include many women. Jan Lee, who plays bass, and with her daughter Juanita sings trios with her husband, said, "I think in the Ozarks it's more family than anywhere, and I hope it stays that way."

Another Ozark characteristic is the emphasis on gospel singing. This is also a natural outgrowth of the family singings, church singing conventions, and the important role religion has always had in Ozark life. All gatherings of folk musicians include gospel music in what is still considered the Bible Belt.

Late Sunday afternoon the audience and musicians reluctantly packed up and one by one pulled out from the shady timber patch. They forded the creek and crawled slowly up the winding road to the highway to return to their homes, jobs, and schools until next weekend, when they would meet in another wooded place transformed for a short time to a campground and theater for bluegrass music lovers.

Credits

AUTHORS

Jim Baldwin
Rick Bishop
Terry Brandt
Doris Brelowski

Suzanne Carr
Jim Conner
Mike Doolin
Larry Doyle

Janet Florence
Diana Foreman
Russel Gerlach
Kyra Gibson

Steve Hardcastle
Jimmy Harrelston
Kathy Hawk
Jay Hillig
Gina Hilton
Alexa Hoke
Nancy Honssinger
Daniel Hough

Stephen Hough
Jenny Kelso
Verna Lucas
Jay Luthy
Teresa Maddux
Ruth Ellen Massey
Sally Moore
Karen Mulrenin
Caryn Rader

Teresa Reed
Carla Roberts
Greg Ruble
Rita Saeger
Sarah Seay
Genetta Seeligman
Doug Sharp
Susan Thames

PHOTOGRAPHERS

Jim Baldwin
Rick Bishop
Terry Brandt
Suzanne Carr
Mike Doolin
Larry Doyle
Janet Florence

Gina Hilton
Ronnie Hough
Stephen Hough
Stephen Ludwig
Robert McKenzie
David Massey

Ruth Ellen Massey
Caryn Rader
Carla Roberts
Greg Ruble
Emery Savage
Doug Sharp
Terry Tyre

ARTISTS

Jay Hillig
Alexa Hoke
Nancy Honssinger
Jeff Jaynes

Patti Jones
Jana Low
Teresa Maddux

Melissa O'Kelley
Emery Savage
Susan Thames
Terry Tyre

OLD PHOTOS FROM COLLECTIONS OF:

Lois Roper Beard
Gene Chambers
Ann Hough

Myrtle Hough
Buddy McMahan
Emma Niewald
Kirk Pierce

Janelle Smith
Lillian Hall Tyre
Ellis Wedge

CONTACTS

Quenton Adams
Alice Mae Alexander
Mr. and Mrs. Loren Alloway
Ralph and Lorene Amos
Grover Ballard
Helen Barr
Al Bealer
Helen Beard
Lois Roper Beard
Betrice Bennett
Don and Betty Betts
Charley Brittain
Harold and Bertha Brown
Ilene Brown
Lottie Broyles
Inez and Charles Calton
Deryl Caswell
Gene Chambers
Helen and Mildred Clark
Marie Corrington
Hazel and Lavern Cravens
H. W. Davis
Ella Dunn
Jess Easley
Belle Farthing
Annie Fike
Elizabeth Fishwick
I. L. and Elsie Florence
Hazel Foreman
Adley and Edith Fulford
Roy Gage
Fuget Garrison
Bill Graves
Esther Griffin
Sylvia Gunter
Essie Hamilton
John Hill
Charles, Jolene, and Cindy Holloway
Junior and Betty Holloway
Ino Honssinger
Ashford and Ella Hough

Letha Simpson.

Cora Hough
Myrtle and Elva Hough
Jim Hufft
Clay Humphreys
Eppah Humphreys
Tom Jennings
Bill Jones and the Bluegrass Travelers
George Kastler
Albert and Ila Lamkins
Ralph Laughlin
Charles and Juanita Lee
Tim McBride

Ewin "Rusty" McClure
Wilma and Buddy McMahan
Charlie and Dorothy McMicken
Lynn McSpadden
Fred Manes
Hazel Martin
Emmitt and Pearl Massey
Ethel Massey
Julie Massie
Quentin Middleton
Keith Mizer
Earl Moore
Mary Moore
Russell Moore
Richard Nichols
Emma Niewald
Ray O'Dell
Joe O'Neal
Freda Parks
Art Patterson
R. D. Patterson
Jessie Peterson

Warren Robinson
Mr. and Mrs. Charles Roper
Ruth Seevers
Jim Smith
Marie Smith
C. H. "Dutch" and Della Snyder
Vivian and Charlie Southard
Mabel Stephens
Gerald Stowe
Ferrell Stowe
Dwight Sutherland
Edith Sutherland
Suns of Bluegrass and Bill Klug
Twyla Thomas
Ellis Wedge
Lenora West
White Oak Pond Cumberland Presbyterian Church ladies
Curtis Wilson
Eula Wilson
Ralph Withers, Harold Rowden, and the Bluegrass Five